Tower in the Sky

SOME AAUP BOOKS CURRENTLY IN PRINT

- Alemayehu Geda. *2011 Readings on the Ethiopian Economy*
  Br. 160.00
- ሰሎሞን ደርጋ፡፡ ጀሺህፒ ዓ.ም.፡ "ስለ ብቸኛ ዝርያዎች መንስኤ"
  ብር 85.00
- ጸጋቡ ገብሬ መድኃን፡፡ ጀሺህፒ ዓ.ም.፡ የጸጋቡ ገብሬ መድኃን ታሪካም ተውኔቶች
  ብር 83.00
- Ian Campbell. 2001. *The Plot to Kill Graziani*
  Birr 91.00
- መንግሥቱ ለማ፡፡ 2ሺህ3 ዓ.ም.፡ መጽሐፈ ትዝታ ዘአለቃ ለማ ኃይሉ ወልደ ታሪክ፡፡
  ብር 50.00
- አዶልፍ ፓርለሳክ (ተጫኘ ጆብሬ መኮንን)፡፡ ጀሺህፒ ዓ+ም+፡፡ የሃበሻ ጀብዱ፡፡
  ብር 40.00
- አለቃ ተክለ-ኢየሱስ ዋቅጆራ (አዘጋጅ) ግርማ ጌታኹን፡፡ ጀሺህፒ ዓ.ም.፡ የጉጃም ትውልድ በሙሉ ከአባይ እስከ አባይ፡፡
  ብር 58.00
- ፀሐፊ ትዕዛዝ አክሊሉ ሀብተወልድ፡፡ ጀሺህፒ ዓ.ም.፡ የአክሊሉ ማስታወሻ
  ብር 35.00
- ጌታቸው ኃይሌ (ተርጓሚ)፡፡ ጀሺህፒ ዓ.ም.፡ ደቀ እስጢፋኖስ ገሕግ አምላክ"
  ብር 65.00
- Legesse Negash. 2010. *A Selection of Ethiopia's Indigenous Trees.*
  Br. 105.00
- Demel Teketay. 2010. *Edible Wild Plants in Ethiopia.*
  Br. 100.00
- ነጋድራስ ገብረ ሕይወት ባይከዳኝ፡፡ ጀሺህፒ ዓ.ም.፡ ነጋድራስ ገብረ ሕይወት ባይከዳኝ፣ ሥራዎች
  ብር 30.00
- ሊቀ ጉባዔ ፈቃደ ሥላሴ ተፈራ፡፡ ጀሺህፒ ዓ.ም.፡ ጥንታዊ የበራና መጽሐፍት አዘገጃጀት
  ብር 42.00
- Biadgelign Ademe. 2010. *General Learning-Teaching Methods and Techniques.*
  Br. 70.00

- ልዑል ራስ እምሩ ኃይለ ሥላሴ፡፡ ጀሺህፒ ዓ.ም.፡ ካሆሁት ከማስታውሰው
  ብር 80.00
- ኃይሉ ወልደ ጊዮርጊስ፡፡ ጀሺህፒ ዓ.ም.፡ ለዛባይ ውሃ ሙግት
  ብር 60.00
- ታደሰ ወልደ ጊዮርጊስ፡፡ ጀሺህፒ ዓ.ም.፡ ኢትዮጵያዊያን በአሜሪካ፣ ማገበራዊና ሥነ ልቡናዊ ትንተና
  ብር 65.00
- Daniel Kitaw. 2009. *Industrial Management and Engineering Economy: An Introduction to Industrial Engineering Textbook*
  Br. 80.00
- ቴምድሮስ ገብሬ፡፡ ጀሺህፒ ዓ.ም.፡ በይኑ-ዲሲ ፐሊናዊ የሥነ ጽሑፍ ንባብ
  ብር 35.00
- Dessalegn Rahmato. 2009. *The Peasant and the State. Studies in Agrarian Change in Ethiopia 1950s-2000s*
  Br. 40.00
- Tenalem Ayenew. 2009. *Natural Lakes of Ethiopia*
  Br. 40.00
- አሌክሳንደር ቡላቶቪች፣ ትርጉም ዶ/ር እምባቸው ከበደ፡፡ ጀሺህፒ ዓ.ም.፡ ከሰሜ ምንልክ ሠራዊት ጋር
  ብር 40.00
- ባህሩ ዘውዱ፡፡ ጀሺህፒ ዓ.ም.፡ የኢትዮጵያ ታሪክ ከ1847—1983
  ብር 30.00
- Alemayehu Teferra. 2008. *Principles of Foundation Engineering*
  Br. 80.00
- Solomon Tadesse. 2008. *Mineral Resources Potential of Ethiopia.*
  Br. 40.00
- Bahru Zewde. 2008. *Society, State and History: Selected Essays*
  Br. 95.00
- Demissu Gemeda and Seid Mohammed. 2008. *Fundamental Concepts of Algebra*
  Br. 20.00
- Emebet Mulugeta (ed.). 2008. *Urban Poverty in Ethiopia: The Economic and Social Adaptations of Women*
  Br. 15.00

- Andrew J. Carlson and Dennis G. Carlson. 2008. *Health, Wealth, and Family in Rural Ethiopia.*
  Br. 15.00
- ጌትነት እንየው፡፡ ጀሺህ ዓ.ም.፡ እቴጌ ጣይቱ፣ ታሪካዊ ተውኔት
  ብር 15.00
- ገብረወልድ እንግዳወርቅ፡፡ ጀሺህ ዓ.ም.፡ ማይፀልሙ የማይደፈሩ ዘመቻና የጉተዙ ታሪክ
  ብር 15.00
- ብላቴን ጌታ ኅሩይ ወልደ ሥላሴ፡፡ ጀሺ ዓ.ም.፡ ወዳጅ ልቤ እና ሌሎችም
  ብር 25.00
- መርስዔ ኅዘን ወለደ ቂርቆስ፡፡ ፲፱፻፺ ዓ.ም.፡ የሐያኛው ክፍለ ዘመን መባቻ፣ የዘመን ታሪክ ትዝታዬ ካሆሁት-ና ከሰማሁት 1896-1922
  ብር 90.00
- ተፈራ ኃይሉ ሥላሴ፡፡ ፲፱፻፺ ዓ.ም.፡ ኢትዮጵያና ታላቃ ብሪታኒያ የዲፕሎማቲክ ታሪክ ከ፲፱፻፶፭-፲፱፻፷፮ ዓ.ም.
  ብር 50.00
- Abebe Dinku. 2007. *A Textbook of Building Construction*
  Br. 40.00
- Bahru Zewde. 2007. *A History of Modern Ethiopia 1855-1991 (2nd edn.)*
  Br. 35.00
- Balsvik, R. 2007. *The Quest for Expression: The State and the University in Ethiopia under Three Regimes, 1952-2005*
  Br. 15.00
- Mulugeta Eteffa. 2007. *The Bitter Honey*
  Br. 25.00
- Tsegaye Tegenu. 2006. *Evaluation of the Operation and Performance of Ethnic Decentralization System in Ethiopia: A Case Study of the Gurage People, 1992-2000*
  Br. 5s.00
- Ydlibi, M. 2006. *With Ethiopian Rulers: A Biography of Hasib Ydlibi*
  Br. 40.00

Forthcoming

☞ ቀኛ ጌታ ዮፍታሔ ንጉሤ በዮሐንስ አድማሱ

NB: All prices are at local wholesale rate.

Tower in the Sky

Hiwot Teffera

Addis Ababa University Press

Addis Ababa University Press
P.O. Box 1176
Addis Ababa, Ethiopia
Tel. + 251-011-123 97 46
Fax. + 251-011-124 32 91
E-mail: aau.press@ethionet.et

ISBN 978-99944-52-48-4

Printed in Ethiopia

Acknowledgements

First and foremost glory be to the Almighty for giving me a second chance at life. I'm also forever indebted to my family for being there for me in those trying times. A boundless gratitude is due to my late aunt Mamite Minda and to my sister Almaz for playing a crucial role in saving my life.

My sincerest thank you goes to so many of my friends for their encouragement, support and inspiration while writing this book.

Samuel Kiros, Woldeloul Kassa, Girma Getahun, Abdisa Ayana, Fitsum Alemayehu, Birku Menkir, Alula Yimam, Aster Fisseha, Bahru Zewde and Asfaw Seife, please accept my sincere appreciation for reading the manuscript and for your valuable and critical remarks.

Meron Alemayehu, Yeweyneshet Suraphel, Seifu Yirga, Yemesrach Fantaw, Engudai Bekele and Wongelawit Tefera, I am most sincerely grateful to you for your support. Ambaye Kidane, thank you so much for always believing in me and for the encouragement you have given me to try my hand at writing. I hope I haven't failed you.

Tadelech Hailemichael, the idea of writing this book was conceived with you at the *Emechat Bet* over thirty years ago. As the saying in the Ecclesiastes goes - *There is a time for everything...*- let me just say that the time has finally arrived. You were there for me in those difficult years. I was blessed to have a good friend and mentor like you at the time I needed it most.

Professor Masresha Fetene, Vice President for Research and Technology Transfer at Addis Ababa University, I offer you my deepest appreciation for your tireless work to get this book published.

I sincerely thank Getachew Maru's friends and others, whose names I would rather not mention (they know who they are), for their interviews and unceasing support. Many thanks also to Mitch Moldofsky for doing editorial work on the manuscript.

I have changed the names of most of the people, except for a few and for those who are dead, to protect their privacy.

Farewell to you and the youth I have
spent with you.
It was but yesterday we met in a dream.
You have sung to me in my aloneness,
and I of your longings have built a tower
in the sky.
But now our sleep has fled and our dream
is over, and it is no longer dawn.
The noontide is upon us and our half
waking has turned to fuller day, and we must part.
If in the twilight of memory we should
meet once more, we shall speak again
together and you shall sing to me a deeper song.
And if our hands should meet in another
dream we shall build another tower in the sky.

-Kahlil Gibran, *The Prophet*

To my hero Getachew Maru

For what will it profit a man if he gains the whole world and forfeits his soul? Or what shall a man give in exchange for his soul?
        -Mathew 16:26, *New American Standard Bible*

To speak of this is painful for me: to keep silence
Is no less pain. On every side is suffering.
        -Aeschylus, *Prometheus Bound*

Mystery and innocence are not akin.
            -Hosea Ballo

I was afflicted with an illness when I was in high school. I didn't know the word affliction then. But I knew how it felt. It left me with a physical and psychological scar. I was broken and despaired of ever filling the fissure.

I grew up and went to school in Harar (a town in eastern Ethiopia) and to say that my last year of high school was disastrous would be an understatement.

In the middle of the school year, I started getting severe headaches and excruciating pain in the right side of my back, my neck and my shoulder. I would go to school and find it difficult to stay till the end of classes. I was either depressed and kept to myself or put up a fight with everyone at home. I behaved erratically with my friends. Nobody knew what was wrong with me, not even the doctors.

Finally, lumps as big as puffballs sprouted on the right side of my neck, on my right elbow and on my leg just below my right knee. I had had a bicycle accident the previous year and had hurt my right elbow and thought that was the cause of the swelling there. As for the one on my neck, I believed it was just an angry gland. I didn't even bother to learn what had caused the lump on my leg. To me, it was more a matter of how I looked than anything else, and I just made sure no one noticed the lumps I was carrying around.

My friend Martha Legesse noticed the swelling on my neck one day and urged me to tell my mother. I did not until about a month later when Martha saw it again and explained to me that it was a disease. She told me she knew a woman who had a lump on her neck, just like mine, and later passed away. I was suddenly seized with a violent terror and flew home to shock my mother out of her depths. Seeing her scream holding her head with her hands, I thought I was going to drop dead right there and then.

I came to Addis Ababa (the capital city of Ethiopia) right away to seek treatment and saw a doctor. He gave me some pills and I returned after a month to take my ESLCE (Ethiopian School Leaving Certificate Examination – a requirement to enroll at the university). The swellings seemed to have gone down for a while.

Soon after, my life took a sudden downturn by the unexpected death of my younger brother, Minasse, who was eight years old and was born with a congenital heart disease. We knew all along that my little brother did not have long to live but we never expected him to die so young. One ill-fated afternoon, his classmate punched him on his chest and my brother fainted. Teachers tried to revive him by splashing water on him. They finally brought him home and he was immediately taken to the hospital. He developed a cough the next day, which the doctors were unable to stop. My only brother died a week after at the hospital. A boy of rare intelligence was my little brother Minasse.

He broke our hearts with his premature death.

After my brother died, I came back to Addis and had an operation on my neck. The tests showed that I had tuberculosis. I was shaken to my core. I had always been the fountain of health, and all of a sudden, there I was hit by an illness. I felt I had contracted the most shameful disease imaginable. I kept my sickness a secret, as if it was taboo.

It was tuberculosis that I had.

The emotional pain was so unbearable; my sole deliverance was to hide it deep in my psyche where even I could not reach. But it took a load off my mind to learn that my TB was outside my lungs. It would have been even more devastating to me had it invaded my lungs.

It has been almost two weeks since we commenced the second semester of the 1972-1973 academic year at the Haile Selassie I University in Addis Ababa. I was elated and proud to have joined the university. Campus life was a distraction for my heart that was throbbing with torment and grief. No one could see the wretched soul behind the cheerful mask I put on in public.

Mid-way through my first semester at the university, my sister Almaz urged me to withdraw until I finished treatment. She worried I might fail and would not be allowed to re-enroll.

I chose to brave it out.

Every weekend I went home from campus with fear and trembling. Besides pills and injections, I took traditional medicine. Some of these herbs caused diarrhea and vomiting. Others were extremely sour or had pungent odor and still others needed special diet. Topical applications were the worst. They were painful, to say the least. I felt as if a red-hot iron rod was driven into my bones when an old man inserted twice a crystal-like substance (*yesemai sibari*) into the small cavity on my elbow. I cried until I could cry no more. I often feared that I would lose my sight for crying but of course I didn't know this could happen just from crying hard.

I would go through that ordeal in the morning and go out on a date in the afternoon with red swollen eyes. Come Monday morning or Sunday evening, I returned to campus, elbow bandaged but looking cheerful. Every day, I sneaked out of Sidist Kilo campus to Arat Kilo (which is about two kilometers away from Sidist Kilo campus) to get my daily Streptomycin shot.

None of my friends knew I did that.

My elbow resisted any types of treatment. Pills, shots, x-rays, incisions, biopsies, alcohol, gauze, hydrogen peroxide, special diet, sour leaves, and bitter roots became my lot. But school was a sanctuary for me. It made me forget the smelly roots, sour drinks, hydrogen peroxide, and cotton swabs. It gave me the freedom to rip the bandage off my elbow and forget about the special diet imposed on me.

It made me forget the ache gnawing at my heart.

How was I going to explain all that to my friends? Besides, taking herbal medicine seemed so backward then that I did not want anybody to know I took them.

I endured it all silently.

I wanted to know everything there was to know about my illness. I read extensively. I even read journals such as Science Digest in the hope of finding an explanation for my plight. On the outside, I looked like any other teenager in the street skillfully hiding my psychological and emotional trauma and heartache from the world; I went on juggling my open and secret lives.

Grand dreams of becoming something or somebody sank into oblivion. Only my positive attitude toward life and books kept me from plunging into the abyss. I learned that life was not a bed of roses. I retired from parties and reduced my movie consumption. I was rebellious at home and patience was the least of my virtues. Nursing my illness, I learned patience and self-composure even when my heart quivered with agony. I saw my life change in a flicker of a moment from a turbulent puberty to a painful and haunted transition to adulthood.

I thought my life had changed forever.

Little did I know that the short trip I made two years later to Sidist Kilo would transform my life in a way I could have ever imagined or that the mysterious world I was suddenly thrust into would erase all that pain.

I was very much intrigued by the sudden intrusion of mystery in my innocent but troubled existence. Agatha Christie mystery novels were the staple of my life in my early teens. That was the kind of mystery I was familiar with, not the sort my head was spinning with that morning of January 1973.

It was told that I was to meet a man that day. The date was nothing like a blind date. My cousin Elsa Woldu always set me up on blind dates with men of all ages and trades, when I was in high school in Harar and came to Addis for summer vacation. The date with the anonymous person was nothing like that.

I was mystified.

I was in lecture hall #405 that January morning in the then new classroom building (commonly called the Arts Building) with over two hundred students. I believe it was a Psychology 101 class. The lecture was as veiled as the thought that had inhabited my head. I was unable to put a bridle on my imagination.

It was wandering to decipher the puzzle.

After class, I hastened to the dorm with the hope of finding my friends. To my relief, I found them waiting for me to go to the cafeteria. I'd wanted them to have lunch early. I was still nervous about keeping secret my rendezvous from them. Had it not been for Tayetu, I could have confided in them. She had warned me not to divulge to a soul that I was going to meet a man. I wondered if she had set them up with anonymous strangers as well.

The cafeteria was noisy and packed to capacity. We got there early and for a change got a thick red-hot mincemeat sauce with *injera* (flat bread) and cabbage, the eternal vegetable side dish on the cafeteria menu. I hastily gobbled down my lunch to make it on time for my appointment with the mysterious person. We went back to the dormitory and I washed my hands at one of the hand-washing tubs in front of the shower rooms. I cast one last glance at the mirror in the hallway before I sneaked out. I quickly tamped down my wild Afro with my hand. There was no time to tame it. I knew I didn't look bad with my dark yellow wrap-around sweater and navy blue thin corduroy pants.

The mystery had started out a few days before. Azeb Girma, Kidist Belay, Sara Habte and I had just come out of the campus cafeteria and were heading toward the dorm, giggling as usual, when we ran into Tayetu Assefa and her friend, Amleset Kibrom. They were our seniors in the university. Tayetu wore khaki pants and a safari coat, her hair wrapped in a headscarf tied in a round knot at the back of her neck.

"Can we talk to you guys?" she said, pasting a smile.

We shrugged our shoulders.

"You are open-minded. We hear your debates at night and we find you very open-minded." She surprised us.

My friends and I enjoyed the fiery debates in the dorm. We argued in earnest, for instance, about how the Haile Selassie regime dismissed thousands of grade twelve and a good number of first-year university students by a brutal scaling system (curved grading). When some of the girls were saying that the government was "doing its best," we accused it of purposely dismissing students to cover up the shortage of classes and lecturers. We had no idea that that debate would make us worthy of the honor Tayetu had just bestowed upon us.

She looked each of us in the eye and asked, "Would you be interested in joining a study circle?"

Study Circle? What is a study circle? "Sure!" We were there to experience life, after all.

"That sounds great. We will touch base again. See you soon," she said and walked away with her friend. Her friend did not utter a word.

We sauntered to the dorm wondering about Tayetu's sudden interest in us. Her "You are open-minded" compliment was so unexpected we did not even talk about the invitation to join a study circle.

It was not for nothing we were taken aback by her sudden coziness to us. Our egos had been bruised by the less than flattering remarks she had made about us on more than one occasion. "Why don't you do it outside? You should be emancipated," she had tried to enlighten us when she came to our dorm one night and found us puffing on perfumed French cigarettes, a few days after classes had started and a couple of weeks before she tried to allure us into her mysterious world.

It was disapproved for women to smoke at the time but most girls did it secretly in the dorm. Only Tayetu and another girl smoked openly on campus. But we didn't think of smoking in public as an act of emancipation. Neither did we like anyone telling us to be emancipated. It was in vogue on campus then to throw the word emancipation around. We thought we were liberated doing things on campus most girls would frown upon. We wouldn't learn the difference between emancipation and liberation until much later, but when Tayetu left the dorm that night we laughed to our hearts' content with, "Oh! I would love to be emancipated!"

We puffed on the cigarettes, courtesy of Kidist's boyfriend, mainly for the sweet smoke, which we blew on our clothes. We kept them in an armoire overnight to retain the scent. Sometimes we breathed smoke into one another's Afros before heading to lecture halls. It wasn't that we didn't have perfume. Thanks again to Kidist's boyfriend; he had brought her three strong French perfumes from Dire Dawa (a small town about 50 kilometers from Harar). But we preferred the scented cigarettes for their soft fragrance.

Tayetu Assefa and her male friends were called Revos. But her male friends were not ordinary Revos. They were said to be "vanguard of the student movement." Rumor had it that they withdrew and re-enrolled at the university every year so that the student movement "would not lose momentum."

They had returned at the beginning of the month and had an authoritative presence on campus. Their serious and purposeful demeanor made the likes of me seem callow. They looked like they carried the world's problems on their shoulders. Their hair was disheveled and they wore safari coats and khaki pants. They always seemed to whisper amongst themselves. They smoked Winston or the locally made Nyala cigarettes and marched with newspaper-covered books clenched under their armpits. I wondered why the books were enfolded in newspaper. It was only afterwards that I learned that they covered political books for security reasons.

Since their reappearance on campus, the "vanguard" squatted at the same spot every day (steps away from the campus cafeteria) and gauged the revolutionary temperament of every passing student. My friends and I knew they called us "jolly Jacks." Jolly Jacks to them were crucibles of bourgeois values and were not up to whatever they were hatching. One day, they were perched on their usual spot when they saw us coming up giggling, as we always did.

"Do you think these girls would join the revolution?" one of them asked in English.

"I don't think so. They probably would become sympathizers," replied another in Amharic.

"Exactly," said Tayetu in English.

A student overheard their conversation and tipped off Yordanos Hailu, my friend Sara's cousin doing law at the university. She couldn't wait to pass on the word to us. We didn't know what revolution they were referring to but we took Tayetu's 'exactly' as another blow to our egos.

It was around mid-December 1972 that I had found out, by sheer accident, about Revos. That was almost a month before Tayetu and her friend Amleset ambushed us on our way to the dorm. I was sitting on a stone bench in front of John F. Kennedy library (the Sidist Kilo campus library built with American aid) waiting for a friend when this guy came over and sat on the lawn, facing me. He acted as if he had known me all his life. I suppressed a smile.

"What is your name?" he asked, stretching out his hand.

"Hiwot," I answered, almost bursting with laughter and shaking his hand.

"I am Ashenafi," he introduced himself leaning back, his long legs stretched out and his hands planted on the ground. He was slightly dark and good-looking with an easy demeanor.

"So...what do you think of campus life?" he asked, studying my face.

"Dormant," I replied, grabbing the opportunity to use the English word that I had recently picked up.

"How so?" Ashenafi asked, raising his eyebrows in surprise.

I had such high hopes of joining the university. When I was in high school, I had dreamed of swirling into the streets with university students shouting slogans at the top of my lungs and waving my fist in the air. I had marched in protest demonstrations in Harar but somehow I always felt that the ones by university students were the real ones. But I was intrigued by the students for not living up to my expectations. *What was all that buzz about university students being militant?* The campus was eerily quiet, with too few students.

"Well, when I was in high school in Harar, I used to hear so much about mass demonstrations and class boycotts by university students. I don't see any of that now!"

"It is because the Revos are not here."

"Revos?"

"That's right. Revo is short for revolutionary."

Revos! They sounded like a separate species. I asked eagerly. "Why do you call them Revos? What do they do?"

"Well...the things you just said."

"So...where are they now?" I was excited.

"They withdrew last February. Many students were taken into custody and the students' union and its organ were banned. They are returning to class next month. Campus life will be different then," he remarked with an air of certitude.

No wonder the campus is so...dormant. Revos! Only a couple of more weeks to go! I can't wait to see these students who sound ever so exotic. "So...if the ones who withdrew last February are Revos, what are the rest of the students? I mean...students other than us...freshmen?"

"Some are fourth-year students who have come back after completing their National Service... the rest are Sabos." There was a tinge of resentment in his voice.

It was getting even more interesting. I had been over four months on campus and didn't even know there were all these types of students.

"Sabos?"

"Yeah, Saboteurs. They stayed behind when the rest of us withdrew," he complained.

"So you are a Revo," I said.

He grinned. "I withdrew with the rest of the students. I'm a third-year Political Science student. I'm coming back next month. I came to the library today," he noted, still smiling.

I was excited. I felt that he had solved the puzzle that so intrigued me. *Now I know why the campus is so dormant.* I no longer had the patience to wait for my friend nor carry on the conversation. I mumbled something and scampered off to the dorm and my friends. I was thrilled to be the herald of such a juicy piece of news. "Hey, did you know many students had withdrawn last February? They are called Revos and are returning to campus next month. And the ones who stayed are called Sabos!" I declared, bursting into the dorm. I got my friends excited. This was information we could use.

The university was at the time a graveyard of many dreams and hopes. Starting in November, first-year students got jittery about their future. Almost half of them would be dismissed at the end of the semester with no chance of ever coming back. What is more, senior students demeaningly called them *Fresh* and taunted them constantly about their imminent adieu to campus as the semester drew near the end. There was even an Amharic song to mark their departure.

አረገረገ ከፍ ጫማዋ
ፍሬሽ ደረሰ መሄጃዋ

With springs in her boots, rocking to fly
Time for Fresh to leave, time to say goodbye!

At the time, male students hollered "Fresh!" at my friends and me when we roved on campus to conquer new territories. Thanks to Ashenafi, we now had a weapon with which to fight back. Whenever they called out Fresh, we shot back with Sabo!

No one dared call us Fresh again.

I joined Haile Selassie I University in September 1972. I was registered at the main Sidist Kilo campus of the Faculty of Arts. The campus was formerly the imperial palace of Emperor Haile Selassie. He donated it to the newly established university. I easily made friends with Sara, Azeb, Kidist, Mekdes, Nurelhouda and Selam.

It was the first time in the history of the university for teenagers to enroll in such large numbers. I was eighteen when I joined the university. We turned the university campus upside down toppling the dress code for women, which was mainly skirt suit, and brought in bell bottoms, mini-skirts, windbreakers, bandanas, sneakers, platform shoes, and flip-flops to an unprecedented degree.

We were pioneers of fresh and casual campus life at least that was how we felt.

Sara, Kidist and I had enormous Afros that covered half our faces. Many students had difficulty telling us apart. We were also nearly the same height. Somebody once remarked that it was as if we were "trimmed with scissors." To make matters worse, Sara and I wore the same kind of pants splashed with crazy colors.

I washed my massive Afro every day and combed only the front leaving the back knotted. "Hiwot's hair would fall off because it is never combed and Kidist's because it is combed too much," Sara used to say.

Kidist was obsessed with combing her Afro. She often dashed out of the dorm to the hallway with an Afro comb where two narrow mirrors were hanging on the wall. If we were in the hallway chatting with girls, she would dart to the dorm and come back with her favorite accessory. On our way to class or to the lounge, if she happened to forget something, she went back to the dorm and took forever to get back. Sara always said, "She is probably combing her hair."

Azeb was the only one with long hair. She was also the tallest and most fair-skinned. She let her wavy hair down and tied a leather strip around her forehead. She wore "Smile! You are on Candid Camera" or "Have a nice day" pins. I teased her it was about time she outgrew "this high school stuff."

She never yielded.

Sara once came out in a miniskirt that drove the campus crazy. Some angry vigilantes who thought she was bringing "decadent bourgeois culture" to campus wanted to teach her a lesson. We got wind of the plot and she ran to the dorm and threw away the offending skirt.

Diligent students buried their heads in books in the library, while my friends and I invaded the student lounge and the kissing pool. As a rule, we came out of the cafeteria around seven in the evening and hung around the student lounge (which used to be the royal stable) until eight o'clock listening to music and giggling. Then we strolled to the kissing pool with our dates.

The kissing pool was located in front of Ras Mekonen Hall, the opulent residence of the Emperor, now housing the Institute of Ethiopian Studies. The fountain was so-called because it was sanctuary to couples who made out in the dark away from the glare of the Revos, who considered romance a frivolous pursuit. It was also the symbol of freedom for us teenagers who had just shaken off the shackles of parental control.

We spent hours on the lush garden, surrounding the fountain, flattering one another and gazing at the stars. We marched back in pairs toward the dorm just before eleven and our partners paid their tearful adieus at the "love" or "separation is death" spot, which was a few meters away from the girls' dormitory. It was so called for boys were not allowed beyond that spot.

We went to the library not so much to study as to join our partners. We giggled, stirring frustration and anger. "This is not a Rendezvous!" cautioned a notice, written in English and pasted on the bulletin board. We besieged the ping-pong table at the student lounge and the tennis court for a while scaring male students away.

No wonder the "vanguard" didn't think much of us.

It was a few days after Tayetu had tried to lure us to join a study circle. I had just gotten back from the kissing pool and was about to climb into my bed when she came to our dorm and motioned me to come. She was standing in the doorway clasping the curtain that separated our dorm and the one next. I passed through the dorm following Tayetu who had disappeared into the passageway. I found her waiting for me beside one of the mirrors in the hallway.

"You are meeting one of the study circle members tomorrow afternoon at quarter past one. He will be waiting for you in front of *Kehas* Hospital," she said, referring to Haile Selassie I Hospital.

"I've got a class at-"

"Don't worry," she interrupted me. "You won't be longer than five minutes. You're going to set up a date to meet another day. He is of medium height and will be wearing a yellowish-brown corduroy jacket."

Why doesn't she tell me his name? The sense of mystery and suspense suddenly enveloped me.

"Nurelhuda Yusuf and Mulumebet Hailemariam would be your other study circle mates. He will tell you when to contact them," she whispered in my ear.

Nurelhuda and Mulumebet were my year-mates. Nurish was a friend of mine. There was no mystery there.

It was the nameless stranger who had become an enigma to me.

I asked for wonder and he gave it to me.
    -Abraham Joshua Heschel

Who is he? Why would a stranger be interested in studying with us in a study circle? What is a study circle, anyway? What can we possibly study with him? I pondered as I hastened to meet the mysterious stranger the next day at Sidist Kilo, where Yekatit 12 Martyrs' monument stood.

    The monument was erected as tribute to the more than 30,000 Ethiopians massacred in Addis Ababa in three days in February 1937 by Fascist soldiers as a reprisal to the assassination attempt by two young patriots on Marshall Grazziani, the Italian Viceroy for East Africa.

    Once I passed the monument, I spotted a young man in his early twenties and of medium height standing in front of the fruit stall across *Kehas* Hospital, which was just outside of the campus. He wore a white shirt, khaki pants and a yellowish-brown corduroy jacket that looked too large for him. He looked confused when I crossed the street and stood before him smiling. For a split of a second, I thought I had come to the wrong person and let my eyes dart around looking for a man fitting the description I was given. But, there was no one around.

    "*Selam*! I am Hiwot Teffera…Tayetu…" I began, smiling and stretching my hand. I wondered why he looked puzzled when he knew very well that he was going to meet a girl.

    "Yes…Yes…My name is Getachew… Getachew Maru. How are you?" he interrupted me, shaking my hand with a timid smile.

    "I am fine."

    "Can we go somewhere…where we can talk over coffee?"

    "I've got a class in a few minutes," I told him, as if skipping classes was not my favorite pastime.

"I know. I've got to go too. But I guess we can talk for a few minutes."

We went to Anbessa Gibi - the garden-rimmed zoo - located just across the square.

"Would you like to eat?" Getachew asked when the waiter came up to our table to take our orders.

"No. I just had lunch. I'll take Coke."

He ordered Coke for me and coffee for himself. I noticed that he was very shy and soft-spoken. I learned that he was a fourth-year engineering student and had withdrawn from the university.

"So you are a Revo."

He laughed. "What do you mean?"

I mentioned to him what I heard about Revos and Sabos. He burst out laughing.

"Why have you withdrawn from school?" I was curious.

"I would like to work for a while. I teach at Shimeles Habte," he replied, scratching his thin moustache.

Why wouldn't a fourth-year engineering student want to finish school? I hated prying into other peoples' private lives and didn't ask any more questions about school.

"Tell me about yourself," he said coyly.

"I joined the university last September. I am originally from Harar...I have two sisters. My older sister lives here and my younger sister is with my mother in Harar. I finished high school at Medhane Alem Secondary School. "

"Medhane Alem is known for its student militancy. Tell me about the student movement in Harar."

Student movement! I'd heard the phrase at the university campus after the Revos have returned to campus but I didn't quite know what it meant even though I could try and make a guess. I imagined it must refer to protest parades and class boycotts. But I had never conceptualized that as a movement. I had no sense of politics and my only 'engagement' with it was when I took part in protest marches in high school. Even then, those titillating rallies were more of an outdoor activity to me than anything else was.

I had other serious undertakings at the time such as going to the movies and organizing parties or being invited to them every weekend and of course reading books. I knew those outings to the streets were directed against the government but I didn't understand any of it. It was the sheer sense of adventure that lured me into the chaos in the streets. Besides, that was what high school students did at the time. Losing face was my Achilles' heel. I knew I had to use my imagination and save me the embarrassment.

I ramped up my confidence and gave it a try. "We held protest demonstrations and class boycotts," I began and looked him in the eye. His eyes smiled at me, which I took to mean a signal for me to go on.

"We were in grade eleven. The boys gave us sticks which they ripped off trees in the back of the classrooms to whip the soldiers with. We marched out of the school compound swinging the sticks. We didn't even go far. The soldiers came out of nowhere and chased us with their clubs. We threw off the twigs and fled!"

He chuckled tilting his head backwards. The lions in the zoo burped and roared. I got somewhat jittery. It was my first time to be in the zoo.

"I loved those rallies," I went on boldly. "My childhood friends Yodit and Martha and I never missed any of them. Our mothers scurried around town looking for us with their *netelas* dangling from their shoulders…"

"I'm sure they were terrified."

"Yeah, but it was annoying to us, you know. One Saturday morning, I was home lying on my mother's bed reading *The Mill on the Floss*, when I heard someone shout my name. I went to open the door but it was locked from outside. I jumped out of the window and saw Martha and Yodit standing behind the fence."

"Wow!"

"I didn't even know why I was locked in. Anyway, my friends informed me that Alemaya Agricultural College students had marched from Alemaya to Harar. Have you been to Harar?"

"Never. I would love to go someday, though."

"Alemaya is a fifteen to twenty-minute drive from Harar. We found the students assembled in front of the Ministry of the Interior."

Saturday morning was a working day in the country in those days and the Governor was expected to be in.

"Many students from Harar had joined them," I continued. "They demanded the Governor to come out and respond to their demands. Somebody else appeared on the balcony and said something which I can't remember and urged us to disperse. I don't know how long we've been there…the police came and drove us out of the area. My friends and I saw a man whom we knew by sight and called him. He gave us a ride home in his Land Rover."

I looked at him and he seemed to be amused. I fancied I could go on hoping what I recounted so far had to do everything with the student movement.

"I once distributed leaflets in the school compound," I said. I didn't know what else to say about the student movement in Harar.

"Leaflets? What kind of leaflets?" He seemed interested.

"They were thin strips of paper torn from exercise books. We wrote about the upcoming demonstration and disseminated them…I was elected class representative to the Student Council when I was in grade eleven. I went to a Council meeting once and I was the only female there. I could understand very little of what was being said. One of the students reported that university students in Addis had boycotted classes and we should too. He said something about the need to 'focus' on something. I forgot what it was. I was so impressed with him for using the English word focus."

Getachew burst out with laughter again.

"Honestly, I guess that was what I took away from that meeting. The next day at the end of class and before we went out for recess, I reported to my classmates that I was at the Council meeting the day before and had to make an announcement. Some of them said, '*Enashinena*, who elected you to the Council?'"

Getachew howled with laughter and bashfully said, "I know *that* is a Harar thing." He couldn't obviously say *Enashinena* out loud, which is almost profanity to non-Hararians.

"I am telling you. They were the ones who elected me. I was so mad I told them to shut up. I received blows from at least four boys that day. I never went back to Council meetings again."

"So much for your political career in high school, huh?" he remarked with a shy smile.

"There was this teacher called Mekonen Hagos," I went on, "he was doing his National Service at our school at the time."

The commonly called National Service was the Ethiopian University Service Program instituted to address the shortage of teachers in the country. University students were required to fulfill this compulsory program upon completion of their third year. Engineering College students were required to do theirs when they completed their second-year. I would later learn that Getachew had done his National Service in Dejen, a small town in the province of Gojjam in the north-western part of Ethiopia.

I immediately noticed similarity between Mekonen and Getachew. He wore khaki pants and Mekonen used to wear khaki too. Besides, I saw something in him…something I couldn't put my finger on…something about him that reminded me of Mekonen.

"Mekonen made political speeches at school," I began. "My friends and I hardly missed any of them. We didn't understand any of it. Actually, we were not in the least interested in his speeches. We just wanted to have a glimpse of his handsome face. We always strategically positioned ourselves in a crowd so that he could easily spot us. We stayed late after school to see him referee a volleyball match. He always greeted us with a smile. One morning, I think it was around recess, we learned that he had been shot dead by a security agent the previous night, while walking with a student. They said that he was shot by a gun with a silencer because the student didn't hear a shot. The only thing he saw was Mekonen falling to the ground."

Getachew listened with a frown on his forehead and signaled for me to go on.

"The entire school went into a frenzy," I continued. "A student was standing in the middle of the school compound that morning carrying a bunch of wilted pink flowers. The students maintained that another student had brought the flowers to Mekonen's class the previous day. When Mekonen saw them, he had said to his students, 'These flowers will shrivel by this time tomorrow weeping for me.' The student who had the flowers was making a speech about socialism and communism to a group of students. My friends and I said to one another, 'Why don't we become political?' We went over and asked him to explain to us what socialism and communism meant. I cannot even remember what he'd taught us. We were grieving at the time; we wanted to convert instantly into something Mekonen believed in. All of us went to the funeral that day and did not return to class for weeks. We were mourning for Mekonen so my friends and I wore black. A few days later, my mother warned me that we would be thrown in jail if we didn't take off our black dress. I refused."

"You were stubborn," he ventured timidly.

"You could say that," I muttered and continued. "Shortly after my mother's warning, I bumped into this police captain on my way home and he cautioned me that we would be in trouble if we kept wearing our black dress. I just shrugged my shoulders and took off. He was so angry he blurted out, 'Who cares...you are the one who is going to rot in jail.' I didn't even look back. He was the one who'd told my mother about the jail thing."

Getachew listened with rapt attention. I gathered I might as well go on with my attempt at explaining the *student movement* in Harar.

"A week or so after Mekonen was killed," I went on, "I think it was around four-thirty in the afternoon...my friends and I were coming from somewhere when Ayele, a student we knew from school, joined us and informed us that his friend, Mamo, has just been apprehended by the secret service. While we were talking about Mamo, a Beetle Volkswagen slowly passed by and we saw him sitting in the back seat! My friends and I hurried home to change our black dress."

Getachew laughed to tears, took out a white handkerchief from his pocket, and dabbed his eyes and nose. I wasn't going to stop. For all I knew, he was enjoying himself.

"There was this interesting student as well at school. His name was Assefa. We were in grade ten at the time. He would lie down on his side on the ground and talk about a Greek philosopher...Socrates? Every day he posted on the wall a drawing of the philosopher lying in bed. He claimed Socrates was on his deathbed after drinking poison. He fascinated me but at the same time, I thought he was cuckoo. He often talked politics, addressed us in English at the morning or afternoon assembly, and always started off his speech with, 'Students, Ethiopia needs its own freedom. Don't you think so? Even a donkey needs its own freedom.' He pronounced needs and students as 'needis' and 'studentis'... the way Tigrians do. He too was political."

"What is your take on the national question?" Getachew asked, recovering from his bouts of laughter.

"The national question?"

"Yeah...for instance the Eritrean question?"

Oh my God! What is this all about? I didn't know there was a question regarding Eritrea. Of course, I knew the government has been fighting with what it called Eritrean "*agamidos*" – an Amharic term meaning bandits. But I had never conceptualized it as a question.

"I know the government is fighting the Eritrean bandits. I've heard from some Alemaya College lecturers that Eritreans want to separate from Ethiopia."

"Alemaya College lecturers?"

"Yes. They always talked politics. They were all educated in America. They used to give us, particularly to one of our friends, pamphlets like *Challenge*, *Combat* and *Tatek*. They said Ethiopian students abroad published the pamphlets. We never really bothered to read them. There used to be fights between Amhara and Eritrean students at the Alemaya College campus. My maternal uncle, who is now a police colonel, used to go there from Harar in the middle of the night whenever a fight broke out. He would make peace and come back. He refused to imprison students, for which he was transferred to Eritrea as a punishment."

"Interesting!" he exclaimed.

We were quiet for a few minutes. He then broke the silence.

"I am sure Tayetu has disclosed to you about what we would be doing."

"She wanted to know if my friends and I wanted to join a study circle. I don't even know what it is."

I still didn't know what a study circle was. Azeb had made a bit of inquiry about it. She'd asked someone thinking that he might know about study circles. All he knew about was "mass organizations" not study circles. We didn't even know what a mass organization was.

"Well...we will form a group and study Marxism and Leninism. Are you familiar with it?" asked Getachew.

"No! Never heard of it."

"Communism?"

"I heard about it for the first time in fourth grade. It was all nonsense, though." I said, waving my hand.

"You knew about communism in fourth grade?"

"It was all nonsense. We had a teacher whose name was Redwan. He used to tell us that Russia and China are Communist. People there do everything together. They even eat in the cafeteria together."

"He told you all that when you were in grade four?"

"Sure he did! He was arrested later on. They said he was accused of planting a roadside bomb, when *Janhoy* was going to Kulubi for the annual St. Gabriel's day celebration. You know the Emperor goes there every year, right? My friend Yodit and I saw our teacher once with other prisoners escorted by police when we were passing by the police station he was held at. Since that day, Yodit and I sat on top of the stone wall surrounding the station every day in the hope of seeing our teacher again. We never did. I don't exactly remember when but we later learned that he was executed."

I knew I didn't make sense talking about fourth grade communism. I needed to say something profound. "I remember reading *Readers Digest*...I was fourteen at the time," I started with mounting confidence. "I learned to hate Communists because of what I read about Alexei, the little Russian prince, who had hemophilia. I cried bitterly when I learned that the boy was executed along with his family. I hated the Communists for killing the royal family."

I was intent on impressing him and making up for my ignorance about communism. "I liked the Black Panthers...Bobby Seale, Jesse Jackson, Hugh Newton, Stokely Carmichael, Eldridge Cleaver...," I went on. "I admire Angela Davis. I have read *Soledad Brother*, which my high school French teacher gave me, maybe five times and I still find it very moving."

I almost let him know that I walked around campus *Soledad Brother* on top of my books making sure that everybody saw it. George Jackson had touched my heart as no one had because of the way he died. Roaming around with his book was my way of telling the world I had outgrown the Harold Robbins and Jacqueline Susanns, unlike some of my year-mates.

There was nothing to stop me. "My cousin had subscriptions to *Time*, *Newsweek* and *Readers Digest*. I used to borrow the magazines from him. That was how I learned about the Black Panthers, Martin Luther King and Malcolm X."

"You know about the Civil Rights Movement; I am impressed," he said with a shy smile.

I didn't know what I knew about the Black Panthers was called the "Civil Rights Movement." I knew what the Black Panthers were struggling for but again it was this inability to conceptualize that exposed my ignorance. Perhaps I was more impressed by the pictures than by the contents of the magazines. *Readers Digest* was different. I read it from beginning to end.

Movement, question! I just met him and I was already learning something new.

It was getting dark. He looked at his watch and shook his head with a smile. "I can't believe we've been here for five hours! It is six o'clock. I forgot all about my appointment."

"I forgot about my class."

When we got up to go, he reminded me to bring "the two girls" at two o'clock Sunday afternoon to a house in Afincho Ber. He accompanied me as far as the main campus entrance and left.

I thought about what had happened all afternoon on my way to the dorm. I was impressed with Getachew for asking me my opinion on serious issues such as the student movement, the Eritrean question and communism. No one had ever asked me my opinion on anything.

I felt important.

He is certainly different. What did he think about those matters, anyway? It didn't even occur to me to ask him. *He looks like the Revos on campus except that he has not returned to campus. I wonder why he has not. He didn't even tell me why we should study what he called Marxism/Leninism.*

I meant to ask him what it meant at some point but I was carried away with my own prattling. *Marxism/Leninism! It sounds exotic!* I wondered what it was all about. I brimmed with excitement with the prospect of studying it and couldn't wait to see Getachew again.

I had always had this sense of wonder, an insatiable thirst for knowledge and self-development in me. I thought books hid in them the key to my quest. I read anything and everything I could lay my hands on. I wanted to read and possess all the books in the world. I read all the time, even during some classes such as math. In grade eleven, I memorized quotations and ran around with *Best*

Quotations For All Occasions tucked in my armpit. I did almost everything my friends did but deep inside I knew none of it was for me.

My friend Yodit Abebe told me that I once said to her, "I would rather do something about my own life than watch somebody else's," when she came home and suggested that we go to the movies as we always did on weekends. We were then in grade ten. I was reading *Montezuma's Daughter*, according to Yodit. I must have been in a bad mood. But she thought it was the most profound thing that ever came out of my mouth.

I was embarrassed for talking so much in front of Getachew whose modesty I found disarming. I couldn't remember blabbering so much in front of anyone. He didn't say much. He just asked questions and listened patiently to my gibberish all afternoon. *Why did I talk so much? It wasn't like me at all.* I hoped he wouldn't think I was talkative, much worse a harebrain!

He seems unassuming but there is something about him…something mysterious. He might be someone who reads books. Reading was the true love of my life and men who read ignited a spark in me. *I would definitely study this Marxism thing with him.*

I had no idea he would open up a new horizon of consciousness for me.

The essence of created things is to be intermediaries.
     -Simone Weil, *Gravity and Grace*

I went home for the weekend and came back to campus on Sunday around one-thirty in the afternoon ready to go and see my mentor in Afincho Ber. I found Nurish and Mulumebet in the dorm. We exited the campus via Prince Beedemariam Laboratory School (commonly called Lab School) and hurried down the street that led to Afincho Ber.

Afincho Ber, a neighborhood located at the west side of Sidist Kilo campus, was known for its large university student population, particularly male. It is steps away from the campus. The university had a dorm shortage and gave a twenty-birr stipend for out of campus rent expenses. Many students rented out "student houses" in the vicinity.

We found the house easily as per Getachew's direction. It was one of the row houses positioned a few meters off the street. I knocked on the door and Getachew opened it slowly and quietly as if trying to not wake someone up. He greeted us with a shy smile, let us in, and closed the door behind him. He politely introduced himself to Nurish and Mulumebet.

The one-room house was tiny and clean but dark, with the lone window closed. There were beds on opposite sides of the room and a small, rectangular table with four chairs in the middle. There was nothing much in the house except for men's clothes neatly stashed in a corner, and books.

A sense of mystery was hanging in the air.

Getachew asked us about campus life, after we had settled on the chairs. Nurish did most of the talking. I remained quiet. I was trying to recover from the embarrassment of talking too much the last time.

"We will be studying Historical and Dialectical Materialism," Getachew announced abruptly, his voice cracking with timidity. "We will start off with Historical Materialism."

He explained Historical Materialism as the study of society whose development is marked by stages, moving from lower to higher forms. Society has progressed from the primitive communal system to slavery, feudalism and then to capitalism, he explained.

"Each of us has to make a presentation on a topic. We should come to the weekly sessions well-prepared, even if we are not presenting. Next Sunday, we will take up the first chapter, which looks at the primitive communal system. I will chair the meeting but chairmanship will rotate thereafter. When we are done with Historical Materialism, we will move on to Dialectical Materialism which is the study of natural phenomena," he stated, looking at us timidly.

Presentation? Chairing a meeting? That was more than I bargained for. I found Historical and Dialectical Materialism intimidating, as they sounded high-flown.

As if that was not enough, he cautioned us with, "Whatever we are doing should be kept secret."

Secret? I was stupefied.

"Read the first chapter and take notes. I will see you all next Sunday at the same time," he added, giving us a handout.

All that took about two hours. On our way out, he reminded us to read the chapter on the primitive communal system. He took the latch off the door, opened it slightly, peeked his head out, and let us out.

We got out of the compound giggling and nudging each other. "He is so shy he made me nervous, wallahi!" Nurish whispered to us. We looked behind us every second to see if he was watching us.

We thought it was funny. Why would he want to study with girls he doesn't even know? We also felt edgy about the seriousness with which he spoke about reading handouts and taking notes. We didn't even take lecture notes properly. I hated the idea of chairing meetings. "Why doesn't he chair the meetings?" I asked. But most importantly, we were mystified and scared by the "It should be kept secret" warning.

It was indeed an uneasy moment.

I got the idea that study circle was not something to joke around with. But I was curious at the same time. I wanted to know what lay behind all that. I didn't say anything to Azeb, Kidist and Sara about our first session when I saw them the next day. If they had been to theirs, they did not say.

The following Sunday, Getachew greeted us with a broad grin when he opened the door for us quietly, just the way he did last time. I suspected he didn't want to draw attention from the neighbors.

He wore an off-white shirt with the sleeves folded up. I noticed his full lips were dry and even chapped. I wondered why he didn't put Vaseline on them to smooth them.

Once seated, he asked after our health and school with a timid beam. I felt he hid his shyness behind a smile. After a brief and awkward silence, he gave us an elaborate description of the primitive communal system.

He comported himself with utmost courtesy and seriousness. He was no longer the bashful man who earlier opened the door for us. He looked bold, businesslike and purposeful. I got a glimpse of his commitment to whatever he was doing. His notes were meticulously written in a hundred-page exercise book. He carefully flipped through the pages, while speaking.

I got the message that he expected us to take the matter as earnestly as he did. I wondered why he had to go through all that trouble to teach us Marxism/Leninism. *Is he ever going to tell us why we should study it?*

When he was done, he became the self-conscious and demure person who let us in earlier. I noticed that he averted his eyes trying to avoid mine. *Why doesn't he look me in the eyes like he does the others?*

He asked us if we had questions or comments. We stared at him with blank faces.

"Who would want to go next? The next chapter deals with slavery," he said at last.

No one uttered a word. We sat there like frightened children.

"Hiwot would you like to go next?"

I thought my heart was going to burst out of my chest. My immediate reaction was to say no but that would be embarrassing myself further. I fixed my eyes on him with a nervous silence. He mistook that for a "yes" and told us he'd see us next week. I took the assignment with fear and trembling. I would rather have had one of the other girls gone before me.

I didn't so much as glance at the handout during the rest of the week. My spare time was divided between the lounge and the kissing pool. I went home for the weekend Friday evening and skimmed through the handout on Saturday.

I was disconcerted, to say the least, by what I read. I found slavery offensive to my sensibility. *How could a human being own another?* I knew a few people in Harar who had *barias* – slaves – but it had never occurred to me they actually owned them.

Getachew must explain to me this scandalous piece of history tomorrow.

The next day, I was uptight upon arrival on campus. Mulumebet and Nurish were not in the dorm. I assumed they had left without me so I threw my stuff on my bed and rushed to Afincho Ber. I had the creeps thinking about the presentation. I wasn't too proud of my preparation. My greatest fear was in exposing my ignorance in front of Getachew. I had boasted so much the first day I met him, I felt the delivery would be the occasion he would put me on the scale and judge me.

I shook his hand nervously when he opened the door for me and went past him and slumped on a chair. I almost confessed I would not be able to go through it. Only pride held me back. Before he even came and sat down, there was a knock on the door. It was Nurish and Mulumebet. We sat around the table. As usual, Getachew broke the ice with inquiries after our health and school, turned to me, and asked me if I was ready to go.

"I think so," I muttered hesitatingly.

He nodded as if to say, "You can go ahead." I started my very first serious talk in a group setting. I was terrified I would say the wrong things and make a fool out of myself. *Oh my God, why didn't I thoroughly read this darn thing? What is he going to think of me now?* It was obvious that I wasn't prepared.

I stole a few sideways glances at him, while talking and saw him nodding his head. I wasn't sure if he did it out of mere politeness or if I was really making sense. I was coy in my own way and hated talking in a group setting. He interrupted me a couple of times and asked the girls if they had questions or comments. That was what he did during his presentation but I wasn't going to look for trouble. The discussion had to be continued for the following Sunday, extending my misery for one more week.

Next Sunday, Nurish and I got there on time but Mulumebet did not show up. Getachew asked us if she was coming. We told him that we didn't know. I had to go on with my presentation, which I hadn't looked at the entire week. He saw that I was struggling so he did most of the explaining.

When we were done, he enjoined us strictly that we should not bring handouts to the classroom or the student lounge. "It is a question of life and death," he promptly added.

I was petrified. *Why would something as benign as a description of societies be a* "question of life and death?" *There isn't any reference to the Emperor.* It was true that we brought the handout to the classroom and the student lounge stuck in our books. I wondered who could have tattled on us.

I couldn't wait to tell Azeb.

Getachew then asked Nurish if she could take on feudalism at the next session. She boldly said yes.

I was impressed.

"See you next Sunday," said Getachew as he opened the door for us.

On our way to the dorm, Nurish and I talked about the, "It is a question of life and death" forewarning. We couldn't figure out what it was all about. I was a bit frightened but curiosity got the better of me.

I needed to know where those sessions were taking us.

The next morning, I revealed to Azeb what Getachew had said about bringing handouts to the student lounge and the classroom. I learned that their "guy" had cautioned them too. Their "guy" was Getachew's counterpart in their study circle. Azeb and I came up with a shortlist of rats. Her boyfriend loomed large. He was our year-mate and active in campus politics.

We would never find out.

1973 was a promising year. It was already March and the atmosphere on campus was tense. The Revos had somehow changed the climate. They seemed ever serious and busy God only knew doing what. The leisurely mood that informed campus life in the first semester was slowly being overtaken by restlessness. There was something brewing. Animated 'interested group' discussions were taking place in the dorms and elsewhere on campus. The reinstitution of the students union – University Students Union of Addis Ababa (USUAA) – was one of the hot agenda items.

One afternoon, my friends and I were coming from the Arts Building when we saw Alemzewd Araya, our year-mate, surrounded by a group of people in front of the campus cafeteria. She was being interrogated about her Pentecostal beliefs and activities. I wondered why they were cross-examining her about her beliefs.

A few days after that incident, a contingent of girls, under the commandership of Tayetu, banged on the door at the study hall where Alemzewd and fellow Pentecostals were singing. Azeb had participated in the banging expedition.

That night Etemete, our guardian, burst into the dorm in a housecoat and a black hair net over her curlers when she learned about the bashing of the study hall door. She lectured us about the rules of engagement in the dorm. She then said, pointing to Azeb, "You should not be led by others!"

Azeb was standing in the middle of the room in her snow-white nightgown and white headscarf. She was so angry; she stepped forward and indignantly shot, "I am not led by others. I can think for myself."

"Wonderful!" cried Etemete with sarcasm. We convulsed with laughter. I was watching the drama from my bed. We mocked Etemete with "wonderful" for days to come.

One morning, quite a few days after the door-banging incident, Azeb, Sara, Kidist and I were on our way to the student lounge when we bumped on Tayetu. She loudly asked us if we would like to come to a clandestine meeting that night. "Come to the Law House," she added when we accepted the invitation. After she left, we made fun of her with, "Oh! I would love to go to a clandestine meeting!"

Even *we* knew it was ironic to say clandestine loudly.

We went to the meeting but did not pay attention to most of what they were saying. We laughed and giggled all the time. We laughed particularly at one of the students in a black dressing gown. We thought he was showing off. We were invited another day and we did the same thing. Tayetu never invited us again to those meetings. We were not sure if it was due to our bad manners or if the meetings were discontinued.

At the time, I did not know there was a relationship between the grilling of Alemzewd about her religious beliefs and the door punching operation and the "clandestine" meetings and those were reflections of the doctrine informing campus politics and part of the overall instability on campus. It hadn't yet crystallized in my head either that there was a connection between what the Revos were doing on campus and my studies with Getachew.

I just took things at their face value.

Nurish did not show up for her presentation on feudalism. That was the fourth Sunday since we started our sessions with Getachew and two of the girls had already dropped out.

"Getachew…I don't think Nurelhuda is coming anymore. She says the session is conflicting with her studies." I broke the news to him.

I felt awkward sitting with him in a semi-dark room. He stole a few furtive glances and cleared his throat several times. I looked up at him every time he did so, thinking that he was going to say something. We sat quietly for a few minutes and then he cleared his throat again. He looked past me. "That is fine. So what did you learn about feudalism?"

I didn't expect he would fire back with a question. I was not supposed to chair the meeting so I had read only random paragraphs of the handout. I fumbled in my bag to look for my new exercise book dedicated to Marxism. I had scribbled a few things, while struggling to make sense of the material.

"I am not prepared. It wasn't my turn to chair the meeting."

"We are expected to come prepared even if we don't have to chair meetings. Does that mean you haven't read the chapter at all?"

There is no getting around this guy! "I have… It is just that I did not read through the entire handout."

I had by now learned new terminologies such as mode of production, relations of production, productive forces and means of production. However, I could not see the relevance of studying all those complex terminologies. I could have dropped out of the study circle like Nurish and Mulumebet were it not for him. I thought he was brilliant. Besides, if he was so keen on what we were doing, there must be something more to the study circle thing, I thought.

He took charge and went on and on about feudalism and introduced me to some new vocabulary such as absentee landlord, serfdom and vassals, but only got me interested when he suddenly made a link between feudalism and Ethiopia. For the very first time, I learned that Ethiopia was a semi-feudal country ruled by an absolute monarch.

It was quite a revelation.

I learned that one percent of the population in eastern, western and southern parts of the country owned over ninety percent of the land. I was incensed when Getachew explained to me that these people lived off the sweat of the majority of the population, who toiled for a meager subsistence and were not even able to send their children to school and they often died of disease and malnutrition.

I felt a nameless feeling surging upon me.

I thought the slave owner was scandalous and odious for treating people as "chattel." I found the feudal lord no less heinous. Sitting in that darkened room I made a mental inventory of all the rich people I knew that could fit the description of the rusty creature called feudal lord. Only one person came to mind.

"I know a feudal lord…I mean based on what you just said. His daughter is a friend of mine at the university. But he is a nice person. He recently brought cake enough for all the girls in the dormitory. I thought it was nice of him," I put forth. It wasn't clear even to me why I said that.

"We are talking about a social system," he said, crinkles forming in the corner of his eyes. "In any case, he might be good as a person but remember that he is part of the system, a system that oppresses and exploits people. Once an egg is rotten…it is rotten. You cannot crack it and separate the good from the bad. You have no use for it once it is rotten."

It was so overpowering, I squirmed. *I will never say anything so stupid again.*

He came along with me to the university campus around seven in the evening. We stopped at the entrance of Lab School.

"I am sorry the girls dropped out. I will ask them if they would like to come back." I didn't know what else to say.

"Hiwot, you don't need to be apologetic. It is not your fault if they don't want to come anymore. We can't force people into something like this, you know. If they want to come back, they are most welcome. If not, that is fine too. We've got to be patient," he advised, looking away.

We stood in the dark silently for a few minutes. It felt so awkward.

"Right now," he began, casting his gentle eyes down, "right now...my only concern is *you.* You have something going on. I see something in you that I haven't seen in the others. I know you will go far. Can we meet Wednesday afternoon? It would be your turn to make a presentation. We will be looking at capitalism."

"Sure, I've got nothing to do."

"See you at five o'clock then."

"My only concern is you." I muttered, almost aloud pacing toward the dorm. *What did he mean by that? The way he said you was so...loaded. Why does he avoid my eyes while talking? He always does that. He seems to be terrified of me.* For a flicker of a moment I had a sneaking suspicion that he might indeed like me. But I dismissed the thought immediately. *That must be the last thing on his mind.* I was in awe of him for expanding the realm of my consciousness and for quenching my thirst for knowledge. I was enchanted by his mysteriousness and fascinated by his brilliance. He was of a different breed and I knew I could fall for that very easily.

He had not yet unveiled to me why we should study all those social systems. But he had definitely aroused interest in me in something I had not yet defined. I felt something stirring in my soul. "I know you will go far." *What did he mean by that? Where am I going?*

I was perplexed, nevertheless excited.

I came home Monday night to read the handout in the privacy of my home. Tuesday morning, I decided to miss my classes and had to pretend that I had an exam on Wednesday so that my sister Almaz would not ask me why I was home. I copied down almost everything from the handout into my exercise book by way of taking notes.

Capitalism appeared to be modern and sophisticated, and its mechanisms much more complex than the previous systems. There was a dizzying array of terms I had to wrestle with: bourgeoisie, petty-bourgeoisie, proletariat, labor power, capital, use value, exchange value, surplus value, alienation, commodity fetishism... *What was Getachew thinking?*

I was apprehensive about the day ahead. I got out of bed early Wednesday morning to go over my notes. I didn't think anything had registered in my head. I left before my sister and my brother-in-law came back from work for lunch. I went to campus and killed time between the dorm and the student lounge, then went to Afincho Ber to meet the young man who'd made me turn pages like no teacher.

I knocked softly at exactly five o'clock. He let me in with a jovial smile. The book he was reading was sitting open on the table. He folded the page, while asking after my health, closed it, and put it on the side.

"So...are you ready?"

Oh my God! He is always in a rush to get started! But then for the first time I realized that he did that because he was nervous.

"I don't know...," I murmured. I hoped he would exempt me from what I figured was a formidable task.

He laughed.

I pulled out my exercise book from my purse but was nervous about opening it so that he wouldn't see my bulky notes. I wished I knew how to take notes like him. His were neat, brief and underlined.

"We will do it together." He alleviated my anxiety.

I was enthralled when he swung me up and down the capitalist landscape. I was fascinated by both the creativity and industriousness of the bourgeoisie and by Getachew, who broke down those intimidating concepts into everyday language. I found the bourgeoisie impressive but a scoundrel no less than the landlord or the slave owner. I reckoned he was sneaky and his machinations subtle when Getachew explained to me he had turned the peasant into a wage laborer and paid him for only some of what he produced, while keeping the surplus for himself.

Nevertheless, it was some consolation to know that the worker would snatch power from the hands of the bourgeoisie through revolution and assume leadership, called the dictatorship of the proletariat. It will then usher us into a mighty age of socialism - the transition to communism - where we will taste the joy of freedom and private property and ownership will be abolished when we open the gates of heavenly communism. What was even more reassuring was that the triumph of this kingdom is inevitable. *Oh my God! Where have I been all this time? Good thing I met Getachew.*

The discussion became even more interesting when Getachew made a connection between capitalism and Ethiopia. He said, "Ethiopia is a semi-feudal country with rudimentary capitalist development." He talked about the "penetration of capitalism" in a "predominantly agrarian society."

When we were done, we sat in an awkward silence. He didn't know what to say to me. The only time he forgot himself was when he started the discussion. He became animated and forgot who I was. I might have been just another man as far as he was concerned.

We left and strolled as far as the main campus entrance. A few students were hanging out at the gate. Getachew slowed when we approached them. He asked if I would want to go out with him for lunch on Saturday. All of a sudden, he seemed to be in a rush. He then asked me if I have ever been to Harar Migib Bet.

I said no. I suspected he didn't want the students to recognize him.

"It is around Nazaret bus station. You know where the Chinese restaurant is...the one around *Legehar*...right? That is where Harar Migib Bet is. Let's meet in front of the Chinese restaurant around noon?" he suggested, talking rapidly and extending his hand.

"I will be there," I said, shaking his hand.

"See you then," he mumbled and turned around.

I took a couple of steps toward the gate and wheeled. He had vanished. *Where did he go? Strange!*

On Saturday, I was standing on the sidewalk in front of the Chinese restaurant when I saw him coming. He was wearing his usual yellowish-brown corduroy jacket and khaki pants. His face was lighted up with a happy smile. We headed toward Harar Migib Bet quietly. The restaurant was small and secluded. We sat in a corner and placed our order.

Getachew seemed a bit more relaxed than usual. I was thinking about this sudden change when he abruptly said with a gentle warmth in his voice, "Hiwot, I am pleased with the way our discussion is going but I am concerned about your increasing quietness."

I looked up and our eyes met. His eyes radiated tenderness. I felt my heart skipping a beat. But he quickly looked away. I was in love with him but had become very much afraid of him. I not only loved him but also admired him. I had never met anyone who talked like him. I was taken by his timidity, humility and decency. As I learned more about him, I talked less for fear of making a fool of myself. I gathered up my nerves. "I'm intimidated by the vast knowledge you have for your age. I am so ignorant and I don't want to make a fool of myself like I did the first day we met."

"I thought you knew a lot more than I expected. I was actually impressed that day. I am only learning myself," he said, warmth mounting in his voice.

We sat quietly for a few minutes. My heart kept beating rapidly. I shifted from side to side in my chair. I was too scared my body language would betray my feelings. In the semi-dark room at Afincho Ber, I had hoped that the darkness would somehow cover what was written all over my face. But here at Harar Migib Bet, I felt it was out for him to read and that made me nervous. I had taken extreme care not to show him the bearings of my heart, not just yet. It wasn't that I had difficulty expressing my emotions. He was so serious and focused on what he was doing, any sentiments of the heart seemed out of place.

I had started thinking less about my affliction since I had started my studies with Getachew. I had been feeling as if the weight was slowly, but surely, lifting off my shoulders.

"So Hiwot, tell me about Harar. I've heard stories about Harar and *ye Harar lijoch*. You are very sociable, gregarious and generous. I know a few students from Harar and I think they fit the descriptions. Now that I know you, I would like to know more about the place." He expressed his interest with his usual gentle and shy smile.

"Oh, I don't know. There are so many funny stories… like what usually takes place at Feres Megala, the bus terminal," I said slowly.

The waiter placed the food tray and our drinks on the table and left. I looked at Getachew once again and his relaxed mood helped my nerves settle down. He laughed copiously when I told him funny stories about Feres Megala.

As of that day, it became a ritual for us to dine at Harar Migib Bet every Saturday or Sunday. He let his guard down when we met there. He was not the serious, awkward, and stiff man he was in the semi-dark room in Afincho Ber. Harar stories broke the ice and eased the tension created by timidity. I often exhorted my brain to remember the funniest stories. I noticed he laughed easily and with abandon. Seriousness gave way to tenderness and the sense of ease.

I often wondered why we went only to Harar Migib Bet. It was a modest place but nothing like the ones I went to. At the time, Lalibela, Harambe, Peacock, Flamingo or Hôtel d'Afrique were the places to be, not Harar Migib Bet. I still didn't know why we had to study Marxism. I still found him mysterious.

Harar Migib Bet added to the mystery surrounding him.

One Sunday evening around mid-Spring, Getachew and I were silently ambling toward the main campus, after our usual session, when he suddenly said, "Hiwot, we might not be able to meet at the Afincho Ber house anymore."

"Oh!"

"Why don't you call me at my parents' house on Tuesday night? I will let you know where our next meeting will be. Have you got a piece of paper?" he asked, grabbing a pen from his shirt pocket.

I gave him my exercise book set aside for Marxism. He wrote the number in the back and returned it to me. I wondered why we wouldn't meet there anymore. It was all in his eyes. He was not going to disclose anything. *He has so much to hide!* I realized that I had to live with what I was given.

"Why don't I give you mine? Just in case…," I suggested.

"Good idea!" He brightened his face with a smile.

I tore a sheet from my exercise book, wrote my phone number and gave it to him. We said goodbye and I hurried to the dorm.

I called him Tuesday night from a payphone. He suggested that we meet the next day in front of Kidist Mariam Church at Amist Kilo (mid-way between Sidist Kilo and Arat Kilo campuses) at five in the afternoon. He took me to one of the student houses behind Engineering College when we met on Wednesday. The house was even smaller and darker than the one at Afincho Ber. It had a bed, a small and dilapidated table, and four chairs. We continued to meet there every Wednesday afternoon for our regular study sessions and had lunch on Saturday or Sunday at Harar Migib Bet.

April 20, 1973 was a momentous day that marked the return of the Revos to the campus political scene and my own ascent to social and political awareness. Mekdes and I were on our way to class when we saw a massive crowd in front of the Arts Building. We stopped by to see what was going on. We heard students speaking animatedly and quickly joined the crowd. Sara, Azeb and Kidist were somewhere behind us. The crowd began to swell. All of a sudden, it turned into the largest gathering I had ever been in.

News about a ravaging famine in the provinces of Wollo and Tigray had been sweeping through the capital city like wildfire. The assembly was called to protest against the famine. It was primed by the shocking pictures of emaciated children and adults posted at the Arts Building.

There had been an influx of the famine-stricken to the capital city. The government had remained conspicuously silent on the famine for months. It was preoccupied with beautifying the capital city for the 80th birthday of the Emperor, celebrated in July 1972.

Standing beside Mekdes, my heart fluttered with excitement. I had been dying to witness a day like this. Mekdes and I pushed our way to the front of the crowd, where I saw a student with a huge Afro, khaki pants and safari coat speaking and wagging his index finger in the air. "Hundreds of people travel hundreds of miles on foot every day from the famine-hit areas in search of food, children among them! Hundreds have perished on their way over and their bodies are strewn along the road, and yet the government was beautifying the city for the 80th birthday of the Emperor!"

Another student came on, angrily accusing the government. "The famine and death from the drought were preventable. The government has deliberately covered up the existence of the famine from the public and the world."

I was mesmerized by the passionate speeches. One by one, students spoke until their Afros appeared as dandelion pappus ready to fly off their heads. They demanded that the government acknowledge the existence of the famine. They recounted harrowing tales of human suffering. "People, including children, are barred from entering the capital, as they had been a few months ago, while Addis Ababa was being electrified with neon lights for the Emperor's birthday," they charged.

We were outraged by such an affront to human dignity.

"Bread!" a shout went up from the crowd. "For the hungry!" we rumbled, raising our fists in the air. "Bread!" somebody yelled out. "For the hungry!" we rocked the campus with a thunderous roar.

I glanced swiftly over and saw an army truck full of *Fetno Derash* – riot police – entering through the main campus entrance. They got off the truck with lightning speed. They had riot gear: white helmets, grey shields and sturdy batons. I had never seen their kind in Harar, where their counterparts had wooden clubs but no shields or helmets to protect them from stones with which students pelted them.

Ever since I saw the *Fetno Derash*, I was thinking about Mekdes. I was worried she might not be able to run fast enough with all that weight. I tried to figure out how I could run and at the same time help her run. It would only be a matter of time before the fearsome soldiers pounced on all of us.

An officer addressed us over a megaphone urging us to disperse. "Stay put!" "Don't move!" shouted some of the students. There was a commotion; no one seemed to know what to do. "Don't move!" "Stay where you are!" the students kept saying. Our eyes were riveted on the riot police, who kept glaring at us like a lion ready to pounce on its prey. The voice on the megaphone once again goaded us to disperse. "Don't move!" someone in the crowd shouted. No one moved. *Boom!* Everyone took flight.

I looked for Mekdes but she was nowhere in sight. I kept frantically looking for her until I saw her sprinting, at least fifty yards away. It was no time to wonder by what magic she had managed to run that fast. I started running before the soldiers could catch up with me, but tripped over blades of grass and fell. I could have been trampled by hundreds of students had it not been for a man who picked me up with one hand and kept running. I didn't even have the chance to see his face.

Dozens of students rushed into a building close to the Law School. I dashed in without even thinking. The place was full of canvases. I found a large one leaning against the wall and hid behind it, occasionally poking my head out. I saw a bewildered looking man standing in the middle of the room watching as his sanctuary was invaded by panting students. I later learned he was a deaf-mute artist.

I came to realize I had made a mistake hiding there when I saw soldiers burst in, swinging their batons. One of them tossed my canvas aside, grabbed me by the arm and pushed me outside. Another came to assist him--as if his colleague was no match for me! They beat me up with their batons and kicked me with their boots even after I fell onto the ground. I thought doomsday had finally arrived. It was the first time I had been beaten up. Compared with this, the demonstration in Harar was a picnic in the park. The soldiers finally left me lying on the ground. I was struggling to get up, when two male students came over and helped me up. They accompanied me to the dorm.

I found Sara, Kidist, Azeb and the other girls in the dorm safe. They were telling their escape stories when Mekdes emerged, tears rolling down her cheeks. Two soldiers had found her squatting behind a car and escorted her to the dorm. When they got to the "love spot," one of them gave her a good lash on her behind as a gesture of a warm farewell. It was so painful she cried.

We had a good laugh on it.

My hands, shoulders and knees were swollen and very painful. My friends had to call my sister's house and *Gash* Tedla, my brother-in-law, came over and drove me home. When I came back after a week, I learned that my status among the "vanguard of the student movement" had been elevated. The day I came back, I was sitting with a friend on the pavement at the "love spot," when a couple of the "vanguard" came over and expressed their sympathy. One of them even wondered how I had survived "those heavy boots."

I indeed survived "those heavy boots." More importantly, April 20 became a landmark in terms of my understanding of social and political action. All the demonstrations that I was part of prior to that were sheer adolescent adventurism. I was never able to grasp their real significance. For the first time, I came to understand that even students could pressure a government to bow to their demands. The government was compelled to acknowledge the existence of the famine and forced to become part of the relief effort.

Nothing could quell the indignity we felt about the famine. We gave up breakfast for the semester so that the money could go towards famine relief efforts. The university formed the Famine Relief and Rehabilitation Committee and teachers gave up ten percent of their salary towards the famine relief.

The "Hidden Hunger" became public knowledge.

After we gave up our breakfast, my friends and I started going in the mornings to a *Pasty Bet* – teahouse – located north of the university campus. Breakfast at the student lounge had become unaffordable. We visited the lounge three or four times a day, and adding raisin cake and tea on top of the daily expense of Coke or Pepsi became beyond our means. My friends often dispatched me to try our luck making money by setting our year-mate Alemzewd's hair. She gave me one birr every time I did; it bought us four bottles of Coke. "It is okay. I will go to the hairdresser," Alemzewd would often tell me. I knew and she knew that I always did a terrible job of setting her hair. She needed me only when she was desperate.

Going to the *Pasty Bet* was cheaper. We had breakfast for only sixty cents – fifteen cents each. We paid five cents for *Pasty* – sweet bread balls fried in oil – and ten cents for tea. I always managed to give a five-cent tip to the young boy, who served us and at times let me pour tea from the dark and huge kettle wiggling on the red-hot embers in the alcove. I loved my tea scalding. We often made a joke out of the yellow Macaroni displayed on the counter. "Oh, I would love to have yellow macaroni!" It was cooked with turmeric and oil and looked very unappetizing.

The *Pasty Bet* was a small place with a dirt floor and a few dilapidated chairs and tables. To our dismay, some campus male students started having breakfast there too. We didn't like the intrusion. In a way, going there was our way of saying we were *liberated*. No self-respecting woman went to a *Pasty Bet* unless you were like Yodit and I, who subsisted on weekends on samosa sold at a *Pasty Bet*. But that was in Harar when we were in our mid-teens.

My friends and I became severely constipated because of the oil drenched *Pasty*. We had to leave our favorite retreat and go to The Castle, next door.

Getachew always gave me a book which he expected me to read, take notes and come for discussion. He would ask me what I thought about it. I unfailingly replied, "It is good." It was one of the most dreaded moments of my life. He would smile and say, "*Good* is not an answer. What did you learn about it? What did you or didn't you like about it?" I read the books over and over so that I would be able to say something smart about them. At times I didn't understand half the contents of some of the books. Other times, I simply hated them but didn't dare tell Getachew. Nonetheless, he would always strike a discussion with passion about any of the books he gave me to read. He would explain everything gently and patiently.

One thing was certain; he had aroused in me an interest in what we were doing and most importantly in being with him. It had been almost five months since I started my apprenticeship under him and I had made strides in my studies. New words and phrases such as "chauvinism," "sphere of influence," "geopolitical interest," "focoism," "protracted armed struggle" and "Soviet revisionism" had been added to my repertoire. I learned about the French, Russian, Chinese, Cuban and Vietnamese revolutions. I picked up names such as Bolsheviks, Mensheviks, Trotsky, Narodniks,

Decembrists, Kulaks, Soviets, Iskra, Pravda, Jacobins, Rosa Luxemburg, Karl Liebknecht, Clara Zetkin, The Comintern, Kuomintang, Che Guevara and Ho Chi Minh.

Those were glorious times on campus too. Books by V.G Afanasyev, Franz Fanon, Amilcar Cabral, Agostino Neto, Régis Debray, Paul Sweezy, Harry Magdoff, Leo Huberman, Ernest Mandel, Edgar Snow, Fidel Castro, John Reed, Granma and Peking Review were widely read, besides Karl Marx, Friedrich Engles, Vladimir Lenin, and Mao Tse Tung. Reeds' *Ten days that shook the world* and *Veneceremos* (Che's speeches and writings) were sensations we were all infatuated with. These books were brought into the country by the student network.

I recall reading a biography of Che, whose title I could not remember. It shook me to my core. I felt an instant identification with his affliction. My heart went out for the revolutionary icon who suffered from asthma. He was not just a guerrilla fighter to me serenaded in the streets and on campus but an afflicted man whose experience resonated with my own.

Getachew once gave me Frantz Fanon's *The wretched of the earth*, from which I scooped ideas about colonialism and decolonization which I had never heard about. Cabral was assassinated a few months earlier and Getachew spoke about him with great reverence and sadness. He said Cabral was one of the "greatest revolutionaries of all time."

One day in early spring, when he and I were having lunch at Harar Migib Bet, I took a book from my purse and asked if he had read it.

"No, I haven't," he said.

There is a book he hasn't read! I was too excited to notice the frown on his face.

"Where did you get it?" he asked, taking it from my hand.

I looked him in the eye and what I saw dampened my excitement. "I bought it from *Mercato*...from second-hand book sellers," I answered resignedly.

He tucked the book into his jacket pocket without saying anything. It was confiscated for all I knew. I didn't know what to think or say. I knew he liked Mao. The book was entitled *The true face of Maoism* by Fyodor Burlatsky. I suspected that he didn't want me to read a critic of Communist literature before I had firmly planted my feet in it. I wondered what possessed me to go out and buy such a book.

That June, I informed Getachew that I was going to Harar for the summer.

"I am sure you will bring Harar stories with you. Are you taking the train?"

I said, "Yes, I always do. I love traveling by train. It is so much fun. The most interesting aspect of traveling by train is the cat-and-mouse game between the contrabandists and the Finance officers."

There was a contraband stretch starting from the port of Djibouti and transiting through Dire Dawa to Addis Ababa. Besides linking the country to the outside world, the railway was key to the thriving of the illegal trade. The railway was built during the reign of Emperor Menilik II with a 99-year lease to a French construction company and the then Swiss advisor to Menilik.

"Tell me about it," Getachew cajoled me eager to hear my train stories. So I did and he laughed until tears were dripping down his cheeks. "When are you leaving?" he managed to say at last.

"As soon as I finish class... that is what...in two weeks?"

"Let's meet on Wednesday and talk about Lenin's *State and Revolution*. I'm sure you've finished reading it by now."

"I have," I lied and quickly added, "I'm not sure I've understood everything." I started reading the book but found it very tedious and didn't have the appetite to go on. I never found Lenin as interesting as Marx. I never dared tell Getachew.

We discussed Lenin's book on Wednesday and had lunch on the weekend at Harar Migib Bet. The following week, I left for Harar to visit my mother, Tenfelesh Demissie, and my younger sister Negede. I spent most of the summer in Dire Dawa with Martha, Mahlet and other friends. Martha worked in Dire Dawa, while I was going to school. She found Mahlet and me summer jobs, where she was working. But we quit our jobs after a couple of weeks just to stay home.

I came back from Harar at the end of August. I called Getachew right away and we met at Harar Migib Bet. We had lunch and stayed there all afternoon. I was excited to see him again. He had become an inspiration to me and I had missed our theoretical discussions. I'd lapsed into my former life in Dire Dawa and hadn't read any of the books he had given me.

A few days later, I started my sophomore year. Azeb went to Business College. Sara, Kidist and I joined the European Languages Department, French as a major and English as a minor. Mekdes went abroad. We learned that Tayetu Assefa had left the country. Sadly, she was later on killed in a car accident in Germany. It was rumored that her friend, Amleset Kibrom, had joined one of the Eritrean Liberation Fronts.

Many students had written off my friends and me at the end of the first semester of our first year. They were taken by surprise to see us in January. They were sure June would be the last time we would set foot on campus. We came back triumphantly in September.

The past year was spent between the lounge, kissing pool and occasionally movies. I had retired from parties after high school, which was one less extracurricular activity. There were also our study circle sessions. We never had lecture notes and the best we could do was borrowing from others at the last minute.

It was a miracle that we survived for as long as we did.

Azeb, Kidist, Sara and Anene moved into a dorm in the main building. Anene Abbas was a high school friend of Sara and Azeb and had enrolled at the beginning of the semester. I got the twenty-birr stipend but stayed in the dorm, most of the time sleeping with Anene and at times with Sara. The dorm gave us a little bit of privacy with only the five of us, unlike the prefab dorm where sixteen girls were cramped in one dorm.

I saw Getachew a couple of days after I started class. We met in front of the zoo, like we did many times, and took a long promenade toward Menilik Hospital.

"I just wanted to tell you that you are going to continue your studies with another person," he informed me.

"Why?" I was disappointed. I couldn't imagine myself studying with another person. I had taken it to mean that the study circle session was something between him and me. I had never looked beyond that and didn't want to study with another person.

"We will continue our study…informally," he said, looking me sideways.

I was relieved. I didn't care whether it was formal or informal as long as we continued our sessions. He gave me a description of this new person and advised me what to say when I saw him.

It had never occurred to me that he would be a messenger of the gods.

I see my calling. It shines forth like the sun.
     -Henrik Isben, *Brand*

A couple of days later, I met my new mentor at the bus station beside the zoo. He was very quiet and serious. He gave me a handout and instructed me to read it and come back for discussion at the end of the week. By then I had soaked up the basics of Historical and Dialectical Materialism and much more that Getachew had drilled into me.

The new mentor gave me the surprise of my life when I saw him toward the end of the week. He disclosed to me that I had become a member of an underground organization called *Abyot* – Revolution. I learned that I was on probation. He gave me a booklet that contained the roles and responsibilities of a member. He warned me not to say anything to anyone about my membership.

I was struck dumb. I shoved the booklet to the bottom of my purse and whisked to campus, my heart thumping with excitement. *How can I keep such an enormous secret?* I thought I would explode if I didn't talk to someone. I resolved to confide in Azeb.

She divulged to me she'd been told the same thing when I broke the news to her. We had a few times said to each other 'my guy' said this and 'my guy' said that, referring to Getachew and his counterpart in her study circle. We'd been good in terms of discipline considering the circumstances. I had never said anything to Sara and Kidist, and neither had they.

The veil was lifted, at last! I saw the gods with my naked eyes. They finally revealed their secrets to me. I found out why I have been studying Marxism-Leninism. Suddenly, the world looked different. It seemed endowed with meaning. I saw the panorama of my life shifting in front of me. I saw it veering toward what I came to believe was my calling. I felt I was one of those chosen to partake in what I envisaged was a magical world. I felt pride rising up in me. I saw myself soaring into the sky like an eagle and landing on the summit of Mount Everest.

I wanted to touch the sky.

But what does working underground mean? My imagination ran wild. I knew what I had thus far been doing with Getachew was a secret but I had never characterized it as *underground*. I remembered the "It is a question of life and death" caution from him. I felt a fleeting sense of fear sneak up on me. But I immediately cast it out of my head. Rather, I wanted to plunge myself into what seemed to me an enchanting and enchanted world. For days, I could not for a second get the word *underground* out of my head. I wondered if every student or lecturer crossing my path worked in the underworld. I peered into their faces for cues that betrayed a secret subterranean existence.

Now that I was a member of an underground organization, I equated the organization with Getachew. They became one and the same. A sudden burst of flame ignited in my chest for both. I felt Getachew was the shining star who led me through the darkness into the luminous road ahead of me. I had long stopped asking myself why I was studying Marxism. I was enjoying what I conceived was a fascinating way of looking at the world. *Why didn't Getachew himself tell me this exciting news? Why did he have to do it through a messenger? Maybe that is how it is done.* I felt the window to Getachew's mysterious world was tossed open. *Now I know why he is so different and so enigmatic.* I started piecing things together and his strange behaviors suddenly became intelligible.

The next day, I did something unbecoming of a person working underground. I had recently learned that a certain law student was asking why I wouldn't wear a skirt. He kept saying I would have if I had "the legs." I wanted to respond to this slap to my self-esteem with action. I went home and came back the next day with my four-year-old niece's brand-new Scottish skirt, which her father had gotten her from England.

I came to the dorm, put on the shockingly short skirt and scurried to the student lounge to make a daring spectacle. It was after lunch and I knew the lounge would be packed. I walked in deliberately slowly so that law student, and frankly everybody else, saw me. I went to buy a drink first and joined my friends at their table. I had made a statement and it was time to go to the dorm and change into something less revealing.

I turned back at the "love spot" and went to the Arts Building instead. I went into the building, came back out, and hastened toward the dorm. I whirled around when I felt someone tapping on my shoulder. It was Getachew! I was shocked to see him. I felt I had dishonored my underground title. I felt blood rush to my cheeks. I burned with shame. He was wearing a black berretta hat and white-rimmed reading glasses that made him look beyond his years. I wondered why he wore those funny reading glasses and that ugly hat that made him look old.

"Getachew, what brings you here?" I asked almost angered by his unceremonious appearance on campus.

"I didn't get to see you on the weekend. I tried to call you several times. I figured I might come and look for you," he said with a shy smile.

"I am sorry. I wasn't home..."

"I saw you running down the stairs a few minutes ago. I tried to grab you by the hand but you pulled back and kept running," he said, laughing.

"Oh!" The weight of shame pressed on me even more.

"Can we go somewhere…maybe find a classroom where we can sit and talk?"

I noticed that he looked uneasy. I figured the hat and reading glasses were camouflage. Tottering beside him, I wondered what he thought of my skirt. He had never seen me dressed like that. Up to that moment, I had managed to skillfully conceal my campus life from him. I searched his face for a hint of disapproval. There wasn't any. If there was, I wasn't able to see it for he walked with his head down as if he didn't want to be recognized by anyone. We climbed up the stairs to the third-floor and went into an empty classroom. We sat next to each other on the wooden armchairs in the first row.

Neither of us spoke. The silence was deafening. I didn't know what to say. I kept pulling down on my skirt nervously. I looked at him sideways to see if he had seen my bare thighs. He was blankly gazing ahead of him. I saw beads of perspiration forming on his forehead.

"Hiwot…" he began abruptly in a cracked voice. "I meant to tell you this for quite a while… but….I just couldn't…couldn't pull myself together…My nerves are a wreck."

I looked at him questioningly. *Oh no!* I was terrified of what I was going to hear.

"I don't know how to put this. I am…I am…I am desperately in love with you!" He spoke in English, his lips quivering.

I was speechless. I almost fainted with trepidation when he held my right hand. I felt his moist hand shaking. He wanted to speak but his lips trembled. There was silence for a few minutes.

It felt like eternity.

"I wanted to tell you how much I loved you the day you told me about those train stories…that was before you left for Harar," he said, wiping his forehead with his hand. He paused and then added, "I just couldn't. I was a complete wreck. I relaxed only when you started telling me those funny stories. It has been ten months since we've met. I vividly remember the day we met and getting confused when I saw you coming toward me. I didn't expect to meet someone like you."

"What do you mean?" The confusion written all over his face the day I met him at Sidist Kilo came to mind.

"I mean you know…I didn't expect to meet someone like you. 'Why are they sending me this one? What am I going to do with her?' I said to myself when I saw you coming up to me. I still remember your huge Afro and the yellow sweater you were wearing. I kept saying, 'No, It can't be her.' You didn't look like the kind of person I was expecting to meet. However, I must admit I was mistaken. You cannot judge people by the way they dress or by the way they do their hair. It did not take me long, though, to realize what kind of girl you are. I had to go somewhere that day but after I met you, I could not resist the temptation of staying. I actually fell in love with you on the spot…right when you extended your hand smiling to shake mine. Remember? We went to the zoo for a drink. I still have fresh memories of everything you told me that day."

"I know I said a lot of nonsense. I feel ashamed-"

"Why? What for?" he interrupted me. "I enjoyed every minute of it. But most of all, I found your innocence disarming. I was touched. You have matured in every sense of the word. I really admire your discipline and commitment for what you are doing even though you didn't understand much of what was going on. That is really admirable. I meant to tell you a long time ago that I loved you but I struggled with myself thinking it might conflict with what we've been doing."

I indeed secretly loved and admired him but I didn't have the courage to show it to him just yet. I respected him almost with awe but his ready smile and easy demeanor assured me a sense of ease. I often thought he lived in a world of his own, a world that was enigmatic and impenetrable.

I was drawn to him, nonetheless.

He stimulated my brain and warmed my heart. I was charmed by his gentle soul and timid nature. I marveled at his thirst for theoretical clarity. He made a conscious effort to furnish my mind with Marxism. I always looked forward to our discussions even though he often assailed me with questions. Most importantly, he did it all quietly and humbly. When I talked, he listened with enthusiasm and rapt attention, which made me feel like I was on top of the world. I'd loved reading novels but he had kindled a new flame in me, a passion for theory. Without realizing it and without even being told in so many words, I was tempered with discipline, commitment and hard work.

I made my way back to the dorm subdued. I was in an adventurous mood when I had left. But I found it all too much to bear and confided in Azeb when I saw her.

"My guy confessed to me that he loves me! I don't know what to say. I am scared."

"I don't believe it! It is so nice," she said with excitement. "But why are you scared?"

"I don't know. I didn't expect that from someone like him."

"Why not? What are you talking about? Isn't he human?"

"He is… but I don't know…he is so serious…oh…I don't know. I can't imagine going out with someone like him."

"You like him too, right?"

"Yeah, I do… but…I don't know…I just didn't expect anything like that from him."

"Tell me what he actually said to you…in a dialogue form," she coaxed me, laughing and placing her fingers on her lips, which was a habit with her.

By "in a dialogue form," she meant what we did every night in the dorm. Azeb, Kidist, Sara and I sat on a bed every night in the dorm after returning from the kissing pool and repeated in turn the conversations we have had with our dates.

"Maybe some other time. Right now, I am too overwhelmed. He saw me in that skirt and I don't even know what he is going to think of me."

She burst out laughing. "Was he in the lounge when you came in?"

"No, I went to the Arts Building before changing. That was where I ran into him. He said he had come to look for me…today of all days!"

"But why did you go to the Arts Building?"

"I don't know."

It might have been the next day or the day after, Sara, Kidist and I were in the dorm chatting. We had just come back from the cafeteria after having supper and were waiting for Azeb to go to the student lounge to mark our presence. Azeb poked her head through the curtain that hung on the door and beckoned to me. I was sitting on her bed, got up, and followed her to the hallway. She looked pale. I wondered what could have happened.

"I heard people have been arrested," she said in a whisper.

"What? Who are they? I hope my guy is not one of them. His name is Getachew Maru," I blurted out, forgetting that I was not supposed to mention his name.

"He is. Mine is arrested too."

"How do you know my guy's name?"

"I heard Abebech mention his name."

"Abebech? How does she know? Are you sure he is one of them?"

"I know for sure he is one of them because I heard her say, 'The Getachew Marus.' I can go and ask if you want."

While Azeb and I were talking, Abebech came out of her dorm and went to the toilet. She was our year-mate. When she came out, Azeb dashed up to her dorm. She may have been there two minutes but it felt like ages.

"Yeah, he is the one," she confirmed to me when she came back.

"So he is arrested?" I literally felt my heart sinking. I became frantic. *Why is he arrested? What is going to happen to him? Are they going to arrest us too?*

I was startled by the turn of events. I thought it was like a dream. It was as if an extra-terrestrial being had just landed into my life, changed it forever within a few months, and disappeared, suddenly with no announcement or warning. I wondered if he would ever come out of prison alive. I wondered if my underground career had ended even before it had begun. I wondered if the bearer of the news of my *Abyot* membership, whose name I had never learned, was arrested too.

Tension and restlessness were building up on campus since classes started in September 1973, and right to the end of the semester. A series of class boycotts, assemblies and meetings took place at the Sidist Kilo, Amist Kilo and Arat Kilo campuses. Around the time Getachew was arrested, an assembly was held at the Science Faculty campus in Arat Kilo. Kidist and I did not go but Sara and Azeb did. Many students were beaten up that day, but Sara and Azeb escaped unscathed.

Class boycott reached its peak in November and December. The university administration had had enough of our boycotts; in December, they announced the cafeteria would be closed until we returned to class. The students' demands were the reinstitution of the banned union and its organ (*Struggle*), academic freedom, the release of political prisoners and larger issues such as "Land to the tiller" and "Democratic rights for all." The day the cafeteria was closed, the students decided to raise money for food allowance for students from the provinces. Meles Tekle, one of the "vanguards of the student movement," invited Azeb and me to participate in the fundraising.

We were thrilled.

The two of us were standing on the opposite side of the entrance of the Arts Building, holding out caps to solicit money from evening class students around six o'clock, when the *Fetno Derash* came out of nowhere. They hounded everyone out of the area. They pushed Azeb and me into an empty classroom and seized our caps and money. A soldier opened the door every now and then and threw some more students inside. That was when it became clear to me that we were indeed arrested.

A few minutes later, I peered through the window and saw Hailu Mulatu, my year-mate and friend Selam's boyfriend, coming toward the building. He took evening classes. He went past the *Fetno Derash*, standing in the dark outside, holding their shields up. I immediately pushed open the window rail and called him. I went to the door and opened it to talk to him, unaware that two soldiers were posted on the opposite side of the door. They ordered me to close the door and stay inside.

Moments later, the door was flung open and Hailu asked me what I was doing there. I told him I was arrested. He asked if there were other girls with me. I gave him Azeb and Hirut's names. He left and came back a few minutes later carrying a piece of paper in his hand, which he gave to one of the soldiers standing at the door. They let the three of us go. On our way to the dorm, we asked Hailu how he managed to get us out. He said he knew the Lieutenant in charge of the campus Police Station.

The campus has been turned into a ghost town with the lights out. Hailu asked us if Selam was okay. We didn't know. We didn't even know where Sara and Kidist were. He said goodbye at the "love spot." He asked us to convey his greetings to his girlfriend. We thanked him and rushed to the dorm.

We found them all safe and sound. We learned that Kidist and Sara had been hiding in the washroom at the Arts Building. "All that bravado was for this?" this lecturer mocked them when he saw them sprinting toward the washrooms. Everybody in the dorm laughed. The *Fetno Derash* later chased them out.

The following morning, we heard that the male students arrested with us the previous night had been taken to a Police Station. Just after lunch, Azeb and I were summoned to the campus Police Station. They interrogated us individually about the fundraising and our meal cards were confiscated.

It was no problem for us eating at the cafeteria without a meal card for the rest of the weeks. I knew one of the servers and he always gave us extra food whenever we had friends over. It wouldn't have been a problem even if he wasn't there. We could have shared with Sara, Kidist and Anene. It was fun for us to go to the cafeteria. It opened at twelve o'clock for lunch and at six for supper. If you were in line before noon or before six, you could definitely get better sauce. However, a watery stew would greet you if you came late. There would often be three pieces of meat floating around. Students called it *therefore* – after the three dots in a triangle symbol used for therefore in mathematics.

My friends and I always arrived late at the cafeteria. It was tacky to stand in line when you were "jolly." We were rewarded with a watery sauce for coming late. We did not mind. What mattered was that we kept our "jolly" pride.

There was usually a long break in the line up between the last girl and a male student queuing up behind her. Servers, all male, usually loaded a girl's tray and shoved a pathetically small portion of food into the tray of a man trailing her. So a male student lined up behind a woman usually left a wide gap between them, hoping that she would recede from the server's mind by the time he got there.

It was the end of December. We had finished the semester and had gone back home. Azeb called me at home and suggested we go to Sidist Kilo campus and get our grades. We agreed to meet in front of the Arts Building. I arrived there first and waited for Azeb a little while and climbed the stairs up to the Faculty of Arts on the third-floor.

I had not the slightest suspicion of what was in store for me when the Faculty secretary gave me two envelopes. I opened up one of them, which happened to contain my grades. I was curious about the second one. I presumed it was some sort of congratulatory letter for passing with distinction. Instead, it stated that I've been suspended from school for one year!

I was stunned.

The allegation was that I was 'agitating' and 'intimidating' students in the dorm. I walked down the flight of stairs pensively and went outside and stood near the entrance of the building. I saw Mr. James Lee, Assistant Dean of the Faculty of Arts, striding toward the building. The Englishman had taught me English 111 in my first year. He came over when he saw me.

"Did you get your grades?" he asked, his face turning red as a tomato.

"Yes, I did."

"Come to my office. We will talk about that nonsense."

I followed him.

"First, congratulations on a job well done," he said, sitting on his chair. "I am so sorry you are suspended. I don't understand what kind of nonsense that is. Don't worry. I am going to fight on your behalf. I will take it to the Dean's office and, if that does not work, I will take it to the Faculty Council. They can't do that."

I didn't know what to say. I simply said, "Thank you."

"You know what Hiwot? Even if you are suspended, you will still be in third-year when you come back. I will see to it that you don't lose a year." He promised.

While he was saying this, Monsieur Chaume, head of the European Languages Department, came in. "They can't suspend my best student! We have to do something about it," he shouted, speaking English in a French accent.

Mr. Lee did not seem to like the Frenchman's presence. The latter got the message and left asking me to come to his office when I am done. I went to the French Department a few minutes later.

"You are the best student in my class. I was looking forward to seeing you graduate with flying colors. They can't do that to you. You are not going to lose a year. When you come back, you will be in third-year. I will give you lessons and all the materials you need."

"I think I have lost the *Mauger* book. I will pay for it," I said, remembering about the textbook I was supposed to return.

We were warned we were not going to get our grades unless we returned the textbooks.

"I don't care about the book. You have your grades, anyway."

Not all those promises allayed my anxiety. I was nervous about how to break the news to my sister Almaz. I came out of the

European Languages Department and went outside. I saw Azeb coming. "Guess what! I am suspended for one year!"

"You've got to be kidding. What for?" she asked with furrowed eyebrows.

"I guess because of the fundraising thing. But the letter says for 'intimidation' and 'agitation.' I don't know what intimidation and agitation they are talking about."

"Oh, my God! I must be suspended too. *Etiye* would kill me for it," she cried, referring to her mother.

We ran up the stairs to the fourth-floor where the Faculty of Business was located. The secretary gave her two envelopes. She too was suspended for one year. We later found out that fifteen of us (three girls and twelve boys) arrested the night of the fundraising event were suspended, Meles Tekle among us.

I broke the bad news to my sister and my brother-in-law over dinner that night. As I expected, my sister was upset about it. She was upset even more because I had done well that semester.

The year ended with a suspension from school and a scary dream. I had the dream a couple of days before we vacated our dormitory. I had slept on the top bunk with Sara that night. "Oh my God, I am glad it is only a dream." I breathed a sigh of relief when I woke up, drenched in sweat. I didn't know what time it was. The room was bright and the sun was at its peak and came through the tiny window that had no curtain. I sat up in the bed gasping for air and shaking. I heard voices in the hallway. It was Kidist, Azeb and Sara.

"You are alive! We thought you were dead. We tried to wake you up. We tried everything but nothing worked. What happened?" Sara asked, putting her hands on the bed.

"What time is it?" I asked, trying to breath.

"It is past noon. Get up, take a shower and let's go have lunch," Azeb insisted.

"I had this horrifying dream. I am glad it is just a dream. Every time I tried to wake up, I just couldn't. It felt like I had dreamt all night and all morning."

"It must have been a nightmare," Sara said, laughing.

"What did you dream about, anyway?" Kidist asked me.

"I saw this white thing that looked like an inflated balloon. It came into each person's house through the door and came out of the window or vice versa. People tried to pop it with sticks but it kept flying in the sky. Then *Janhoy* came out and addressed a multitude of people. 'A terrible thing is happening to our country. We need to pray. We need to pray,' he implored them. They knelt on the ground and prayed with the Emperor. He ordered soldiers to shoot at the balloon. They shot toward the sky non-stop but none of the bullets hit it. It actually went further up in the sky. Finally, when they managed to hit it…it popped and fourteen crescent-shaped stars spread across the sky. Everybody was scared and knelt down saying, '*Egzio!*' They prayed and prayed."

"Wow! What a long dream? It is spooky too. It must have some kind of meaning," Sara said.

"I don't know. I am glad it is just a dream. It was so scary."

We met Yordanos, Sara's cousin, at the cafeteria and told her my dream. She said she would have her mother interpret it for her when she goes home in the evening. Yordanos' mother said that something terrible was going to happen in the country that would spread throughout the fourteen provinces.

We couldn't figure out what possibly could happen to the country that would spread throughout the fourteen provinces.

It is possible to predict the time and progress of revolution.
It is governed by its own more or less mysterious laws.
    -Vladimir Ilyich Lenin

Had I known the whirling wheels of history were about to shake up the rhythm of our leisurely existence, January 1974 wouldn't have felt like the longest month of my life. Alas, those January days dragged by painfully slow.

Azeb and I were not even allowed on campus since we didn't have ID. We met Kidist and Sara off campus. It was painful not to be able to go to school. We didn't know what to do with ourselves. It was then that the suspension had sunk into our head. We had no choice but to look for a job. We didn't even know where to go. We went to the Central Personnel Agency (CPA) in Arat Kilo once and found the lineup dreadfully long. We turned back vowing never to return. Finally, I got a tutoring job through my brother-in-law, teaching Amharic to a British woman.

February 18 started as a day like any other when I left home in the morning to meet Azeb in Piassa – Piazza. We had planned to go to Reis Engineering to apply for a job. I was standing in front of Mona Lisa Bar in Abware, a few steps from home, wondering where all the taxis had gone until a passerby told me that I was wasting my time waiting. He informed me the taxi drivers had gone on strike.

They went on strike protesting high gas prices precipitated by the Organization of Petroleum Exporting Countries (OPEC) oil embargo. The price of oil had skyrocketed overnight because of American and other Western countries' support to Israel during the war with Egypt and Syria at the end of 1973.

Later that day, I learned teachers had joined the taxi drivers protesting the new education reform bill, which they believed would have scaled back the strides the country had made in education.

It wouldn't have been complete without the participation of students. They were out in the streets to give the protest a political color. The day after the strikes by taxi drivers and teachers, people spontaneously poured out into the streets. We didn't realize that it was the revolution that was igniting. We didn't see it coming. It caught us all by surprise, including those who diligently worked underground to ignite one in their own time.

The cabinet of Prime Minister Tsehafi Tizaz (Minister of pen) Aklilu Habtewold (educated in Alexandria and France) resigned and was replaced by that of Lij (title given to men of royal blood) Endalkachew Mekonen. Endalkachew was an Oxford-educated member of the aristocracy. He was the son of Ras Bitwoded (meaning military officer of the highest rank) Mekonen Endalkachew, the first Imperial Prime Minister in the country. Pressured, Endalkachew promised reform and pleaded for time.

Demonstrations and strikes paralyzed the country at the end of the month. Factory workers, civil servants, small businessmen, and lower and middle-rung officers of the armed forces, some of whom had already mutinied in January, jumped on the bandwagon demanding better wages and living conditions. Demonstrations and strikes reached their peak in March. Workers, deacons, nurses, students, teachers and women came out with demands. Women demanded "equal pay for equal work."

The university campus seethed with turmoil. Once again the students' demands included the reinstitution of the union and its organ and the release of political prisoners (such as Getachew and others), as well as the unconditional return of the fifteen students suspended in December of the previous year--meaning us. A leaflet was distributed on campus calling on students to rally behind the suspended 'militants,' such as Meles Tekle, Azeb Girma and me. Azeb and I were not too pleased with such publicity. But I found myself once again on campus shouting slogans and raising my hands in the air.

The ban on the union and its organ was lifted on 21 March. We, the fifteen students, were allowed back without any conditions. The university campus had never been so animated. There was a sense of triumph and jubilation in the air. Preparations were started for the election of USUAA congress and officials. Newspaper and magazine clippings were pasted everywhere. Electrifying and bold campaign speeches were delivered by candidates in English, the official language of USUAA. Some of the speakers dazzled us with their eloquence, others held us in thrall with their oratory, and still others struck us dumb with their good looks and command of the English language. My friends and I whisked from one campaign speech to the other, feverishly applauding every speaker. I had always dreamt of participating in demonstrations and class boycotts at the university, but never had I imagined I would witness anything like these campaign speeches.

My entire being quivered with excitement.

Meles Tekle, who was on campus for eight years and may have been set to go for another eight or so, asked Azeb and me to help out counting ballots at the Ras Mekonen Hall. We felt it was the ultimate honor.

The day USUAA was inaugurated at the Christmas Hall (adjoining the Sidist Kilo campus cafeteria), Eshetu Chole, a former student activist and university lecturer with a PhD in economics, and Girmachew Lemma, a law student and former president of USUAA, left us spellbound with their intoxicating speeches. But it was Eshetu Chole who captured our imagination. We roared in total rapture when he revealed to us that all we needed to do was three things: "Organize! Organize! Organize!"

It was a delirious moment.

Impassioned debates raged on campus over whether or not to withdraw. Most students favored withdrawal but, at a rally at Arat Kilo campus, Meles Tekle pleaded with us to remain on campus. We would have no power once we were scattered, he warned, and that tipped the scale in favor of staying. Withdrawal was deemed the most potent weapon for pressuring the university administration and the government, and those who pushed for withdrawal held their ground. The debate went on for days.

Our friend Ephrem Kebede was one of those students who ardently supported withdrawal. Kidist, Sara, Azeb and I were on our way to the dorm one day when we saw him scurrying, a piece of paper on hand.

"Hey Ephrem, where are you going?" we called out.

"I'm going to the registrar office to submit my withdrawal form," he shouted.

"What are you talking about? We haven't yet reached a decision." We burst out laughing.

"I don't care! I am going to withdraw, anyway," he cried. He went ahead and withdrew but stayed on campus.

Such was the vigor with which withdrawal was held.

We held a one-day sit-down hunger strike in front of the Arts Building, hollering slogans and demanding the resignation of a myriad of ministers, including the new Prime Minister. We gave that day's breakfast and lunch to the famine-stricken, squatting near Alert Hospital. They had come from afar in search of food.

Sara, Kidist, Azeb, Anene, and I volunteered, along with other students, to distribute the food to the hungry. When we came back, we found the campus almost deserted. Most of the students had gone home after a grueling day in the sun. Kidist and Sara went home too. Azeb, Anene, Meles, the recently elected president of USUAA, Getachew Begashaw, and I went to an eatery close to the university and talked about the events of the day. Azeb, Anene and I spent the night at the dorm.

The strikes and protest rallies persisted through April. Muslims held the biggest demonstration on the 20th, demanding equality of religions. A great number of Christians came out in solidarity. Azeb and I were astonished at the number of housewives who came to the rally that day. Housewives went to church, the market, funerals, and *mehaber* (self-help association). The revolution threw them out in the streets babies strapped to their backs, shouting slogans, raising their arms in the air, waving flags or umbrellas and ululating.

Something new was happening.

Placards fluttered high up in the sky bearing slogans such as: "Land to the tiller," "Democratic rights now," "Education for all," "Peoples' Government," "Equality of religions," "Lower food prices," "Down with feudalism" and "Down with imperialism."

I chanted slogans with others until my lungs burst like balloons, demanding the resignation of a countless number of ministers most of whose sins I didn't know. "Resign!" was perhaps the most shouted slogan at the time.

Every day, teachers, workers, civil servants and students thrust themselves into the streets and burst into spontaneous demonstrations. I quit my tutoring job. Taking to the streets became a full-time occupation.

Onward we marched fervently shouting slogans and condemning our enemies with one voice. We demanded change and a better future with the same zeal and determination. The camaraderie and sense of solidarity among demonstrators was unsurpassed. Our communion with one another brought out the best in us all.

We felt suspended in time and space.

The phrase 'peoples' power' was abstract to me until I witnessed real people rising up collectively. They had neither weapons nor ideology, neither party nor leader, they were, nonetheless, a formidable force. I came to realize that their power and fearlessness was a product of their unity. It was that unity that shook the very foundation of the age-old system. What was believed to be an Addis Ababa phenomenon swept like a tsunami through other major cities and towns in the fourteen provinces, submerging the country in turmoil.

My friends and I recollected my dream. I felt I had seen it all about two months ago. I told people around me about it. They were all amazed.

I felt proud.

The Emperor appeared on TV pleading for calm and making promises and concessions, but no tangible changes or swift action. His pleas fell on deaf ears. The high tide of the revolution had stripped him of his godlike aura. Nothing could abate the tempest. Nothing could appease the people.

It was obvious that the monarchy was on its death-bed, fighting for its last breath. The system couldn't cater to the needs of the modern social forces and of the radical elements by fulfilling their revolutionary demands. Even though the Emperor was widely recognized a pioneer, in modernizing the country, he was no longer able to keep up with the changing social and political environment and effect any meaningful change. His government was in disarray and its inability to control the situation undermined its legitimacy. The famine in Wollo and Tigray had made people question its moral fiber.

Change was needed. Change was in the air. Change was inevitable.

Like any upheaval, the revolution had moments of tragedy. Some people died and many more were injured during the violent suppression of demonstrations by government forces. Hundreds were put behind bars. In the process, hooligans destroyed and looted private property.

There was no lack of moments of comedy either. After a massive demonstration was over in Dire Dawa Lefe, a street woman a little weak in the head, trudged down a deserted street under the scorching sun holding a piece of blank cardboard and shouting "Resign! Resign! Resign!" at the top of her voice.

"Who should resign, Lefe?" a bemused passerby asked.

"All of them! ማን ወርዶ ማን ይተራል!"

The revolution swept everyone off their feet. Normal life was in a limbo, its rhythm shaken to its core. Euphoria and exuberance became the norm. Spirited debates exploded about the course of the revolution in newspapers, cafés, work places and school compounds. Everybody wanted to throw in their two cents worth. For a brief period of time, we enjoyed a taste of freedom of the press never before seen in the history of the country. Leaflets were everywhere. It seemed like they were coming down like rain from the sky and sprouting from the earth like mushrooms. New words such as *Abyot* – revolution - were coined. Parents named their newborns *Abyot*. Students from abroad rushed back to the motherland to partake in this historic and momentous event.

All of a sudden, we found ourselves in a new and unexpected situation. Awe and reverence for the crown gave way to a sense of defiance and liberation. The future looked bright. The rainbow was cast on Ethiopian skies.

There was hope.

Every revolution was first a thought in one man's mind.
         -Ralph Waldo Emerson

The boundless hope that poured out of our hearts into the streets in those revolutionary days had its roots in the sixties. The decade in Ethiopia, as in many countries in the world, was a threshold to change. It had ushered a new kind of people with new ideas, hopes and aspirations for themselves and for their country. It was the coming of these new people with new ideas that had sparked the revolution.

In the sixties, as Ethiopia was embarking on the road to modernization, a new class of people, a working class, was emerging, heralding the development of a new system, capitalism. Manufacturing and other industries expanded, leading the way to capitalist development and the growth of the work force. As Getachew had taught me, the pace of growth of the industrial sector was too slow to guarantee a developed capitalist system and accommodate the ever-increasing number of the unemployed.

The local capitalist, whom Getachew told me was known as the *comprador bourgeoisie* – in communist parlance - was dependent on foreign capital for his own growth. The expansion of industries and the growth of the working class were inhibited as a result. The first workers' union, the *Franco-Ethiopian Railway Company Workers' Association,* was founded in 1947. Unionization had heightened since then, and the late sixties and early seventies brought in labor unions and strikes to an unprecedented degree as workers hoped and fought for better wages and living conditions.

In rural areas, commercial farming, though on a small scale, caused rising expectations, while creating discontent among many peasants rendered landless or unemployed by the process. It also led to the increased export of certain items to fulfill the ever-growing demands of foreign exchange for the government.

Young modern or commercial farmers, with loans and incentives from the government, were new phenomena in the country in the mid and late sixties and early seventies. The formation of large agricultural projects such as Chilalo Agricultural Development Unit (CADU) and Wolayita Agricultural Development Unit (WADU) and the Upper, Middle and Lower Awash basin projects opened the door for the transformation of traditional peasant agriculture into large-scale commercialized farming.

Farmers, to me, were the illiterate in the countryside, with rough hands and wide Bermuda shorts that looked like skirts. The new farmers were educated, drove expensive cars, wore jeans, danced at discotheques, and spoke fluent English or French.

Commercial farming promised growth, modernity and a new life in rural areas.

The middle-class was meanwhile developing its own idea of a new and modern Ethiopia with rising expectations and aspirations. It was educated and employed by the government and the private sector. It saw itself as modern, at odds with the aristocracy, which it deemed archaic and a roadblock to the modernization of the country and to its own growth and advancement. It was young, feeble, and very small in number (not even one percent of the population), but it was growing slowly and surely, with a relatively strong purchasing power compared with the majority, whose life was plagued by poverty and illiteracy.

This modern class adopted a distinctively Western life style and values. They were keen on material possession, purchased new cars and appliances and built exquisite villas with chimneys sticking out into the sky. Trimmed gardens dolled up the paved, brick-walled, fenced-in and guarded yards of their villas.

The middle-class clearly distinguished themselves from the rest of the population, most of whom lived in shabby cluster or mud houses. They changed, within their own circle, traditional interpersonal relationships, brought women to the public sphere and reinterpreted fatalistic elements in the culture, introducing the idea that one can change one's circumstances through one's own effort, secular education being the main avenue to social mobility. They were a consumer class with taste for all things Western. Piassa was the miniature world that symbolized the new Ethiopia that they had envisioned. There was no other place in Addis Ababa that so captivated their imagination.

I had seen Addis rapidly change since I first set foot in it as an eleven-year old girl. I came to Addis for the first time right after I wrote my grade six *Ministry* – national examination. I still have memories of the huge advertising signs – Shell, Mobil, Agip and Cerelac – reeling in front of my eyes when the train accelerated toward the city. I stared at them in awe.

They surely gave Addis a modern feel.

I remember going to Piassa every Saturday afternoon with my cousin Elsa, who is my age, when I came in the summer from Harar. I stared at the exquisitely dressed young married couples leisurely strolling and enjoying the pleasant late afternoon weather. Besides ordering clothes from Sears catalogues, they swarmed stores owned by Greek, Armenian and Italian expatriates such as Ariston, Hermes, La Bergerie, Moda Nova, Allonesta, Maria Koshasha, Bartolotta, Sasso, Darmar and by nationals such as *Mecheresha* Fashion. These chic stores flaunted Greek, French and Italian fashionable clothes, fragrances and shoes.

The modern couples bought Scandinavian furniture from Mosvold and had it delivered right to their doors in a matter of days. I remember being impressed, since I never saw anything delivered to anybody's house in Harar.

They purchased dazzling Italian white and opaque red, green and purple crystal glassware from Novis. They bought crayons, spelling worksheets, children's books, flowered notepads and fancy exercise books from the Artistic Printing Press. As a little girl, I bought my exercise books in Harar from Aberash *medeber* – kiosk – and there was nothing fancy about them. Their covers had the pictures of the Emperor, the Empress and their sons. The shoppers at Artistic sent their children to private, prestigious schools like Sandford (English School), Nazaret, St. Joseph, and Lycée Gebre Mariam with fancy exercise books, and their little ones with crayons to kindergartens such as Jack and Jill, La Fontaine and Peter Pan.

The men developed a taste for new sports. Saturday morning, they played tennis at Juventus Club showing off expensive sportswear, while their wives were talking about the latest coffee grinder and Dr. Spock at Ghion or Hilton Hotel, watching their children swim. After lunch, Russian women gave piano lessons to the children, when their wives shopped at Chico and got their hair done at Francesca's before heading over to Piassa. Some bowled the night away at R.E.C.E or dined with their wives or friends at Castelli, Sangham, Omar Khayyam, Lombardia, and Buffet de la Gare.

They drove their families to Sebata, Gefersa, Koka or Debre Zeit Sunday afternoon and went on vacation to Sodere or Langano. They flashed polished Mercedes Benz, Alfa Romeo, BMW, Citroën, Peugeot, Renault, Opel, Taunus, and Volkswagen. As a young girl, I looked with utter wonderment when they got out of their cars and inserted coins into parking meters.

The parking meters added a tinge of modernity to the drama unfolding in Piassa.

Piassa was also home to the new modern youth that were as much consumers as the finely dressed men and women. They shopped at Petit Paris or La Bergerie. Petit Paris was their Mecca as Mode Nova was to the modern couples. Piassa was the promenade where these elegant and stylish youngsters picked up their future dates and made fashion statements. They indulged in hamburgers, club sandwiches, baklava, banana shakes, ice-cream, pizza, and the uniquely Ethiopian *macchiato* at cafés, creameries, tearooms, pastry shops, delis, and pizzerias.

There was an art exhibition at the Belvedere Art Gallery in Piassa featuring the works of distinguished artists such as Afework Tekle and Zerihun Yetmgeta. Modern couples and singles streamed into the gallery to witness celebrated works of art and even buy some. Among the pieces hanging on the wall was Zerihun Yetmgeta's "After Six" that made female viewers look away in embarrassment. It depicted a group of women, squatting in the woods, their dresses hitched up to their knees, cleansing themselves. My friend Mahlet and I watched the reaction of every woman with amusement. We were standing at the door handing out exhibition brochures. I had never been to an art gallery and I felt so modern.

Piassa promised a new life. Piassa promised modernity and affluence. Piassa gave hope to its pilgrims.

But Piassa was an oasis in the middle of poverty. You would be amazed to know what it unabashedly hid in its bosom: *Serategna Sefer*. *Serategna Sefer* was home to hundreds of sex workers. It was the hotbed of sexually transmitted diseases. Squalor, disease, utter poverty, dense population, illiteracy, and sexual wantonness characterized the ill-famed neighborhood.

I thought *Serategna Sefer* was a scandal to Piassa that glittered with gold, silver and fashionable Seiko and Roamer watches.

The mid-sixties and early seventies were boisterous years. Discotheque, Cottage, Saturday Night Fever, Stereo Club, The Cave, Osibisa, Sheba, Venus Cub and Hôtel d'Afrique were jammed with youngsters, who frenziedly shook their booties to the tunes of The Beatles, Rolling Stones, Tom Jones, Temptations, James Brown, Tyrone Davis, Elvis Presley, Beach Boys and The Archies.

My friends and I threw parties in Harar and called ourselves *Evergreen Friends*. Our parties began and ended with Cliff Richard's *Evergreen tree.*

The joint concert of the various bands in Addis was a novelty in those days. My aunt took me to the then new *Mazegaja Bet* – City Hall – for the New Year's Eve concert when I came to Addis for the first time. Since then, it became a tradition for my sister, my brother-in-law and my aunt to go to the evening concert every year, and for my cousin Elsa and me to go on New Year's Day.

The screens of the Ambassador, Haile Selassie I Theatre and Cinema Empire in Addis Ababa, and Haji Ahmed Bomba Cinema Bet in Harar, enchanted us with the faces of Paul Newman, Clark Gable, Sidney Poitier, Tony Curtis, Doris Day, Elizabeth Taylor, Greta Garbo, Lana Turner and Marilyn Monroe.

My friend Yodit and I collected bubble gum cards of our favorite actors and actresses. I bought bubble gum after bubble gum to find the Roger Moore and Michael Landon cards.

I never had enough.

In Addis, after a movie, fashionably attired youngsters jammed Post and Meskel Rendezvous, where they exchanged pleasantries, winks and phone numbers.

Shashi Kapoor, Nargis Dutt, Raj Kapoor and others made us weep and laugh with Indian movies such as Mother India, Waqt, Sangham and Duniya. We didn't always understand the words, as some of the films didn't have sub-titles. But we understood them enough to laugh and weep. My friends and I went to Haji Bomba Cinema Bet with handkerchiefs whenever an Indian movie was on. We knew we were going to cry for the young newlywed girl inevitably abused by her old and stern mother-in-law.

I remember going to the Drive-in-Theatre in Addis on New Year's Eve with my sister and my brother-in-law, who were then young newlyweds, to see *The Yellow Rolls Royce*. I was only twelve but I recall gaping when my sister got out of the car and brought in a speaker from the dual speaker pole.

I was bewitched.

In Harar, my friends Martha, Yodit, Saba, and I made egg sandwiches and *buna be wotet – caffe latte* – every Saturday morning, spreading a blanket in the garden beside Saba's house to "study." We sat so close to the street that we got easily distracted. Saba's mother spied on us from a distance. She was never able to figure out how we could study sitting so close to a main street.

Street kids roamed the town carrying a *reclame* with the weekend's movie. We always asked with excitement, "What is on this afternoon?" when they passed by Saba's house. They shouted, "Elzabet Teller!" or "Rock Hudson!" or "Shashkapoor!" There was no need to find out the title of the movie. The names of the actors and actresses were enough to make us jump to our feet. We gulped down our sandwiches and *caffe lattes*, gathered our things, changed our clothes and off we went to Haji Bomba movie theatre in Feres Megala.

TV was a novelty, then, and we were glued to the screen watching *The Fugitive, Perry Mason, Bonanza,* and *Mission Impossible*. There was no TV in Harar, and I only got the chance to see all those series in Addis in the summer. I was almost in tears the day I had to return to Harar at the end of one summer. The last episode of the *Fugitive* was showing. I was so curious, my cousin Elsa had to write me the ending.

Listeners' Choice program was new on the radio and we went wild listening to Etta James, Bettye Swann, Roy C, Bobby Bland, Dean Martin, Frank Sinatra, Aretha Franklin, The Supremes, Jim Reeves, Otis Redding, Wilson Pickett, Clarence Carter, Albano Carrisi and Gigliola Cinquetti. Indian radio listeners' choice program also brought us Mohammed Rafi, Lata Mangeshkar and Asha Bhosle. My friends and I memorized the lyrics just as we did the English ones, even if we didn't understand them.

We also had our own "soul music," with Ethiopian singers such as Tilahun Gessesse, Mohamed Ahmed, Buzunesh Bekele, and Alemayehu Eshete. Unlike Western singers, for whom love was the major theme of their songs, our singers pointed to the crisis of moral values, the loss of culture and tradition and the intrusion into our society of materialism, greed and decadent values. Singers were believed to be the forerunners of the revolution.

Writers had their fair share of contribution in prodding peoples' consciences and sensitizing them to social ills as well. Abe Gubegna's *Aleweledem*, burnt by the government and precipitating the long time detention of the author in Mocha, in the province of Ilubabor, was an instance. Whilst in exile there, he is said to have written a book, 'Mocha allehu,' a pun with an apparent meaning of 'I am in Mocha,' but pronounced as 'mochallehu,' conveying the hidden meaning: 'I am dead,' describing his existence in limbo. Bealu Girma's *Yehilina Dewel* and Hadis Alemayehu's *Wonjelegnaw Dagna* are other examples of the upsurge not only of the literature of the time, but also of moral and social criticism. Hadis Alemayehu's, *Fiker Eske Mekabir* – Love unto grave – was another example. It exposed the exploitation, oppression and backwardness of the feudal system. In a poignant poem, it subtly provoked peoples' sense of indignation.

It was fashionable to go abroad at the time. But those who made it to the airport were mainly sons and daughters of the rich. Their parents paid an astounding amount of money to American and European universities and Swiss finishing schools to give their children the best possible education.

Youngsters awaited anxiously the arrival of their I-20 forms to go to the favored destination – America. They threw farewell parties when their F-1 Visas arrived. They sent back pictures from the dreamland leaning on opulent cars, while wearing winter jackets, scarves, mitts, and winter hats. They looked to us like they had just stepped out of a movie screen or a Vogue or Marie Claire fashion magazine.

When Piassa teemed with modern couples and the sons and daughters of the rich boarded planes, the university (a kilometer away from Piassa) was like a cauldron simmering with student unrest. The University College of Addis Ababa, nucleus of what later became Haile Selassie I University, was founded in 1950, and since the early 1960s, the students had been challenging the regime. Their demands initially revolved mainly around their own immediate needs, such as better cafeteria food or the safeguarding of academic freedoms.

It was the December 1960 coup d'état led by Germame Neway, a former university student with a Socialist orientation and a Masters degree from Columbia University, and his older brother, Brigadier-General Mengistu Neway, commander of the Imperial Bodyguard, that changed the way the monarchy was perceived.

Students came out in support of the coup, seeing it as the beginning of a "new era" in the history of the country. The coup showed them that change was indeed possible, that kings did not rule by divine mandate. Their demands shifted from their immediate needs to larger social, economic and political issues. Even then, their demands were more reformist than anything else. They still saw the Emperor as a father figure, on the road to modernizing the country.

However, the formation of the Eritrean Liberation Front in 1961, the Russian, Chinese, Cuban, and Vietnamese revolutions, decolonization in Africa, the struggle against apartheid in South Africa and the Civil Rights Movement in the United States, left indelible marks on the imagination of the students, encouraging them to challenge the regime. Students from other African countries studying at the university through a scholarship program, established by Emperor Haile Selassie, also contributed to the heightening of the social and political awareness of the university students.

The Ethiopian Students Union in North America (ESUNA) and Ethiopian Students Union in Europe (ESUE) played a significant role in raising the social and political awareness of university students and the development of the student movement at home. They published pamphlets such as *Challenge, Combat, Tenesh Ethiopiawit, Tiglachin, Yetigil Senselet* and *Tatek*, which were smuggled into the country. These pamphlets were hand copied, distributed and widely read by students and teachers.

Marxist-Leninist thought was seeping into these publications and a clandestine group, named Crocodile Society, was formed in the early sixties. The Crocs, as its members were called, studied Marxism-Leninism and helped its spread among university students.

As their social and political awareness heightened, the students became incensed by the inequality, injustice and political repression they saw around them and rebelled against the regime.

They were particularly appalled by the living conditions of the peasants, who were robbed of their lands and produce by a land tenure system that privileged the royal family, aristocracy, nobility and the clergy. They spoke out against the suppression of political freedom demanding freedom of speech, the press and of assembly.

They began to see themselves as children of the people and champions for their causes.

The mid-sixties were a defining moment in the history of the student movement when a new kind of student burst on the scene, reshaping the political landscape on campus, Marxism-Leninism as the guiding ideology. Karl Marx, Friedrich Engles, Vladimir Ilyich Lenin, and Frantz Fanon were widely read. The movement decidedly took on an anti-feudal and anti-imperialist posture. In February 1965, the students demonstrated in front of the parliament, where a bill to regulate tenancy was being debated. They fluttered placards reading "Land to the tiller," thus setting the year as a watershed in the history of the student movement. It was the first time that the students had come out with such a radical slogan.

The students also looked beyond their country and espoused anti-apartheid, anti-Zionist and anti-Vietnam war stances and supported the Civil Rights Movement in the United States and Socialist and National Liberation Movements in Africa and Latin America.

The late sixties saw enhanced radicalism and militancy as this new breed of students took center stage. They demanded no less than radical change. They saw the problems and solutions of the country through a Marxist lens. The new ideology was credited as being panacea to all social, economic and political ills. It promised to bring heaven down to earth and the students, seduced by its utopian vision, yearned to transplant it in their country.

And so the idea of igniting a revolution was born.

In January 1967, USUAA (the University Students' Union of Addis Ababa) was set up a month after its organ, *Struggle*, was published. The students had achieved many victories but had difficulty uniting the student body under one union, since it would have to include all the different colleges in Addis Ababa. The students defended and shielded USUAA like a mother protecting her child.

It became the reason for their being.

Students were boiling with hatred for the West, too, and anything Western aroused their indignation. When some of the female university students staged a fashion show at the Sidist Kilo campus in March 1968, students threw eggs and tomatoes at the invited guests and disrupted the show. Police shot tear gas and many were arrested, leading to the closure of the university and the banning of the students' union and its organ.

The students saw the fashion show as a shameless subscription to Western cultural imperialism and the girls as a dumping ground for bourgeois luxury that benefited imperialists. Besides, fashion was seen as a way of distracting women from the problems of the country, just as religion was regarded as the 'opium' that blinded students from the harsh realities of life. That was why my year-mate, Alemzewd Araya, was harassed for her Pentecostal beliefs after the Revos returned to campus. Pentecostals were then an endangered species in a place where Marxism was the de-facto religion.

For many years, the cycle was repeated: university students boycotted classes, came out into the streets and distributed underground pamphlets. In the process, they faced many confrontations with the government. The university administration would ban USUAA and its organ in retaliation, only to reinstate it when students again boycotted classes or poured out into the streets.

Eventually, it dawned upon USUAA radicals that the movement should go beyond throwing stones and reciting poetry. The drill was that they recited poems, debated in debating clubs, boycotted classes, took to the streets, chanted slogans, held up placards and pelted stones on buildings and at soldiers. Truckloads of them would be taken to Sendafa, a small town outlying Addis Ababa, and those who remained boycotted classes calling for the release of the detained. The vicious circle that defined the movement became a dead-end.

The idea that the student movement was the 'vanguard' of the revolution had been churning around in their heads for a while. But as Marxism-Leninism illumined the trajectory of the struggle, the students realized that only a Marxist-Leninist party could safeguard the interests of the workers and peasants.

A group of students, with the prominent student activist Berhanemeskel Redda, hijacked an airplane in August 1969 to be mid-wife to the birth of this Marxist-Leninist party. They became known as the Algeria Group because they chose Algeria as their temporary home after they forced an Ethiopian airline to land in the Sudan. Ethiopian students within the country and abroad hailed the hijacking as a courageous revolutionary act.

Another group of students attempted another hijacking in December 1972; that ended with the tragic mid-air death of six students, one of whom was the intrepid student activist Waleligne Mekonen, who was working at the time. A female student survived, wounded. Another female student, Marta Mebratu, was killed.

December 28, 1969 was another turning point for the students. Tilahun Gizaw, a celebrated student activist and the incumbent president of USUAA, was shot and killed one night near Sidist Kilo campus, while walking with his girlfriend and his brother. This unleashed a huge uproar of anger among university students, teachers, intellectuals, high school and even elementary school students throughout the country.

Thousands of university and high school students and teachers assembled in the university campus the next day. They carried Tilahun's coffin (which they took from the hospital) and chanted slogans. Soldiers came into the campus and fired at them as a scuffle ensued to gain possession of the coffin. Hundreds were arrested and tortured and some were killed.

In response, even more high school and elementary students and teachers burst into the streets of cities and towns across the country in violent protest. Thousands more were arrested. Ethiopian students studying abroad protested in front of the Ethiopian embassies across Europe and North America, condemning the brutality of the government. Nothing could abate the rage kindled on December 28, 1969. Tilahun Gizaw's murder radicalized thousands of students and intellectuals across the country overnight, making it another turning point in the radicalization of the students.

As Gabriel Tafesse, a former university student activist, imparted to me, "It was customary for USUAA congress candidates to raise political issues such as land to the tiller. Tilahun spoke about the national question that touched upon the sensitive question of the right of nations to self-determination and up to secession. I think that got the security nervous. Up to that time, the Haile Selassie regime had been tolerant. The killings on campus sent a shockwave through the student body. The very idea that the government kills was a shocking revelation to us. The killing of Tilahun became a turning point."

The Eritrean question was on the hot burner at the time and the government was certainly nervous about these claims.

Despite all of that, the students were for the most part alienated from the general population, as their struggle was generally limited to the university campus. The abstract and elitist language they used couldn't penetrate the hearts and minds of the people.

In the late sixties and early seventies, high school students across the country flooded the streets of many cities and towns demanding "Land to the tiller" "Lower food prices," "Education for all," and "Political freedom," bringing these issues to the streets and raising the consciousness of the people in the process. They took the issues to homes, offices and factories sensitizing the public about the plight of the peasants and the urban poor.

Ironically, the National Service program was instrumental in the politicization of these high school students, as university students were dispatched across the country to address the shortage of teachers. Mekonen Hagos, killed in Harar in 1969, was one of those students, who played a pivotal role in politicizing the students.

Harar, for one, was tossed upside down with student unrest when I was in high school at Medhane Alem. Never a semester passed by without class boycotts or protest demonstrations. Parents' committees were set-up by schools so that parents could keep an eye on their riotous teenagers. Medhane Alem was known for its student militancy as were other high schools in the country, such as Menilik II, Teferi Mekonen, Medhane Alem, Etege Menen, Leul Mekonen, Kokebe Tsebah and Shimeles Habte in Addis, and Woizero Sihen in Dessie, Atse Gelawdios in Nazaret and Hailemariam Mammo in Debre Berhan.

Meanwhile, the student movement at the university was beset by internal strife and became fraught with division, character assassination, labeling and ostracizing. Extreme radicalism, fanaticism, intolerance and dogmatism overrode common goals and aspirations.

The divisions were not limited to the students on the home front. The Ethiopian Students Union in North America (ESUNA) and the Ethiopian Students Union in Europe (ESUE), whose visions for their homeland were the same, squabbled over which "strategies" and "tactics" the revolution should follow, dividing the students into two antagonistic camps, which would later turn bloody. The unions also suffered from division and fractures within themselves, realigning allegiance to differing stances of the times.

The Marxist theoreticians at Haile Selassie I University scoffed, to put it mildly, at the liberals, moderates and reformists, as well as at one another. The Marxist-Leninist pen became the means for thrashing dissenting voices, just as the gun would later become the weapon of choice for settling scores. However, the general student population was not that versed in Marxist literature. Their consciousness was, for the most part, limited to political propaganda.

Marxism was not only taken as the only Truth but also canonized. Questioning or doubting it amounted to blasphemy. Professor Andreas Eshete, Yale University philosophy graduate, giving a lecture as part of his course, *From Hegel to Marx,* in the 1971/1972 academic year at Haile Selassie I University, asked a packed lecture hall, "What is scientific about socialism?" Seyoum Belachew, one of the students who attended the lecture, recalled, "We were not too happy. We saw it as an affront to Marx!"

It was the very belief that Marxism was *scientific* that gave it the mandate to be the Truth and the only Truth. Such was the sense of irrefutability the students had internalized about the theory. Such was the grip that Marxism had on their minds.

Such was the mind-set that paved the way for what was yet to come.

Marxist-Leninist underground study circles sprouted in the early seventies in the country, recasting the political landscape with the underground struggle as the main path of resistance. The professional revolutionary, who would later rule the underworld, organized clandestine study circles inside and outside of university campuses and work places, setting the stage for the emergence of a Marxist-Leninist party. The Crocodile Society was the precursor of these clandestine study circles. *Abyot*, the underground organization I had joined, and other Marxist-Leninist groups inside and outside the country, were born of such a movement.

Many years elapsed before Matheos Abera, a close friend of Getachew Maru and a former student activist, related to me about the new move within the student movement to getting organized and the division that ensued as a result.

He was a freshman when Tilahun Gizaw was president of USUAA, after a one-year indoctrination of being a Revo while in Beedemariam School. Tilahun insisted that, instead of boycotting classes and coming out with petty issues, they should go in a different direction. One day at a general assembly at the Christmas Hall at the Sidist Kilo campus, he cautioned them to be careful... that they are alone... and that they have to organize and rally the people behind them. "Suddenly," Matheos said, laughing and went on, "Getachew Maru sprang to his feet and thundered at Tilahun. 'Nearly a billion Chinese are with us! The whole world is with us!' he said and reeled off Mao Tse Tung's thought!"

"What was his point?" I asked, bursting out with laughter.

"He was saying to Tilahun 'What are you afraid of?' You know, Marxism-Leninism as a concept, as a guide to the student movement, was not officially talked about before. In fact, Tilahun was more leftist than Mekonen Bishaw in 1968, when he ran for USUAA presidency and was defeated. In previous years, the 'I solemnly swear' oath was taken by raising your right hand. The following year, when Tilahun came back, the oath was recited with your left fist clenched. It was okay for us. Socialism was okay with us. But when Getachew came with Maoism, he shook the whole atmosphere! We said, 'We have somebody with courage.'"

Tilahun was killed and the students withdrew and took make-up courses in the summer. When they came back to school the next year, with Getachew now a third-year and Matheos a second-year student, the first thing they did was re-establish USUAA. Matheos was on the election committee. He said, "We knew who to have as secretary. We were the movers and shakers of the union then. Getachew had to be the secretary."

Mesfin Shiferaw, a close friend of Getachew and a former student activist, had stated to me about Getachew's preparation for USUAA congress candidacy. Before Getachew went to Dejen for his National Service, he was saying to his friends that he would run for USUAA congress. The whole year he stayed at Dejen, all he did was hone his public speaking skills. When he came back after a year, his friends were surprised at how a better speaker he had become.

1970, the year Getachew became secretary of USUAA, was known as the year a bitter division was born between the junior and the senior radicals. Getachew and Matheos belonged to the junior and students such as Tselote Hezkias and Tsegaye Gebremedhin to the senior radicals. The younger radicals wanted to radicalize the student movement even more, through increased class boycotts and demonstrations, in order to politicize the general public. The older radicals, on the other hand, were in favor of getting organized and gaining access to the people in order to educate and organize them. They wanted to remain on campus to realize this goal.

"We couldn't figure out why all of a sudden the Debteraw group didn't want to boycott classes," Matheos told me. "It was around the second semester, and the crisis in the student movement was looming. High school students boycotted classes. Getachew became a sensation among them. He became a symbol among high school students at Teferi Mekonen, Leul Mekonen…among students like Mekonen Bayisa, even in places like Dessie. Getachew was it!"

There was once a meeting on campus. Getachew got up and gave a speech Matheos says he will never forget. "'Our dear calculators,' Getachew criticized the senior radicals in the graduating class, 'you have come here calculating how much money you are going to make, when you are going to buy a car, when you are going to buy a house…' Our group was so happy."

"When the conflict between the 4th year left and the 2nd and 3rd year left became bitter, mediation was started," Matheos continued. "Getachew said he wouldn't even bother. We met on the second-floor of the Engineering College. Tselote and Debteraw came. You know, there are historical accidents. Guess who was picked up to mediate between the junior left and the senior left? Girmachew Lemma! He was considered liberal. Somehow, we couldn't come to an agreement. Insults were hurled around. I must have threatened Tselote with a stone. Anyway, something silly happened."

Getachew and some students boycotted classes but the Debteraw group stayed on campus. Then high school students boycotted classes protesting the soaring price of butter. University students were supposed to initiate the boycotts. They lagged behind and the university was "exposed."

But Mesfin pointed out to me that the conflict between Getachew's and Debteraw's groups had started earlier, when

Getachew and Mesfin were in the first year. They had a math class that finished at one o'clock and they always ran to the cafeteria so that they didn't miss lunch. One day, while running, they heard a student among the Debteraw group say, "I wish Christmas would come and we could be rid of these." Getachew answered back, "Those who are on academic probation..." Since then a friction was created between the two groups. The Debteraw group spread a rumor about Getachew being Pentecostal. Mesfin said, "I don't know where that came from. I grew up with him. What is more, the guys were showy and adventurous. We had reservations about them."

Later, the younger radicals came to realize that there was a move within the student movement toward organized revolutionary struggle.

It was with great interest that I listened to Matheos when he reminisced about their last days at the university and how they too started getting organized. "When we got into third-year in 1971, Girmachew Lemma became president of USUAA. I was in the National Affairs Committee. Getachew had finished his term. By the way, Getachew never had close friends from among the USUAA radical circle. All his friends were from Engineering College. We noticed that he was distancing himself from the student movement. He became serious. He spoke less and you could see his radicalism and rhetoric waning. In February, all of us, USUAA executives, were thrown into jail. We were hoping to get out soon but we were detained for almost six months. We were held in Gibe. After I was released, Getachew and I met at Varsity Café in Amist Kilo. At the time, he was living with Abiyu Ersamo and Shimeles Retta in Afincho Ber. He invited me to their place. He cooked pasta. He liked cooking pasta...you know chopping onions...He was very good at it. I was surprised. I didn't know how to cook."

"There was a study-material in nine series on Historical and Dialectical Materialism, Political Economy, National Question and so on," Matheos went on. "He gave me one of them and said that he would give me more. 'Am I going to study this again?' I asked. He said, 'You have no discipline! We've got to be serious.' Then I sensed it had something to do with an organization. I had studied Marxism-Leninism when I was in grade twelve at Beedemariam Lab School, long before I met him. It was Tesfu Kidane who had taught us Marxism-Leninism. Getachew then asked me to organize study circles for all those who were in prison in Gibe and Kolfe, and especially for students in high school. Woldeab Haile, Getachew Assefa, Belay Kebede and I formed a core study circle."

"We helped Alemayehu Egzeru form a study circle in Gulele, Nadew and Getachew Embusu formed one around Kebena, Berhanu Gola established one around Shola and Abebe Gelashe organized one in Teklehaimanot," continued Matheos, "Some went to the provinces to do the same. Agere Miheretu went to Woldya, Atalelegn and Marilgn went to Hosana, Alemayhu went to Harar, Getachew Kumsa went to Adwa, Girma Bucher went to Wolayita Sodo and Tsegaye Zerihun went to Jimma. When we were supposed to be admitted in September, the six of us – ex-active USUAA officials - were suspended. We were hired as teachers. I went to Ambo. Everybody quit university. Getachew started teaching at Shimeles Habte. Girmachew Lemma joined the labor force. We started teaching because we were suspended. We had no choice. Even those who were not suspended started working."

The reason the students quit school was to pursue the struggle professionally. That was how *Abyot* was born.

"Endreas Mikael came to Ambo," went on Matheos. "He was Abiyu Erasmo's friend. He was a fourth-year Alemaya College student and was already recruited by *Abyot*. We became roommates.

We were also in Gibe prison together. Later, Shimeles Retta came to Ambo as a teacher. The three of us established cells in Ambo and in various towns such as Gouder, Nekemt, Shambo and Chincha. We also established cells in Debre Sina and Fiche. Endreas went to Wolayita to link with other teachers. I went there too and did organizational work. What can I tell you? *Abyot* literally became large. It became an organization. The network was expanded. You could feel it."

"Was there an organizational structure?" I asked.

"Absolutely not! There were only cells. The nucleus focused down to a few people – Getachew and students in Engineering College and in Gondar."

Organized, albeit rudimentarily, and armed with Marxist theory, the students wanted to take their struggle to an even higher plane. It had been quite a while since they were shouting, "Freedom is won through struggle and violence." Che Guevara had cast his spell on them and the jungle became bewitching and transcendental. Mao's 12,000 kilometer Long March gave hope and inspiration and Dien Bein Phu symbolized victory in all its glamour.

The most celebrated revolutionary song of all time, *Fano Tesemara* – onward rebel – was sung on campus and in the streets of Addis, inciting marchers to go into the woods and lead the struggle like Ho Chi Minh and Che Guevara.

ፋኖ ተሰማራ ፋኖ ተሰማራ
ፋኖ ሜካ ግባ ትግሉን ልትመራ
እንደ ሆቺምን እንደ ቼ ጉዌቫራ

The Ethiopian Students Union in Europe (ESUE) promptly hurled its scathing criticism at the students at the university calling their action "left adventurism," "left infantilism" and "ultra-leftism." They also charged USUAA leaders of "ultra left errors" when the university students commemorated the one hundredth anniversary of the Paris Commune. No matter what criticisms were thrown at them, the university students were determined to emulate Che Guevara.

Armed struggle became the unmistakable avenue to radical social transformation.

It was from Matheos that I learned about their preparations for armed struggle. "Getachew talked to me about scouting and things like that. I had a couple of cameras, a sleeping bag and a tent. I got those things I guess when I was working as a Research Assistant at the Faculty of Science. Getachew used to come to Ambo on the weekend and one day asked me if he could borrow the tent. I will never forget this. I was pitching the tent in the front yard of our house in the morning. A cigarette was dangling from my mouth. I used to smoke like crazy. I saw this man coming. He wore a black coat, a hat, a black tie, and sunglasses and carried a cane. He looked like a Mafia debt collector. It was my dad! I threw away the cigarette. '*Duriye*, pick it up!' my father said. 'You see, I've been telling him to quit but he refused…' Getachew said. What do you know? He became friends with my father! Oh! How that guy bonded with my dad! He then informed me that a student called Eshetu would introduce Endreas and me to someone who would give us commando training. The fellow was a retired Paratrooper Sergeant. He trained us in Taekwondo in Ambo for three weeks in a trench after school hours."

"Endreas had a gun…a Beretta," went on Matheos. "Getachew suggested we should get one too. A gun cost 250 birr at the time. I had friends in *Mercato*. We bought one for me and one for Abiyu Ersamo. We started getting serious. We got permits for our guns. You could easily get a license if you went to the provinces. You get your gun registered but you are penalized for buying it contraband. That was it."

"In the summer of 1973, it was suggested that we get in touch with the Sergeant again. It was around *Filseta* fasting season. The four of us – Getachew Maru, Abiyu Ersamo, Endreas Mikael and I – went to Langano with the Sergeant. The place was behind Aklilu Habtewold's summer house. It was about three kilometers from Bekele Molla resorts. Getachew had surveyed the area ahead of time. We stayed there in a tent getting military training for one month."

That was the time I went on summer vacation to Harar. I had no idea Getachew was involved in something like that.

"We did not go out except for more training," Matheos went on. "I had started dating then. I wanted the training to end sooner. I used to sneak out in the middle of the night and have a Sprite at Bekele Molla's. There was a discussion every night. Our trainer didn't understand much. We had interesting discussions, more on social and interpersonal issues. At some point I said, 'This is a poor country and it would be a problem when socialism comes. How are we going to feed the people let alone build the economy? I don't think it will be that easy.' At the time, there was famine in the country. Abiyu said, 'It is easy to feed the people.' We asked him how. He said, '*Kocho* – *enset* – grows easily in dry soil. If only the people could get used to it.' I said, 'Getachew! I was thinking of feeding the people *injera* with chicken sauce! If we are feeding them *kocho*, why am I struggling? I was thinking of giving them a better alternative. There is no need to fight to eat *kocho*.' He said to me, 'What kind of person are you?' I said, 'Getachew, I'm telling you the truth. There is no need for bloodshed to feed the people *kocho*!'"

I burst into a roar of laughter. *Kocho* is flat bread made from pulverized and fermented false banana.

"We had near misses when training," Matheos continued. "One day, we were practicing air pipe chock with a rope. You are not supposed to turn when you do that. Getachew turned his head and he had this scar on his neck. We suggested to him to wear a turtleneck sweater. When you throw kicks, you lift your leg up and kick and the other person is supposed to retreat or defend. I hit him on his side. He stopped breathing for almost five minutes. I didn't know what to do. This is training. You hit unintentionally. We even practiced how to kill and revive. We used real knife too. We took the training seriously. Well, we returned from camping after a month. Something about Taekwondo is that it teaches you self-discipline and inwardness. We were young – we were in our early twenties. The year was 1973. We were physically strong and we came out tempered. That was also how great our friendship was."

What was interesting was that, without communication of any kind, at exactly the same time *Abyot* members were training in Taekwondo in Langano, some members of the Algeria Group, the group that hijacked an Ethiopian airline in August 1969, were taking military training with Nayef Hawatmeh's Popular Democratic Front for the Liberation of Palestine - and the rest with Yasser Arafat's Al Fatah in Syria!

The students had labored for many years to incite a revolution. They were the only organized body and the sole vocal opponents of the Haile Selassie regime. But a new era had begun by which the people, mainly urban dwellers, took matters into their own hands but were haunted by the specter of another organized body.

What we call the beginning is often the end. And to make an end is to make a beginning.
The end is where we start from.
    -T. S. Eliot

On April 23, 1974, a little over two months after the revolution had erupted, Endalkachew's government declared that the party was over. It prohibited demonstrations and strikes. Some ministers and high-ranking officials of the previous government were thrown into jail accused of corruption and mismanagement. The government was not unified and had no full control over the military.

That was its undoing.

As for us university students, even before we made up our minds whether or not to withdraw we were ejected out of campus with the excuse that there was not enough time to complete the academic year. Closing the university was one less headache for the government that was simmering in a pressure cooker. The radicals were impatient with a reformist government and demanded the resignation of Endalkachew and the establishment of a Provisional Peoples' Government.

Nothing short of regime change was acceptable to them.

We had taken it for granted that the army would have rallied round the people, when it had earlier staged a series of mutinies across the country. However, it had gone back to its barracks after the government had tried to satisfy its demands. We accused it of betraying the revolution and the people. It came out again, this time in support of the people, and held a series of mutinies and watched demonstrations with their muzzles pointed down - a bad omen for the government.

The Seven-man Committee, set up earlier by the armed forces and led by a Major named Tefera Tekleab, sent a telegram in June to members of the army to send their representatives. Thus was born the Derg, the Coordinating Committee of the Armed Forces, comprising middle and lower-rung officers. Lieutenant-General Aman Mikael Andom, a man with an illustrious military career, became chair of the Derg. An obscure Major, Mengistu Hailemariam, dubbed a "trouble maker" by some, became the vice-chairman. Even though Aman Andom, who was not a member of the Derg, was the chairperson, Mengistu was the real leader who maneuvered behind the scene.

When it became clear that the Derg was poised to fill the vacuum created by the revolution, uncertainty, anxiety, fear and ambiguity began diluting the hopes, optimism, sense of euphoria, and aspirations of the people. A military government was by no means desirable but they didn't know what to make of the Derg's promises of respecting their rights and realizing their dreams.

It kept telling them that it was born in their bosom and was there to serve them and protect the revolution from those who wanted to turn back the tide. However, many were suspicious of its motives. Particularly the students and progressive forces warned that it would hijack the revolution, as there was no civilian organized body contending for leadership. Others wanted to give it the benefit of the doubt and hailed the vice-chairman, Mengistu Hailemariam, as the "man of the people."

All too soon, events would prove their naiveté.

The Derg took power unofficially in June and did some housekeeping until August, setting the stage for its ascent to power. In July, it replaced Prime Minister Endalkachew with *Lij* Mikael Imiru, son of *Ras* Imiru Haile Selassie cousin of the Emperor. *Ras* Imiru was briefly leader of the Resistance in western Ethiopia after Emperor Haile Selassie went into exile during the occupation of the country by Fascist Italy in 1936. The Derg issued a series of warnings and imprisoned members of the aristocracy, royal family and some of its radical members. It coined its first slogan, *Ethiopia Tikdem* – Ethiopia First. It took control of the media and other government establishments – a bad omen for the country: it foreshadowed the beginning of the end of the revolution.

Getachew had missed out on all of that. It was only during those tumultuous months that it got through my head that what was happening was what he had worked so hard to bring forth. I marveled at the irony of life. I often wondered what he did, what he ate and how he felt. I dreamed of the day he would come out. I hankered for our theoretical discussions in the tiny and semi-dark room and our endless talk and laughter at Harar Migib Bet.

I missed his timid smile and his gentle soul.

I wondered what had happened to the gods' herald who brought me the tidings of my *Abyot* membership. I later learned that he might have been Nolawi Abebe. Nolawi was one of the founding members of *Abyot*. He was in prison with Getachew at the time.

I had not read a single Marxist book since Getachew was arrested. In many ways, the revolution itself was my teacher. I had learned so much more about revolution and change from life itself than I did from books.

I felt I had come of age.

It was sometime in June, almost five months after the revolution had erupted. I was home and casually picked up the phone when it rang. I couldn't believe it. All I could say was, "Getachew!" He was released after nine months of imprisonment. We met in the afternoon in the small house behind Engineering College. He looked thinner and darker but cheerful.

"I don't believe you are out, Getachew. I didn't even know where you were held," I said.

"We were held at the *Kerchele*. They accused us of subversive activities. I'm not sure if you had heard about it, there was a riot by inmates in March. Many were killed. It was terrible."

"Was it the first time for you, to have been arrested?"

"I've been in and out a few times but only for short periods."

I wanted to tell him how I felt about him but I was terrified. I then mustered my courage and said, "Remember what you told me in that classroom just before you were arrested? I meant to tell you how I felt about you the next time I saw you. I was too shy and too overwhelmed to say it that day. Besides, I was ashamed you saw me in that skirt. I felt bad when you were arrested before I even got the chance to tell you how I felt about you. So you can take this as a confession..." My heart almost burst asunder. He clamped my mouth with his hand as if what he was going to hear would be too much to bear.

"I thought about you all the time. I don't remember a day that passed by without thinking about you. I am so glad to be with you again," he said.

It was only years later that I learned from Mesfin, Getachew's childhood friend, why "Getachew Maru's group" was thrown into jail.

"Ten of us - eight from here and two from Gondar – were arrested," Mesfin reminisced. "We were accused of plotting to overthrow the government and of producing and distributing divisive and subversive leaflets. A letter, actually a twenty-eight page hand-written propaganda material, was mailed to someone with whom we had communication in Gondar and it was intercepted by the security. However, when we appeared in court, they could not present that twenty-eight page letter as evidence for the accusation because it was considered a personal letter and intercepting individuals' personal letters was illegal then as long as the material was not duplicated and distributed to others. We were also accused of supporting a group of people who protested the Emperor's intention to give up a piece of land to the Sudan. One of the documents confiscated from us was an explosives manual. We were studying about explosives and weapons. Let me tell you something about Getachew. When he was arrested, he and Tadesse took all the responsibility upon themselves to save the rest of us. Some of us were taken away later. They were ready to die and save the rest of us. They told us not to admit anything and that they had taken the responsibility for everything."

Matheos had misgivings about the letter intercepted by the security. "Getachew… and the rest of the *Abyot* inner circle – all of whom were in Engineering College - were jailed. Endreas and I were not. You have no idea how angry I was. All that organization…the training we took…Getachew Maru was a demi-god. 'How is it that things got so messy?' I thought. Anyway, I couldn't forgive him."

He refused when other *Abyot* members, such as Endreas and Getachew Assefa, suggested they talk. He told them they had to reengineer the whole thing from scratch. He made some people dissociate themselves from *Abyot*.

I promised myself that now Getachew is out, I would be a good revolutionary. The past few months had taught me what it meant to be a revolutionary and why I was studying Marxism/Leninism. We went back to our weekend ritual of going to Harar Migib Bet and studying Wednesday evening. We discussed articles, pamphlets and books. He gave me three books that transformed my life. While reading, I felt I was spellbound and transported to a magical world. I even found the danger embedded in the stories beguiling. Maxim Gorky's *Mother* was actually the one that gave me an idea of what I would be doing in the underground organization. Pavel Vlassov became a model revolutionary to me. More than anything else, I was inspired and moved by the story of his mother.

Nguyen Van Troi, a book about the story of a young Viet Cong who attempted to kill Robert McNamara, the then US Secretary of Defense, and Henry Cabot Loge Jr, gripped me from beginning to end. Troi's "Long live Vietnam!" during his execution remained engraved in my imagination. I was amazed at his audacity to shout a slogan in the face of death. He became the ultimate source of inspiration to me. *Song of Ariran,* the story of a Korean man who had joined the Chinese Communist Party, was another book that I found fascinating and inspiring.

Those were one of the best times of my life.

. "Why? Why me?" I asked during my illness and before I met Getachew. My restless heart had kept on searching for an answer. There was no answer, but healing later came in the shape of a young man named Getachew Maru. Every book he discussed, every word he uttered, every concept he defined and every sentence he completed had a healing touch. It awakened my brain and soothed my troubled heart.

Getachew was the shaman who resuscitated my lethargic soul and solved my existential riddle.

I never told Getachew about my illness. Neither did he say much about himself. I learned about him only in bits and pieces. He had come from a large family of eight brothers and sisters. He was rebellious when he was in elementary school. One day he ground a pinecone and put it in the house. The house smelled so bad everybody had to leave. His father, a colonel in the army, even contemplated putting him in *Tebai Maremia* – youth correctional institute. He completely changed when he went to high school. He retreated to his room and buried his head in books. He either read or wrote when at home. When he was in grade eight, he brought home a typewriter and taught himself how to type in one day! He may have been unknowingly preparing himself for what was to come. He was recognized as "best teacher of the year" when he was teaching at Shimeles Habte.

Mesfin and Getachew were friends since seventh grade. They went to Arbegnoch School. "He used to call himself Communist when we were in grade eight," Mesfin laughed. "I've never heard anyone say anything like that at that age. He didn't even know what it was."

Getachew used to fight in elementary school and no one could beat him. One day, he had a fight with a boy who was older and bigger than he was. He threw him on the ground and Mesfin and other friends laughed. The boy got up and wanted to hit him but Getachew flung him to the ground again. The boy's mother later said, "I know Getachew. He is *kechero*!" In grade eight, this teacher was about to beat him one day but Getachew got up and held both his legs. The teacher couldn't do anything so he let him go.

When Getachew and Mesfin finished grade eight, Getachew went to Beedemariam Lab School. Mesfin remembered, "In Lab School, Getachew became a different and disciplined person and excelled academically. He didn't do that well in elementary school because he never took school seriously. When he graduated from Beedemariam, he was the best student and was the valedictorian of 1966. At the university, he was brilliant and the best in the department of Mechanical Engineering just as Abiyu Ersamo was in the Faculty of Education. We were members of the Science Club and we used to do things in the lab such as rockets. Getachew was very creative."

Getachew Maru giving his valedictorian speech at Lab School,
1966; left to right Kassa Woldemariam, President, Haile Selassie
I University, Akalewold Habtewold, Minister of Education,
Mulugeta Wodajo, lecturer Haile Selassie I University.

Getachew Maru
as freshman, 1967   Getachew Maru, 1969

Hiwot, 1972

Hiwot, 1972

*Around the time I met
Getachew, 1973*

Kissing Pool

Ras Mekonen Hall

Beedemariam Laboratory School was inside the Sidist Kilo university campus and students with the highest grades from all over the country were sent there.

"I was introduced to Getachew when we were in our freshman year in 1967," Shimeles, a friend of Getachew, recollected. "We were dorm-mates and later rented a house together. He didn't come to class for one week when we were in our freshman year. When he came back, he had his hair almost shaved off. We didn't know what had happened. We later learned that his mother had passed away."

Getachew did not eat or talk for several days after his mother died. He must have been deeply affected by her death.

"Getachew's father drove a Volkswagen and used to come to campus whenever there was a mass demonstration," Shimeles went on. "He always happened to see me first and asked me if his son was okay. He used to worry about him so much. I always went to look for Getachew and brought him to his father. Getachew was younger than I was. He was an outstanding student and very good at giving response instantly. He slept at the desk in the classroom covering his head with his jacket whenever he found a lecture boring. The lecturer would feel that he had not motivated him. When we studied and worried about exams, he would sit and draft his speech but had a 3.86 average!"

Shimeles was referring to the speeches Getachew made when he was secretary of USUAA.

"When we were in our freshman year," Shimeles continued, "Getachew had a lawyer's briefcase in which we put loose tea, a kettle, a spoon, and a ball. We would then go to room number 237, one of those larger classrooms, and play soccer and go to our rented house at Amist Kilo around one in the morning without turning a single page. Getachew used to read Peking Review. His mail slot was always jammed with subscription magazines. He was funny and was a man of iron discipline. He had firm adherence to what he believed to be genuine principle. He also had high regard for his friends."

This was also what Matheos had told me about Getachew. "For instance, if I asked him to meet at Kryiazis or have ice-cream, he would say, 'Are you out of your mind? That is jolly Jackism.' When we pushed it, you could see him becoming uneasy. Getachew was an introvert. He was serious and disciplined. He had strict standards of revolutionary behavior and about anything personal. He did not smoke, he did not drink... we did everything. He was dogmatic about Maoism too."

Right after Getachew was released, *Abyot*, the organ of the organization I had joined, started coming out. It was only later that I learned Getachew was its editor. One day, not too long after he was released, we met at the bus station adjoining Anbessa Gibi and took a long walk toward Menilik Hospital.

"A discussion is going on in our organization about a possible merger with other groups with similar goals," he said. "There are progressive groups that we can potentially work with such as the *Democracia* group, *Meison* and the Red Flag."

"I know a little about *Meison* and the Red Flag but nothing about *Democracia*," I admitted. I have recently been reading issues of *Democracia* but I knew next to nothing about the group. *Meison,* the Amharic acronym for All Ethiopian Socialist Movement – AESM - was also circulating its organ, *Voice of the Masses*, at the time.

"It is a small group. The Red Flag is a very small group too. Actually, there is a joke about the Red Flag. They say their membership is not even 'enough for one *bercha*.'" Getachew laughed. "Jokes aside, we have common goals. We are by far the largest group. We have organized particularly the youth. We are even thinking of preparing ourselves for the ultimate."

"The ultimate?"

"You know, no ruler gives up political power willingly," he explained softly. "In a country like ours, rural armed struggle is the main avenue through which the masses seize political power. Some of the groups have differing views on this. For instance, *Meison* says that we should first focus on educating and organizing the people. They say the time is not ripe for armed struggle. We say it is. We may have differences with all of them on certain issues, but to my mind, we should be able to work together. Our twin enemies are feudalism and imperialism and we should work with all anti-feudal and anti-imperialist forces, including the military junta. There is no group capable of giving leadership to the revolution at this point. We were caught off guard by it. Because of the power vacuum, you could say that the military junta has assumed power even though it is not yet official. We have to work together for a common goal. Think about all the groups and cast your vote. I don't want to influence your decision. If you have questions, I can answer them."

All the groups claimed to be Marxist-Leninist and it was difficult for me to make up my mind. There was already a negative rumor spreading about *Meison* for its position of support to the Derg when *Democracia* pushed for a civilian provisional government. I did not like the Red Flag because of an individual, who looked down upon my friends and me. I needed to talk to Azeb. I wondered if that would be a violation of discipline but I didn't see any harm in it. I found her in the same situation. Finally, we cast our vote in favor of the *Democracia* group even if we didn't know anything about them. We had read *Democracia* and liked it and that was enough for us.

It was only later that I learned that *Abyot*, the *Democracia* group and *Meison* had actually been working jointly, before the revolution, for a short period. They had an internal publication called *Ewneta* –Truth.

The *Democracia* group, so called then by its organ, belonged to the Ethiopian Peoples' Liberation Organization (EPLO - a merger of various groups, one of which was the Algeria Group). Unlike *Abyot*, which was founded in the country, EPLO and *Meison* were established in Europe. All of them had eminent names attached to them. Getachew belonged to the young generation of radicals that came on the university campus political scene in the late sixties and early seventies. He was the most famous member of *Abyot*. The celebrated student activist, Berhanemeskel Redda, was Secretary-General of the EPLO. Haile Fida, another distinguished student activist, was *Meison*'s leader.

It was Matheos who enlightened me about the early days of the various organizations and their publications. "We duplicated leaflets with *adefris*," he reminisced. "*Adefris* was a wooden frame with a silk screen on top and a cutting-board like wood at the bottom. *Democracia* started coming out in June 1974. *Abyot* came out later, in July or August. Like *Democracia* the *Voice of the Masses,* the organ of *Meison,* had come out earlier. *Abyot* was hard-hitting, while *Democracia* was more moderate. The content was the same, though. We later found the first real duplicating machine, which could print the *Democracia* logo in red. We duplicated *Democracia* and *Abyot* in shift. One day, somebody from *Meison* came and asked me to duplicate *Voice of the Masses* for them. He told me that their duplicating machine was broken. I duplicated it for them."

"I hadn't seen Getachew for a while," Matheos went on. "Merger between *Abyot* and *Democracia* was in the air. I met Getachew Assefa one day and he asked if Getachew Maru has gotten a "promotion over there?" I told him I didn't know."

Getachew Maru was one of the two negotiators sent from *Abyot* when negotiation about the merger took place between *Abyot* and the *Democracia* group. That was the "promotion" Getachew Assefa was referring to. *Abyot* members had reservations about the *Democracia* group and were not yet ready for the merger. The *Democracia* group, with people like Tselote Hezkias, Zeru Kishen and Tsegaye Gebremedhin (Debteraw), was associated with the EPLO.

"I had dissociated some people from *Abyot* and brought them to *Democracia*," Matheos told me. "This was after Getachew and the others went to prison. When it was asked who had brought *Abyot* members to *Democracia*, my name came up. Getachew was angry with me and he did not want to speak to me."

"One day, I saw him at Sidist Kilo around the zoo. He was with a girl. I was astonished because I had never seen him with a woman. You have no idea! I think it was you that I saw," Matheos said, looking up at me. "You know, you are off guard when you are with a girl. He nodded to me with a sense of bashfulness and a half smile. Apparently, when I saw him with a girl he had a sinking feeling of what I was thinking of him. All that inhibition had left him. I was in a hurry to go to town and spread the news. Later I heard that he was saying, 'Dating is good. It is good for the revolution.' I was surprised. Then the merger took place and he joined the Politburo."

The merger between *Abyot* and the EPLO took place and some members of the Red Flag joined them. The organization took the name EPLO, retaining both *Democracia* and *Abyot* as its organs.

Abyot was directed at workers and *Democracia* targeted the general population.

We, university students, returned to campus at the beginning of September 1974, but there were no classes. Azeb and I stayed in the dorm. One day, we flocked to the Christmas Hall to watch *A luta continua*, the film about FRELIMO, the Liberation Front of Mozambique, struggling to free Mozambique from Portuguese rule. I saw Josina Machel's –Samora Machel's first wife's – epitaph on a tomb. In a moment of madness, I wished it were mine.

Even death has its seductive moments.

I saw myself in the jungle, a rifle dangling from my shoulder, just like the FRELIMO guerrilla fighters. I was so excited I wanted to scream. When the film ended, the audience was enraptured. Some ran wild and threw chairs; others pushed and shoved to get out. My friends and I were terrified of being trampled. We made it out safely. We had watched *October*, the silent film about Lenin and the October revolution, earlier. It was nowhere near as arousing as the FRELIMO film.

The jungle had its own fascination.

On the 12th of the month, the Derg deposed Emperor Haile Selassie, ending fifty years of rule and the Solomonic Dynasty. The Derg filled the vacated throne, called itself the "Provisional Military Administrative Council" and promised it would return to its barrack after transferring power to the people.

Nobody believed it.

After seven months of turmoil, the revolution, as many feared, was officially hijacked by the military.

The conflict between students and the Derg became apparent. On 16 September, university students organized a demonstration that commenced from Arat Kilo campus. It was going to be the litmus test for the Derg's patience. Azeb was already there in her white thin corduroy pants, white T-shirt and white snickers when I got there. Students carried placards with slogans: "Democratic rights now!" "Provisional Peoples' Government!" "Down with feudalism and imperialism." We marched peacefully toward Piassa.

All of a sudden, we heard shots when we reached Berhanena Selam Printing Press in Arat Kilo. There was total chaos. We ran in all directions. Many tried to scale the barbed-wire fence of Berhanena Selam, to no avail. Others, including me, fled toward the street that led to Amist Kilo. We invaded the compound with a cluster of houses just across Princess Zuriash Building. I thought of running into one of the houses but got into a mud wall kitchen instead. I saw a huge barrel behind the door and hid beside it, leaving the door open.

I tried to peep through the crack in the door to see what was happening outside but something was in my way. A soldier passed by the kitchen door and suddenly I heard a cry. I looked toward where I suspected it had come from. A boy, about eight years old, was squatting beside me! "Shush! What are you doing hiding here? They are not going to do anything to you. You will get me arrested instead," I said in a whisper.

I saw through the crevice on the door soldiers knocking on peoples' doors and dragging out students. A soldier came into the kitchen carrying a baton. I watched him clamping my hand tight over the boy's mouth. He scanned the kitchen and left. Another soldier came in, did the same thing, and darted out. It never occurred to them to look behind the door.

After about twenty minutes or so, everything became quiet. I asked the boy to go out and see if the soldiers had gone. He never came back. After I made sure it was all quiet and after seeing demonstrators coming out of their hideouts, I emerged from the kitchen and stepped out of the compound. I saw soldiers hauling off and kicking students in front of the Second Police Station, which is just across the street. I took the small street that led to Amist Kilo and hailed a taxi from there.

It was already lunchtime when I got home. I changed my clothes before my sister and my brother-in-law came home from work for lunch. It was when I took off my brown pants and beige jacket that I noticed that they were marred with soot. I heard my sister's footsteps coming toward my bedroom. I was sitting on my bed.

"Have you been at the demonstration?" she asked.

"No, I didn't even know there was one," I lied.

"What is on your hair?"

"I don't know," I said, touching my hair with my hand.

She left without saying anything. I rose and went to the mirror. My hair was covered in spider webs!

A few days after the protest rally, the Derg declared a state of emergency prohibiting protest demonstrations and strikes. It held union leaders and members of the armed forces in custody, accusing them of calling out for Provisional Peoples' Government, and killed peasants in different provinces for demanding land. In October, it threw teachers and others into jail, on charges of pushing for a Provisional Peoples' Government. Five members of the armed forces were killed, and several wounded, in Harar. A number of people standing in front of the office of the workers' union looking for a job were mercilessly shot dead.

The Derg's motto, *Ethiopia Tikdem yaleminim dem –* Ethiopia first without bloodshed – became tainted with blood.

The Derg realized right away that it was not going to consolidate its grip on power as long as it kept the students in its bosom. Before October was out, it openly talked about dispatching us to rural areas in the name of a *Zemecha* – National Campaign for Development through Cooperation. We were to educate the peasantry about the spirit of *Ethiopia Tikdem,* and prepare them for land reform and conduct a literacy campaign. University and high school students (those in grade ten and above) and teachers would be sent off to rural areas for ten months.

At the university, we were divided over the question of the *Zemecha.* Some saw it as an opportunity to educate and organize the peasantry. Most students, however, were suspicious of the Derg's motives. They saw the *Zemecha* as nothing but an ingenious plot to stifle the struggle and solidify the Derg's power. We assembled at the Christmas Hall and saw debates seething on whether or not we should go. We took lunch breaks and packed the hall for days to continue talking.

My friends and I were against the *Zemecha,* but each position had its own merit. One morning, Meles Tekle, a vocal opponent of the *Zemecha,* gave the speech of his life. There was a thundering applause when he said in English, "Try to teach the Eritrean peasant how to wash his hands; he will instruct you how to pull the trigger!" We became ecstatic and kept clapping feverishly and non-stop.

We overwhelmingly voted against the *Zemecha.*

On November 22, the Derg's brutality was officially unleashed. I was home when the radio announced the execution of sixty people, over fifty of whom were ministers and high officials of the former regime; the rest were members of the Derg. Lieutenant-General Aman Andom, chair of the Derg, was also killed. Among the executed were also the two former Prime Ministers, *Tsehafi Tizaz* Aklilu Habtewold and *Lij* Endalkachew Mekonen. I stood unable to say anything, while my sister Almaz was crying and shivering. She kept saying, "They killed them all. They killed them all!"

The entire country was gripped by shock, fear and terror. All progressive forces condemned the brutal act through their publications. *Democracia* declared that Fascism reigned in the country.

I was sitting and chatting with Getachew in the small house a few days after the executions. Suddenly, he asked, "So Hiwot, what do you think of *Democracia* claiming that Fascism prevails in the country?"

"Oh I don't know…."

"The measure the junta has taken on the sixty people is definitely fascistic," he began, in his usual gentle voice. "There is no doubt about that. But can we say that Fascism has reigned in a country where capitalism is only now budding? I don't claim to have knowledge of Fascism, but I know that we are merely being pedantic. The problem is that we are not theoretically equipped to grasp some of the emerging issues. We have to have a clear understanding of the objective conditions of the country, the nature of the military junta and all the anti-feudal and anti-imperialist forces that we can work with. Right now, we are merely throwing around terms and labels we don't even know much about."

"I don't know. I don't know anything about Fascism," I admitted.

"Besides," he went on, mixing Amharic and English, "besides, we need to be clear about our characterizations of the Derg. We have to be careful too. It is not a unified entity. There are democratic forces in its midst. There are also individuals with militaristic dictatorship tendencies and others loyal to the previous regime. We will alienate the democratic forces and push the Derg toward more political repression if we continue to characterize it as such."

I promised myself I would read about this new thing called Fascism. I had heard the word in association with Benito Mussolini of Italy.

It might have been around the end of the month or beginning of December, Azeb and I were heading toward the Arts Building when we ran into Meles Tekle in the parking lot in front of the building. Our group had become friends with him lately. He had taken a liking to our friend Mekdes even though he saw her as his class enemy. One day, he even took Azeb and me to a place where *Struggle*, organ of the students' union, was duplicated. We helped out with stapling the pamphlet.

"You contradicted Abebech on the national question last night. How dare you? Don't you know that she is your *mastermind*?" he screamed at Azeb.

Azeb had a debate with Abebech on the national question the previous night. That was what he was referring to. Azeb became flustered and simply stared at him. I became indignant.

"How can you talk to her like that? Who do you think you are? And who do you think Abebech is? She is not our mastermind! We can think for ourselves and can say whatever we want to say and it is nobody's business." I poured out my anger.

I could not usually summon that kind of courage to talk to people like that. But I was so outraged by the way he treated Azeb, I couldn't control myself. We decamped, leaving him there.

"How could you allow him to talk to you like that?" I asked her on our way back to the dorm. She didn't say anything. I saw her eyes moist. I felt bad about the whole situation. I didn't like talking to Meles like that but neither did I like the way he treated Azeb. I looked at her one more time and my stomach churned. *I will talk to him again when I see him next.*

The next day we were stupefied when we learned that he'd been arrested. He had recently become more popular because of his electrifying speech against the *Zemecha* at the Christmas Hall. We suspected they arrested him because of that speech or for ridiculing Derg members, Captain Sisay Habte, Captain Endale Tessema and others, who had come during the revolutionary days to talk to the students at the Arat Kilo campus. Students signed petitions for his release, to no avail.

On 19 December, the Derg officially declared its version of socialism, Ethiopian Socialism and subsequently nationalized all the country's banks and insurance companies. It cloaked itself with leftist slogans and spoke the language of the left in order to find currency among them.

During the revolution, EPLO and *Meison* had emerged as the two main organized and most vocal forces in the political landscape of the country. EPLO, on one of its organs *Democracia* (*Abyot* being the other), repeatedly demanded the Derg to return to its barrack and called for the transfer of power to the people in the form of a Provisional Peoples' Government (PPG). *Meison,* on the other hand, maintained that the people have to be educated and organized first before they assumed political power. As a result, it took the position of "support" to the Derg, which would later be revised as "constructive criticism," that is, encouraging the Derg on certain issues and criticizing it on others. *Meison* insisted that its support was rather to progressive elements within the Derg.

The *Zemecha* was declared, and no one who refused to go would be able to go back to school or be able to work, the Derg had warned.

It was launched on December 20 at the Jan Meda. Many students went. My friends and I did not. Mengistu Hailemariam, vice-chair of the Derg, addressed the *zemachoch* – campaigners – and they shouted "Menge! Menge!" Many still believed he was the "man of the people." It was obvious that day that Mengistu took this endearment to heart.

Even though we had overwhelmingly voted not to participate in the *Zemecha*, the Derg was heedless of our decision. *Zemach* – campaigner – assignment list was posted right away at the Arts Building. Kidist, Sara and I were assigned to the Southwest, in the province of Wolega. I was assigned to a tiny village called Guliso, Kidist to Gimbi and Sara to Nejo. Azeb was to go to Shilabo to the East, in the province of Hararghe.

Before the end of December, I took the train to Harar to say goodbye to my mother and my younger sister Negede. I came back to Addis a week later, thinking that I would soon be dispatched to Guliso.

All is not well.

                    -William Shakespeare, *Hamlet*

In January 1975, the first batch of the 60,000 *zemachoch* was
dispatched to the South. They kept us on standby with a twenty-four
hour notice to leave. We tuned into the radio, watched television
and pored over the papers every day to catch on our departure dates.
Sara and Kidist left toward the end of the month. A few days after
they left, I learned that Guliso *Zemecha Tabia – Zemecha* Station –
was being renovated and my departure date had indefinitely been
postponed. Azeb was not called either, for reasons I cannot
remember. In the mean time, I found out that there was an
exemption from the *Zemecha* for those with genuine reasons.

       When the issue of the *Zemecha* came up, my family's
greatest concern was my health. How was I to deal with the lack of
balanced diet and regular visit to the doctor and continued supply of
medication?

       After I found out about the possibility of exemption from the
Zemecha, I consulted my sister Almaz and visited my doctor to get
a medical certificate. I took the certificate to the *Zemecha Memria* –
Campaign office – right away. Engineering College, in Amist Kilo,
has once been the seat of higher education but had been turned into
a *Zemecha* office, swarmed by people clad in uniform. It was the
first time I set foot on the campus.

       I waited in the hallway until it was my turn to be attended to.
Looking at the classrooms, I wondered which ones Getachew had
taken courses in. I was then asked to come into an office. A man in
a military uniform sitting behind his desk pointed me to a chair to
sit down. "How can I help you," he asked, fumbling through a stack
of papers. I gave him my medical certificate without a word. He
examined it for a few seconds, put it on the desk, went through a
list, and told me I was assigned in Addis Ababa at Ba'ta Mariam

Zemecha Tabia. It wasn't what I had hoped for but staying in Addis was not a bad idea, after all. But I was rather surprised that it did not take the man that long to approve my application. The certificate was signed by Dr. Taye Mekuria, one of the two renowned surgeons in the country at the time, the other one being Dr. Asrat Woldeyes. Azeb too applied for an exemption and was assigned in Addis at Etege Mesk *Zemecha Tabia.*

By the beginning of February 1975, I was already registered at Ba'ta Mariam *Zemecha Tabia*, located in Ba'ta Clinic, a Family Planning Clinic located beside Ba'ta Mariam church, just below the Parliament Building. We held meetings in the morning with the *Azmach* – the *Zemecha* Secretary – my former teacher at the Woizero Yeshimebet Elementary School for girls in Harar.

In the afternoon, we taught literacy as part of the Derg's literacy campaign. I started volunteering at the clinic right away, helping distribute milk and hygiene items to poor mothers. I was later elected Assistant Secretary of the *Zemecha Tabia.* In the afternoon, I worked in the office for an hour or so and went to the YMCA where I held a literacy class with children.

Just after I was registered at Ba'ta Mariam *Zemecha Tabia*, the day I've been dreaming about finally arrived. Getachew told me that I would be working with women when we met one day at the small house. He had told me to recruit *zemachoch* into study circles, thinking that I was going to Guliso. Now that I remained in Addis, he told me that the focus would be on Addis Ababa *zemachoch.*

"You will be meeting the comrade tomorrow. She will be waiting for you in front of Meskel Rendezvous," he told me.

I noticed that members of the organization called one another comrades, just like Chinese Communist Party members.

"Oh great!" I uttered gleefully.

He gave me a secret code and I met the comrade the next day. We talked and set an appointment for another day. We met a few times after that. She even took me to her apartment once. I later learned that she had come from abroad. As for our underground work, there was nothing much we did except talking. I was eager to roll up my sleeves and get on with it. After we met a few times, I felt my eagerness ebbing away.

At the time, I lived with my sister Almaz and family in Abware, which was within walking distance from Ba'ta Mariam *Zemecha Tabia.* I often walked to and from the *Zemecha Tabia* and heard someone call out "Teacher!" It was always one of my female students sitting under the sun selling charcoal or vegetable in the market. I felt sorry for the girls, who came to class in the afternoon after a trying day in the market.

The girls lived in the neighborhood just below the parliament. It was one of the poorest neighborhoods in Addis. I became acquainted with their mothers, who sometimes welcomed me into their homes. Tears welled up in my eyes to see the girls, looking hungry, their clothes torn and their hair dusty but assuming family responsibility at such a tender age. They swept the floor, did the laundry and ran errands. They were seven, eight, nine or ten years old.

I stole flour, oil, onions, coffee, sugar, hair oil, just about anything I could lay my hands on, from home and gave it to the mothers of my students. My sister once gave me children's clothing and I distributed it all to the kids. The humility of the mothers of my students was so touching; I often wiped my tears leaving their houses.

My literacy class was the noisiest and the kids got the most breaks. The classrooms were located behind the YMCA building and were made of corrugated sheet metal. It was dark inside and the heat was intolerable. Unless one kept them active, most of the kids dozed off because of the heat. Most of them were palpably hungry too. They farted every second, which I often found unbearable.

I would have them go to the toilet and then wash their faces, arms and legs under the standing water pipe in front of the classroom. They always looked as if they were just excavated out of the ground, with their tattered clothes and dirt on their faces, hands and legs. I would let them prance around for a few minutes and, once they were refreshed, shepherd them back to the classroom. Now and then, I made it easy for them, and asked them to tell stories or what they wanted to do with their lives when they grow up.

"Fassil?"

"Folice!"

"Befekadu?"

"Folice!"

"Weinshet?"

"Teacher!"

"Sintayehu?"

"Teacher!"

The boys wanted to become policemen and the girls, teachers. The world they lived in was so limited; there was "no scope for imagination." Only one boy was different, passionately beating the desk with two pencils. He wanted to be a drummer.

Some of these kids were not lucky enough to start school, as their parents could not afford to send them to *Yeneta's* – a priest – who charged one birr per child per month to teach the Ethiopian alphabets. But when news reached the neighborhood about a free *Zemecha* school, many parents pulled their kids from *Yeneta's* and brought them to us. However, the *Zemecha Tabia* could absorb only so many.

Our priority was to register those children who didn't know their alphabets. Mothers came and told us how poor they were and how many children they had and how they could not afford to send their kids to *Yeneta's*. The kids lied, pressured by their parents, that they were not going to *Yeneta's* and didn't know their alphabets. We turned a blind eye to some of the children obviously going to *Yeneta's*.

A priest came into the *Zemecha* office one afternoon, swishing his *chira* – fly-whisk – his white turban neatly wrapped around his head. He wore a *netela* – shawl – over his white long sleeve shirt and white breeches. I was sitting at the desk in the corner talking on the phone. I hung up the phone and sprang to my feet. A priest normally held out his cross for people to kiss. This one did not. It was obvious that he was not on a sacred mission that afternoon.

"Who is in charge around here?" he asked, looking me up and down.

"The *Azmach* is not here. I am the Assistant…*Azmach*…How can I help you? Have a seat," I said, using the polite you and pointing to a chair.

He continued standing in the middle of the room. Then he asked, a look of disappointment setting in his eyes, "Can I talk to someone older?"

"I am the only one around."

"What kind of injustice is being done around here? How could you throw me out of business? Do you think God would appreciate that?" he lamented, laying his *chira* on his shoulder and still standing in the middle of the room.

"I am not sure what you are referring to," I pretended, knowing very well what he was talking about.

It was the first time for me to talk to a priest. I was never fond of them because of my mother's *ye nissiha abat* – soul father – who came to our house once a month and blessed our house with holy water. I always covered my face with my hands or with my book when he sprinkled me with holy water. I had no qualms about showing him my annoyance. Embarrassed by my behavior, my mother would apologetically say "*yezare lijoch*" – today's young people. She would tell me I had "the devil" in me after he left.

"You took away all my students and put me out of business. That is what I am referring to. May I know how you expect me to feed my children?"

I was stunned.

"We wanted to enroll only those children who were unable to start school. When we made the screening, we asked the parents if their children went to school. We were told none of them did.... Now classes have already begun. We can't send them away," I said firmly in spite of my sympathy for him.

He made an inventory of his mishaps swishing his *chira* from side to side as if to ward off flies. I did not know what to say.

"Where do I go to complain?" he asked, frustration obviously mounting in his voice. "But what is the use? No one is going to listen to me. Things are upside down these days."

"The *Azmach* is available mornings," I told him. I knew there was nothing she could do for him. I just wanted him to leave. His pleading eyes had made me uncomfortable.

"Let God give you what you deserve," I heard him say when he left. He never came back.

We kept all our students. Our plan was to enroll them, which we later succeeded at, into public school.

Fassil, one of my students and who was about seven, had a terrible infection on the inside part of his right elbow. The infection was so bad he scratched his arm ferociously. I feared that his arm would be lopped off in a matter of days. I wanted to help and asked a health worker at the Ba'ta Clinic to give me hydrogen peroxide, cotton swabs, gauze and an antibiotic ointment. She looked at me with a grin on her face and asked me what I would be doing with all those supplies. When I told her, she said the boy had to go to the hospital. Hospital was a luxury for the little boy. I begged, pleaded, and finally won her heart.

Every day, I brought the boy to the standing water pipe and washed his arm with soap and water, rubbed it with hydrogen peroxide, spread ointment and swathed it in gauze. My students stood in a circle, watching with the utter fascination only children are capable of. I did that for a couple of weeks. At first, the infection seemed to be unrelenting. Finally, I began to see improvement. I went back to the health worker and asked for more supplies. She was not convinced but gave in, anyway.

About a month after I started my medical experiment on him, I was about to go into the classroom when Fassil ran after me and cried, "Teacher! Look! Look!" I looked at his arm and tears pooled in my eyes. The infection was gone! I bent down to kiss him. Suddenly, something fell at my feet and I looked down to see. It was a woman with a red headscarf kissing my feet! I was moved. I helped her up and looked at her questioningly.

"I am Fassil's mother. I don't know how to thank you. My boy had suffered so much for so long. I feared that he was going to lose his arm one day. May the Mother of Our Lord reward you for what you have done for my son? I have no way of rewarding you. I am utterly poor."

Tears rolled down my cheeks. "It is nothing....I just..." My lips quivered.

She wished me a thousand blessings and left, wiping her eyes with her *netela*. I was humbled by her humility.

Such moments solidified my commitment to the struggle.

On March 3, the Derg proclaimed its land reform program, changing the age-old social relationships between landlords and peasants. It had quickly realized that it could stay in power only so long as it appropriated the language and goals of the progressive elements of society. A few days after the proclamation, EPLO stated on its organ, *Democraica*, that the proclamation was the right step forward but doubted its practicality.

The land reform, according to *Democracia*, was supposed to herald the arrival of a new system. However, the people who should have reaped the benefits of such a proclamation were not allowed to get organized under the leadership of the proletariat, and democratic rights (that would pave the transition to socialism) had not been guaranteed to the people. By "the people," *Democracia* meant workers, peasants and all progressive elements. To that extent the proclamation, *Democracia* maintained, "is like giving the meat but denying the knife," meaning giving with one hand and taking away with the other.

Right after the proclamation, Getachew and I met at the small house. He was wearing his dark red jersey top and jeans. I settled down on the chair beside him and we talked about the land proclamation. "The proclamation has implications on the tactics and strategies we have devised. We have to understand the meaning of all this and give appropriate leadership to the revolution," he stressed.

The land question was the most important issue of all. Revolutionaries of the time had pinned their hopes on rallying the people around the slogan: "Land to the tiller." It had been the single most important slogan in a country where 90% of the population lived in rural areas and whose lives were tied to the land.

A few days after the land proclamation, a seminar was held for women; eighteen of them were elected to form a Women's Coordinating Committee. The purpose of the committee was to organize a seminar to raise the political consciousness of women of all walks of life.

The Derg took another brutal measure in the same month. Meles Tekle, under custody since November, was executed with Gidey Gebrewahid and Rezene Kidane. They were accused of throwing bombs at the City Hall and Wabishebele Hotel and of attempting to set a gas depot ablaze. They were killed along with feudal lords, who were accused of sabotaging the land reform. Another wave of shock ripped through the city. I felt bad for a long time for parting with Meles Tekle the way I did that day in the parking lot in front of the Arts Building.

Before the end of March, Addis Ababa *zemachoch* were called for a meeting at Christmas Hall at the Sidist Kilo campus. They told us that a seminar would be held for 360 women in April and that we should select three female participants. Amsale Tamrat, Azeb and I were selected.

Getachew was excited when I told him about the seminar. The seminar, he explained softly, would create the perfect opportunity for me to work with women. Since all kinds of women would be represented at the seminar, he instructed me to focus particularly on factory workers. I was to learn about their working and living conditions and recruit them into study circles.

The Women's Coordinating Committee, which had recently been formed and most of whose members came from the EPLO and *Meison*, organized the historic seminar. The two-week seminar began on April 17 at the parliament. Participants were recruited from among factory workers, sex workers, housewives, teachers, businesswomen, civil servants and students. Azeb and I were thrilled to be part of this historic event. Like every participant, we got complimentary bus passes and free lunches at the Theological College cafeteria for the duration of the seminar.

Mengistu Hailemariam gave the opening remarks the day the seminar started but left as soon as he finished his speech, to the disappointment of many eager to ask him questions.

I met the female comrade I was assigned to work with at the seminar. She was one of the organizers. Azeb and I also got to see some of the notable names in the political circle such as Nigist Tefera from EPLO and Atnaf Yimam from *Meison*. The organizational affiliations of these women were not public knowledge but we associated them with the organizations because of their positions on the issues.

Most importantly, Azeb and I were excited to talk to factory workers. I was not able to recruit anyone and didn't know if Azeb had succeeded on that front. But we learned so much about their lives by simply talking to them. We had lunch with them every day and after lunch, we sat down with them on the lawn in front of the cafeteria until we got back to the afternoon session. The women were from factories such as Diabaco Cotton Spinning Company and Lazaridis Cotton Ginning Company.

The seminar led to the formation of a Women's Association under the Chairmanship of Nigist Tefera (a Haile Selassie I University graduate). The Derg later hijacked the Association and started harassing the former leaders, mainly EPLO members, forcing individuals like Nigist to go underground.

Our main responsibility, as seminar participants, was to go back to our respective organizations and groups and educate our peers. I made a presentation of whatever I had learnt at my *Zemecha Tabia.*

In the same month the seminar was held, my friend Kidist returned from the *Zemecha.* She had a job at the Political Science Department at the university. Since Azeb and I were staying on campus, we went to visit her often in her office. She got married right away and rented a house around Teret Sefer.

One afternoon around the end of spring, I tapped the door of the little house and pushed it open. Getachew always left the latch off the door, while waiting for me. I closed the door and pushed the sliding lock into the latch. I sat down beside him. We chatted for a while about recent events and the situation in the country in general and about the book that he had recently given me to read.

"Hiwot, I would like to invite you to see *Enat Alem Tenu.* I want us to go see it on Saturday," he said, taking my hand in his.

I was thrilled.

Enat Alem Tenu was an adaptation of Bertolt Brecht's *Mother Courage* by the celebrated Ethiopian playwright, poet, Laureate Tsegaye Gebre-Medhin. I was startled he asked to go to the Theatre. We've never been to public places. Harar Migib Bet was the most public place we've been to.

On Saturday, we had lunch at the restaurant, and then walked together to Haile Selassie I Theatre. At the Theatre, I was surprised when he held my hand. He had never done that in public. The only time he did that outside the small house was when we were in the streets in the dark. We later came back to the restaurant and talked about the play and other issues until dark.

"How is the assignment with the women coming along?" he asked after a while.

"Oh…I don't know. We haven't been doing anything. We met a few times but we haven't done anything. I wanted to mention it to you…"

"Are you telling me you haven't yet met anybody else?"

I nodded in the negative.

"Why didn't you tell me?"

"I was going to one of these days."

He didn't say anything. He sounded disappointed. "Some of our comrades are only Social Democrats," he said in English after a brief silence.

I didn't know what to say. I was familiar with the term from my readings and discussions with him about the Russian revolution but I wasn't quite sure what he was trying to tell me. I didn't ask for an explanation. I felt it would be prying for me to ask.

I hoped he would go on. Instead he said, an ironic smile glinting in his gentle eyes, "There is also this subtle division among comrades…between homegrown revolutionaries and those returned from abroad. The ones who had come back from abroad look down upon the homegrown. I don't think that is fruitful. Only our actions will testify to what kind of revolutionaries we are…not where we come from." He was a homegrown revolutionary.

All is not well. I thought.

All was not well in the country either. For the first time in our history, May Day was celebrated but it was punctuated with bloodshed. At least 21 workers and students were shot dead at the parade that day for demanding Provisional Peoples' Government (PPG) and democratic rights.

After the execution of Meles Tekle and others in March, the Derg had gone on a killing spree of students, workers, military officers, and peasants across the country. It claimed that many of the executed were former feudal lords engaged in "counter-revolutionary activities." It accused them of sabotaging the land reform. Some of them had indeed taken up arms and fled to rural areas to restore their confiscated land. But the Derg had no qualms about killing progressive elements along with the so-called counter-revolutionaries. EPLO and *Meison* denounced the imprisonment and killing of progressive forces.

Executions were unabashedly announced on TV and radio. The dreadful and hateful *Yefiyel Wotete* was played along when executions were announced.

> የፍየል ወጠጤ ልቡ ያበጠበት
> እንዋጋ ብሎ ለነብር ላከበት
> የማትረባ ፍየል ዘጠኝ ትወልዳለች
> ልጆቿም ያልቃሉ እሷም ትሞታለች

Yefiyel Wotete was a traditional incantation of bravado – a sort of war cry – until the Derg turned it into a doomsayer. It is the story of a cocky kid goat that challenged a Leopard to a showdown. The moral of the story is closer to Aesop's *The Donkey, the Rooster and the Lion* fable: *false confidence often leads to misfortune.* I always listened to that song with a sense of utter dread. Even if I had seen him the day before, I always feared that Getachew might be executed.

Azeb and I had moved in earlier to our previous dorm when we (Addis Ababa *zemachoch)* found out that we could stay at the Sidist Kilo campus dormitory and dine at the Science Faculty cafeteria at Arat Kilo. We went to *Emama* University's with our male *zemach* friends, all of whom were university students, when we tired of cafeteria food and whenever there was *Yefiyel Wotete on* TV.

The eatery was in Amist Kilo, right behind Engineering College near the little house where Getachew and I met. The owner was nicknamed *Emama* University, as the overwhelming majority of her customers were university students. She was illiterate but knew names of university students, turned-lecturer students, campuses, cafeterias, and buildings. She had several anecdotes about debtors and campus trips. "Do you know Bekele Asfaw? Hailu Ashebir? Ketema...Ketema Sebsibe? Ketema owed me five birr... Bekele two-fifty...and Hailu seven-fifty. They all stopped coming here. I once went to the Arts Building to look for them. I bumped into Worku instead, who stopped coming here a long time ago. He owed me two-fifty," she would spill out her frustration.

My friends and I went to *Emma* University's, counting every penny, not only to eat but also to watch TV. *Emama* was heavy set and told her endless debtor stories sitting on a chair, her back against the TV, making it difficult to watch. Filled with dismay, we often left.

Varsity, which was also in Amist Kilo, was our main hang out. Sometimes we had no money to buy each of us a drink. Henok Belew, my high school classmate and friend, was bold enough to order a bottle of *Ambo Wuha* – mineral water – and five glasses! The waiter served us with a suppressed smile. We went to the Varsity mainly to listen to the Derg's execution list accompanied by *Yefiyel Wotete*.

With Azeb Girma in front of the prefab dorms, 1976

During the Zemecha, 1976

On August 27, 1975, Emperor Haile Selassie died at the age of 83. Rumor was circulating that Mengistu Hailemariam himself had killed him. People had anticipated that something might befall the country when he died. Nothing happened.

His death symbolized the end of an era.

Two days later, EPLO officially declared its existence under the name of the Ethiopian Peoples' Revolutionary Party (EPRP). Its program was distributed in several ethnic languages. The need for a New Democratic Revolution aimed at overthrowing feudalism and imperialism, a Provisional Peoples' Government, the safeguarding of democratic rights, redistribution of land, ensuring the right of nations to self-determination, right up to secession and nation building, were put forward in the program as the main goals of the Party. There was jubilation among members and supporters.

Soon EPRP called for all *zemachoch* to evacuate their *Zemecha Tabias*. But the Derg extended the *Zemecha* by one year, even though many *zemachoch* were at the time evacuating their *Zemecha Tabias*.

On 12 September, Addis Ababa *zemachoch* were forced out for the parade commemorating the first anniversary of *Abyot Ken* – Revolution Day – the day the Derg usurped power. Thousands of people, Addis Ababa *zemachoch,* workers, peasants, civil servants, teachers, students, representatives of ethnic groups and others from all over the country, marched toward the former Meskel Square, christened *Abyot* Square, the equivalent of the Russian Red Square.

I marched with Ba'ta Mariam *zemachoch* and Azeb with Etege Mesk *zemachoch*. We wore our khaki uniforms, scarves and hats. The parade moved painfully slowly. There were hundreds of spectators standing on the pavement marveling at the human ants surging toward the square.

When we reached the United Nations Economic Commission for Africa Building, I thought I saw a familiar face among the crowd. Before even I ascertained who he was, he stepped out of the crowd and came toward me. He was smiling. That was when I realized it was Eshetu Chole, the university lecturer who gave the sensational "Organize! Organize! Organize!" speech at the USUAA inauguration. He had been arrested in October 1974, along with a number of teachers accused of demanding a Provisional Peoples' Government. He was released when amnesty was given to some prisoners on the occasion of the commemoration of the first anniversary of *Abyot* Day. "How are you?" he said, shaking my hand with a huge smile.

I was stupefied. I never thought he knew me, let alone that he would recognize me amidst hundreds of *zemachoch*. "Congratulations!" I cried.

"Thank you." He stepped aside when the parade started to move.

I did not know if Azeb was ahead of me or behind me but I wanted to shout to her, "I just shook hands with Eshetu Chole!" I remembered the times Azeb, Kidist, Sara and I whispered *"Gash Eshetu! Gash Eshetu!"* walking behind him, nudging, and giggling like school girls in our university days.

In the same month, Kidist gave birth to a baby girl. We were all overjoyed, saying, "the first child of the group is born." She quit her university job and got another one. Azeb and I stopped going to the *Zemecha Tabia* after the *Abyot* Day parade as more and more students returned from the rural areas, evacuating their *Zemecha Tabias*.

September 1975 was marked by agitation among workers. The Confederation of Ethiopian Labor Unions (CELU) which had spearheaded the struggles of workers since its inception in 1963, made a resolution demanding democratic freedom, Provisional Peoples' Government and the release of political prisoners. CELU had thus far perhaps received the harshest blow from the Derg, including disbandment in May of that year and imprisonment and execution of its leaders.

At the end of the month, the Derg declared a state of emergency. Strikes, demonstrations, producing and distributing, and even the reading of leaflets became illegal. Anyone caught committing such a "crime" faced severe measures. Even schools were closed. Another state of emergency, declared in October, lasted until April 1976.

Just as the Derg was quashing political opposition, my own underground career was gaining momentum. October of that year was another milestone in my underground career. Getachew said to me when we met one day in the tiny house, "From now on, you will be working with the youth – in the Youth League – the youth wing of the Party. You are going to meet a comrade tomorrow afternoon. He will be waiting for you at three o'clock at the bus station adjacent the zoo. He will pretend he is reading a newspaper. You will ask him what time it is. He will say, 'Sorry, my watch is broken.' Remember, you have to use a code name."

I rejoiced with the prospect of working in the Youth League. I could not wait till I met the comrade. I picked the Muslim name Alia as my code name. I got to Sidist Kilo at exactly three o'clock the next day and saw a young man with a huge Afro, a brown turtleneck sweater and a black leather jacket standing beside the bus stop. He was reading a newspaper.

There were a few people at the bus station. I immediately remembered what Getachew had told me about meeting people in public, "You are meeting the comrade at a bus station and it is likely that other people will be around. You have to make it appear normal not to arouse suspicion."

"What time is it, please," I asked the youngster casually and politely, pretending to be a passerby.

"Sorry, my watch is broken," he recited.

That was how I met Tito Hiruy. We talked, taking the street that led to Menilik Hospital. He told me I would be working in a cell and that I was going to meet "other comrades." We exchanged telephone numbers and I told him my name was Alia. Later, I learned he was a student at General Wingate School and had just returned from *Zemecha*.

"Who? Alia? Mummy, he is asking for Alia." I heard my nephew say in the evening a day or two after I met Tito. The phone was sitting on a small table in the hallway in the house. I darted out of my bedroom and snatched the phone from the little boy. "Hello!"

"Alia? It's Tito…"

"*Selam*!"

"The boy-"

My nephew stood there looking puzzled. Then I heard him say, "Mummy, Hiwot has changed her name to Alia!"

Wey goude - woe to me! "Oh, he is my nephew," I said to Tito, interrupting him. I knew that I had blundered. I should have given him my real name once I had given him my phone number. I wondered if my sister and my brother-in-law had heard my nephew. They were sitting in the living room. The TV was on and they were chatting. Nobody seemed to have heard my nephew. I was relieved. Tito told me to come the next day to a place I could not remember. I hung up the phone and ran into my room, unable to contain my excitement. I had a feeling that it was going to be different this time, but I had no idea the gateway to heaven had been thrown wide open before me.

It is not a garment I cast off this day, but a skin that I tear with my own hands.

-Kahlil Gibran, *The Prophet.*

The next morning, unable to even imagine what would await me, I knocked on the door of the house Tito had told me to come to. My heart was pounding. When I stepped in the small and semi-dark room, I saw three young men sitting around a table. They looked businesslike and serious for their age. I instinctively adopted a formal demeanor. Tito introduced me to Samuel and the two brothers, Sirak and Dawit Tefera, as members of the cell. The cell had just been formed and Tito was the contact person.

He said that Addis Ababa was divided into four Zones and that Sirak, Dawit, Samuel and I would each be responsible for a Zone. The three of them have already been assigned Zones. Dawit was responsible for Zone One (comprising *Mercato*, Gulele, Teklehaimanot etc. areas), Sirak for Zone Two (Nifasilk, Kera etc.), Samuel for Zone Four (Arat Kilo, Sidist Kilo, and Entoto) and I became responsible for Zone Three (Bole, Casanchis – a corruption of Case Inces – etc.). Our primary task was to establish committees in our respective Zones. The committees would be responsible for organizing and directing the activities of each Zone. Members had been randomly recruited thus far and had to be shuffled around the four Zones. We were given codes that would allow us to meet members, who would populate our Zones.

When I left at the end of the meeting, I was immensely enthused by the prospect of doing actual work. I had the sense that this was the beginning of the underground life that I had been waiting to throw myself into.

The Youth League was fashioned after the Komsomol – the Russian Communist Youth League. It was a semi-autonomous organization and contact with the Party was established at Central Committee levels. Its organizational structure was parallel to that of the Party. The supreme body of both organizations was the Congress, even though it was a much later development for the League.

After the merger with EPLO, *Abyot* had sent a large contingent of youth that saturated the League leadership and other higher committees. Many of its members had filled higher Party committees as well. Contrary to the belief that EPLO was the largest group that "swallowed up" other smaller groups, it was *Abyot* that had the largest membership, not only compared to EPLO but also to all the groups that had surfaced during the revolution.

The cell I joined later became the Addis Ababa Youth League Inter-Zonal Committee, with Tito as secretary. The Inter-Zonal Committee was below the League Central Committee in the hierarchy of the organization. It played a major role, providing leadership to the League in planning, organizing, directing, coordinating, and facilitating communication among members.

When I had enough people to populate my committee (with individuals transferred from other Zones), I formed Zone Three Committee. Semegne Lemma, whom I met through a code, was one of the committee members. We clicked right away and became best friends. Like me, she was originally from Harar and lived with her wealthy uncle, at the time kept in prison by the Derg.

Each Zonal Committee was responsible for forming sub-Zonal committees below it. Sub-Zones formed Regional committees below them and Regions created sub-Regions. Below sub-Regions were Cells: the very foundation of the organization. One of the most important tasks of cells was expanding the base of the organization through recruitment of members. Each cell comprised five members. The secretary linked the cell to the sub-Regional Committee above it.

Once the framework of the organization has been laid down, recruitment took place at lightning speed. Cells sprouted in neighborhoods like hydra tentacles. The League wasted no time in absorbing in its hierarchy *zemachoch* back in town with their enormous Afros, abandoning their *Zemecha Tabias*.

They were the perfect raw material. Some were already 'handled' in study circles at their respective *Zemecha Tabias*. Others were pushed around by the Derg and were highly politicized. They boasted 'knowledge' of the peasantry and saturated the League structure in a flash. There was a sense of urgency to speed up recruitment partly because of the need to beat rival *Meison*, which the Ethiopian People Revolutionary Party (EPRP) kept at arm's length from the youth with wicked labels.

One had to be between the ages of fifteen and twenty-five to become a Youth League member. An individual was recruited to study circles and required to study the basic tenets of Marxism-Leninism. An individual can become a League member after a three-month probation period. At least two members, who studied in the study circle with the candidate and are themselves League members, had to write recommendation letters for membership. Anyone who had been in the League for ten months could be recruited to the Party. To become a Party member, committee members who had worked with the individual and were Party members had to write a recommendation letter to the IZ (Inter-Zonal Committee).

Strict discipline was required of us. The League, like the Party, upheld the principles of democratic centralism. We were taught that individuals were subordinate to the League, and the minority to the majority. Members could discuss and debate policies and issues, but once a majority decision was reached, we were obliged to uphold it.

We used code names to minimize danger. Unless we happened to know one another before, we did not reveal our identities. Neither were we supposed to know more than what was necessary. Only the chair of the committee knew the people who worked in the committee immediately above.

We had to use a secret code when meeting a new member. The codes were memorized and if they were on paper, the paper was destroyed immediately. Telephone conversations were brief and coded. Punctuality was of utmost importance. As far as appointments were concerned, we were not expected to wait for a person for more than ten minutes. If appointments failed, they were reestablished through a 'mechanism' - we met again at a certain designated place and time. We buried incriminating documents in our backyards, mattresses and in boxes with false bottoms.

We had to be vigilant at all times. Scanning a café before entering was indispensable. If I went into a café and saw a member whom I knew sitting with anyone, I turned back and went elsewhere. Mere association with a known League member might confirm an individual's membership. Paying attention to our surroundings helped us spot security agents, who went in and out of cafés in search of prey. If a member was arrested, those who worked with that individual would leave their homes for a few days, or at least be cautious, in case the detainee succumbed to interrogation.

Cafés sprang up like mushrooms in the city, as if in response to our need for meeting places. Committees met once or twice a week under normal circumstances (these regular meetings were held in houses), but committee chairs met with individual committee members daily in cafés or in the street, often more than once a day to ensure League members were kept abreast of events. Situations changed daily or even hourly. They needed to know pertinent security information such as license plate numbers and makes of vehicles driven by secret service agents, descriptions of agents, targeted cafés, and bus stops.

All major instructions flowed from the League leadership via the IZ to committees all the way down the chain of command. Instructions were disseminated throughout the organization in a matter of hours.

The beginning of 1976 saw spurts of League activity, as well as new and sensational ways of attacking the government. The end of 1975 had been a time of organizing the youth more or less "quietly" in cells and committees, hosting *Zemecha Tabia* evacuees and refining and adapting the organization's structure. The League made significant strides in recruitment of members during that period.

It was time to go on the offensive.

"There will be a graffiti and banner hoisting day. Banners with slogans should be hoisted at night on electric poles and walls should be painted with slogans. It is going to take place city wide simultaneously. The date will be announced later," Tito told us at one of the IZ meetings in early 1976. He gave us the slogans to be painted.

We diffused the instruction throughout the League structure that very day. Preparation started for the big day with utmost secrecy. No one, not even the IZ, knew the day of execution. Every neighborhood formed its own Intelligence Unit that assessed the security situation in its locale. Once an intelligence report was gathered, the IZ passed on a favorable report to the *Yebelay Akal* - higher body - that is the League leadership.

Tito revealed to us at a meeting one day that the big day had arrived. When the meeting ended at five-thirty in the afternoon, we raced to meet our Zonal Committee members. By eight o'clock, the word had crackled throughout the League structure. The next morning, the entire city was submerged in a sea of red with banners hoisted everywhere and walls ornamented with slogans.

Addis looked like a carnival city.

The graffiti and banners were as much the delight of members as they were the Derg's nightmare. Outside the League structure, neighborhood juveniles littered walls with EPRP slogans, taking matters into their own hands. As an unintended result, graffiti became their preferred pastime, often complicating the League's plans.

The Derg declared the mass organization proclamation in April 1976. *Kebeles* – urban dwellers associations – and Youth and Women's Associations arose in neighborhoods. *Kebeles* were Administrative Zones that divided the city in various units. A political school was set up and manufactured cadres, dispatching them across the country to spread the tidings of socialism and counter EPRP's activities. *Wuyiyit Kibebs* – discussion forums – were established in factories, companies, government offices, hospitals, schools, and the army. People were forced to attend these forums during working hours.

At some forums, quizzes were even given. An older man I knew one day asked, "When was that Eleni born?" when preparing himself for a quiz at the *Wuyiyit Kibeb*. By Eleni he meant Lenin. Eleni is a woman's name. I burst out with laughter when Getachew one day told me that he saw their *Kebele* chairman going to his office, a few days after he was elected, holding a page of Selected Works of Marx and Engles between his thumb and index finger. He was assuring the government and the cadres that he was indeed sipping from the fountain of Marxism!

The League also created mass organizations, such as the Students Association, Women's Association, and the Youth Vanguard, that ran parallel to its structure. Almost every secondary school in Addis had a Students' Association Committee. Women's Association Committees were set up both in schools and in *Kebeles*. The Youth Vanguard initiated boys and girls, between the ages of eleven and fourteen, into the world of underground life.

Besides other Associations, the Party later formed what it called the Democratic Front to expand its networks among teachers, workers, civil servants and the military. The mass organizations were as much underground as the Youth League or the Party. They were the main recruitment fields for the Party and League. Tens of new recruits were funneled into the League each day from these organizations, eventually reaching the point where it became difficult to coordinate the activities of the manifold cells blossoming in each *Kebele*.

The IZ once spent an entire day trying to figure out how to coordinate the activities of the cells in each *Kebele*. After an all-day deliberation, we came up with the idea of Basic Organization. It was a "Eureka!" moment. The Basic Organization became the foundation of the entire League structure and of the Party that coordinated and directed the activities of all cells in each *Kebele*.

Creation of mass organizations was one of the Derg's strategies to rally mass support and smother "counter-revolutionary" activities. *Kebeles* would later become the most effective machinery of control and repression. Every *Kebele* resident was required to have a *Kebele* residence identification card, which the Derg used to control the movement of people. Travelers had also to obtain travel permits from their *Kebeles*, another ploy to curb mobility. But *Kebele* associations, such as Youth Associations, became recruitment fields for the EPRP and helped it spread its Gospel. They also became the battlefield between EPRP and *Meison* for conquering souls and were instrumental in "exposing" League members to *Kebeles,* cadres, and security agents, just as *Wuyiyit Kibebs* had become responsible for revealing the political affiliations of participants.

The Derg called for a United Democratic Front at about the time the mass organization proclamation was made. For EPRP, a Democratic Front is possible only when it is representative of the proletariat, peasantry, petty-bourgeoisie, mass organizations, political groups and National Liberation Fronts. Therefore, EPRP demanded that the Derg should first guarantee democratic rights before trying to forge a United Democratic Front.

In early 1976, EPRP and *Meison* engaged in a sizzling debate (without claiming authorship) on the government owned Amharic daily *Addis Zemen* – New Era – and *Goh* – Dawn – magazine over the kind of democracy needed at that particular point in time. The question of political freedom was one of the most important issues that has long been championed by students and all progressive forces. The eruption of the revolution made the issue even more pressing.

Meison advocated for limited democracy, claiming that unlimited democracy would help reactionary forces turn the tide of the revolution. For *Meison*, the people were not yet savvy enough of the democratic process and needed to be educated, organized and armed first. Unlimited democracy could only be guaranteed in a Democratic Republic, according to *Meison*. It accused EPRP of opening the door to reactionary forces that would enable them highjack the revolution by advocating unlimited democracy.

EPRP, in addition to its response to the debate on *Addis Zemen* about what kind of democracy was needed and for whom, clarified its position in a late June issue of *Democracia*. It proclaimed democracy to be a basic human right, but at the same time acknowledged that there was no such thing as absolute democracy. By demanding unlimited democracy, EPRP was asking the Derg to lift the restrictions that it had imposed upon the rights of the people. In answering the question of democracy for whom, EPRP stated that democracy is, in essence, partisan. It has a class nature. Therefore, it was advocating for the institutionalization of democracy only for workers, peasants and progressive forces. The institution of democracy was not the goal, claimed *Democracia,* but the establishment of a classless society. There is no democracy in a classless society. There is not even the need for it.

Political power was one of the burning questions that arose since the outbreak of the revolution. EPRP was at odds with the Derg and *Meison* over what kind of government should be forged at the time. The Derg had made it clear that *it* was the "provisional government." EPRP called for the immediate establishment of a Provisional Peoples' Government. By that, the Party meant a popular government representing all anti-feudal and anti-imperialist forces: political organizations, National Liberation Fronts and mass organizations. *Meison,* which was the champion of the slogan earlier on, gave support to the Derg on the premise that the people were not yet ready to take power in their hands. A bitter squabble arose over this between the two organizations.

EPRP ended up on the Derg's blacklist over this.

The other crucial issue the revolution brought to the fore was the kind of revolution needed and who the friends and foes of this revolution would be. In Marxist thought, a bourgeois revolution paves the way for socialism. Even though this revolution ultimately benefits the bourgeoisie, it helps the proletariat get organized and prepare itself for a socialist revolution. Freedom of expression, institutionalized to facilitate bourgeois competition, helps the proletariat heighten its consciousness and facilitates the way for the struggle for socialism. At the end of the day, the idea is for the proletariat to make a bourgeois revolution in conjunction with the bourgeoisie, then turn against it, and abolish capitalism through a socialist revolution.

Both EPRP and *Meison* advocated a New Democratic Revolution targeted at feudalism and imperialism, bringing on board all of the anti-feudal and anti-imperialist forces. According to EPRP, a New Democratic Revolution can take place only when the proletariat assumes political power. This revolution would pave the way for socialism, vanquishing feudalism and imperialism rather than completely destroying capitalism, maintained EPRP. The goal was to build communism where there was no class structure. However, a series of revolutions should take place before the establishment of communism.

The idea of a New Democratic Revolution was taken from the Chinese Communist Party leader, Mao Tse Tung. Mao claimed that a bourgeois revolution could not take place in the so-called Third World countries because of imperialism. The growth of the national bourgeoisie in developing nations is stunted by imperialism and is incapable of carrying out a bourgeois revolution. Therefore, in semi-feudal and semi-capitalist countries, the New Democratic Revolution overthrows feudalism and imperialism and prepares the transition to socialism. This revolution brings on board all anti-feudal and anti-imperialist forces struggling under the leadership of the proletariat and the Communist Party.

The difference and antagonism between *Meison* and EPRP rose to a crescendo with polemics, innuendos and name calling becoming the primary means of exchange. *Democracia* labeled *Meison* members petty-bourgeois opportunists or *Bandas* – after

Ethiopians who collaborated with Italians during the five-year occupation of the country by Fascist Italy – for supporting the Derg. *Meison* labeled EPRP *Achir guzoyists* – for demanding Provisional Peoples' Government, which it saw as nothing but a shortcut to power. It also called EPRP members anarchists and *Temenja nekash* – literally meaning gun biters - for picking up arms. EPRP had a military wing – the Ethiopian Peoples' Revolutionary Army (EPRA) –already operating in the terrain of Assimba in the province of Tigray.

This squabbling was just a prelude to what was yet to come.

One spring afternoon, I went to see Getachew at the small house. He was as usual reading a book. He got up to greet me with a broad smile and we chatted for a few minutes, catching up with what had happened in our lives since we saw each other last.

He then said casually, "Hiwot---I would like you to develop a study-material."

"What do I know about developing a study material?" I murmured. I was bewildered. I thought developing a study material was beyond my reach.

"You will know. I have brought you a handout. Read it and then develop a draft and show it to me. I know you can do it. If you don't try you can never learn the skill. If you really think you can't do it on your own, ask the *comrade* to work with you," he insisted, giving me the handout.

I knew he was referring to Azeb when he said the *comrade* in the feminine.

There was silence.

"There is a title for you," he said and scribbled on a piece of paper – *Yesetoch ekulnet: yekeberte setoch kimtlenet* – Equality of women: overindulgence of bourgeois feminists.

The title scared me even more. I listened with trepidation.

"The idea is to show the limitation of bourgeois feminists' conception of women's oppression and emancipation. They believe that the root cause of women's oppression lies in patriarchy. For Marxists the root cause of women's oppression is economic. Women's emancipation comes when they, like men, become owners of the means of production," he explained.

I took the piece of paper, put it in my purse, and leafed through the handout indifferently. I was not too happy with the assignment. I have been studying with him for so long and I felt the assignment would be the acid test of my knowledge. He had always praised me for my performance and I felt he had placed great expectations on me.

I worried that I would not measure up.

"I haven't seen you in a dress since that day I saw you on campus," he sighed, looking down at my brown skirt. He was alluding to my outrageously short skirt.

"I was so ashamed of myself that day...," I said absent-mindedly, still thinking about the assignment.

"Why?" he asked, putting his hand around my neck.

"Well, because you were not supposed to see me dressed like that. I was worried you might think I am-"

"Why would I think anything of you? Besides, I didn't even know what I was doing that day. I was choking with fear not knowing how to express my feelings to you. It is not that I did not notice, though. I was actually going to tell you not to wear this skirt again," he said, touching the hem of my skirt.

"Why not?" I asked, leaning on his shoulder.

"There is a comrade who resembles you. She wears the same kind of skirt. The security is after her and you might end up in their hands by mistake."

I didn't think there was an immediate threat so I did not say anything. Instead, I picked up the book sitting on the table that I wanted to look at ever since I got there. It was covered with a white paper. I leafed through it and saw the title. It was about Fascism.

I put it back on the table when he said, "*Democracia* still claims that Fascism has reigned in the country. If you ask me that is sheer pedantry. To say that the Derg takes fascistic measures and Fascism has reigned in the country are not altogether the same. The way we characterize the Derg and define the situation has implications on our political and social analysis of the country and the strategies and tactics we design. If we want to lead the revolution, we have to have an accurate assessment of the objective conditions of the country. We have to identify our real enemies and all anti-feudal and anti-imperialist forces that we can work with. The way I see it, we are antagonizing everyone."

"Doesn't the leadership know that?" I ventured.

We had never talked about Party leadership and wasn't sure how he was going to take it. I had no doubt that the Party knew what it was doing. I believed that whatever was on *Democracia* was inerrant.

Getachew did not say anything about the leadership but talked about Fascism and Bonapartism and the similarities and differences between the two and between Egypt's Gamal Abdel Nasser's "brand of socialism" and that of the Derg's. "Nasser's regime was Bonapartist. To my mind, the Derg is akin to Bonapartism than to Fascism," he maintained, throwing around many words and phrases like imperialism, state capitalism, National Socialism, scientific socialism, militarism, NCOs, Fedayeens...

This was the second time he had raised the issue of Fascism. But since my mind was on the assignment that day, I did not give it much of a thought.

In the evening, we hailed a taxi in front of the German Cultural Institute. I went in by myself and looked through the back window as he got into another. I sighed deeply. *Why did he have to burden me with such an assignment? What made him think I can do it?*

The idea of not delivering made me cringe.

I told Azeb when I saw her the next day. "He thinks we can do it, huh?" she said, laughing. She agreed to work with me, but we worried we might not do a good job. We divided the parts between us so that each of us came up with a draft. We rummaged through Kennedy Library looking for books.

The handout that Getachew had given me contained Engles' *Origin of the Family, Private Property and the State*, and excerpts from Betty Freidan's the *Feminine Mystique* and Germaine Greer's *The Female Eunuch*. Azeb and I were put off by Greer's obsession with the "Temple of Venus." We thought she was frivolous and obscene. We wanted to tear her apart if only we knew how. After an incredible toil, we finally came up with a draft and I gave it to Getachew. He praised our work. He told me it was "beyond" his expectation. I thought he was humoring us, as I never saw the material being used in the League or anywhere else.

Long afterward, however, I saw it in a booklet form. I told Azeb and we remembered the agony we went through putting it together. It was the first time we had written anything, and the experience gave us both the opportunity to understand the various ways of looking at women's oppression and liberation (or emancipation, in Marxist terms) as well as experience doing research and of course writing. All that brought my commitment and dedication to the Party to a higher level.

Having plunged myself into the League, I now saw the texture of my existence changing rapidly and completely. I had peeled off the layers of my former self and felt like a new person was emerging out of the old skin. Life became imbued with meaning. It seemed that I was leading a conscious, purpose-driven, value-laden, fuller and richer existence.

A feeling of plenitude ascended in me.

Almost before I knew it, I had been tossed into a solemn but fascinating and fulfilling adulthood. I took myself seriously and aligned my behavior to the new person that I had become. I made significant changes to the way I looked, keeping to bare essentials and denying myself things that my peers indulged in.

My Afro shrank. I descended from my platform shoes.

Let me quickly say that I did not even try that much to make changes in the way I looked. Rather, it sprang out of the depths of my being. Besides, living dangerously was the mode of existence of the underground life and it commanded that I remained as inconspicuous as possible. I felt I had found my essence, my soul's vocation and my true self in the struggle. I came to believe that I was cut out just for that. It was as if my journey for knowledge and self-development has been consummated.

My wandering soul finally found an abode.

Indeed, my preoccupation to become a dedicated and single-minded revolutionary reached the point of obsession. Pursuing my education suddenly seemed selfish and inconsequential in light of the plight of the masses that needed to be lifted out of poverty. What was education when the people needed me? How could I aspire to have it all when there were millions who had not even a hope to hold onto?

The struggle was my present, my future, my life.

It did not matter to the Party whether or not I was educated, or so I thought. I believed with all my heart that the Party was all-inclusive. Anyone committed to the good cause was welcome. The story of students returning from abroad, abandoning their education, inspired me.

The revolutionary times had called return to the motherland a moral duty.

I often thought of my vanity over my physical affliction. How could I ever have been so conceited? I forgot about the issue that once upon a time shook me to my core.

I was a great admirer of the French language and culture when I was in high school. I fell in love with the language in grade nine. I learned about French culture from our textbook, *cours de Langue et de Civilisation Françaises,* and mostly from my readings of English translations of Maupassant, Zola, Dumas, Flaubert, and Victor Hugo.

When I was in grade eleven, I almost jumped in excitement when my French teacher promised to find me a scholarship upon his return to France. I never heard from him again. He had even had me apply at the *École Normale Supérieure*, in Addis. I never knew what happened to my application. I would have given anything to go to France and pursue my studies. I had often imagined myself promenading on the Champs-Élysées and reading in the Jardin des Tuileries.

After I joined the League, I longed to visit Karl Marx's grave in Highgate Cemetery in London instead of reading in the Jardin des Tuileries. I found meaning in Gorki and Sholokhov, when it was revealed to me that my teenage passions - Dickens, the Brontës and Jane Austin and all those French authors that I adored - were indeed bourgeois writers, whose literature served the ruling class. I recognized that I had actually been subscribing all those years to "decadent bourgeois culture," aimed at brainwashing and duping people through books, film and clothes.

Azeb and I often watched movies at and borrowed books from the British Council during the *Zemecha*. We stopped going to this bourgeois institution as our consciousness increased.

I had never been religious even though I grew up with my mother, a devout Christian, and knew the scriptures by heart. Even my sister Negede, almost six years younger than me, knew the scriptures by heart at a tender age. She went to church, sang in a choir and fasted in a way that made me look like a heathen. When I was in Harar, my friend Yodit and I must have owed the Trinity hundreds of birr from promising a ten-cent incense for every trifling.

That had been the closest I had come to religion.

Marxism had become my religion. I was baptized by those poetic words in *The Communist Manifesto*, the *Economic and Philosophic Manuscripts of 1844*, *Theses on Feuerbach* and the *Holy family*. Marxism opened my eyes to the injustice around me and inspired me to fight and destroy the oppressive and exploitative system and build a better one on its ashes. I did not look out for my own salvation but wanted to live and die for the liberation of the masses.

Marxism brought out the best in me.

It gave me hope. It promised me victory would be ours in the end, when the proletariat prevails and brings happiness and love not only to our land but also unto earth. Our great spiritual fathers, Marx, Engels, Lenin and Mao had assured us that the "Kingdom of Heaven" was not only within reach but was inevitable.

Many of us did not even know any more than the basics of the theory. It did not matter. We believed in it and that was what counted. I did not reject the existence of God outright nor did I find it particularly necessary to do so. I was too busy making history to worry about the existence of God. There was no more need for me to make promises to the Trinity. I knew I could rely on my own resources, the guidance of the League and the Party, and faith in the people.

We were the supreme masters of our destiny.

Marxism was the lens through which I saw the world. What I saw was a world portioned out into black and white. The people, whom I passed on the street, rode in a taxi with or saw dining in a restaurant, were no longer individuals with their own worries, anxieties, ambitions, and sorrows. They were workers, peasants, feudal lords, petty-bourgeois, bureaucrats, and lumpen proletariats. They were either enemies or potential allies. I did not see rich or poor people any longer. I saw poverty, oppression, and exploitation. I did not feel compassion toward blind or maimed beggars. I went past them without giving alms as I used to. Instead, I felt outrage at the system that rendered them so utterly poor and robbed them of their dignity.

I walked past them with a renewed sense of commitment to the struggle.

I often visualized in my mind the "shining city on the hill," where justice prevailed. That was the "tower in the sky" we had set out to bring down to earth. I would have set the foundation for this "tower" with my blood, flesh and bones if need be. It did not matter if I did not live to see it. What counted was that I fought the good fight then and dedicated my life to the cause. I had no doubt in my mind that we were struggling for a just cause. I believed in my heart and soul and with every fiber of my being that victory would be ours in the end.

It was so fulfilling, so promising.

I found the thought of struggling alongside a multitude of comrades inspiring. I was bound with them by the promise of the future. We were the true sons and daughters of the masses – their heartbeat.

The feeling was heartwarming.

The very sight of my comrades assured me that I am indeed part of something bigger and greater than myself. I felt a sense of solidarity and oneness with them even if I did not know them personally. The very knowledge that they were out there struggling alongside me was inspiring. I didn't even know the real names of many of my comrades I was working closely with nor did I know what they liked or disliked, whether or not they were happy or sad on a particular day. But I knew more about who they were and how they felt than I did about anybody else. I knew them because I knew the Party. I knew what the Party stood for and where it was taking us. That was what I knew about my comrades. That knowledge was what bound me to them. I did not need to know anything else.

To my surprise, it was the friends I grew up with that I had difficulty understanding any longer. I could feel an abyss separating us. I felt sorry for them for living in darkness, for not realizing their true selves by joining the struggle.

It was my comrades for whom my heart leapt every time I saw them in the streets. They were easily recognizable. They dressed the same way and had the same drinks (coffee or tea) or ate the same thing (bread) in cafés. All I needed was to glance at the streets and I could easily identify them standing at bus stations reciting codes or in cafés leaning over tables and speaking in undertones. They walked briskly with their jackets zipped or buttoned to hide paper stuffed in their faded jeans. Their eyes darted around streets and cafés to outwit the enemy and to avoid undesirable identifications. They looked serious and purposeful and had aged beyond their years, saddled with the heavy responsibility of transforming a country at such a young age. I came to believe that comrades were not ordinary human beings; I thought they were a bit above ordinary mortals and a bit below angels.

They were in a league of their own.

All the sentiment I had for family and friends was channeled into this new breed of humanity. What bound us with family members was blood, with friends it was love. What bound us with comrades was ideology, the revolution, the Party, and the future. It did not mean we had no sentiments for family and friends. It meant they came second. The Party came first and comrades embodied the Party and what it stood for. They were the new family and friends, with the Party as the Father. They were in fact more than family and friends. The sense of camaraderie, selflessness, devotion and trust we had toward one another was unparalleled.

Our relationship touched the sublime.

Powerful slogans stirred my sense of justice. *Democracia* became my Bible. It was like manna, whose revolutionary power was magically transferred to me. It inspired reverence for the Party, and its magical words helped me rediscover my sense of justice. It guaranteed me triumph and the undoing of the enemy. It exulted and glorified the Party and the people and demeaned the adversary.

I hung on every word in it.

The very sight of red banners adorned with our emblem – the hammer, sickle and the red star – evoked in me a deep sense of joy and pride. The emblem was the totem that bound me to my comrades. There was something mystical about it. It roused awe and inflamed fervor in me. It promised me that the Party was indeed powerful and invincible.

I felt reassured.

Revolutionary songs rekindled in me a sense of sacrifice, altruism, justice and human dignity. They excited my senses and warmed my heart. Just as Mao warned, "revolution is not a dinner party," they cautioned me that the road to freedom is "paved with thorns." *Ewagalehugn le mebte* inspired me to stand up for our rights and to partake of the struggle.

እዋጋለሁኝ ለመብቴ ላንገብጋቢው የእግር እሳቴ
የትግል መርሀ ቅኘቴ ትግል ነውና ሕይወቴ

Le Zemenat, the most famous of all revolutionary songs, wheedled me to take up arms and vanquish the oppressor.

ለዘመናት በጭቆና ማጥ በግፍ ሰንስለት ታስራ
መብቴን ሳስከብር ጨቋኙን ልጥል
ተነስቻለሁ ዛሬ ይኸው ታጥቂያለሁ ዛሬ

I regarded the Party with profound love and veneration. It became the embodiment of what I stood for. My comrades and I spun and wove stories about its power and invincibility.

We idolized and deified it.

I learned to love Getachew passionately as our relationship grew and deepened. His complexity enthralled me. The man who was frighteningly disciplined, ascetic and had rigorous standards was soft-hearted, timid, affectionate and passionately loving, but not as demonstrative. Romance was considered as a trivial pursuit by the revolutionary culture of our time. We worked under austere conditions and what came first was the struggle. We had little time or interest to indulge in personal flatteries and almost all our time together was spent on talking about our work.

Even from the beginning, I had seen something in him that I had not seen in other men. As I got closer to him, I knew I was destined to be with him. He represented to me not only the Party but also what was best in it. The love I had for him was meshed with the love I had for the Party. It was hardly possible to distinguish between them. Social justice, oppression and political freedom were not my idea of conversation before I met him.

He put an edge on my sensibility.

I wanted to emulate him and become a dedicated revolutionary. I took pains to copy his asceticism. Whatever I did, I had always had him in the back of my mind. He was both my inspiration and my conscience. I always felt that I had to say something intellectual or talk in Marxist terms whenever I was with him. I wanted to impress him as he did me with words and phrases like "ideological," "bourgeois conception of," "Che's focoism," or "war of attrition." First, I was not as conversant as he was about those things and second I was afraid he might think I was an echo. Therefore, I preferred to be myself. As I got to know him better, I learned that I could talk to him just about anything. I was no longer mystified and intimidated. We talked and laughed in abandonment in the little dingy place or at Harar Migib Bet. He laughed like the innocence of a child, often with tears trickling down his cheeks.

Our love was as underground as the organization we belonged to. It was something special. It seemed profounder, richer, and grandeur, just as I believed the Party was.

...these must be gods who could fly through the air.
    -Ovid, *Metamorphoses*

May Day 1976 was even bloodier than the previous year's had been. A number of students, workers, teachers and others were killed and imprisoned in their hundreds, followed by more executions and imprisonments in June and July. EPRP repeatedly condemned the escalating repression and continued to call the Derg Fascist.

It was around the end of May 1976 that Semegne Lemma and I fancied that we could form a Women's Association in *Kebele* 18 and later in *Kebele* 19, which were both in Bole. My sister and family had by then moved to Bole, and Semegne and I lived close by. She lived in *Kebele* 19 and I lived in *Kebele* 18. Since there were only a few youth in the area, it was difficult to form a Youth Association. The middle and upper middle-classes populated *Kebeles* 18 and 19. The *Kebeles* were also home to many of the embassies.

I brought the idea of forming a Women's Association to Tito and he gave me the go-ahead. When I mentioned it to Getachew, he said, "You should target peasant women living in the area as well. Ask the *Kebele* to invite them to the meeting. That way, you would have a good turnout of peasant women."

He was referring to the peasant population in the outskirts of Bole. The peasants were from the Oromo ethnic group and many of them came to town every Saturday to sell their produces and craft such as clay pots and baskets.

Semegne and I went to *Kebele* 18 one afternoon and announced our intentions to the chairman. He was far behind many *Kebeles* in organizing the youth and women and was happy and enthusiastic about it. We prepared flyers, which he printed for us, and disseminated them throughout the *Kebele*. We asked him to mobilize the peasant women in the area. He sent out criers, who announced the time and date of the meeting.

The open-air meeting was held around the beginning of June, just across the *Kebele* office. There was an unexpectedly large turnout. Semegne and I made speeches over the megaphone explaining the purpose of the meeting. Two interesting things happened that day. First, all the middle and upper middle-class women sat on one side and the peasant women on the other, making it clear that they had nothing to do with each other. Secondly, their husbands accompanied the peasant women. The husbands sat on one side, their sticks planted in the ground, and listened to the speeches, suspicion written all over their faces. They said they had come to find out why only their wives had been invited.

A Coordinating Committee was set up. Almost all the committee members were from the middle and upper-middle classes. Some of them were my sister Almaz's friends. My sister did not come to the meeting since she was expecting a child. She gave birth to her third child a couple of days later.

To our dismay, none of the peasant women was represented in the committee. Their husbands refused on the grounds that they could not accompany their wives to meetings. Semegne and I learned that it was going to be a long journey toward the emancipation of women.

I gave a written report to the IZ about the meeting. I also told Getachew what had happened at the meeting. He said it would take time to educate people and above all organize them. Our focus should be, he insisted, "on getting access to the peasant women. It wasn't bad that the men showed up, after all. They would learn something and when they understand the purpose of the association, they would allow their wives to come to meetings."

I agreed.

"*Ajirit*, you would be working in the Party Women's Inter-Zonal Committee," Tito told me around the end of June. "Things are very slow there. They need someone with organizational experience and you will be a great asset to the committee."

Ajirit in the feminine and *Ajirew* in the masculine were terms of endearment that we used to call one another.

"Is that in addition to what I am doing?" I asked Tito.

"Yes, of course. I know you can handle it."

I met Nigist Tefera a couple of days later. She was wearing a brown skirt, which was the same as mine. I remembered what Getachew had told me about a comrade that had a brown skirt. I'm not sure what Nigist has been told about the skirt but Tito had also once told me that a *Yebelay Akal* had told him to warn me not to wear the brown skirt because they might arrest me mistaking me for a comrade who resembled me. I would later learn that *Yebelay Akal* was Getachew.

I had seen Nigist at the women's seminar held at the parliament in April of the previous year. She had become chair of the Women's Organization until the Derg snatched the leadership from them and gave it to its cadres, driving individuals like her to the underground. We had also bumped into each other on several occasions in back alleys and cafés.

I went to the women's IZ meetings a few times. The women in the committee were older than me and educated in the United States, or had graduated from Haile Selassie I University. I had met Nigist individually several times and would rather have met her alone than go to those meetings. They were nothing like the ones in the fast-paced League. I was not sure if I could say so to Tito. One day, I summoned my courage and told him my misgivings about working in the committee.

"You know what? I don't think I like working in the women's IZ. First, I feel that I am not contributing anything. Second, it is not like working in the League."

"What do you mean?

"I can't see how I can help. It is so different from working in the League. Things are so slow…so laid-back."

"So, are you saying you don't want to work there any longer?"

"It is nowhere near like working in the League."

"Well, if you feel that way, then you should stop going."

I breathed a sigh of relief.

It was around the end of August. Getachew put the book he was reading face down on the table and rose to greet me cheerfully when I pushed open the door of the tiny house. I went in, sat beside him on a chair, and threw a furtive glance at the book sitting on the table. It was Antonio Gramsci's Prison Notebooks. I picked it up and leafed through it as I always did when I saw a new book. Getachew told me about Gramsci and his difference with Marx. He then picked up a recent copy of *Democracia* lying on the table.

"Have you seen this? It states that we have to defend the revolution through both rural and urban armed struggle. As a result, the whole concept of the Provisional Peoples' Government (PPG) has changed," he expressed his discontent, waving the leaflet.

"PPG has been a tactical slogan," he went on. "It was meant to rally all anti-feudal and anti-imperialist forces behind us. When discussions took place for the merger between *Abyot* and EPLO, the agreement has been to treat the PPG as a tactical slogan. The PPG is something that may or may not be formed. Now it has become the end game. If it becomes the end result, then conducting urban armed struggle could be justified. It is dangerous to even think of embarking on military activities in the city."

I had never seen him talk so serious. "What is the justification for conducting urban armed struggle, anyway?" I asked, taking the leaflet from his hand.

I had noticed for quite a while how feudalism, imperialism and Fascism were redefined as enemies of the revolution instead of the long-standing enemies – feudalism and imperialism. Besides, discussion was taking place in the League about urban armed struggle and the phrase "defense squad" was swirling around.

"The comrades say that the objective conditions have changed," Getachew paused, then added. "They say the land proclamation has complicated our role in rural areas so they claim that the focus of the struggle has shifted to the cities. Besides, they say the Derg is killing our members and we have to defend ourselves. We are not even equipped to carry out military operations in the cities. What we should be doing is intensifying the rural armed struggle and weakening the junta's power through attrition. There are quite a number of strategic areas that have been studied and are being studied. We should educate and organize the peasantry and attack the Derg from different directions and force it to spread itself thin. The Derg does not have any mass base. That is where our advantage lies. We are the ones who have mass support. What we need to do in the cities is limit our activities to political organization and propaganda and prepare the people for the final struggle. Instead of concentrating our forces in the cities and getting our members needlessly killed, we should send them to the army."

I loved those discussions. That was my only opportunity to discuss theoretical issues. I agreed with all what he said but did not know what to do with that knowledge.

A "Rectification Movement" took place throughout the League structure. IZ members were asked to talk to lower committee members and identify weaknesses and strengths. We learned criticism and self-criticism. I recall reading Mao's Little Red Book on Criticism and Self-Criticism. We documented all our strengths and weaknesses and passed them on to *Yebelay Akal*. We continued our work with renewed zeal and determination.

Near the end of the summer, in order to strengthen League and Party relations and encourage horizontal communication, a Party Inter-Zonal Committee member joined the League IZ. One day he told me to work in Party Zone Three Committee. I met with Adane, whom I knew by sight, with a code. He was my senior at the university and was later arrested and killed at the checkpoint in Wukro, in Tigray province.

I went to the Party Zone Three Committee meeting on a Saturday afternoon. I had great expectations about the Party. If the League was that efficient and dynamic, I imagined how much more the Party could be. To my dismay, it was not at all what I expected. By the time I left I was a bit disappointed, if not disillusioned. The laid-back attitude in the committee put me off.

Of course, Tito and I usually gossiped about the Party. We enjoyed our small talk during our individual meetings in cafés. We talked about the paternalistic attitude of the Party and how things were much slower there in contrast to the League that glided on the fast-track. Meetings in the League IZ were full of fire and enthusiasm. Tito's dynamic personality inspired vigor and ardor. He brought energy, radiance and the sense of urgency to meetings.

I told him about my new assignment (working in the Party Zonal Committee), when I saw him next. He was outraged. "This kind of paternalistic attitude is not acceptable. The IZ would lodge a complaint against the Party. The League is an autonomous organization. The party cannot say I want this person or that person. If it needs individuals, it has to request through the proper channel, not horizontally. They should give us the criteria and we would recommend individuals based on the criteria," he fumed.

He raised the issue at the next IZ meeting and I was criticized for not informing the League IZ before I took orders from the Party IZ.

I was embarrassed of what I had done.

Each Zone submitted an annual report to the League IZ the first week of September 1976. Membership had skyrocketed along with membership contributions. The League started with a few individuals in October 1975. In one year, membership had risen well over 9,000 in Addis alone. This did not include those embraced in study circles, members of the Women's and Students' Associations and the Youth Vanguard, ready to embark on the boat, nor the hundreds in prison.

The Party gained organizational momentum in all the major cities. It made headway in establishing study circles in factories, the army, offices and school compounds. It taught discipline, hard work, commitment, self-sacrifice and altruism to a legion of youth and others. It embraced members of many ethnic groups in its ranks. Its members and supporters spoke out at *Wuyiyit Kibebs,* raising levels of political consciousness among workers, the army, teachers, and civil servants.

The League sent out a squadron of youth to *Kebele* Youth Associations, where they ignited fiery discussions and recruited members in thousands. It introduced graffiti and banners, which turned out to be effective tools for conveying messages. Banners inscribed with slogans were hoisted east and west, north and south, with the red star, hammer, and sickle inscribed in the middle. *Democracia* added glamour to the magic of banners and littered walls. The government's socialist propaganda, designed by its Marxist mentors, paled beside the biting and blistering *Democracia*.

All this took place in a very inspiring international situation. 1975 was the year FRELIMO declared itself a Marxist-Leninist state in Mozambique. 1976 was the year South Vietnam was unified with the North that Cambodia became Democratic Kampuchea, Guinea Bissau was preparing for parliamentary elections and Communist and Socialist parties in Western Europe such as Italy, France, Portugal and Finland, were making strides in parliamentary elections. It was also the time they sought independence from Soviet domination.

EPRP reached its zenith of popularity in 1976. Its fame crossed land and water. Everybody whispered its name. It appeared mighty and invincible. It soared into the sky. The clouds and the moon seemed to fall under its dominion.

But, like Icarus, who flew too close to the sun and got the wings of his chariot burned, it came too close to the "sun" for its own good, too.

We mustn't consider assassination – after all- as the chief path to political truth.

-André Malraux, *Man's Fate*

The day was September 23, 1976, a few days after the League IZ had received the annual report. A chill went through my bones when I heard on the radio about the assassination attempt on Mengistu Hailemariam, the vice-chairman of the Derg. I was bewildered by the actions of the Party.

I was frightened to go out.

Getachew came to mind. *What did he think of the attempt on the vice-chairman's life?* I know he wouldn't approve of it. I wanted to see him right away. I figured that he might be hiding. A few days later, three *Meison* members were gunned down by EPRP squads followed by the assassination of Fikre Merid, a Central Committee member of *Meison*. I had met Fikre once, when I was in high school. He had just arrived from Paris with a PhD in law and his family had thrown a welcome party for him at his parents' house in Dire Dawa. My friends and I were invited through his younger brother.

The Derg declared war on EPRP officially. Instead of the usual counter-revolutionaries, CIA agents and anarchists, it called it by its name for the first time. The pro-EPRP magazine, *Goh*, was shut down. The "Revolutionary Platform" on *Addis Zemen*, which had become the theoretical battlefield between EPRP and *Meison*, was discontinued, followed by arrests and official executions.

The omens warned of a catastrophe.

A few days after EPRP's bullet ripped through Mengistu's pelvis, I was standing on the steps of the front door of our house, when I saw a notorious security agent surveilling the neighborhood. He was standing in the middle of the road adjacent to our house. I ran into the living room and opened the tiny window behind my niece's piano. I struggled to move the heavy instrument so that I could have a full view of the security agent. I couldn't. I knelt on one knee on top of it and spotted the agent's car, with the infamous license plate number, parked at the roadside. I saw the agent going to the late General Abebe Gemeda's house on the opposite side and talk to the guard. The General was one of the fifty-two officials of the previous regime executed by the Derg in November 1974.

There were no EPRP activities in the upscale *Kebele*. I had never seen a single leaflet or slogan littered wall in the neighborhood. I could not sleep that night. *Who was he looking for? What was he talking to the guard about?* I thought of the trouble that might befall my family on my account.

A few days later, my sister Almaz called me to her bedroom. "I've been trying to figure out what you are up to. You leave home at six in the morning and come back late at night. I can't say you go out on a date at six in the morning. You go out rain or shine. Where are you going? What are you doing? Even your telephone conversations are brief and business like. What are you up to?" she asked, looking perturbed.

I stood there silently.

"Well, you can't go out as of tomorrow."

"I can't." How could I have told her about my underground life?

"What do you mean you can't?" I saw terror inscribed in her face.

I had always respected her and had never disobeyed her. I did not want to disobey her now. But what about the struggle?

"Well, you can't leave home without my permission," she said firmly.

I went back to my bedroom in silence. What she did not understand was that I was carrying Ethiopia's problems upon my back as Atlas did "the vaults of the sky."

I did not sleep that night. I knew I had to leave home but wondered if I would ever have the resolve to do it. I drifted into sleep around dawn. When I woke up, I reminded myself that I still had to make up my mind. I got up, bathed, listlessly packed a few things in a bag, wrote a note to my sister ending it with, "You will understand someday," put it in an envelope with her name on it, flung it on the coffee table in the living room and left. I was in tears when I stepped out of the compound. I loved my niece and nephew and always enjoyed playing house with them. Then there was the youngest, only a few months old, and it was even harder to part with him.

I had to leave because my obligation to the revolution was beyond and above family love.

I didn't know where to go. I took a taxi to the apartment that my friends from Harar, Martha, Mahlet and Hanna, had rented in Piassa. I chose to stay there until I found a place to settle. I knew the League provided "shelter" - a home (a member's or supporter's house) - for members who needed it. I told Tito that I had left home when I saw him later that day. He told me that I could work for the Party "full-time" and that I would be given 70 birr for my upkeep. I had become a professional revolutionary! I was unable to contain my excitement.

I flew up to the heavens.

Classes resumed in October for the first time since the *Zemecha* started. Sara, Azeb and I re-enrolled. We were given a crash program to make up for the lost time during the revolutionary upheaval. I changed my major from European Languages to Governmental Affairs, a new department merging Political Science and Public Administration, which meant I still had to be in second year. I didn't care. I re-enrolled only as cover for my underground activities. But I decided to stay in a campus dormitory for as long as I could. Azeb, Sara and I moved into the new dormitory, built not too long before. Kidist changed her major to Economics, took evening classes and worked during the day. Semegne enrolled in the Faculty of Science at Arat Kilo campus.

Preparation for the declaration of the Youth League was underway, despite the harsh repression by the Derg after the assassination attempt on the vice-chairman. I met Tito one day in mid-October, after an IZ meeting at Noh Café on Churchill Road, across Lycée Gebre Mariam, the French language school.

"*Ajirit*, you have to go to Alamata to deliver a stencil," he told me. "It contains the declaration statement of the Youth League. It should be duplicated and distributed simultaneously everywhere. They should prepare banners and paint slogans on walls. Everything should be kept secret until the day of the declaration. They will be notified of the declaration date later."

I was both thrilled and proud to be entrusted with such an assignment. It also came at the right time.

I was out of reach of family control.

I got the communication code from him a couple of days later. I memorized it and discarded the piece of paper. The day before I left, I committed a cardinal sin of breaching discipline. I told Azeb about my trip. We talked about our underground activities in general terms but I had never told her in what capacity I worked and neither had she. I told her about my trip so that in the event that something happened to me, she could notify my family.

I took the Mekele bus to Dessie attired in traditional apparel, which I stole from my cousin Elsa. I wore a headscarf and put on white sneakers and red socks, the only ones I could find. I hid the stencil in my pantyhose and a few papers in my sneakers.

It was my first time taking that route and I was looking forward to seeing Dessie, about which I had heard so much from my mother. She was born there but came to live with her grandfather in the province of Hararghe, when she was still a young child.

I arrived in Dessie, the capital city of the province of Wollo, located in north-central part of the country, about 400 kilometers from Addis. Dessie was a historical place, home to prominent and historical personalities such as Negus Mikael (a war hero and member of the nobility) and *Lij* Eyasu (son of King Mikael and an uncrowned Emperor). Dessie's *Woizero* Sihen was also the school best known for its student militancy. It had produced students of great revolutionary credentials, such as the famous Berhanemeskel Redda and Waleligne Mekonen.

I got there around four-thirty in the afternoon and checked in a hotel not far from the bus station. I took a cold shower from a pail of water sitting in the toilet. Refreshed, I went out to look for something to eat. I took a stroll up and down the main street to see what was available.

I finally came across the Etege Hotel, which looked impressive by Dessie's standards. I went in, my head covered with a *netela*. There were only a few men seated at scattered tables. I could tell what kind of people they were from the way they were dressed. They were office workers, teachers, cadres and bus drivers. I was the only female there. I sat down at a table in the corner and placed my order – *injera* with *key sega wot* – hot and spicy beef sauce. I went to my hotel as soon as I was done and went to bed.

When I woke up I thought it was still the middle of the night and was about to go back to sleep, when I thought of consulting my watch instead. I squinted at it and it read a few minutes to six. I jumped out of bed and dashed to the toilet and used water from a pail to wash myself. I dressed up in a hurry and ran to catch the Mekele bus. I was a bit late but fortunately, I made it before the bus left. The buses never left on time.

The bus came to a halt at the Woldya checkpoint, a two-hour drive from Dessie. Men were asked to get off the bus but women were allowed to remain on board. While they were searching luggage, I went with the men to an eatery called Zerai Deres, named after a folk hero.

Zerai Deres, a man of Eritrean origin who worked as a translator in Rome, was marching in a parade when Italy was commemorating its fourth anniversary of the establishment of the Fascist empire in 1937 and saw the statue of the Lion of Judah, symbol of the Ethiopian monarchy, pitched as war booty. He was incensed and is said to have killed five Fascist soldiers with his sword. He was shot and wounded. He later died in prison.

Zerai Deres was a small place with mud wall and dirt floor but apparently famous for its *dulet* – minced lamb, liver and tripe with butter, salt and hot spice (my favorite dish). One could get *dulet* for one birr and yogurt, in a *Kibur Zebegna* glass – named after the Imperial Guard for its tallness – for twenty-five cents. One had the choice of sprinkling *berbere* or *mitmita* (hot spices) on the yogurt. I had mine with *berbere*. The yogurt was thick and smooth, just the way I liked it.

It was heavenly.

It was only after I drained the last dregs of my yogurt that I became conscious that what I was actually doing was uncommon. My attire was meant to make me look like a traditional housewife. The red socks and white sneakers alone could have betrayed my efforts, let alone lunch at an eatery unchaperoned.

I had always wanted to see Wollo, particularly places like Bati, Ambassel, Yeju and Wadla ena Delanta, subjects of Wollo songs. I took it upon myself to see Woldya around. I took the street that led to the centre of the town and wandered around. Woldya was bigger than I had imagined. I came back from my touristy excursion just on time.

Two soldiers searched male passengers boarding the bus and peered through their ID cards. I was not searched but one of the soldiers asked me to show him my ID. I fished in my plastic bag and produced my student ID. He took it from my hand, examined it and gave it back. I climbed into the bus and went back to my seat. When I sat down, it struck me that what I had just done could have put me in trouble. I was in a jeans jacket and a T-shirt in the picture with an Afro hairdo, which did not altogether go with my new look. The soldier wasn't smart enough to pick up on that one.

There was no incident and the bus sped to Alamata, a small town about hundred-twenty kilometers from Dessie. Upon arrival, I got off the bus and went to the hotel I had been told to check into. It was only a few yards away from the bus stop. Tito had told me, "The comrade won't be at the bus stop to fetch you as originally planned. She teaches in a nearby town and won't be there before dusk. You have to check into a hotel until she comes to get you."

Two or three sex workers were sitting on the lawn when I entered the hotel compound. They looked very unfriendly. I ran into a woman on the veranda and asked her if they had a room available. She ignored me, went over, and sat with the women. Thrown off by her rudeness, I went into the bar and found a man who helped me check in. He gave me the key and told me the room number. I turned to see the women and saw them laughing. It was obvious that they were laughing at me. Once in my room, I wanted to rinse my body off the dust from Woldya and went to the toilet. There was no water. I was also dying for a glass of water. The hot and spicy *dulet* at Zerai Deres had made me extremely thirsty. I went outside and asked a woman standing on the veranda if she could please get me *Ambo Wuha* and a pail of water. She gave me a "Who do you think you are?" look and climbed down the stairs to sit on the lawn beside her colleagues. They all broke into a hysterical laughter.

I couldn't figure out why they were so hostile. I went to the bar, got myself a bottle of mineral water, and came back to my room. I told myself I would take a bath at the comrade's house later. I lay down on the bed and was dozing off when I heard a knock on the door. For a fraction of a second, I thought the women had come to tear me apart. I tiptoed to the door in utter dread and looked out through the crevice. It was a man. Relieved, I flung the door open. He recited the code I was supposed to exchange with the female comrade.

"*Selam*! Come on in!" I said, smiling.

"The comrade who was supposed to come and get you teaches in another town and won't be back until much later. We did not want you to stay long in the hotel for security reasons. So I came to fetch you," he told me, coming in.

That was how I met Mekonen Bayisa for the first time. Mekonen was an EPRP member and had come from Addis to work in the area. He deposited himself on a chair, we talked for a bit, and then I grabbed my plastic bag and went out with him. I went to the bar, settled my bills and returned the key. I glanced fearfully toward the women when we approached the gate. They did not look as hostile any more. As soon as we stepped out of the compound, I told Mekonen what had happened.

"You know why?" he asked.

"No."

"They thought you had come to become just like them. That is what they do when they first arrive here. I mean they check in as guests and become hosts after a couple of days. So when they see a woman checking in by herself, they automatically assume that she has come to compete with them. Now that you are leaving, they are happy," he said, smiling broadly.

I burst out laughing. I imagined myself coming from Addis to dusty and sedate Alamata to become a sex worker!

Mekonen took me to a house, where we spent the afternoon. He told me about the area and general Party activities. The female comrade came in the evening and the three of us headed to her house. There were no streetlights and I couldn't see in the dark. I stumbled every second in the deep grooves of the dirt road, interrupting the conversation. Mekonen held my arm and practically led me through the dark streets of Alamata. At home, the female comrade served dinner and we talked about the situation in Alamata and surrounding areas.

After Mekonen left, I wanted to ask the female comrade if I could take a bath but was afraid it might look bad on me. There was no electricity and the only lighting in the room came from a hurricane lantern sitting on a small round table in a corner of the room. While I was contemplating the best way to ask, she brought warm water in a plastic bowl and put it under my feet. I thanked her and started taking my sneakers off. She brought a stool over, and sat down to wash my feet! I was touched by the extent of her hospitality. Tears welled up in my eyes. I pulled my feet up and refused to have her wash them.

I came to learn that the organizational structure in Alamata was very rudimentary. The Party had many members and supporters but, being a small town, everybody knew everybody else. That caused serious security problems. My assignment was to deliver a stencil. When I heard about the way things were done, I offered to share my experience. The female comrade organized a meeting with all the representatives of the surrounding towns in the following days. I drew the League structure and explained how it worked, the way information was relayed, and how secret service surveillance was maneuvered and "exposure" minimized.

The comrade representing Dessie asked me to come to Dessie and share my experience with the rest of his committee members. I went there after a few days' stay in Alamata.

I stayed longer than I had intended to because of my trip to Dessie. After I came back to Addis, I wrote an eleven-page report about the organizational limitations in Raya ena Azebo – a region bordering the provinces of Wollo and Tigray. I also reported the lack of organizational activities in the so-called "peasant areas." I wrote that the membership and support to the organization has not been properly harnessed and the comrades needed experienced people who could work with them. There was enthusiasm and commitment, but compared to Addis, the level of organizational experience left a great deal to be desired. I offered to go back and work there. Tito told me I was needed in Addis more and somebody else would be sent instead.

"It is from *Hadis*," he said when he gave me a piece of folded paper, a few days after I came back from Alamata. I suspected it was from Getachew but didn't know who Hadis was. I opened the folded note. It read, "Tomorrow - six o'clock - Abune Petros Square - Hadis." I recognized Getachew's handwriting. For the first time I learned that his code name was Hadis.

I was happy to hear from him. I have been worrying about his safety after the assassination attempt on the vice-chairman. I hadn't heard from him for a while. I had left home and he had no way of reaching me. I did not know how to contact him either.

I met him the next day at the square dedicated to Archbishop Abune Petros, who was executed for his support to Ethiopian resistance fighters during the five-year occupation of the country by Fascist Italy.

We checked in at a hotel. I was anxious to hear his thoughts on the assassination attempt. "I saw the report," he said, hugging me as soon as we went into our room. "It was excellent. I am so proud of you. I was really impressed by the maturity of your assessment. You did an excellent job."

How does he know I wrote it? Being the youngest member of the Central Committee, he linked the League Central Committee to the Party Central Committee. That was how he learned about the report. He teased me for saying Raya ena Zebo in the report. The correct name was Raya ena Azebo.

The waiter knocked on the door and asked if we would like to order something.

"Yes, we would like to order supper," said Getachew. He turned to me and asked me if I wanted to have the usual. I shrugged my shoulders. He ordered *Yebeg tibs* and *Yedoro firfir*.

"You can get us tea after supper," he told the waiter, closing the door behind him. He came back and sat next to me on the couch.

"I want to go back. I really want to. There is so much to do over there. But I was told I was needed here more. So many people can take my place here. I don't understand why I am told I am needed here more every time I ask to be sent," I complained.

"When was it that you asked to go and you were told you were needed here more?" He grinned, looking amused by my seriousness.

"Well, for one, now. I also asked more than once to be sent to Assimba. The *comrade* and I even hiked to get fit but we were both told we were needed here more."

The *comrade* in the feminine was Azeb.

"If you were told you were needed here more, it was because you were needed here more," he said, flashing a smile.

Joining EPRA, the army in Assimba – our *Sierra Maestra* – was the ultimate dream of every League member. Azeb and I wanted to go there so badly we went on hiking from time to time. She had more physical endurance and used to be upset when I struggled to climb a hill. I would say to her, "If ever I get to go to Assimba, I will remain in the base area cooking and washing." She would laugh, covering her mouth with her hand.

I would have loved to continue the discussion about going back and working in Raya ena Azebo but realized that Getachew would not say anything more about it. Instead, he looked at me from top to bottom with a concerned look.

"Are you okay? You look pale and you seem to have lost weight."

"I haven't been feeling well since I came back from Alamata. I have a stomach ache and have lost my appetite."

"You should see a doctor. You might have picked up a parasite. You don't look well at all."

The waiter brought supper and put it on the table and left. I got up to wash my hands and came back. He went to wash his hands too. He had left his glasses and berretta hat on the couch. I had never seen him in those glasses and the hat since I saw him at the university campus. When he came back, I asked the question that had been on my mind for the past few weeks.

"So what do you think of the attempt on Mengistu?"

He sighed heavily. "It was utter insanity. There is no explanation for it. An assassination attempt on a leader amounts to a coup d'état. Killing individuals amounts to terrorism. A Party such as ours should not be engaging in things like that. The idea of urban armed struggle is a departure from the path of the struggle outlined at the beginning. The Party is treading a dangerous avenue. If we follow that course, the struggle for which so many have already shed their blood would be derailed. The very existence of the Party will be imperiled. We have no capability of defending ourselves from what is to come. Some of us have expressed our opposition to the assassination attempt as well as the whole idea of urban armed struggle."

I loved it when we talked about issues. That was when my brain cells were awakened. I listened intently.

"What we should be doing instead is strengthening our army in Assimba, building armies at various strategic areas and intensifying the rural armed struggle. Rural armed struggle is protracted. You weaken your enemy through attrition. The peasantry, in a country such as ours, is not only the backbone of the army but also of the revolution. We have to educate and organize it in order to win its support. If we don't do enough in the rural areas and if we can't organize the peasantry on time, we won't be able to rally it behind us and we will have nowhere to retreat. We have recruited thousands, particularly the youth. Where are we going to hide all those young people when and if the Derg becomes more repressive?"

We sat quietly for a few minutes. A feeling of uneasiness enveloped me. "But what was the point of killing Mengistu? If anything, it would backfire on us, as we are already seeing. Killing one person wouldn't make a difference," I said.

"All I can say is that it is very shortsighted."

"We had a discussion about urban armed struggle at our last meeting. There was talk about the need for staging a Paris Commune type insurrection," I put in eager to prolong the discussion.

The Party had recently popularized the Paris Commune. In the May 1976 issue of the EPRP-dominated *Goh* magazine, the Paris Commune was hailed as the first seizure of power by the proletariat and as having no equal in the history of revolutionary struggles, setting the tone for urban armed struggle.

"I know it has become fashionable these days to use the phrase. We don't even have a clear idea of what it is. We are again being merely pedantic. The Paris Commune was a failure. How can we model our revolution after something that has failed? The Commune is useful only as far as it teaches us a lesson. Thousands of people have died in the insurrection. The idea of insurrection is adventurous. Do you have any idea how many lives would be lost in an insurrection? We have neither the military capability nor the political and organizational readiness to stage an insurrection. We are underestimating the power of the Derg and overestimating that of ours. We think the Party is invincible. But that is not the case. I can tell you that much. All this talk about insurrection is a rush to seize power at any cost. We are looking for a shortcut to power; the PPG is our shortcut to power. We want to achieve the PPG through insurrection even if it means bloodshed."

I wished he could eat and talk but he stopped eating as he started getting agitated. I wished I had not raised the subject before supper.

The room had a gloomy cast. A feeling of despondency began to swell in me.

"It is not that we do not want the PPG. It is more than welcome if it must come," he went on, "but not through a bloody insurrection! But our comrades want it at any cost. There is a clique in the Party dominating the leadership. It is that clique that is pushing the idea of urban armed struggle. You know, Hiwot, some of our comrades are power-mongers. Power, at any cost, is what they are after."

I didn't know what to say. I was frightened by the magnitude of his frustration.

He explained to me briefly, what the Paris Commune was and reiterated his discussion on the Chinese rural armed struggle. I very well knew that he was impressed by Mao's idea of "protracted armed struggle." That was the path the revolution should pursue in order to guarantee the formation of a Democratic Republic, he believed.

I noticed that his gentle soul has been stirred. I did not know how to help. *Who are the members of the clique?*

"One thing I am concerned about is that our members do not read," he said after a brief silence.

"There isn't enough time to read now. There is so much organizational work to do," I pointed out.

I loved the theoretical discussions I had had with him. My love for knowledge was rekindled only when I was with him. That was what I had been missing after I transferred to the League. But it had been a while since we had stopped our informal study as both of us became busy. Security issues were also becoming a problem on his side. In addition, there was no meeting place like before. So I did not read any more Marxist Literature. I read only Amharic translations of Russian books by Pushkin, Gogol, Dostoevsky, Lermontov, Korolenko, Belyaev, and others to satisfy my hunger for reading.

"I know we are overwhelmed by fast moving events. I understand that perfectly. But the dilemma is how we can interpret situations if we don't have the theoretical clarity. That is one of the things that bothers me," he said.

We stopped eating. He was too agitated and I was too ill to eat. The waiter came and cleared the table. He came back with tea and put the tea glasses on the table and left. Getachew locked the door, came back, and sat down beside me.

"I left home. I saw this agent spying on our neighborhood one day. I did not want to endanger my family," I said to change the subject.

"That is why I couldn't get a hold of you. I tried to call you several times. Have you found a shelter?"

"Not yet. I called you too...at your parents' house."

"Where are you staying?"

"At the university...They said they would find me a shelter soon. I won't need it right away, anyway. I am staying at the dorm."

"You still wear this skirt, I see," he said, shaking his head but smiling.

I was happy to see his timid smile on his face again. "This is the only skirt I've got," I said, holding out the hem. "The security people think women comrades wear pants and sneakers. They say that is one way of identifying us. I'm trying to look different. We're telling our female members not to wear pants all the time."

"I understand. My fear is that they might get the idea that you are *her*."

I knew he was again referring to Nigist Tefera. "I know. You've already told me that."

"I always worry about your safety. You don't seem to care. You don't pay attention to your surroundings. I'd noticed that when you walk with me. You've got to be vigilant."

"You seem to be preoccupied and frustrated. I've never seen you so preoccupied... so disturbed. I don't like to see you this way. I want you to smile and laugh as you used to. You have to take it easy," I said, changing the focus from me to him.

"I'm sorry to take it out on you. I'm sorry to make you feel bad. I didn't mean to burden you with all that," he said, smiling ruefully and tenderly drawing me to him.

I felt emotion rising in me. The tender gaze in his eyes touched me. We've had discussions like those before. He had before pointed out what he thought were the mistakes of the Party. But never had I seen him so engrossed.

"It is not about me. It is about you. But what do you mean when you say burden me? Am I not part of it? Is it not my life as it is yours? Is it not what I do? "

"Of course it is your life. It is what you do. That was not what I meant. If I am frustrated, it is because of what I see around me. What is at stake is the struggle…the revolution so many are fighting for…so many have died for. We have claimed leadership of the revolution and we have to do it right. I understand there are vicissitudes. That is a given. But we are responsible for the lives of people we bring on board. We can't totally avoid imprisonment and execution but we should do our best to minimize it. I would have loved it if we saw each other more. I feel bad about that too because I want to see you more and spend more time with you like before. But you know how it is."

"I have no problem with that. I know why we can't see each other as we used to. That is not even an issue for me. It is *you* I am worried about."

"Don't worry about me. I am already feeling good. I am already happy."

"Yeah, but tomorrow you will go back to your worries," I said.

We laughed and everything seemed to be like before. We talked for most of the night and then went to bed.

I couldn't sleep.

The Party can never be mistaken…You and I can make a mistake. Not the Party.
        -Arther Koestler, *Darkness at Noon.*

He was tossing and turning too. I kept thinking. *Can the Party make a mistake?* Suddenly, I wanted to turn the light on and ask him that very question but did not. I had always believed the Party was infallible. I had refused to believe that it would make a mistake. What Getachew had been saying all along made sense. I believed it too. I just could not come to terms with the idea that the Party could make a mistake. Getachew always gave me a copy of the *Red Star*, the internal organ of the Party. It was only later that I learned he was Secretary of its editorial board, as well as being editor of *Abyot*. *Red Star* raised theoretical and organizational issues, but its publication had recently been discontinued for reasons I did not know.

I knew that there was no viable training for defense squad members in the League. I'd believed all along that Party defense squads had better training and enough ammunition. I could gather from what Getachew said that the Party was not even equipped to engage in military activities in the city. *Who is doing all that? Who are the people Getachew called the "clique?" They must be the ones who are making such blunder, not the Party.*
        The Party cannot make a mistake.

I lost weight drastically in the following weeks. There was something in my stomach that gnawed at me. Tito asked me what was wrong and I told him I had stomach problem. He said it was "gastritis" and advised me to drink milk. As advised, I bought milk and went to my friends' apartment in Piassa. It came out even before I emptied the glass. I did not want to go to the hospital.

Tsege, one of the girls who lived in the Piassa apartment, told me that she would ask her doctor if she could see me. The doctor agreed to examine me without going through the regular procedure. She was from Eastern Europe and worked at Menilik II Hospital. She wanted me to do various tests the day I went to see her. I was sitting in front of the laboratory waiting for my test results, when one of the technicians came out with a contorted face.

"It is scary! Where did you get it from?"

"Get what?"

"I can't tell you what it is. But oooooh…it is disgusting!"

"What is it?"

"I am not supposed to say," he said and went back in.

I went back to the wait area and sat on the bench. After a few minutes, the doctor came out and signaled for me to come in.

"Have you been outside Addis lately?"

"No," I lied, afraid of giving out information.

"You can't have this here. You must have been traveling outside Addis. You have Strongyloidiasis. It is a nasty parasite. If it is not treated, it will obstruct your intestine and kill you. Come, I will show you something."

She took out a huge medical book and showed me an x-ray of the parasite in a human intestine. I wanted to throw up. I was both scared and disgusted at having such an abominable creature in my gut.

I left the doctor's office, went to the hospital pharmacy to buy the prescription drug and proceeded to the apartment in Piassa. I spent the night at Aster's, Martha's older sister and my friend. She lived on the second-floor of the same building as her sister.

The next morning, I took two tablets as prescribed. About two hours or so later, I started having severe cramps, nausea and diarrhea. Fortunately, Aster had taken the day off from work and was home. The pain got worse and I started sweating profusely. I became so weak I couldn't even get up and go to the bathroom anymore. Aster wanted to take me to the hospital but I refused. In the afternoon, I was so sick I began slipping in and out of consciousness. Every time I opened my tired eyes, I saw Aster and her little boy kneeling down and praying in front of an image of the Virgin Mary. The whole thing seemed to me like a dream or something that I was watching from a faraway place. Finally, I drifted into sleep. In the morning, I was too scared to take the remaining two tablets. I felt weak and drained. My lips were chapped. I began to feel better after a couple of days of taking the rest of the tablets.

It was the morning of November 17. I went to see Semegne at her dorm at the Arat Kilo campus, as I did almost every day whenever I spent the night at the dorm. Semegne's dorm had two double-decker beds and she slept on the lower one. The dorm was quiet and I found her alone lying on her bed and reading. She put the book away and sat up when she saw me. I sat on the edge of the bed. We chatted for a few minutes and I said, getting up, "I should get going. I have a meeting in less than twenty minutes. I will see you tomorrow." We stood in the middle of the room and a chill ripped through my spine when I looked at her eyes. Something told me that I was not going to see her again. I wanted to say something but the words refused to come out. I stopped at the door and looked at her one more time. There was something disturbing in her eyes.

I left with an unsettling feeling. I trudged toward the gate debating with myself. I stopped for a few minutes to make up my mind. *Should I go back and tell her? But what am I going to tell her?* I exited the compound absorbed in deep thought. I flagged a cab almost reluctantly, when I came out onto the street.

I couldn't shake the premonition from my mind all day.

The next day, I learned from Tito that Semegne has been arrested the previous day. The news of her arrest had come from "our people" in the secret service. She went to the airport but turned around at the checkpoint, when they asked her to open her pouch. Suspicious why she did not want to be searched, the soldiers stopped her and searched her and found a copy of *Democracia* in the pouch.

She must have endured a horrible torture but nobody had come to look for me, the other Zonal Committee members, or her sub-Zonal Committee members, proof that she had never given in to torture. She was an incredibly committed and disciplined person. It was so hard to go on after she was arrested. She had a great sense of humor and we laughed all the time at home, in a café or in the street. She had the knack to notice the most unnoticeable but funny things about people or places and we used to burst out laughing every second walking in the street. Bole Mini was our hang out when we didn't have meetings and when we were not at my place or hers. That was where we laughed the most. We had become inseparable living close by and even after we moved into the campus dormitory.

I learned only later that she was executed sometime in December, about a month after she was arrested. She lost her life over a copy of *Democracia*! She was only twenty-two. I was distressed by her death. I felt bad for a long time for not telling her about my premonition. I often wondered if I could have prevented her death by warning her. But I didn't know what to say to her. It was the first tragedy I had to deal with after joining the Party. It was the first time I had lost such a close friend, as well. Every time I thought of her, that disturbing look in her eyes kept coming at me, at times making me blame myself for her death. However, most of the time, it was her bashful laughter that kept coming back into my mind. Only my commitment to the Party helped me cope with such a tremendous loss.

It was still November. Tito said to me, "*Ajirit*, you are going to Mekele. I know you just got back from Alamata but you have to go. From now on you will be doing liaison work for the Party as well as for the League. This time, you are going for a League assignment. You have to deliver documents."

"When am I supposed to leave?"

"In a couple of days…I will get back to you with the details of your trip."

The next day he gave me travel allowance and the name and phone number of the comrade I was supposed to meet. He also gave me the communication code and papers that I must deliver to the comrades in Mekele. I didn't know the contents of the papers. I confided in Azeb again so that she could notify my family in case I never returned. I rushed to my cousin's to steal back the traditional dress and *netela* that I wore during my trip to Alamata. I left before I got the chance to see Getachew. I didn't know how to reach him.

Mekele is the capital city of the province of Tigray. It is about 770 kilometers or so north of Addis Ababa. Mekele was then a two-day bus ride from Addis. I made it safely to Dessie the first day. I spent the night at a hotel with a woman called Abeba, with whom I had made friends on the bus. Abeba asked me if I wanted to share a room with her so that we could save money. I agreed, thinking it might even reinforce my appearance as a regular traveler. We shared the same bed. She told me that she was a housemaid and was going to visit her mother in Mekele, whom she had not seen for years.

The next day, we started our long ride to Mekele. The bus stopped at the Woldya checkpoint as it did during my trip to

Alamata. I asked Abeba to come with me to Zerai Deres to have *dulet* and yogurt. She told me that she had *agelgil* – lunch in a traditional lunch bag. She had brought dried food. I reluctantly had the *agelgil*. My heart was at Zerai Deres. The men came back from the eateries and boarded the bus after being searched and their IDs scrutinized. The women were neither searched nor asked for ID. I did not have an ID. I did not dare bring my student ID with me again.

The bus stopped at Korem, a small town past Alamata. A few people got off for a drink, food or to relieve themselves. Abeba and I ran to an eatery to use the toilet and came back. Once we passed Korem, I was in for a surprise. I marveled at the beauty of the magnificent and rugged Alamata mountain chains, particularly Amba Alaghe. It was breathtaking. I saw a plateau for the first time in my life.

It was a hair-raising experience riding through those majestic mountains. Many passengers threw up as the bus curled and twisted through the steep road. My heart stopped beating when the bus ascended what seemed to me like the summit of the mountains. I thought it was soaring into the sky. I covered my face with my *netela* to avoid looking below but, unable to resist the temptation, I would now and then look down and tremble like a leaf when I saw buses and cars slowly climbing the formidable mountains. That was when I knew how high we were going. The seemingly bottomless pit would send a chill up my spine every time I looked down.

Before I knew it, the bus arrived at Endayesus, which is about ten kilometers away from Mekele. Endayesus is buttressed by walls built by the Italians during their invasion of the country in 1895, before they were defeated at the Battle of Adwa in March 1896. The place was intimidating with its fortress and solemnly standing soldiers. The bus stopped and male passengers were asked to get off. Two soldiers came in and conducted a massive search, asking for identification cards and rummaging through luggage. One of the soldiers asked Abeba to show him her ID.

I had a window seat and pretended to look out, my *netela* over my head to hide my face. *What is my excuse for not having an ID? What am I going to say if he asks why I am going to Mekele? Why hadn't I thought about it before? How could I be so stupid?* Abeba did not have an ID. The soldier asked her where she was going and why. She told him she was going to Mekele to visit her mother. He asked her to get off the bus with her belongings.

I was shocked.

I knew I was next. I was happy when Abeba said she did not have an ID, which would make the two of us. I could no longer pretend I was not aware of what was going on beside me. I turned around and stared into the soldier's eyes. He peered into my eyes. I kept staring at him. He did the same thing. The unthinkable happened. He swung around and left without saying anything! I followed him with my eyes until he got off the bus. I could not believe it. Once he stepped out, I gave a sigh of relief. Then I remembered that Abeba was standing outside, surrounded by soldiers. I waved at her when the bus started moving. I drew my *netela* across my face to hide my tears.

The bus arrived at Mekele around four-thirty in the afternoon. The town was highly militarized with police, army, *Abyot Tebaki* – the Revolutionary Guard recently formed by the Derg under the aegis of *Kebeles* – and *Nebelbal* – Blaze – Mengistu Hailemariam's version of a Red Army that he had recently built. It was answerable only to him.

I got off the bus and looked for a public phone. I went into a drugstore and asked the man in a white smock if there was a payphone nearby. He let me use his telephone. I made the call but there was no response. I thanked the man and went out. I didn't know where to go. I was hungry and had a terrible headache. I was dying for a cup of tea and wondered about going into the café a few steps away from the drugstore. I went in even before I paused to make a conscious decision.

The youngsters in the café stared at me curiously when I went in. I knew I would be completely out of place with my traditional dress, *netela*, red headscarf, sneakers, red socks, and a plastic bag. Adding surprise to their curiosity, I took a seat at a table near the door and ordered hamburger and tea. I hadn't had such a delicacy for quite some time and I wasn't going to miss the opportunity. Besides, I wouldn't have known what to order in a place like that. The youngsters seemed to be innocuous and were giggling and flirting.

They reminded me of my own recent past.

When I was done, I went back to the drugstore and asked the man if I could use his phone again. I dialed the number and the phone kept ringing but there was no answer. I didn't know what to do. I went back to the café and ordered pineapple juice. I stayed there for about twenty minutes and went back to the drugstore to try my luck one more time. Again there was no answer.

I got nervous.

What am I supposed to do if I can't get a hold of the comrade? What if the line is down? Where is the nearest hotel? I might need an ID *card to check into a hotel. I don't even have one!*

"I don't think it is a wise idea to go back and forth. Please stay here until you find the person you are looking for. Have a seat," the man said, pointing to the bench in the corner of the room when I was about to step out.

I thanked him and sat on the bench. I felt bad about my behavior. *I shouldn't have done that. What if he was a security agent?* After about fifteen minutes, I told the man I was going to try one more time. My heart was pounding, holding the telephone receiver to my ear. It was getting dark and the drugstore would soon close. I didn't even realize that the call has been answered.

"Hello!"

I couldn't believe my ears. I asked for the comrade. When he said "speaking," I recited the code.

"Where are you?"

"I am close to the bus station. I'm calling from-"

"You know what? Go up a few meters and you will find a drugstore. Wait for me there. I will be right there," he said, interrupting me.

I went back and sat on the bench. A young man came in after about fifteen minutes. He came straight to me and after we exchanged greetings, he went over to the man, for all I know was a pharmacist, and talked to him for a few minutes. I suspected the man was one of our own. I thanked him when I went out with the comrade. The comrade took me to a restaurant. I had already eaten so I just had a drink. I gave him the documents when we got to his place. He showed me around Mekele during my stay. Mekele is small but had its own beauty with houses made of stone. I left after a few days. I passed the Endayesus checkpoint without any incident. I was not asked to produce an ID. I was not searched.

We arrived in Maichew after almost a three-hour ride. Maichew, hilly and green, was the place Ethiopia lost a battle (after a fierce resistance and victories elsewhere) to the Italians during the Italo-Ethiopian war in 1936. I was just wondering about the historical significance of the place when the bus stopped in the middle of nowhere. An older police officer came in and asked the men to get off. After all the men disembarked, a tall and burly *Nebelbal* came in. The *Nebelbal* and the police officer searched peoples' belongings. I was sitting by the window seat; an older woman was sitting beside me. The *Nebelbal* asked every woman for an ID. He was loud, brusque and authoritative. He demanded the woman beside me to show him hers. I hoped that she did not have one. I was disheartened when she produced a *Kebele ID*. I looked through the window to give the impression that I did not know what was going on.

It was dangerous to travel to Tigray at the time, even with an ID. Mekele was the gateway to Assimba, home base to EPRP's army, and to the mountains where the Tigray Liberation Front operated. It was also one of the routes to Eritrea, where the Eritrean Liberation Fronts have been operating.

"Madam, your identification card," I heard the *Nebelbal* say, using the polite you.

I turned around and saw him standing beside the woman.

"Your identification card!" he repeated with the familiar you.

"I don't have one."

"How come?"

"Our *Kebele* has not yet issued the cards to everyone," I said. Many *Kebeles* were quite behind on issuing ID cards at the time I was traveling. I knew that and I thought I might give a shot at that excuse.

"Get off the bus!"

I leapt to my feet.

"Get your belongings," he commanded in a gruff voice.

I grabbed my plastic bag and got off the bus. Two young soldiers were standing outside. I went over and stood beside them. It will be all right as long as they don't touch my belly or ask me to remove my sneakers, I said to myself. I had papers stuffed in there. But I was suspicious of the *Nebelbal*, whose eyes had an evil cast. He was abrasive and had a no-nonsense approach. The older police officer and he got off the bus and the *Nebelbal* ordered the bus driver to go. The bus did not move. The young *Autanti* – ticket collector – stood at the door watching us.

"Sir, I said you could go. There is no reason for you to wait," the *Nebelbal* glared at the driver, his rifle slung over his shoulder.

"Why are you telling him to go, while the girl is still standing here?" asked the older policeman, tapping his palm with his policeman's club.

"Close the door!" the *Nebelbal* snarled at the *Autanti*.

The *Autanti* closed the door. But the bus did not move.

"What about the girl? Why are you asking him to go?" The older policeman asked again.

"She is under arrest," the *Nebelbal* said, giving me a baleful glance. "She is traveling without an identification card. Take her away," he ordered the two young soldiers, pointing his index finger behind me.

The two young soldiers grabbed both sides of my arms, one on each side. I managed to turn my head toward the direction the *Nebelbal* pointed at and saw a small grey building with a huge sign that read *Marefia Bet* – rest area. I knew it was a police station. The *Marefia Bet* was the only sign of human existence in the area. The very sight of it shot an icy wave of terror through my body. I imagined myself in that dreadful place and what would become of me. My brain raced with an incredible speed. It was a moment of decision. I had to do something dramatic to save my life.

"Oh my child! My poor child!" I suddenly screamed at the top of my voice.

"Poor thing, you have a child?" asked the older policeman with palpable sympathy.

His sympathetic question induced in me a deluge of tears. "I have a one-year old boy. I left him with my bedridden mother," I said, wiping my eyes with my *netela*.

"Where do you live and where are you coming from?" asked the burly *Nebelbal* unmoved by my torrent of tears.

"I live in Addis Ababa and I am coming from Mekele."

"Why did you go to Mekele?"

I knew I had to be convincing and above all, I had to say something that would probably soften the diehard's heart. I said, sobbing violently, "I went to look for my husband. My husband is a soldier and had gone to Eritrea to fulfill his *gedaj*. He left just before our son was born. He didn't even have the chance to see him. I haven't had news from him for over a year. I was told that he was sent to Mekele for some kind of training so I wanted to come and look for him. I went to the division he was said to have been staying at but...I was told that he has never been there. Now I know for sure he is dead...How is it possible not to hear from him for over a year? My poor son! Who is going to look after him? My mother is an invalid."

I believed my own story. I took a risk by saying that my husband was sent to Mekele for training. I didn't even know if soldiers were sent to Mekele for training. Besides, I wouldn't have known what to say if asked which division I've been to. But I hoped the word *gedaj* might somehow save the day. *Gedaj* —obligation to the motherland in Derg's parlance – was their treasured word and I hoped to bet my life on it.

"Please let her go. What harm can she possibly do? She is just a child?" said the policeman to the *Nebelbal*, genuinely feeling sorry for me.

I felt the two young soldiers loosening their grip on my arms after my stage act. They too seemed touched by my story. The *Nebelbal* was the only one who didn't buy it.

"She is lying. I don't believe a word she is saying," he said, throwing a suspicious look at me.

"What do you mean? Can't you see her tears and her pain?"

"I know her kind. I have worked in Eritrea. I have seen the bandits. It is women like her that do the most damage. They are the ones who transport ammunition from one place to the other. I can tell when I see one. You will see she will spill out everything under that…," he said unflinchingly.

"What do you gain by getting this poor child in trouble? Don't you have a mother? Don't you have a sister? Aren't you born of a woman? Don't you have any compassion in you? Let me beg you in the name of the Mother of our God. Let her go. Your soul will be damned if you arrest this innocent girl," the police officer pleaded, looking disgusted by the behavior of his colleague.

I was touched by his kindness. I couldn't control my tears watching him talk. I looked at the *Nebelbal*. I thought I saw a glint of softening in his eyes! I had to seize the moment… dramatize even more to win his complete sympathy. "I know my husband is killed in a battle. How could I've never heard from him for so long? He died for his country fulfilling his *gedaj*. I am being detained in an unknown place. Who is going to take care of my son when I am in prison or if I die in the wilderness? I know my mother does not have much left to live. The God of my child, please look after my little boy. That is all I ask of you!" I wailed convulsively.

That did it. "Go! *Askonagne!*" he shouted, lifting one leg to kick me on my behind. The *Autanti* opened the door and I dived into the bus. He barely missed me. The *Autanti* closed the door and the driver speeded up.

The people in the bus were glued to the window watching the drama. When I got inside, some of them congratulated me. I went back to my seat and I became emotional and cried anew as people around me showered me with congratulations. I knew that the bus driver was instrumental as much as the policeman saving my life. Had he left, I would have ended at that sinister place in that evil man's hands. That was what I thought of him then.

I wanted to go over and thank the driver but I could not move. I felt sorry I did not even get the chance to thank the policeman. I knew many of our comrades came that way and I wished that the policeman always worked with the *Nebelbal* who seemed vicious. *How much blood that man must have spilled?*

I shuddered by the magnitude of the danger I was in. It was that glance to the *Marefia Bet* that prompted my theatrical performance. It wasn't death alone that spurred me to act but also the idea of being forcefully violated by the burly *Nebelbal*. *Who knows how many of them could there be...?* They would have later killed me and hurled my corpse over a top of a hill. Nobody would have ever known what had happened to me.

I was amazed by the survival instinct in all of us when we are faced with danger. I was never aware I was capable of such a theatrical performance. I became convinced that there was an actor in every one of us. Up to that moment, I had danced around danger but had never really come face to face with it the way I had that day. I knew there was the possibility of being arrested or even of dying before I left for Mekele but that was only a fleeting thought that crossed my mind. I was more into the excitement and adventure aspect of it and of course undertaking a dangerous task for the sake of the Party than anything else. This was my first real brush with death (because there would have been no chance of getting alive out of that situation was I apprehended) and I found the whole experience tempering.

When we arrived in Korem, we stopped for lunch. I had a terrible headache and my eyes were swollen after the Maichew incident. I was nauseous as the bus zigzagged through the Alamata Mountains. Everybody got off except for a few women. I didn't want to have lunch. I could hardly open my eyes because of the pounding headache. The bus driver, a tall, heavy-set man, who seemed to be in his late forties or early fifties came over and asked me to go have lunch with him.

"By the way, thank you so much. I really appreciate what you've done for me. I don't feel like eating now. I have a severe headache. Thanks you anyway," I said.

"Come have lunch with me. I will buy you *Aspro* and coffee. You will be fine," he insisted, pulling my hand.

I had little energy to resist. We went to the eatery and he ordered lunch. I went to wash my hands.

"I didn't want to leave you with those men," he said when I came back and slumped in a chair. "I said to myself, 'I can't leave this girl in the middle of nowhere with all these men. I should stay till the end.' I have daughters your age. I just couldn't do it. That was why I stayed. I am glad it turned out for the best."

"I can't thank you enough. I would have ended at the police station were it not for you. The police officer was a kind person too. It is because of you two that I am here now."

He smiled flirtatiously. "How could I have left a girl like *you* in the hands of that beast?"

I pretended I did not get the message. I could hardly eat so I had tea instead. The driver went out and came back with Aspirin. I went to the toilet, washed my face, came back, and took the Aspirin. He ordered another cup of tea for me. After an hour, we went back to the bus. I looked at my face in the tiny mirror I had brought with me. My eyes were still red and swollen. I leaned on the window and closed my eyes when the bus started to move.

I woke up at the Woldya checkpoint. I did not get off the bus. I didn't feel like eating. Even the *dulet* and yogurt at Zerai Deres couldn't appeal to me. The driver came and asked me to go with him and have *"konjo dulet."* I told him I was not feeling well. When he left, I covered my face with my *netela* and leaned back on the window. I woke up around five in the afternoon in Dessie.

I got off the bus and scurried as fast as my legs could carry me to avoid the driver. I knew I would have to return in-kind the favor bestowed upon me in Maichew. I checked into a different hotel than the one I stayed at with Abeba on my way to Mekele. A young man, the son of the owner of the hotel, helped me check in. I went to my room and washed myself with a bucket of water sitting in the toilet. I felt fresh and the headache had gone away, thanks to the Aspirin and the long nap I took on the bus. After what I had been through at Maichew, I needed a bit of relaxation. Besides, I was hungry.

I went to Etege Hotel throwing my *netela* over my head. As soon as I sat on a chair, I saw someone waving at me. It was the driver! He was sitting with a group of men who appeared to be drivers. He signaled to me to join them. I politely declined by shaking my head. The waiter came and took my order. I saw the driver waving at him. When the waiter came back, he brought all sorts of food that I had not ordered. I looked up to ask him and saw the driver coming toward my table. We had dinner together and I rose up to go. He told me he had reserved a bed for us. I was gracious about declining the pass. He said he would catch up with me after having a few laughs with his friends.

How does he know where I am staying?

I went to bed as soon as I got to my room. I was in a deep sleep when a loud and incessant knock on the door woke me up. I looked at my watch and it was past midnight. I tiptoed to the door, peeped through the crack, and saw the driver. The youngster, who had helped me check in earlier, came and asked him not to disturb me. They walked down the hållway; I waited until their footsteps died down before heading back to bed, thanking the young man all the while. A few minutes later, I heard a light knock on the door. I cursed the driver - *would he never let up?* I tiptoed and looked through the crack. It was the youngster! I went back to bed, smiling.

The next day, when I got back to Addis, I went straight to the campus dormitory. Sara, as alert as she always is, said to me, "Have you been to Wollo? You have a Wollo accent. Where did you pick it up?" I was amazed.

I was more amazed by what I was about to learn.

Citizens, did you want a revolution without a revolution?
    -Maximillian Robespierre

It was around the end of November, just after I came back from
Mekele. Dumbstruck, I stared at Tito when he read out from a
"circular." We were at an IZ meeting at one of our meeting places.
Tito said the "circular" had come from the Party Central
Committee. It read that *Ha* and *Le* – A and B – were expelled from
the Central Committee. We knew who they were. *Ha* was
Berhanemeskel Redda, and *Le* Getachew Maru. I could not bring
myself to believe that the Party could do such a thing. I could
faintly hear Tito saying *Yebelay Akalat* would come to our meeting
to explain the "new policy."

    I wanted to see Getachew immediately but I didn't know
how to reach him. *What did he think about his expulsion?* I thought
of asking Tito after the meeting if he could set up an appointment
for me. *Getachew had sent me a note through him. Can I do it? But
Getachew has been drummed out of the Central Committee!*

    I went out to the street, shock, disbelief and confusion
pressing on my shoulders. I was profoundly disturbed not just by
the shocking news but also by the very idea of confusion creeping
into my heart. I had been wondering these past few months if the
Party could ever make a mistake. Now that I heard about the
weeding out, I felt the very fabric of my being shaken.

    The *Yebelay Akalat* came to our meeting a few days later. I
recognized one of them, Girmachew Lemma, who had spoken at the
USUAA inauguration at the university. He was wrapped in *gabi* –
handmade wrap made of cotton – as camouflage. He did most of
the talking. The talk centered on the Party's new policy: the need
for staging urban armed struggle. The justification was that the
"objective conditions" of the country had changed and that the Party
had to defend itself from the repression and executions perpetrated

on it. They said that *Ha* and *Le* were expelled for disciplinary reasons.

My heart sank. I knew why they were expelled. They were expelled because they were against the launching of urban guerrilla warfare. Their words left a bitter taste on my mouth. I had been almost excited to see them, but when I realized that those were the very people who had expelled Getachew and Berhanemeskel from the Central Committee, my excitement vanished.

It was early December. The situation in the city had become tense following the assassination attempt on Mengistu Hailemariam.

"*Ajirit*, you are going back to Mekele. You have to explain the new policy to the Tigray Youth League Zonal Committee. You're going to meet a comrade tomorrow who is going to tell you the details of your trip," Tito told me.

"When am I expected to leave?" I asked anxiously.

I was eager to get in touch with Getachew. I didn't want to leave before seeing him. But I didn't know how to get in touch with him. I couldn't think of anything else except for seeing him. Berhanemeskel and he were branded *Anjas*-factionalists. Things were getting serious.

"Soon. The committee is meeting in a few days. You have to be there before the meeting ends. Anyway, the comrade will tell you the details," Tito said, giving me the communication code.

I met Aklilu Hiruy, Secretary-General of the Youth League, in *Mercato* the next day. He wore a green blazer with black pants. I could tell he was Tito's older brother. The resemblance was striking. Unlike Tito, who was outgoing, Aklilu was soft-spoken, reserved, and shy. His Afro was not as enormous as his younger brother's was.

We went to a café in the *Adarash* – shopping area – in *Mercato* and talked about my trip. We set up an appointment for the next day and parted. We met at a café in Arat Kilo the next morning. We ordered our drinks and sat quietly. He looked nervous. I watched him, sipping my tea. He then pushed a piece of folded paper across the table and stuck it underneath my teacup saucer.

I opened it right away. I knew it was from Getachew. The note said to meet him the next day at the same time and place. I beamed with obvious excitement. Aklilu watched me silently.

"Some *Yebelay Akalat* may be theoretically advanced, but they have misguided views on certain issues," he said, looking at me pointedly and patting his mouth with his hand. "We should be vigilant and not subscribe to their views."

I held my tongue. I knew he was referring to Getachew. "I understand I'm going to Mekele, but I don't have a *Kebele* ID," I said, changing the subject.

"I will surely get you one, but you've to get a new picture and give it to me later today. I'm sorry to tell you, though, I won't be able to get you a real *Kebele* ID. I can only get you a fake one. The chair of the *Kebele* who was supposed to get us a real one is away."

"That is okay, but I can't travel without an ID to Mekele again. It is extremely dangerous. I will definitely end up in jail this time around."

"You will be fine. You look innocent and nobody suspects you of anything of that kind. Besides, you have done it before," he said with a shy smile.

We came out of the café a little later and I took a cab to Piassa to have a one-hour picture taken at Photo Berhan. It was late afternoon when I saw Aklilu again. I gave him the picture.

I met Getachew the next day at Abuna Petros Square. I couldn't even wait until we got into our room. "Getachew, I am so sorry! I couldn't believe it when I heard of your expulsion!" I said with a crack in my voice.

He smiled and asked me after my health. We crossed the street and advanced to the hotel. We checked into a room. He tossed his reading glasses and berretta hat on the couch. I put my small bag, with change clothes, on the floor and settled on the couch. He came and sat beside me and put his arm around me.

"I kind of sensed it was coming," he said. "The saddest part is the reason the comrades gave for our expulsion. Among other things, they accused us of talking to individuals outside the proper channel. They want to continue with their dangerous idea of urban warfare no matter what the consequences. Our members and supporters are paying for it every day. The Derg executes forty or so people in retaliation for any one person we kill. The ratio is forty to one. Tell me if there is any sense in that ratio."

He was referring to the two recent killings of over fifty of our members by the Derg in retaliation for the assassination attempt on the vice-chairman and the killings of *Meison* members by the Party. The executions had been announced, accompanied by the infamous *Yefiyel Wotete*.

Among the executed was Wubishet Retta. He was our neighbor in Harar, a brother and uncle of my childhood friends. He was studying in Russia but had abandoned his studies to join the EPRP army. I remember the picture he had sent home wearing a Russian fur hat. This framed picture sat on an armoire in the living room. I peered at it with admiration every time I went over. At the time, he was the only one I knew of in Harar who had gone abroad to study.

Getachew went on, "They make it sound as if we've infringed upon the principle of democratic centralism. The issue is not disciplinary but political. The comrade and I are expelled because we are against the idea of urban guerrilla warfare, the assassination of Mengistu Hailemariam, the use of PPG as a strategic question and, frankly, a host of other political issues. We also suggested that we should accept the Derg's recent call for a United Front. They accused us of reconciliation with a government whose hands are smeared with blood."

He continued, "Our members need to understand the implications of the policy of urban armed struggle. I am sure they will not support it once they know what is at stake. I am positive that things will be rectified and resolved once a congress is called. The problem is the comrades don't want to call a meeting of congress. CC meetings are not held as often as they should be; decisions are made by the clique and communicated to others by phone. Their excuse is "security problems." It is all the doing of the clique."

I didn't know what to say. I was startled that he still called the people who kicked him out "comrades." I was amazed by his confidence that the differences would be resolved. *Is he naive?* I knew how passionately the *Yebelay Akalat* defended the idea of urban guerrilla warfare the day they came to our meeting. "Three *Yebelay Akalat* came to our meeting the other day to explain to us the new policy. They talked about your expulsion too. They were Girmachew Lemma, Tselote Hezkias and I think the third one was...Kiflu Tefera," I said.

Tselote and Kiflu were Central Committee members. Girmatchew was not. He was a member of the Addis Ababa Party Inter-Zonal Committee. One of his own comrades would later kill

Tselote in Assimba, and Kiflu Tefera was destined to meet his end at the hands of the Derg.

"How did you know their names?" Getachew asked taken aback. I knew I had disregarded discipline.

"I know Girmachew. I heard him speak at the USUAA inauguration. As for the other two...uh...We are told to explain the new policy to committee members all the way down the League structure. I am going to Mekele to do the same," I said, switching to a different topic.

"When are you leaving?"

"I am not sure yet, but very soon." I told him about my recent trip to Mekele and the Maichew incident.

"Make sure you get a proper ID. They won't let you get away with it this time," he warned.

He had changed even more than when I had seen him a few weeks ago. He looked tired and drawn. "I would like you to meet the *comrade* and his wife one of these days. I have told him so much about you," he said.

I looked at him quizzically. I knew he was referring to Berhanemeskel Redda but I didn't know Berhanemeskel was married.

"He is married," he said as if he had read my mind.

"I didn't know he was."

"His wife has recently come back from abroad. She is very nice and interesting. I can see you two becoming good friends. I want you to meet them both soon."

I was thrilled with the idea of meeting the legendary Berhanemeskel Redda. He had become a household name for quite a while. "Wow! It would be nice to meet the comrade."

There was a considerable age difference between Berhanemeskel and Getachew, the latter being the younger one.

However, there was a parallel between what they did and the views they held about the course of the revolution.

"I know. The comrade is a great and committed revolutionary. It is sad that things have come to this level in the Party," Getachew sighed. "By the way, I would like to see you before you leave. Why don't we meet tomorrow afternoon?"

"Sure, we can do that."

He said he was thinking of inviting the *comrade* for a discussion about "the so-called" new Party policy. By the *comrade* he meant Azeb. "We are talking to members individually to ignite discussion in the Party and the League," he said. "We would like them to see the mistakes of the comrades and where they are taking us. Particularly, those members in the higher hierarchies could push through their channels to urge the Central Committee to call a meeting of congress. Can we meet tomorrow in front of Leul Mekonen School at six o'clock? We will take a long walk rather than sit in a café. I hope the *comrade* will make it."

In the morning, we checked out of the hotel and I saw him off. In the good old days, he was the one who made sure I was in a taxi safely. Now that security had become tight, I became the one who remained behind and saw him off. I took a taxi to *Mercato* to see Aklilu.

I wondered about the fate of our relationship riding in the cab. *Could I continue my cherished relationship with him or would I be expected or even be forced to sever it? What am I going to do if they expect me to stop seeing him? Leave him or run away from the Party?* Neither of them were options to me. I was equally committed to both. On the one hand, I couldn't have left the Party because the ultimate thing was not my personal life but the struggle. The Party came first, more than anything else in the world.

On the other, I couldn't leave Getachew just because he was expelled from the Party's CC. It was due to his inexhaustible efforts that I was involved in the Party in the first place. Beyond that, my life was tied to his with a love as unbreakable as the revolutionary spirit he had instilled in me. I had not yet seen any changes towards me among the comrades except for the little "advice" from Aklilu. Tito had played the mail carrier for Getachew, and later Aklilu had taken over.

I decided to keep my poise and see what the future held in store for me.

Democracia would later make a vitriolic attack on Getachew and Berhanemeskel, calling them "spineless," in one of its issues. It stated that, "Some individuals, who started the struggle by mistake, want to shun us when the going gets tough... those who would like a struggle without sacrifice...they say the Party is responsible for the death of the youth...they want to discontinue the struggle..." I was astounded and appalled by what the Party said in public about two of its most famous and senior revolutionaries. None of the Party CC members, for that matter anyone in the organization, was as famous as those two.

When I saw him that morning, Aklilu gave me the communication code, my forged *Kebele* ID, money for transportation, food and accommodation, and the name and phone number of the comrade I was supposed to meet and said, "We called the comrades in Mekele several times but there was no answer. I think the line is down. Here is what you can do- Go to the house and knock at the door- I will give you the direction..."

"What? You want me to..."

"Hold it, hold it…it is pretty easy," he said in his gentle voice. "The house is right by the bus stop. All you do is get off the bus and make a-"

I burst out laughing. "You've got to be kidding. You want me to go to Mekele and knock on a door?"

"I am telling you it is easy. Besides, we will keep calling them even after you have left. The committee starts the meeting the day after tomorrow. You really have to be there," he said, giving me the direction.

I knew I had to go.

Azeb and I took a cab to *Mercato* to meet Getachew in the evening. I used to confide in her everything that Getachew had been telling me. We wondered what was going on inside the Party, but we didn't have the courage to say anything. We just wished the problem would go away and the leadership would come to its senses.

We met Getachew in front of Leul Mekonen School. He was wearing his yellow-brown corduroy jacket, a book stuck in one of his pockets. I hadn't seen him in that jacket for a long time. We meandered around the neighborhood. He talked about the Party's policies on urban armed struggle and the PPG. He explained again how the two were interrelated and how it was damaging the Party and how it would lead to intensified repression, how it had to stop before our members were wiped out.

Neither Azeb nor I said anything. We were overwhelmed. When he was done, he told me to stay behind. I told Azeb to meet me in Piassa in front of Cinema Ethiopia in an hour.

"When are you leaving?" he asked as soon as she left.

"Tomorrow."

"Did you get your ID?" I nodded, saying nothing.

"I was just going to ask you if you could deliver a note to the comrades in Mekele. The letter is from the *comrade*. If you feel you can't, it is okay. I understand. Read it now and decide whether or not you would want to take it," he said.

I knew the *comrade* was Berhanemeskel Redda.

"I don't mind," I said.

He took a folded paper from his pocket and gave it to me. "Tell them to pass it to Tsehaye. Please take care of yourself. Send me a message as soon as you get back." He wished me a safe trip and hopped into a taxi.

I met Azeb in front of Cinema Ethiopia around eight o'clock. We went to my friends' apartment in Piassa. I had earlier asked her to spend the night there and that I was going to Mekele. We talked about what Getachew said on our way to the apartment. We were scared, and wondered how we could raise the issue in our respective committees.

Everybody was home when we got to the apartment, a dark cloud hanging over our heads. We had dinner with the girls and went to bed early. We got up around four in the morning and left around five. Azeb came with me to the bus station to see me off.

The bus arrived in Dessie, after an eight-hour ride. I got off and checked in a hotel not too far from the station. I went out to look for something to eat. I had dinner, came back around eight o'clock and went straight to bed. I fell asleep right away, but woke up in the middle of the night. I had been thinking all day about the note Getachew had given me. I had not read it out of sheer discipline, but I'd somehow sensed what could be in it. I couldn't be sure of the repercussions of delivering a letter sent by Berhanemeskel Redda to Party people in Mekele after he was expelled from the Party's Central Committee.

Getachew and Berhanemeskel were branded *Anjas* and were accused of wanting to collaborate with the Derg. Berhanemeskel, in particular, was accused of staying at the Derg office when he didn't have a proper shelter after being expelled from the CC. Years later, I learned that Getachew also didn't have a place to stay, after he was expelled, and once even had to spend a night in the woods by himself!

Finally, I decided to read the note and make up my mind. I unfolded the paper, a feeling of shame hovering over me. I thought it would be a breach of discipline on my part even though Getachew had asked me to read it. The note, in three or four lines, condemned the killings of *Kebele* officials and of *Meison* members, calling it "utter terrorism" and "senseless killing" and saying "It is costing us lives." It appealed to the comrades in the army to "pressure the Party Central Committee into calling a meeting of congress."

I was reading a note written by Berhanemeskel Redda! I reread it. What was in it was the very reason he and Getachew had been expelled from the Party Central Committee.

I crumpled the piece of paper and closed my eyes. *What should I do?* I wished I had read it when I was still in Addis, or at least told Azeb about it. The very idea of passing it over would be incriminating. *What is going to happen to me if they find out? I will become a fugitive!* I wished Getachew was there with me. I knew he would not have left me agonizing. *Why didn't I read it when he asked? Am I going to let him down?* I did not know Berhanemeskel personally and that made it easier for me. But Getachew? I went back to bed but I couldn't sleep. Finally, I sat up in the bed, shredded the paper slowly and burst into tears.

I felt I had betrayed Getachew.

In the morning, I took the bus to Mekele. When we arrived at Woldya, the bus stopped for a routine search. The men were asked to get off but not the women. I ran to Zerai Deres to have the usual *dulet* and yogurt, while the soldiers were ransacking our luggage. When I came back, men were being shaken down and asked for ID. I was neither searched nor required to produce an ID.

We resumed our trip and braved the Alamata Mountains. I shuddered when I saw the *Marefia Bet* at Maichew. I was terrified of seeing the burly *Nebelbal*. *What kind of excuse am I going to give this time?* He would have definitely arrested me. Thankfully, the bus did not stop at Maichew but at Endayesus, which was as intimidating as ever. I arrived in Mekele safely. When I got off the bus, I went into a store and made several calls to the comrades' house. There was no answer. I went to the house as per the direction. I knocked on a red gate and a man came out to open it for me. I recited the code.

What a relief! I was at the right place.

I met the Tigray Zonal Committee members (who came from various districts) the next morning and spent all day with them. It was tough for me to explain to the group, after all the discussions I had had with Getachew, about the new policy. *What can I do?* I rationalized to myself. *As long as I am in the Party, I have to do what the Party asks.* I focused my talk more on organizational issues and shared the League experience. I enjoyed my stay with them. I returned to Addis a few days later without any incident.

I met Aklilu in the afternoon, the day after I got back. I asked him if he could arrange an appointment for me with Getachew. He said he would try. I met Azeb in the evening, and she told me that she had a discussion with Aklilu about the new Party policy after I left. He told her that she should not "waver." He had no idea she had met Getachew. We agreed not to say anything to anyone.

Azeb had never told me that she knew Aklilu, and neither had I told her. I saw them together only once, at Lidet Biskut Bet, a café and pastry shop at Teklehaimanot Square south of *Mercato*. I came in with one of my Zonal Committee members. They left right after we came in. That was how I learned the two knew each other.

Aklilu and I met most of the time in a café near Tourist Hotel in Arat Kilo. I once saw Azeb with a man in Arat Kilo when Aklilu and I were heading to the café. Azeb and I pretended we didn't know each other. That was how Azeb found out I knew Aklilu. Since that day, Azeb and I referred to him as "the comrade - Arat Kilo."

A couple of days after I asked Aklilu to arrange the appointment with Getachew, he gave me a piece of folded paper. I slipped it into my breast pocket of my jacket without reading it.

"It might be a good idea to distance ourselves from some *Yebelay Akalat*," he said. "They maybe theoretically advanced but they have misguided ideas on certain issues. We have to be careful and not subscribe to their views." He repeated word for word what he had already told me.

I pretended not to understand. I could see that they were not going to stop me from seeing Getachew. I had never done or said anything to implicate myself, except for seeing him. I took out the note the minute I parted with Aklilu. It read, "Same place, same time, tomorrow-Hadis."

I met Getachew in front of the hotel the next day. He looked relieved to see me. There was always danger in traveling to Tigray at the time, more than any other place in the country. Lately, it had become even more dangerous for anyone who was not Tigrigna speaking. I knew he worried. I worried about him too, particularly since his expulsion, which I still had difficulty understanding.

After we had finished dinner and the waiter had cleared the table, Getachew ordered tea. I thought it was time to break the news about the note.

"After reading it at a hotel in Dessie, I tore up the note you gave me," I said, speaking slowly. I felt ashamed of my cowardice.

"It is okay. Don't worry about it. I told you to read it and make up your mind. In any case, I admire your honesty. You could have told me you had delivered it. I would have no way of finding out." He took my hand in his. I wasn't sure if he had noticed the troubled expression on my face. He said, "Thanks anyway." His voice was full of warmth and affection.

I felt a lump in my throat.

The agony I was going through was obvious, even if I didn't say it in so many words. I had felt bad when I tore up the note. I felt wretched when I heard him utter those words and even show tenderness. I would have almost preferred to be criticized for my failure to understand the implications of my actions for the revolution. I would have felt I deserved it.

But it wasn't like him to say that to me. Instead, he thanked me for my honesty. Honest! I would have preferred to die right there than lie to him. The guilt and shame that had gnawed at my heart since I destroyed that note troubled me even more. His words could not console me.

I knew I would live with the guilt and shame for as long as I lived.

What triggered shame and guilt was the idea of letting down Getachew. What was happening in the Party or the course of the revolution was too abstract to me at that point. I did not tell Getachew the agony I went through before I tore up the paper or when I made the confession.

It wouldn't have made a difference. I had let him down. I was ashamed of what I did and did not have the words to express my feelings. Even, "I am sorry" or "I feel bad about what I did," would not have been good enough.

I chose to remain silent.

"As I told you, I want you to meet the *comrade* and his wife. I want you to meet them one of these days. Actually, we will go see them next time we meet. I really want you to meet him. I have told him so much about you. I know you can become good friends with his wife," he said as if to make me feel at ease.

I still wanted to meet Berhanemeskel, but my burning desire was tempered by what I had done to his note.

The revo*lution needs the enemy.*
   -Fidel Castro

The day was February 4, 1977. I had spent the night at the apartment in Piassa. Martha and I were waiting for a taxi at the bus stop opposite Cinema Ethiopia, when we saw our friend Sewasew Tewahade coming toward us.

"What are you doing here? Why don't you leave?" Sewasew said, waving his hand.

It was around eight-thirty in the morning. Martha was going to work and I to my underground enterprise. "We are waiting for a taxi. What are you doing here? Where is your car?"

"My car is in the garage. Why don't you leave? It is over."

"What are you talking about? What is over?"

"It is over! Your people, Lieutenant Alemayehu Haile and Captain Moges Woldemikael, have been killed. The coup has failed! What are you waiting for? You should go. *Aleke dekeke!*"

The expression *aleke dekeke* – "It is now all over" – alluded to the 1960 announcement on the radio of the coup d'état by Girmame Neway and his brother Brigadier-General Mengistu Neway. Alem Mezgebe, the then radio host, had proclaimed that the era of oppression, *aleke dekeke* – "It is now all over," – when the Neway brothers detained ministers and took key government posts under their control. Alem Mezgebe then fled into exile when Emperor Haile Selassie restored his government. The Emperor had been on a state visit in Brazil when the coup took place.

Before we even got the chance to absorb what Sewasew had just told us, our hilarious friend yelled, "Taxi!" When the taxi came to a halt, he shouted at the top of his voice, *"Hulet sew Assimba!"*

It was rush hour, and there were dozens of people at the bus station waiting for taxis and buses. To shout out at the top of one's voice to a cabbie to take two people to Assimba was utter madness. Many people by then knew the rugged terrain was the home base of EPRP's army in the province of Tigray.

"You want us get killed?" We screamed at him and jumped into the taxi. It was only after the taxi drove away that we started laughing. He was still standing and cackling at the bus stop when the taxi disappeared into the traffic.

That was how I learned about the carnage at the Derg offices.

February 4, 1977 was the day the Ethiopian revolution took a frightening turn to darkness and savagery. Mengistu Hailemariam became the undisputed, supreme dictator. He massacred seven members of the Derg, who had been called to a fake meeting at the Derg offices. It was the talk of the town that EPRP had supporters in the Derg. At least one of the two officers Sewasew mentioned was an EPRP member (That was why our friend Sewasew told Martha and me to leave town. It was rumored that EPRP had a hand in the alleged coup).

At the time, there was a move within the Derg to restructure and redistribute power that had accumulated in Mengistu's hands. Members of the Derg, including Mengistu, had approved the restructuring plan. But, apparently, Mengistu was not all that keen to let all that power slip through his fingers. He was plotting to get those people out of the way.

So he accused the slaughtered Derg members of plotting a coup d'état to oust him, and eliminated all those whose political views he believed to be "left" or "liberal." One of the slain was Brigadier-General Teferi Benti, the incumbent chair of the Derg and said to be "liberal" and "conciliatory." He had, a few days before, called for a "national reconciliation," and a "United Front," in the speech he gave at *Abyot* Square. The Derg approved his speech, but Mengistu considered it "too conciliatory" to the EPRP. EPRP had immediately rejected the call for a United Front on the grounds that democratic rights had first to be guaranteed.

"Our enemies were planning to eat us for lunch, but we had them for breakfast," Mengistu bragged at a speech he had made at Revolution Square two days later. "The revolution has moved from the defensive to the offensive," he trumpeted. He shouted slogans until the veins on his neck bulged. "Revolutionary Ethiopia or death! We will fight until the last man and the last rifle," he roared.

At the time, he was at war with the EPRP, the Eritrean Liberation Fronts in the North and the invading Somali army in the East. Once he had cleaned up the Derg, he fancied that it was time to stamp out the rest of the pests. That was the only way he could consolidate his power. When America had earlier turned down his plea for help he had turned to Russia, and was not disappointed. Russia then promptly brought its people and ammunition and paraded them at his doorstep. He not only had immeasurable power in his hands but also all the armaments he needed to wipe out an entire people.

Fidel Castro's advice to create a one-Party system was taken to heart by the new dictator. He had recently formed the *Abyotawi Seded* – Revolutionary Flame – a Party with people who had proven their loyalty to him. His monster army, *Nebelbal,* along with the *Abyot Tebaki* – Revolutionary Guard – would play a pivotal role in his "White terror will be vanquished by Red terror" campaign.

Mengistu would later in 1977 give a crushing blow to the invading Somali army, but his bitter and bloody war with the Eritrean Liberation Fronts would continue. He galvanized all his armed forces, and when that did not seem enough, boys as young as fourteen were rounded up and taken from their homes and streets and sent to war, with little or no training. Most of them perished in the wilderness.

As for EPRP, the piecemeal executions were not enough. For them, he had another plan in mind.

On March 23 1977, the Derg launched a five-day *assessa* – search. The Derg, *Meison, Nebelbal, Abyot Tebaki,* the army, and Marxist groups such as *Woz League* (Workers League) and *Malerid* (Amharic acronym for Marxist-Leninist Revolutionary Organization) all rolled their sleeves up to crack down on the common enemy – the EPRP. All the Marxist groups around the Derg, including *Meison*, had their own differences and were in one another's way, but what united them was hatred of the EPRP.

Driving became illegal within certain hours. House-to-house searches were conducted to disarm the EPRP. Many of its members and supporters were thrown into jail or killed. Anyone suspected of "counter-revolutionary" activity was subject to *netsa ermeja* and could be shot by cadres and *Abyot Tebakis* with impunity.

Meison and EPRP had reached the zenith of their enmity. Even siblings sought one another out for blood. *Meison*, formerly on the receiving end of EPRP bullets, struck with a vindictive zeal.

The table was turned.

Warnings about the *assessa* had been disseminated in the League structure to make the necessary precautions. The Youth League had boldly declared its existence at the beginning of the month under the name The Ethiopian Revolutionary Youth League, amid an impending clampdown. Gutsy League members had braved *Abyot Tebakis'* bullets and distributed pamphlets, littered walls and hoisted banners.

I spent the *assessa* eve at the apartment in Piassa. I went to bed wondering where I would be spending the next five days. An idea popped into my head in the middle of the night. I woke up around five in the morning, took a shower and left. I took a cab to the TB Centre. I figured a hospital would be the last place to be searched, and I could at least spend the first day of the *assessa* there.

Sitting on a bench in the garden, I was amazed by the sheer number of people suffering from TB. Some of them were wasted away to skin and bones. I looked back at the days I suffered, which I had been so ill at ease talking about. I had completely forgotten about it. I had stopped taking medication long ago. "There are people amidst you who pretend to be patients," I suddenly heard a male voice say over the megaphone, around eleven o'clock. *Oh my God! I thought I was being smart hiding in a hospital!*

The voice continued, "They pretend to help the sick or show them around. They target especially the very ill and those from the countryside. Beware of them. They are pickpockets!"

I laughed, relieved.

I didn't have breakfast when I left the apartment. I was hungry but didn't feel like buying food in the compound. The whole place had an ominous feel to it. I wanted to leave but I had to choose between the sinister place and jail and or even death. I emerged out of my sanctuary around quarter to six in the evening. The street was deserted and there was no taxi in sight. After what seemed like time without end, I found one that would take me only as far as *Mercato*.

The usually bustling place was abandoned. Only a handful of people scurried around mostly *Nebelbal* and soldiers. I tried to talk the cabbie into taking me to Piassa, offering to pay more. I got off when he told me one more time he couldn't. While I was scampering and anxiously looking for a taxi, I saw two soldiers advancing toward me. I accelerated my speed. They caught up and I heard one of them shout, "Halt!"

I couldn't pretend I didn't hear him, so I stopped. "Your identification card," one of them said with an air of authority. I didn't want to bring my fake *Kebele* ID with me, for all practical purposes. I fished my university ID out of my purse and handed it to him with a confidence that matched his authoritative posture.

The card had been washed several times, stuck in my pocket; it had lost its color and had become cloth like. "You can go!" he said, after glancing at it for less than a second. I knew he did not read English, or he would have known it had expired at the end of December of the previous year. I flagged a taxi and hopped in. I had a good laugh with my friends at the Piassa apartment when I told them where I had spent the day.

On the second day of the *assessa*, I heard that EPRP Central Committee and Politburo member Tesfaye Debessay had jumped to his death from Kidane Beyene Building, near Ambassador Theatre, when *Kebele* and *Meison* cadres were chasing him. A wave of shock went through the Party and the League. Tesfaye was chair of the Central Committee and had a PhD in philosophy. He had come back from Europe to take part in the revolution.

That day, I went to my cousin Elsa's around six-thirty in the evening. Days before the *assessa*, I went there to spend the night and saw a man sitting on the couch in the living room. I instinctively knew he was a Party member. I made friends with him easily and since that day, I sat and talked with him whenever I went there. I became his window to the outside world. At times, people came, took him in a car, and brought him back. He had an infirmity of his legs and I often wondered how he could survive those horrible conditions with those legs. I wondered if he was still there.

He was not. My cousin sadly told me that he had been killed trying to leave town before the *assessa*. I learned that his name was Nega Ayele. He was a university lecturer in the department of

Political Science and had co-authored a book, *Class and* Revo*lution in Ethiopia*, with John Markakis (the Greek Social Scientist and lecturer at Haile Selassie I University). Nega was killed with Dr. William Hestings Morton, an Englishman (a lecturer at Addis Ababa University – Haile Selassie University was renamed Addis Ababa University by the Derg), who drove the car. They had been heading to Langano (a resort area) to avoid the search but returned when they heard shots. They were gunned down by *Abyot Tebakis*. Party Central Committee member Yohannes Berhane and Party member Melaku Markos were also killed that day.

The death of Nega and other Party members sent a chill up my spine.

Ououta, Yowling, Committees were set up by the Youth League to counter the *assessa*. Mothers yowled at night and youngsters broke streetlights when soldiers and *Abyot Tebakis* raided homes. This was meant to mobilize the people against the *assessa* and imprisonment and killing of the young by the Derg. The yowling led to chaos and the arrest and murder of even more youngsters. The *assessa* ended after the detention of hundreds and the death of many EPRP members.

Jail was coming closer to home. I hadn't seen Sara since she came out of prison. She had been arrested at a meeting held at the university campus over a month ago. She was released but was arrested again, this time for a longer period. She, Azeb, and I used to go to Kidist's house for lunch, when running EPRP errands. We used to say, "Let's go to Kidist's and have a balanced diet." It had been a while since we had done that and since I saw Sara and Kidist.

It was sometime in April. I had an appointment with Tito in front of the old Post Office Building. I saw him coming up, smiling, and then turning away and going back down the street. I was wondering why he did that when someone tugged at my elbow. I turned and saw Getachew!

I was happy to see him.

He had his usual camouflage: the white rimmed reading glasses and the berretta hat. He wore khaki pants, a light blue shirt and a khaki jacket. There was a taxi beside him and the door was open. He spoke rapidly with a buoyant smile, "Tomorrow, same place, same time" and dived into the taxi.

I had desperately wanted to hear from him. All I could think of at the time was him. *Is he still alive? How is he faring? Did he get a proper shelter? Did he leave town?* The questions replayed in my head. Every time I heard somebody had died or had been arrested, I quivered, fearing that it might be him.

I had recently heard that Berhanemeskel had gone to Merhabete (in Shoa) and had started an armed struggle. *Has Getachew gone with him? Anja*s are the recent enemies the Party has created. The war with them was escalating by the day. I have had this ominous feeling that the Party might hurt Getachew. It was quite a relief for me to see him again.

I strode down the street to meet Tito who was waiting for me at the far end of the building. It was then that I understood why Tito turned back. It was because he saw Getachew. I met Getachew the next day in front of the hotel. I knew he was not going to tell me how and where he had spent the *assessa*.

But his childhood friend, Mesfin, told me years later, "Let me tell you about Getachew. After he was expelled from the Central Committee and during the first *assessa*, they sent me to ask him if he wanted a shelter...that is, to go out of town. He said to me, 'I cannot ask kids to throw Molotov cocktails and yowl at night and then go out of town to save my skin. I am not going anywhere.'"

Getachew did not ask anyone to throw Molotov cocktails but took responsibility for others. That was exactly who he was.

"I was worried about you too. Where were you during the *assessa?*" he asked when I told him that I was worried about him. He burst out laughing when he learned where I had spent the first day.

"Getachew....I heard the comrade is gone," I said, referring to Berhanemeskel. We were sitting side by side on the couch.

"I am sure you did."

"Why didn't you go?"

"Why would I go?"

"I don't know. I thought...actually...I was hoping you would."

"I have a lot of respect and admiration for the comrade. We share common ideas. But I see no reason for me to go."

"Why don't you join him? Maybe it is better if you did?" I suggested.

"Why? Why do you say that?"

"I don't know. I fear for you. I have a feeling *they* might hurt you," I told him, sighing heavily.

The waiter knocked at the door and Getachew leapt to his feet and opened it for him. The waiter brought our order and placed it on the table and left. Getachew locked the door, whirled around and said, "What did you say again?" He stood there a look of surprise written all over his face.

"I said... I fear for you. They might hurt you. You know."

He came back and sat beside me. "We have disagreements, without a doubt, but that doesn't mean they are going to hurt me. Why would they want to hurt me, anyway? We are comrades! Comrades who fought side by side for so long."

I was looking for a way to explain my forebodings to him but I felt embarrassed at what I said, but at the same time, I had this vehement urge to say it. I forewarned, "I don't know why, but I have this unsettling feeling…a feeling…that *they* might hurt you."

"No, they are not going to hurt me. Don't worry. Right now, two or three individuals are leading the Party. They are the ones who make decisions. Yes,…it has come to that. Some of our comrades in the CC have gone abroad, some have died, some have gone to Assimba and the comrade and I have been expelled. There is no Party leadership to speak of."

I looked at how he had changed. He looked even more haggard. A feeling of frustration and fear started to compound in me.

He went on, "If you ask me, it is the League that is providing leadership to the revolution at this point. The comrades still don't want to call a meeting of congress. That would have been the solution. I believe we will be able to iron out our differences once a congress is called. As it is, the comrades are not willing to do anything to rectify the situation. They still want to hang onto their ideas, even if they are witnessing the death of hundreds of our members. I just wonder how much blood will be spilled before they realize their mistakes."

I wondered if he was naïve or if I was being bad for suspecting my comrades of foul play. He still believed that they would "iron out" their differences, after all what he had been through. His positive attitude amazed me. I was moved by his innocence. Tears came to my eyes. *Why does he have to suffer so much? All the things he and Berhanemeskel said have come true. The Party is witnessing the death and imprisonment of so many members and supporters. What went wrong in the Party? It was so beautiful. Things have become murky and ugly. I want him to go! How am I*

going to make him change his mind? Why should I think badly of
the comrades when he trusts them?

The thoughts reeled through my head.

"How long is this going to go on? You have changed so
much. You have lost so much weight. How long are they going to
keep you this way?" I managed to say without looking at him. My
eyes were wet and I didn't want him to see them. He stared at me,
smiling, and I had to look up. He must have seen my tears. He took
my hand in his. "It is okay. We will work it out," he tried to put my
mind to rest. But I was not to be easily reassured. We stayed up late
talking and went to bed.

When I woke up in the morning, I felt this strong urge to
insist that he should go. I felt I had to press him to go away. I
wanted to tell him what I had heard at a recent IZ meeting, but was
afraid. *How can I say something like that about the Party? Am I*
going to defile its name? Should I tell him or shouldn't I? Would it
have any bearing on his decision? "The other day, I heard one of
the comrades say at an IZ meeting that this comrade interrogated a
former comrade, accused of being *Anja.* He said he put out
cigarettes on him, when interrogating him. I was staggered when I
heard that. I never thought we could do something like that. That is
why I insist you should go."

I got it off my chest.

"I don't want you to worry too much about me," he said,
without batting an eye. He was tying his shoelaces. He stood up and
put his jacket on. "I will be fine," he tried to reassure me again and
went on, "I actually worry about you. Often, I shudder when I think
about what might happen to you."

What did he think about the cigarette burning? Why doesn't
he listen? Why doesn't he see the danger? How can he not sense it
even when I can? There was no ground for my fear. It was just a

hunch based on what was going on against *Anja*s. If *Anja*s were blamed for everything that had gone awry in the Party, and if Getachew and Berhanemeskel were the "creators" of *Anja*, then it was easy to glean for me that the Party may turn against them with vengeance. I understood that much. *How could he not?* "I would have loved if you had gone somewhere," I entreated him. When he did not respond, I asked, "How are we going to meet again, anyway?"

"We will find a way. I haven't been able to send you a note through the comrades. I will try to find a way. The problem is neither of us has a permanent address. Don't worry. We will find a way," he said, smiling and patting on my shoulder.

We came out to the street and flagged a taxi. He looked me in the eye and told me he would send me a note soon and got into the taxi. My heart gave a violent leap. Something told me I was not going to see him ever. I wanted to shout and beg him to go somewhere but the words would not come out. Something choked my throat. The taxi moved and he waved at me smiling.

I did not wave back.

I stood there watching the taxi disappear through the mist of the tears in my eyes. I thought about my premonition. *Why am I feeling this way? It is the same feeling that I had when I saw my brother and Semegne for the very last time!* Tears trickled down my cheeks.

The first time I had a premonition was when I went with my mother to visit a relative at the hospital when I was in grade seven. The lady was sitting up in the bed when my mother and I got up to go. I gave the woman one more look before we left and my heart jumped. Something told me she was going to die. She died the next day.

Before Getachew's expulsion from the Party CC, I always worried that the Derg might kill him. After his expulsion, I feared that the Party would somehow hurt him. I kept thinking about what might happen to him. In as much as I didn't want the Party to hurt him, the very idea of having these thoughts about the Party troubled me. Why am I having these thoughts about the Party that I love so much? I kept asking myself.

Three days later, I was sitting in the café in Arat Kilo with Aklilu. He looked me straight in the eye. He had a strange countenance. I could hear my heart suddenly start pounding. I sensed there was something wrong. "Do you know where the comrade is?" he asked after a brief silence. I knew he was referring to Getachew.

"I don't know. You know I have no access to him. Wasn't it through you he sent me notes? I met him three days ago and that was by sheer accident. Why did you ask, anyway? Is he okay?" I could feel alarm choking my throat.

"Well...*they* couldn't find him. *They* don't know where he is. I thought you might know."

My heart quivered at the idea the Party might do something grave to him. I could barely talk. "I don't," I managed to say.

"In case you find out, let me know," he said.

I said nothing further. My tea was sitting on the table untouched. I could not stay a minute longer after that. I hailed a taxi and went to the apartment in Piassa, tears in my eyes. I didn't know what to think. I hoped he had joined Berhanemeskel in Merhabete. I felt relief surging in me. *Maybe that is where he is!* I knew better than that. He had told me only three days ago that he wouldn't go. Besides, if he thought of doing anything like that, I was confident that he would take me with him. *Where is he? Is he in jail?* He was in danger on both sides: the Derg and the Party. I was paralyzed with fear. I didn't know what to think nor who to ask about him or where to look for him. I met Azeb the next day. She looked distraught.

"I saw the comrade last night at the Casanchis house. The Party has detained him. A squad is guarding him. I was stunned to see him," she said tears in her eyes.

I couldn't believe my ears. "Getachew is detained by the Party? A squad is guarding him? What are you talking about?"

"Yes, I saw him. I saw him last night," she said.

I told her what Aklilu had said to me the day before. "I knew *they* would do something like that to him. I asked him to go away, to go somewhere... But he didn't listen," I poured out my frustration.

"What is going on in the Party? Where is this leading us?" We said to each other.

We were perplexed.

"I heard that the comrade has been detained by the Party," I told Aklilu when I saw him later that day.

"I know."

"You know? Why did you ask me his whereabouts if you knew?"

"I wanted to find out if you knew."

My heart sank. Aklilu is a nice person. We had become friends ever since we have met. We met twice a day but we had nothing in particular to do. I often wondered why we met. It was futile to try to get anything out of him about Getachew.

Azeb told me the next time I saw her that Getachew was no longer at the Casanchis house. That was bad news. She could have brought news about him had he stayed there. I was desperate. I wondered what his fate might be. I often imagined him guarded by a squad. I missed the good-natured man whom I'd been with for four and a half years. I had never been with a man that long. I had become attached to him. Above all, I looked up to him. These and other thoughts racked my brain and tormented my soul but I continued my work with the same zeal and commitment.

It was just before the second round of *assessa* started. Azeb and I went to the Piassa apartment one day around mid-morning. It was safer to be there than being in a café. Besides, we didn't have money so we had to stay there until our appointments. We found Askale Nega chatting with Meskerem. The latter was one of my friends at the Piassa apartment. Asku was our year-mate at the university and an EPRP member. I had never worked with her but had crossed paths with her in back alleys. I was toying with the zipper on my pouch, while we talked. The pouch fell and hundreds of safety pins were scattered on the parquet floor. Azeb, Asku and I scrambled to pick them up. We used the pins to hoist banners. I was supposed to pass them on to my Zonal Committee members later that day.

Meskerem was bewildered. We had laughed when she said earlier, "Look at Hiwot's cheeks. They are red like ripe tomatoes. She roams every day in the sun. She is always on the road. Asku...you will end up having red cheeks like her...you too...Azeb."

She was concerned about us getting red cheeks. We worried about ducking bullets.

"What are you going to do with all those safety pins?" She was puzzled.

I did not respond.

I was the only one amongst my Harar friends who was politically involved. Even though I had never said I was an EPRP member, they knew I was somehow involved with the organization.

Martha always begged me to tell her "frankly" if I was a member. I always told her that I was a "sympathizer."

My friends made all kinds of jokes about my EPRP activities and me. Meskerem always said to me, "When EPRP seizes power; I know they are going to make you Minister of Foreign Affairs. I beg you to give me a passport so that I can leave the country."

One day, Kidan, one of my friends living in the apartment, was sitting by the window in the living room. I was chatting with the other girls, when she asked me to come over. I ran to look out the window. "Look...Look," she cried. "That is what you want to turn us into." I looked down the street and roared with laughter. I saw four Chinese men sauntering in their drab blue uniform Another day, Martha said, "I hate revolution. I want to leave this country and go to another one."

I asked, "What if a revolution breaks out there?"

"Then I will go elsewhere. By the time I go around the world, I will get old and die." That was how much my friends at the Piassa apartment hated revolution and politics.

After the safety pin incident, Azeb and I left the apartment and agreed to meet in the evening. She went her way and I went mine. Azeb said she might find us a shelter for that night. She showed up late, as usual. We met in *Mercato* in front of Leul Mekonen School. We had had nothing to eat all day and we were desperately hungry. We had only one birr and thirty-five cents between us. We could only spend thirty-five cents on food. The rest was our taxi fare for the next day.

The 75 birr stipend given to us by the League was spent mainly on transportation, as we constantly moved from one appointment to another. The substantial financial support for me came from my cousin Elsa. I couldn't ask my sister Almaz for money after I ran away from home, even though she always asked after me and even came to the Piassa apartment to look for me. Martha also gave me money for transportation now and then. As for a place to stay, the door to the apartment was always open for me. There was also my cousin ever ready to have me over. She was married by then and had a baby.

Azeb said she knew a place where we could buy food for thirty-five cents. We zigzagged through the area looking for it. We couldn't find it. I became nervous. It was dark and the area was one of the breeding grounds of League members and the epicenter of EPRP activities. The *Abyot Tebakis* and the secret service closely watched it. I didn't know my way around *Mercato*. Almost all of my appointments were in the *Adarash* and they were with Aklilu.

"You don't know where the place is?" I asked impatiently.

"Of course I do. It is just I couldn't find it. It's got to be around here… somewhere."

"I hope you won't get us arrested or shot. I think we should go to the shelter. Forget about the thirty-five cent meal," I lamented.

After so many twists and turns, we finally found it. The place was a dungeon. The people sitting in the semi-dark room were apparently beggars or homeless people. We ordered *injera* with split pea sauce. The food did not look palatable. It was even worse when I tasted it. The portion was so small it did not even appease our ferocious hunger. Afterwards, we went to the shelter, which was not very far from the eatery. It was a tiny, dimly lit room with a dirt floor. There was nothing but a dirty straw mattress and a wooden box. The place was swarming with bugs.

"I am not going to sleep on the mattress," I declared.

"Where are you going to sleep, then?" Azeb asked, looking at me in surprise.

"On the box," I said, pointing to the wooden box.

"When are you going to learn?"

"Learn what? First, the mattress is too small. Second, it is obviously infested with bugs. They are already all over my legs," I said, bending down to scratch my leg.

Azeb lay down on the mattress, giving me her back and putting her sweater on her shoulder. "Let's sleep now. I have to get up early in the morning," she said after a pause.

"I have a meeting at seven o'clock. I have to get up early to go to the apartment, shower and change."

"I have a meeting too. I have to go first to Casanchis to take a shower."

I used my purse for a pillow and lay down on the box. Azeb was tossing, turning and scratching. I felt sorry for her. I too was scratching. The wooden box was not comfortable either but I couldn't say anything after refusing to sleep on the mattress. The cracks on the door and the mud wall were so large one could see what was going on outside. I stared through a crease, unable to sleep. Just when I was about to drift off, I felt a violent cramp in my stomach. I sat up to figure out what was wrong with me. Suddenly, I felt an intense urge to go to the toilet. I also wanted to throw up. "Azeb! Azeb!"

"What?"

"I am sick. I am going to throw up. I think I'm having diarrhea too."

"*Sebebegna*. That is why I hate to go with you anywhere."

"What are you talking about? Is it my fault that I am sick? It is your thirty-five cent food that made me sick!"

She laughed. "I don't even know where the latrine is. I made a grave mistake bringing you here, anyway."

My head spun and I barely heard what she was saying. "Can you take me or not? I am going to throw up right here!"

She got up reluctantly and helped me get up from the box. We went out to look for the latrine. We were heading toward where we thought it might be when we saw four *Abyot Tebakis*. They were conducting their night patrol. We found the latrine but I was too scared I might slip into the pit. It was dark and I couldn't see the hole. When I was done, we came back and halfway through I said to her, "We've got to go back."

She was indignant. "You will get us killed tonight. Look how they are watching us. They will know we are not from around here if we hang around too long."

I didn't care. I was too ill to worry about them. "Can you please take me back?"

"She is going to get us killed tonight!"

We had to go back and forth four or five times, closely watched by the *Abyot Tebakis*. The only reason they didn't stop us was, I believe, it was obvious that I was in distress. Finally, I curled on the box and drifted into sleep. I was too sick to get up in the morning. I dragged myself out and we took a taxi as far as Piassa. I got off in front of Cinema Ethiopia and she continued her ride to Casanchis.

I figured I might sleep over at Aster's (Martha's older sister) that night. I didn't bother to go to Martha and friends' apartment on the third-floor. Around midnight, the doorbell rang. Aster and her husband Demissie and I woke up. I was sleeping on the couch in the living room and went to the bedroom. The little boy was still sleeping. The bell rang incessantly. We didn't know what to do. Aster and Demissie suspected it was the secret service looking for me. Who else would ring the bell after midnight when a strict curfew was in effect?

Demissie struck upon an ingenious idea: send me down the building by a rope through the window. They lived on the second-floor. He said he could braid a rope out of their bed sheets. I looked at the snow-white linen. I held a smile in check. I went over and drew the curtain and saw three *Abyot Tebakis* in front of Omar Khayyam restaurant, their Kalashnikovs slung over their shoulders. I saw myself shot in mid-air and plunge to my death down the building and my body sprawled in front of Gebre Tensay Pastry Shop, where I had my daily cream horn fix. "There is no way I can do that," I said. I wanted to burst into a loud laughter.

The bell kept ringing. They would definitely break in if no one answered the door. The couple and I stood in the bedroom trying to come up with a sensible escape plan. They wanted to hide me under the bed or in the armoire. But those were places the *Abyot Tebakis* and secret service first searched. Finally, Demissie decided to see who was at the door through the bathroom window, which faced the elevator. But there was full moon and whoever was at the door could see him. He tiptoed to the bathroom, while Aster and I were watching him in silence. I thought he would never get there watching him drag his long legs. Finally, he reached the window and leaned over to the side, lowering his head to have a glimpse of who was at the door.

The doorbell suddenly ceased ringing and Demissie saw Martha and Mahlet hopping into the elevator. He shook his head and grinned. Relieved we went back to bed. The next morning, I went to the third-floor to find out what the girls were ringing the bell for after midnight. They were angry with Aster and Demissie for not answering the door. They had no idea I was there. They had a visitor and had come to borrow a mattress!

The incident led me to believe that I really needed a shelter. I didn't like the idea of subjecting my friends to what Aster and her husband had gone through that night.

Not long after that, Tito found me a shelter at a *Kebele* adjacent the Derg office. The owner of the house was a teacher whose name I never learned. The infamous Solomon, who had killed and imprisoned a squadron of youth, was the cadre of the *Kebele*. He rambled through the *Kebele* with a machine gun in his hands and often stopped people and searched them. He even shook down women's baskets when they came from the market.

One night, I was on my way home when I saw this tall man leaving a kiosk, located off the street. He was carrying a machine gun in his hands. I knew it was Solomon. He never liked people behind him. We were the only ones walking in the street. I didn't want that machine gun aimed at me so I ran down to the kiosk to avoid him.

"Weird guy!" the shopkeeper said when I asked for chewing gum. I pretended I didn't hear him. I paid for the gum and looked in the direction Solomon was heading. He had disappeared in the dark but I lingered behind, just in case. I didn't want him to ambush me. Thanks to God, I got home safely.

All the youngsters in the *Kebele* had left home. Solomon once called a *Kebele* meeting. These meetings were mandatory. Anyone who did not show up was labeled "counter-revolutionary" or *adhari* – reactionary – if the person was well-to-do. People were also punished in various ways for not attending the much-hated meetings. At the gathering, Solomon asked the people to hand in EPRP members. He told them that it was easy to identify them. "You will find them at bus stations pretending to read newspapers, telling the time, scratching the tip of their noses. In a café, they order either tea or coffee. They whisper amongst themselves. They look shabby - girls with Afros, *netelas* and sneakers, and boys with worn-out jeans and dirty sneakers."

That was largely an accurate description of EPRP members. What was interesting was that he was asking parents to hand in their own children! The Derg later executed him. That was how the Derg paid its gratitude to its zealots.

But it saved its monstrous brutality for EPRP members and its supporters.

And behold, a great wind came from across the wilderness and struck the
four corners of the house, and it fell on the young people and they died...
     -Job *1:19, New American Standard Bible*

On the eve of May Day, April 30, 1977, the Derg committed the
most atrocious crime in Addis. It was a Saturday afternoon, and the
Youth League had organized small demonstrations in each *Kebele*.
By six o'clock, hundreds of youth had been killed and many more
arrested.

That night, I was at my shelter when *Abyot Tebakis* went
door-to-door, searching and arresting more youth. A youngster from
the neighborhood, the teacher who gave me the shelter and I were
sitting at home when we heard their footsteps. The house was tiny,
with two-rooms but no back door. Since there was no route to
escape, we awaited our fate in death-like silence. The *Abyot Tebakis*
would definitely take away the young man and me, should they
come in. Finally, we heard them knocking at the house next to ours.
We waited in silence. They skipped our house. We were spared
because the teacher was a *Kebele* official.

The entire city was gripped with shock by what had
happened that evening.

The next day, I left home early for a short IZ meeting. We
talked about the tragedy and all Zones were asked to bring the tally
of the dead on Monday. When I came back home that night, I heard
the wailing of a woman next door. I learned that she'd been looking
for her missing son since the previous night. He was neither among
the dead nor among those in prison. Like hundreds of parents, this
woman has been scouring the city night and day to find her son.

Parents who went to the hospital to claim the bodies of their
dead children were asked to pay 120.00 birr for the bullets wasted
on their sons and daughters.

The level of atrocity was unfathomable.

We, IZ members, were busy tallying the number of the dead on the afternoon of May Day. When I returned home in the evening, I saw women coming in and going out of the compound next door. I knew the boy was dead because the women looked solemn, wearing their *netelas* upside down. I learned that the family dog had been howling all night, and when they let him off the leash the next day, he ran into the hedge surrounding the house. When they followed him, they found the boy's body stuck in the hedge. Nobody knew what time the body had been shoved into the hedge. It might have been the previous night or early in the morning. The body must have been there when I left in the morning.

It was mind-numbing.

The IZ met Monday morning. All Zone representatives submitted the number of the dead in their respective Zones. Five-hundred youth have been slain in less than two hours!

"We are the only people in the entire world who know the number of the dead," the Party IZ representative said.

One family lost five children in one *Kebele*, four of their own and the uncle of the four kids, who was young himself. Children as young as ten and twelve were killed that day. Wollo Sefer, the poorest neighborhood in Bole, which was also in my Zone, suffered the highest causalities in the Zone. *Mercato*, known for its dense youth population and youth militancy, suffered the highest number of fatalities in Addis. The five-hundred did not include the number of those killed after that fateful day. Hundreds had ended up in jail and many more on death row during the house-to-house searches that took place that night and in the days following.

The second round of the *assessa* started in May. The joint effort to wipe out enemy number one, the Party, was gaining momentum.

Firing squads inundated the city. Targeted raids took place; hundreds and thousands of young people and others were thrown into jail, and hundreds more killed. The Derg unleashed its bloodthirsty force in frenzy. *Meison* was still on the offensive, avenging the blood of its members spilled by the EPRP. Its vendetta knew no bounds.

The streets of Addis and other major cities turned red with blood.

I started working in the Field Committee which facilitated the sending of members to the army in Assimba. We had to provide money and contact names for members on a daily basis. The comrades had left home and had no place to stay, as members and supporters were "exposed." The number of members that needed to be sent to Assimba became overwhelming, a logistical as well as a financial nightmare. Some members spent nights under bridges, exposing themselves to danger. Many of the members sent to Assimba did not even make it. They were heard of no more.

Cafés became dangerous, as more and more were identified as EPRP hang outs. I had to meet Tito at Noh café one morning, just before our seven o'clock meeting. When I got there, the door, which normally opened at six in the morning, was closed. I wondered if Tito had already been there and left. I looked around. He was nowhere in sight. I waited for a few minutes and went to the meeting. I found him there.

"Sorry! I had no way of informing you of what had happened."

"What happened?"

"The cashier at Noh was taken away this morning just after they opened the door. They shot him several times. But they said he was still alive when they took him away."

"No wonder the place was closed."

"I got there a few minutes after they left. I couldn't wait."

Another day, I went to Lidet Biskut Bet, the café and pastry shop at Teklehaimanot Square. The place was always jam-packed with League members. One of the servers always greeted me enthusiastically; as soon as he saw me coming in he would yell, "Tea for one!" He might be serving customers or simply standing, tray tucked under his arm. When I looked in the direction of the voice, he would wink at me and get me tea as soon as I sat down. When I came in that day, he did not shout his usual, "Tea for one!" He came to my table with a somber face.

"You should leave quickly. They came in about fifteen minutes ago and took one of the young people. I have seen the guy with you before. That is why this place is empty."

That was when I noticed that the place was indeed deserted and eerily quiet. There were only a few older people. "What did he look like?"

"He is of medium-height. He was sitting over there," he said, pointing to a table in the corner. "A young man came in and sat with him for a few minutes and then left. Just after, men in civilian clothes came in and took your friend away. Please leave. We are alerting all."

I bolted from the pastry shop and took a cab. I wasn't sure who the person was that was taken. I feared it might be the Zonal Committee member I went to meet. I later found out that it was him. I had missed jail by a few minutes.

Luck was what kept us alive, for the most part. As the hunt for EPRP members reached a peak, meeting places became hard to come by. The IZ often scrambled to get one. We went to a house, once, for a day meeting, around seven in the morning. It was locked by a padlock. There had been a raid the previous night; some members had been taken away. If the soldiers had still been there, the IZ would have landed in jail. A few days later, the soldiers raided another house a few minutes after we had left. Another five minutes, and we would have been caught with incriminating materials.

"Let's go to the *Ij meschia*," we often said when we ran out of meeting places. *Ij meschia* – a place where you surrender – was a tiny, dark, one-room mud house in Gola Mikael. The *Kebele* knew it was as an EPRP nest. Going there amounted to surrendering.

Ij meschia had a tiny bed and a chair. Most IZ members sat on the bed when having a meeting. Tito sat on the chair. There was always a soft knock on the door around noon. Tito opened it halfway and a dark wrinkled woman's hand passed on a tray to him. Without fail, there was one coal black *injera* with a handful of yellowish macaroni in the middle of the tray. That was lunch for five people, four men and a woman. The yellowish macaroni reminded me of the *Pasty Bet* my friends and I used to go to during our university days.

Once, the IZ found a meeting place on the second or third-floor of a building just above Omar Khayyam Restaurant in Piassa. In the middle of the meeting, we heard men's voices and footsteps in the hallway. A deafening silence fell over the room. We scrambled to stow away our papers. The parquet floor in the hallway squeaked much louder as the footsteps came closer and closer. We stared at one another. The lone escape route in the house was the tiny window facing my friends' apartment. The only chance of getting away would have been jumping two or three stories down through the tiny window. That meant hitting the ground beside Omar Khayyam and being greeted by the bullets of the soldiers guarding the Electric and Power Authority Building, which is just across the street. There were also *Abyot Tebakis* and soldiers, rifles flung over their shoulders, pacing up and down the neighborhood on the lookout for a kill, not to mention soldiers on machine gun-mounted patrol cars.

There was nothing we could do but wait.

We heard two men talking, but we couldn't figure out what they were saying. We then heard papers shuffling and the men walking away. We waited in silence until the sound of their footsteps died away. We wondered if we should leave or carry on with the meeting. We figured they wouldn't come back so we decided to stay. We finished our meeting around five in the afternoon. When we opened the door, it was sealed with a paper with a *Kebele* seal. Tito bent down to read it. It was an eviction notice.

The tenant was in rent arrears of two months!

It was time for me to leave the shelter at Solomon's *Kebele*. Tito told me that they had found me another around Kidist Mariam in the house of one of the League CC members, Gezahegn. Gezahegn's mother lived with her three daughters, two of whom were in their mid-teens and the youngest of whom was six years old.

Etiye, as I called Gezahegn's mother, told her neighbors that I was her oldest daughter from a previous marriage. She said I had come from Arsi where I lived with my father. Gebeyehu Dagne, a League CC member, used to come there to play cards. I thought he was trying to lighten up the kids' and their mother's lives. *Etiye* was always worried about Gezahegn, whom I had never met. He had left home some time ago. It was safer to be there than at Solomon's *Kebele*. But my heart was somewhere else. I was worried about Getachew.

Father, forgive them; for they do not know what they are doing.
      -Luke 23:34, *New American Standard Bible*

*Anja*s became the object of the Party's fury. In the same way the Biblical Jewish high priest transferred the sins of the community to the scapegoat on the Day of Atonement (the day Jewish people made atonement for the sins of Israel), the high priests of the revolution transferred their sins to the *Anja*s. *Anja*s, many of whom were falsely accused, became responsible for all that had gone wrong in the Party. In the same way Getachew and Berhanemeskel were driven out of the Party Central Committee, and in the same way the scapegoat was chased away and banished from the Jewish community, *Anja*s were tracked down and killed. The most prominent witch-hunt was conducted against former *Abyot* founders and members.

Their own comrades shot them dead at night or in broad daylight.

Abiyu Ersamo, one of the founding members of *Abyot*, and other *Abyot* members, such as Endreas Mikael and Bekri Mohamed were gunned down after Getachew was detained. Getachew Assefa was never heard of after he went to North Shoa with a Politburo member.

EPRP went on rampage to banish *Anja*s from the face of the Earth. The rank-and-file did not know the political differences that precipitated the purging of Getachew and Berhanemeskel from the Politburo and Central Committee of the Party. What most of them "knew" or rather were told, was that *Anja*s wanted to work with the Derg, that they wanted to break up the unity of the Party and that they denounced members to the secret service.

The threat of or even the existence of *Anja*s was exaggerated.

At a time when morale had gone down and members gave in easily to interrogation, *Anja*s became responsible for every arrest and execution. They became enemies that had to be severely dealt with. In some *Kebeles,* members distributed leaflets with names of suspected *Anja*s, exposing them to danger. They did not realize the implications of their actions. But they did it, anyway. They were blindly and readily following whatever was filtered down to them.

The scapegoating of *Anja*s served a purpose. It diverted the attention of members from the mistakes of the Party leaders who shifted responsibility from themselves to *Anjas*. The hatred against *Anjas* became a unifying factor, even more than the hatred of *Meison*.

Many *Anja*s, chased by Party and League squads, were forced to surrender to the authorities, hoping for mercy. Some of them gave up people and information. They were either imprisoned or executed for their "trouble." Others joined the various Marxist groups surrounding the Derg, such as *Woz League* and *Malerid,* to save their lives. These individuals were not even in the top ranks of the Party, who enjoyed privileged information about the Party or the League.

It was years later that Nebiyu Aynalem, a former EPRP member, told me about the genesis of *Anja*. "The Politburo removed Getachew from the committee," he said. "There was no due process. They just decided that he should not attend their meetings. The CC elects Politburo members but they expelled him, anyway. They expelled Berhanemeskel at the same meeting. They had asked me to give shelter to Berhanemeskel two months prior to his expulsion from the CC. I did not know he was the same Berhanemeskel Redda at the time. I was working in the Addis Ababa Party IZ Committee representing Zone One. Berhanemeskel and I often shared our concerns about the armed struggle staged by the Party in the cities. One day, he confided in me that there were comrades who shared our concerns and that we should meet them. 'We have to save the Party,' he said. So the six of us, that is, Berhanemeskel Redda, Getachew Maru, Getachew Assefa, Abiyu Ersamo, Bekri and I met one day. We had a discussion and an argument all night. That was how I got to meet Getachew Maru. I never knew him personally. Getachew Maru had a resolute position on urban armed struggle. He was saying, 'All this bloodshed is not necessary. It is adventurous. But it can be rectified.'"

"We met again the following week," went on Nebiyu. "At the meeting Berhanemeskel said, 'The existing leadership is illegal. It has no legitimacy. Let's assume the leadership until congress is called.' Getachew Maru said, 'Are you crazy? We cannot create a parallel leadership behind the comrades. This will hurt the Party. It will hurt comrades. Comrades have made a mistake. We should give them counsel not hurt the Party. We cannot endanger the Party.' Abiyu said, 'We can go to Wolayita. There is an area that I know of and we can negotiate from there.' Bekri said, 'I got contact with defense committee members. We can take the ammunitions to Wolayita.'"

"An argument ensued over this," Nebiyu continued. "The three of us, that is Getachew Maru, Getachew Assefa and I said we shouldn't do that. 'As it is, the Party does not have adequate arms to defend itself; we cannot expose it to greater danger. What we can and should do is give advice to the comrades.' I was tired, finally. Around two or three in the morning, I said to them, 'I'm an EPRP member. I am going to report to the Party that we had this meeting. I'm out of it.' Bekri said to me, 'You can't get out of it. They are not going to let you get away with it, anyway.' I went to bed. They went on with their discussion and voted on it around four in the morning."

"On one side stood Berhanemeskel, Abiyu and Bekri, and on the other Getachew Assefa and Getachew Maru," went on Nebiyu. "The next day I told Berhanu Ejigu, my contact person, what had happened. They asked me to submit a formal report. I told them everything…who said what. They expelled me from the IZ. Zeru Kishen told them to let me stay. 'It might look like elimination,' he said. However, Girmachew Lemma said, 'How can we work with such an opportunist?' Berhanu Ejigu took the same position. So I was expelled on the grounds that I was sabotaging the urban armed struggle."

Zeru Kishen was a member of the Party Central Committee and Berhanu Ejigu that of the Addis Ababa Party IZ.

"Abiyu Ersamo, Endreas and Bekri started their own activities," continued Nebiyu. "Getachew Assefa and Getachew Maru maintained their contact with the Party. The Party killed Bekri, Abiyu and Endreas sometime in April. In the same month, they asked Getachew Maru to come to Hayahulet Mazoria and detained him."

Getachew's friend, Shimeles Retta, told me that, all of them that is, Berhanemeskel Redda, Abiyu Ersamo, Endreas Mikael, Getachew Assefa, Getachew Maru and Bekri Mohamed, had the same position on the three questions: urban armed struggle, Fascism and a United Front with the Derg.

"Their difference was on the how," he said. "Getachew Maru had seen the problem ahead of time. From among those I knew, he was the only one who did not want to leave the Party. He used to say, 'Let's have an internal and democratic discussion. Let's put pressure on the CC to allow discussion within the Party.'"

That was exactly what Getachew was saying to me too all along.

"*Ajirit*, you have to accompany a *Yebelay Akal* to Mekele. He cannot travel on his own. This time we will get you a real ID card. Go get a picture and give it to me later today," Aklilu told me sometime in May.

I got my picture taken at Photo Berhan in Piassa and gave it to him around five in the afternoon.

"Here is the code, your ID and money. You are going to meet the comrade around *Somale Tera* tomorrow afternoon. He will be wearing khaki pants and a khaki jacket, a black cap and a black arm band," Aklilu said when I saw him the next day.

I met Fikre Zerga, a Party alternate CC member, the next day at the *Somale Tera*. I got there first and saw him coming from a distance. He was about six feet tall and good-looking. I wanted to smile. The camouflage did not work. He didn't look like the kind of person he was trying to look like. It was obvious that he was an educated person despite his efforts to disguise himself as an ordinary person. I later learned that he had studied law at Haile Selassie I University and went to America for further studies. He told me that we would be leaving the next day around one in the afternoon and I should wear black clothing.

"We will be traveling as a married couple, mourning the death of their son. I want us to avoid the main bus going to Dessie. We will take the *Lonchinas*, one or two towns at a time. If we make it to Dessie safely, then we will take the Mekele bus from there," he told me.

I ran to *Mercato* and bought a black headscarf and went to my cousin's to steal a black dress and a *netela*. I didn't have the time to notify Azeb. I didn't even know how to reach her, since she didn't have a permanent shelter. We had a "mechanism" for meeting, but that was only if our appointments failed. I contacted my Zonal Committee members and some of my "single contacts" and notified them of my absence for a few days. In the event that I did not make it back, my Zonal Committee members knew how to contact Tito.

The next day, I went to the bus station in a long black dress, a black headscarf wrapped around my head. The borders of my *netela* laid over my shoulders, the way mourning women do. I met Fikre at precisely one o'clock at the bus station beside the ticket counter. We bought our tickets and he told me that Debre Berhan, a small town about 130 kilometers northeast of Addis, would be our destination for the day. We didn't have much to say to each other in the bus. He was very tense. There weren't that many people. We arrived in Debre Berhan after two and a half hours and checked into a small hotel. We took a room with two beds. It was only after we retired to our room that Fikre began to relax. We talked about the Party, the League and the situation in the country over dinner. I wondered if he knew where Getachew was and how he was doing. I couldn't have asked, since it would have been an infraction of discipline.

Fikre and I got up early in the morning and rushed to the bus station in the biting morning chill to look for a *Lonchina* that would take us to Kara Kore, our destination for the day. *Lonchinas are* buses that only go short distances. We found one and went to a teahouse at the station to have breakfast until departure.

We arrived in Kara Kore without incident. We had lunch at an eatery, just off the main street and wondered if we should spend the night there or proceed to Dessie. Finally, we decided to leave when a *Lonchina* arrived. We happened to get one around one or two o'clock, and arrived safely in Dessie in the late afternoon.

We checked in a hotel Fikre seemed to know. It was close to the bus station. He called his friend, who came right away. The hotel patron gave us a private room and the three of us dined and talked for a few hours. I was tired and went to my room leaving the two there. I slept through the night and woke up early in the morning.

I wasn't sure if Fikre's friend took a room with him or if he came in the morning. I saw them together at breakfast. The hotel owner had prepared breakfast with coffee and tea, which we gobbled down and rushed to the bus station. Fikre's friend came to the station to see us off. We boarded the Mekele bus, which was filled to capacity. Fikre became relaxed once we passed Dessie. He had worked in Dessie for quite some time and didn't want to be recognized.

Endayesus checkpoint near Mekele was the major challenge after Dessie. The bus stopped in the open space before the fortress and men were asked to get off. Two young soldiers came into the bus and asked the women to open their luggage. Fikre had two suitcases: one green and one yellow. He had given me the keys before he got off. He stood on my side of the window and looked inside. He looked nervous and I saw beads of sweat on his forehead. He wiped them off nervously with a white handkerchief. I didn't understand why he was so tense.

"Whose suitcase it is that," the taller soldier asked, pointing to the green one sitting on the rack.

"It is mine," I said.

"Bring it down," he ordered his colleague.

The soldier brought it down and put it on an empty seat.

"Open it," the taller one said to me.

I unlocked the padlock and opened the suitcase as naturally as possible. There were military uniforms inside! I was stunned but kept my composure.

"What are those?" the taller soldier asked me with a frown.

"They are my husband's uniforms."

"Your husband is in the army?"

"Yes, he is."

"Put it back!" he ordered his colleague and asked, "Whose suitcase is the yellow one?"

"It is mine," I said with an almost flirtatious smile. I knew I was in danger. I didn't know what else could be in the yellow suitcase. I didn't want him to open it.

"It is okay. Leave it there," he said to his colleague and went past me.

I looked at Fikre. His eyeballs seemed to pop out of their sockets. *Who knows what else is in those suitcases? Why didn't he tell me? What if I had made a mistake?* Fortunately, I was poised betraying no emotion.

The male passengers came in after being searched and showing their ID. Fikre came back and sat beside me. He looked relieved but sweat still trickled down his cheeks. He had surmounted the last and most formidable hurdle. He smiled at me, took my hand, and pressed it as a way of saying "Thank you." I smiled but said nothing. We got off the bus in Mekele and went to a house not too far from the bus station. I was standing in the middle of the living room when Fikre came over and embraced me.

He said, "You are a brave girl. I stood there trembling and thinking about what might happen to you, while you were sitting there collected. When you were asked to open the suitcase, I said to myself, 'What have I gotten this girl into?' But you did very well. I was impressed with the way you comported yourself."

"Why didn't you tell me you had military uniforms in your suitcase? I told the soldier they were my husband's. He asked if my husband was in the army and I told him yes."

He laughed and hugged me again. "I had a discussion with the comrades about it before I left – I mean whether or not to tell you about the contents of the suitcases. We decided that it was better not to because if you knew you might become nervous if and when you were searched. There is 12,000 birr, cassettes with revolutionary songs, military uniforms and other things in those suitcases. Everything is going to the army."

I shook my head and laughed. My guardian angel was there once again to protect me. I spent a few days in Mekele, and then it was time for me to get back. The night before I left, Fikre told me he wanted me to come back and work in Tigray with them.

"I will take you to Assimba next time you come. I have written a note asking the comrades to send you up here," he said, giving me an envelope.

I smiled and told him I would deliver the letter. He gave me another envelope to give to his friend whom I met at the hotel in Dessie. I left for Addis the next day. I popped into Zerai Deres when the bus stopped at the Woldya checkpoint. The bus arrived in Dessie late afternoon. Before checking in a hotel, I ran to the Post office to drop off the envelope to Fikre's friend who worked there. Fikre's friend came along and helped me check in a hotel and we went to Etege Hotel to have dinner. We then went for a walk and finally he accompanied me to my hotel and left.

The second *assessa* was in full swing when I came back from Mekele. Addis has never been so tense. People were taken away from their homes, work places and cafés without question. They were stopped and searched in the streets, and often arrested or shot.

I proceeded to my friends' apartment in Piassa from the bus station. I always brought a skirt and a blouse with me when I traveled so that I wore them on my way back to Addis. All I had to do when I got there was remove my *netela* and my headscarf. My friends were home when I got there. I was so tired and all I wanted to do was go straight to bed. "Where have you been? You have become so dark." They bombarded me with questions. I laughed it off as usual. I spent the night there.

The next day, I stayed home all morning. I would have to wait until seven in the evening to call Tito or get in touch with Aklilu. Besides, I was not feeling well. Every time I traveled, I became ill. I brought back all kinds of parasites with me. I had diarrhea and nausea again so I decided to buy the pills that the doctor had once prescribed for me in the afternoon. My friends came back home for lunch and as soon as they left, I changed my mind and wanted to see if I could run into Tito at the *Ij meschia*.

When I got there, I looked around quickly to see if the coast was clear. I neared the house and found the door ajar, which meant there was no meeting going on. It also meant that there could be someone or no one. I hoped Tito or at least someone I knew would be there. Otherwise, I would be making a blunder. I peeked through the door and saw Alemayehu Egzeru standing, his back to the door, sorting through papers. He twisted around when I came in.

"*Ajirit*, you are back! You were supposed to come back the day before yesterday. We thought you were done with!" Alemayehu was a League CC member.

"I got back yesterday. Everything went well."

We chatted for a few minutes and when I rose to go, he asked if I could pass hundreds of leaflets of *Democracia* to Habteselassie, whom he was supposed to meet at five o'clock. Habte was a comrade in whose house the League IZ met a few times. The leaflets were to be distributed that night and I squeezed them in my round straw purse and took off. I hated carrying a purse and when I joined the university, I had bought the straw purse from Harar for its casual look. Only female American Peace Corps carried it then. Azeb and Sara used to tease me saying I was aspiring to be a Peace Corps.

I still had some time to kill before seeing Habte, so I decided to go back to the apartment. It was the first time I had ever taken anything implicating there. I took off the sweater tied around my shoulders and threw it over the round lid on my purse as a precaution. I decided to go via Nyala Hotel, located on a side street just a few meters away from the Piassa apartment.

"Halt!" I heard someone yell when I came into the street leading to Piassa. I wasn't sure where the command had come from. I looked behind me and there was no one. "Halt!" I saw two *Abyot Tebakis* standing on both sides of a small side street off the road leading to Piassa. They had stopped a man and were searching him. The man had both hands raised up in the air. I didn't know what to do. If I turned back, they would be suspicious and pursue me, maybe even shoot me if I attempted to run. If I went up the street, they would definitely stop me. *What am I supposed to do with the hundreds of leaflets I am carrying?*

I went up the hill slowly watching them from the corner of my eye. I made it seem like I was out for a mid-afternoon promenade. By now they had let the man go and were watching my movement. There was a vegetable stall a few yards away, just below Pizzeria, but the question was how to get there before they stopped me. I reached the stall after what seemed an interminable walk and dived in.

I grabbed brown paper bags and threw in fruit displayed by the window so that I could follow the movements of the two predators. I saw their eyes riveted on the window. I got almost every type of fruit without letting my eyes off the window. It occurred to me that I might have more fruit than I could pay for. I had only twenty birr on me.

So I went to the cash counter and the bill came to sixteen birr. I went back to the window pretending to get more bananas. I found the *Abyot Tebakis* still looking through the window. I fumbled with the bananas until a miracle happened. I saw two men coming from the side street behind the *Abyot Tebakis*. I quickly moved to the door but kept out of sight of the *Abyot Tebakis*.

"Halt!" When the two men put their hands up and the *Abyot Tebakis* started to search, their backs facing the stall, I darted out and briskly walked back down the street. The apartment was only a few meters away, but I didn't dare go up there as I would definitely be stopped. I wasn't even sure if that *Kebele* hadn't also been raided. My best bet was to go back where I came from. Once I made a turn on the side street to Nyala Hotel, I dumped the fruit and sprinted. I didn't even look back until I reached Lion Pharmacy, which was quite far from where the *Abyot Tebakis* were. It was only then that I noticed I was running in a quiet street!

I went back to the *Ij meschia*. Well, Alemayehu was still there. "You almost got me nailed with these pamphlets!" I said, breathing heavily and giving back his bundle of *Democracia*. We talked until he had to go to his appointment. I had nowhere else to go so I decided to go back to the apartment. I went up Churchill Road to kill time. If there was a raid at the Piassa *Kebele*, it would be over by six o'clock, I assumed.

When I arrived at the apartment, my friends' housemaid told me I was lucky. The *Kebele* was raided by the *Abyot Tebakis* minutes after I left. They searched every apartment in the building and took away the son and nephew of the owner of the pastry shop downstairs, who lived on the same floor as my friends. Had I stuck with my previous plan of staying home till seven in the evening, I too would have ended in their hands.

I had cheated prison or death twice in one day.

I met Aklilu the next morning and gave him the envelope Fikre had given me. I didn't think I would never see him again when we parted that afternoon.

"Guess what!" Azeb said, looking alarmed when I saw her around one in the afternoon the next day.

"What?"

"I was walking with Aklilu this morning in Teklehaimanot... near Lidet Biskut Bet. We heard men shouting 'Halt!' We turned around and we saw them get out of a car carrying machine guns. Aklilu started running toward Black Lion Hospital. I ran into a *tej bet*. There were men drinking *tej* and the servers hid me in a back room. I later escaped safely. I learned about an hour ago that Aklilu has been arrested at the back of the hospital when an *Abyot Tebaki,* who saw the *Meison* cadres chasing him, hit him on the head from behind. He became momentarily unconscious and fell to the ground. They took him away. "

I was speechless.

Tito and I had an appointment around six in the evening in front of Nyala Hotel that day. I wondered if he knew his older brother has been arrested that morning.

"Have you seen Aklilu today?" I didn't even bother using Aklilu's code name.

"No. Why? Did you have an appointment with him?"

I realized that he didn't know. "I am sorry to tell you that he's been arrested." I told him what Azeb had told me.

"Is that so?" he said in English, his big eyes suddenly turning red.

Aklilu, we later learned, daily faced the most brutal torture imaginable. News came almost every day about the unspeakable torture he had to go through and how he endured it all with silence. He later died hanging upside down from a pole!

As Secretary-General, his loss was a huge blow to the League. His death had a tremendous impact on all of us who had worked with him. He had come from Switzerland where he was pursuing his education. He was one of the most committed revolutionaries I had ever met.

Aklilu, like Getachew, used to be concerned about my laxity as far as security was concerned. He insisted that I should never enter a café with another comrade before I made sure someone I knew was there. But I always ended up making a mistake. There were times that he left a café, like he did with Azeb, as soon as I came in with a comrade or comrades. He became frustrated with me every time that happened. He was a real gentleman and always expressed his frustration politely.

I rarely had appointments in *Mercato* before I met him. We met every day, at times twice a day, at Arat Kilo or in *Mercato*. One day, I was waiting for him early in the morning at a café in *Adarash*. A man came in and sat down beside me and told me that he has been coming to *Mercato* for business everyday and that he has seen me in the same café or in the area. He offered me a job at Reis Engineering if I was not going to school. "It is not a good idea to be seen in a café everyday in these dangerous times," he said. While the man was talking to me, Aklilu came in. I started up when I saw him. He went back out. The gentleman asked if I knew him. I said "No" and took leave right away. Aklilu was waiting for me in the *Adarash*.

He was not too pleased with my behavior. "First of all, you shouldn't have reacted when you saw me. It was obvious from your body language that you knew me. Second, you shouldn't have left the café right away. That is the kind of thing I've been trying to tell you to avoid. What if the man was a security agent? It would have been the end of you... and me too," he chided me with a gentle smile.

"Sorry, I know what you mean," I said and told him what the man had said to me. "Incidentally," I continued, "after I met you here yesterday, I took a cab to Casanchis. The taxi driver told me that was the fourth time that I'd been in his taxi since morning. I wasn't even aware of that. He said I should never do such a thing in these precarious times."

"That is the kind of/thing I am trying to tell you to avoid. You really ought to be aware of your surroundings. I don't know...you just walk around as if nothing is going on. It is by sheer miracle you are still alive. You look innocent and I think that is what is helping you," he said, patting his mouth with his fingertips.

A few days later, I was making a phone call from a payphone in Amede Gebeya, a shopping area in *Mercato*. I was holding the receiver when I swirled around and saw him going down the street with a couple of men. I gave a start, smiled, and unintentionally put the receiver back on the hook. He pretended he did not see me. I re-inserted the coin into the slot, re-dialed and turned. There he was standing beside me unable to control his laughter. "You never learn, right?" he said, shaking his head.

Aklilu had a point. It was mostly through associations that members got to know one another. If a comrade is seen with an individual, that individual is automatically taken as a League or Party member even if he or she is not. Such identifications had serious security repercussions, especially in areas with dense youth populations, which are also hot spots of EPRP activities. Many League members were mostly known to *Abyot Tebakis,* secret service agents or cadres, through associations.

It was the same with labeling others as *Meison* or *Anja.* If someone was seen with a known or suspected *Meison* or *Anja,* the entire League structure "knew" that individual was a *Meison* or an *Anja,* even if the person was not.

Not long after Aklilu was jailed, I started feeling malaise and getting frequent headaches. I was taking a shower one morning when I found a lump on the back left side of my neck. It was as if it had burgeoned in one day. I had forgotten about my health problems. I had stopped taking medication since I left home. I waited to see if the swelling would go down. It actually became bigger. The idea of being sick again terrified me. Not because I was afraid I might die, but because I would be unable to continue my Party activities.

I say this without irony. To understand my frame of mind at the time, you have to understand the prevailing feeling within the movement toward our own mortality. As far as we were concerned, the fear of death had long been vanquished. Our love and commitment to the Party had washed away the stain of fear. There was no terror of the unknown: death caused us neither angst nor fear of annihilation. Death was not a lonely journey: we were interred together in mass graves, comrades-in-arms in death as in life. Death did not concern us. The struggle, the Party was all.

There was nothing enigmatic or mysterious about death, it was simply a sacrifice. We knew what we were dying for. Historical Materialism had taught us that History is intelligible and explainable. It ascends unerringly toward its goal. There might be bumps on the road but we will inevitably get there.

Death had meaning. The meaning was not founded on the sense of being "part of that vast harmonious whole" or "oneness" with nature or God. It had meaning because of the sense of being part of the great march of History. Above all, it was the feeling of "oneness" with the Party. The meaning invested in the Party was too deep and too profound to be destroyed by death.

There was no "Tolstoyan moment" no flash back, no self-analysis when we came face to face with the Reaper. Many endured horrendous deaths, the image of the Party enshrined in their hearts, shouting slogans: "Long live EPRP!" "EPRP will win!" Their stories inspired the rest of us awaiting our turn. We had faith that our deaths were not to be in vain. Other comrades would pick up the torch when we fell. Thousands endured the most gruesome torture so that their comrades could relay the torch to the finish line, so that the Party might continue to fight. They kept silent so that the Party could speak.

They died so that the Party could shine.

Death was the least price we could pay for the noble cause; for the people. Our comrades' unmarked mass graves were etched in red: "I will wash the path to freedom with my blood so that you can live happily ever after."

A testament to the heights to which the human heart could soar.

Oh Marx! How he wounded my heart! How callous of him to say that we "must *perish* in order to make room for the people fit for a new world." We were not like the Jews whom "Moses led through the wilderness." We thought we *were* the new generation! We did not think we were to be surpassed. We chose to *perish* because we believed in the cause, not for glory or to gain immortality. We surrendered our lives out of pure dedication to the struggle.

It was a sublime, even a holy act.

When the swelling on my neck became even bigger, I called my sister Almaz and asked if my mother could get me the traditional medicine that I used to take before. A couple of days later, I met my mother at Arat Kilo, at the taxi stand beside the Ministry of Education. She and my sister Negede had earlier fled from Harar when the invading Somali army started bombing the town. She gave me the herb and plied me with questions, hoping to know where I lived and what I did, perhaps knowing that it was a futile effort. I received the herb and went home. The swelling came down after about ten days I started taking it. I did not have the time to worry about myself so I discontinued the herbal medicine altogether, thinking the rest of the swelling would go away on its own.

It was around mid-June, not too long after Aklilu was arrested. I had to meet Azeb at a bus station. I waited around for her for an hour, knowing very well that it was extremely dangerous to stand in one spot for more than a few minutes. Azeb was always late for our appointments. When she arrived, we usually spent the first five minutes or so arguing over her tardiness. I always said to her, "If ever I get arrested in the streets, it would be when I am waiting for you." She always laughed it off. That day, I left; it was the first time I did that.

The next day, I saw her walking down Churchill Avenue with a couple of men near the Post office. I was going up the hill on the opposite side. She looked at me with a restrained smile. I looked away so as not to see the people she was walking with. I wondered if she had shown up for the appointment the previous day. I was still angry with her for making me wait that long. The next day, I had to see an IZ member, a new addition to the committee. "*Ajirit* is arrested," he said with a grave look on his face when I met him in a café.

"Which one?" I asked alarmed. The first people that came to mind were Azeb and Meron Assefa. Meron, a tall and beautiful girl, and I had not worked together but we knew each other by sight. I always worried about her because I saw her everywhere. Since I saw Azeb the previous day, I didn't think it would be her.

"Azeb!" he said.

I was dumbfounded. "But...I saw her yesterday around five in the afternoon."

"She was arrested this morning at a meeting. One of the comrades did not show up but they went ahead, anyway. The comrade was apprehended on his way there and led the soldiers to the meeting place. The comrades were caught with papers and ammunition. One of the soldiers slapped Azeb on the face and asked her what she was doing there but didn't take her away. She could have escaped had she not hung around. A soldier came back and took her away. The comrade must have told them that she was with them."

I was once again in shock. Azeb and I had come a long way. We had become inseparable the past couple of years. She was clad with iron discipline and had unbounded commitment and dedication to the cause. She was one of the most pure hearted people I had ever met. I wanted to cry out loud. I could not imagine my Party activities without her. Even if we had never worked together, we had always shared money, thoughts, ideas and concerns. Lately, we had shared fears about the way things were going in the Party. I wondered how long I could hold out before I faced her fate.

I dragged myself through the days following her arrest. It was not advisable to go to someone's house who has been arrested, but I often went to visit her mother. Azeb and I exchanged letters, which were secretly smuggled in and out of prison. I wrote to her about the "son" – the League – and the "father" – the Party.

Azeb, like Aklilu and so many others, had to endure the most harrowing torture. She would be taken to the hospital only to render her fit to endure more torture. They said every bone in her body had been broken.

She never gave in.

Besides Azeb's fate, I worried about Getachew's. There was no news about him. There were all sorts of rumors about *Anjas*. The anger directed at them did not seem to let up. I wondered how long the Party was going to keep Getachew under custody. I longed to see him but my instinct had told me that I was not going to see him for the rest of my life.

...in whose name he had sacrificed others and was himself being sacrificed: in the precept, that the end justifies the means. It was this sentence which had killed the great fraternity of the Revolution and made them all run amuck.

      -Arthur Koestler, *Darkness at Noon*

Tito's eyes had something about them. They gave a foreboding import. We were at an IZ meeting. It was only a couple of weeks after Azeb was arrested.

      "Thirteen houses were raided last night. The comrade has died...Getachew Maru...has died," he said, speaking slowly.

      I was speechless. I could hardly hear what he was saying. His voice grew faint. It seemed to come from a distant place. I thought I was going to lose my senses.

      "Getachew Maru...killed...squad...shot..."

      What is Tito talking about? Am I dreaming? It can't be true. Getachew can't be dead. That is not possible. This must be a bad dream. "Can you say that again?" I said in a cracked voice and struggling to clear my head.

      Tito recounted, "Thirteen houses were raided last night. One of them was the house the comrade has been detained in. When the comrades heard the soldiers knocking at the gate, Getachew told the squad leader that they should escape. The squad leader refused. 'You are not going anywhere,' he told him. Getachew asked, 'Are we going to surrender arms folded?' The squad leader then took out his pistol and aimed it at him. Getachew hit the comrade's arm with karate and when the pistol fell on the floor, he jumped out of the window. The squad leader picked up the pistol and followed him and shot him dead."

      There was an eerie silence.

Tito then said, "Girmachew Lemma has also been killed. The Party's duplicating machine was confiscated. It was kept in a house in Abware…"

We got up to go. Tito asked me to meet him at the café around Cathedral School, as we usually did after a meeting. I told him I would rather go home and see him the next day. I didn't feel like talking to anyone. I wanted to go some place where I could be alone and try to make sense of what I had just learned. A boundless despair enveloped me.

The world turned dim.

Getachew is dead? He is killed by the Party? I wanted to scream but nothing could come out. My brain became bleary. I felt like I was standing at the top of a mountain and looking down through a fog.

I didn't want to go to my shelter. I didn't know where else to go. I dragged myself to the apartment in Piassa knowing that there were going to be people there. All I needed was to be alone and a pillow to bury my head in and cry my heart out. I tried to cry on my way to the apartment but my tears refused to come out. I saw the world I had built for the past four and a half years crumbling in front of me. The young man I had loved, respected, admired, and looked up to has died.

I wanted to know about his last moments. *How did he feel when he was shot? What did he say? Did he say anything at all? Did he think about me? What were his last thoughts? What a cruel world it is? Could it have been bearable if the Derg had killed him? What did he die for? For trying to save lives? Is all this in the name of the revolution…in the name of the people? Are we justified to do away with peoples' lives in the name of the revolution? How can we do good if we kill one of our own? We started out with a sense of comradeship, love and trust but where are we going? Have we forgotten where we are going? What about our collective mission?*

The world suddenly turned opaque.

I could not fathom how anybody could pull the trigger on a person like Getachew, who was so peaceful and so gentle. He had never lost his trust in the Party nor in his comrades. *Can I remain in the Party after all this? How can I continue to work for the Party alongside the people who had killed him? Is it going to be the same again?*

Everything became a blur.

I got to the apartment in Piassa dazed. Everybody was home. They were chatting and laughing. I envied them for a fraction of a second. Their world seemed peaceful, bright, and gay. *Can I go back to that life again?* I was too tired to answer the questions that popped in my head. I sat with them for a couple of minutes and went to the bedroom feigning headache. I couldn't even confide in Martha.

How could I tell her that his own Party has killed my boyfriend? Martha used to tease me when she saw me fret over the executions followed by *Yefiyel Wotete* on TV or on the radio. She always asked if I was afraid my boyfriend in the "cave" would be killed. She never knew I was going out with Getachew. She just assumed that I was dating a mysterious man in a "cave," whom I feared might be killed by the Derg. The "cave" for her was the underground. I found out that I was lonely. I wished Azeb was there. I missed her so much.

I felt hollow.

As I lay down on Martha's bed, I wondered what was happening to me. *Why am I not able to weep for Getachew?* I was a cry girl who shed tears over every trifling but when I needed my tears the most they would not come. I wondered if it was normal.

I wanted to get up and run away but didn't know where to go. *Will they hunt me down and kill me if I run away? Where am I going to run? Should I run away? What about the struggle?*

I pretended I was asleep when Martha slipped in beside me. I stared at the ceiling in the dark. I didn't want to close my eyes. Closing them amounted to forgetting Getachew. I wanted to stay wide awake so that I could feel the pain. I kept thinking about how we met and the times we spent together. His shy smile, his tender gaze, his trembling hands, his quivering lips, his pounding heart, his peculiar laughter, his noble soul, his loving heart, and his serious discussions paraded in front me. It all seemed like a dream.

I looked back at the love we had, a love that was underground…a love that was intense, always threatened with danger but all the more profound. He was my mentor, the lamp who led me through the darkness and showed me the new life stretched ahead of me.

I wondered about destiny. *How was it that I met him instead of somebody else?* I went back to the first day I met him to look for an answer. There was no answer. Even though the pain was unbearable, I was happy I met him. After knowing him, I wouldn't have wanted to meet anybody else. I wouldn't have traded the time I had spent with him for the world.

Why is all this happening to me? I had lost another friend, Afework Demissie, before Getachew. He had asked me to come with him to Amsterdam when he went to do his Masters degree in Geology. I didn't want to because going to Amsterdam at the time meant getting married at seventeen. Afework died in a car accident a few months after he came back from Holland. I went to his funeral in Harar and cried until my tear ducts dried up. Only Getachew and my involvement with the Party had helped me come to terms with his death.

I remembered Minasse, my little brother, whose death I had never come to terms with. I thought about my affliction. *Why are these things happening to me? What have I done wrong? Why I am chosen for all this tragedy?* For the first time, I realized how precarious existence was. I discerned that life was full of tragedy and some people are chosen to shoulder the better part of it. I thought I was one of them.

I felt life had closed in on me.

I saw Getachew coming with his shy smile. He had his ugly berretta hat and white rimmed reading glasses on. "Getachew is alive! He is alive! Why did I think they had killed him? Why did I think he was dead? He is alive!" I heard myself say. I sat up on the bed shaking and sweating. I looked around and the girls were sleeping. I must have drifted into sleep for a few minutes. *It is only a dream! Getachew is dead!* That was the last time I dreamt about him. It was already morning. I wanted to wake up the girls and tell them Getachew had died. I wanted to tell the whole world that the Party has killed Getachew. I had no strength left. The words would not come out. My tears had still refused to come out.

Something had snapped in me.

In the morning, I dragged myself out of bed, took a shower and left with a heavy-laden heart to see Tito. *How am I going to face him?* For the first time since I joined the Party, my faith in it was shaken. I had two alternatives: to renounce it or to continue to fight beside those very people who had killed Getachew.

I was confounded.

I met Tito at the café in front of Cathedral School. He looked crestfallen. His eyes had the same expression they had when I told him about the imprisonment of his brother, Aklilu. We sat with a sullen silence for a few minutes.

"I'm sorry about the comrade. It is unfortunate," he said a while later, shaking his head.

I looked away. I did not say anything. There was nothing to say. I wouldn't bear mention Getachew's name to any EPRP member. I knew Tito would feel as bad about Getachew's death. He was an *Abyot* member. He probably knew Getachew from the time he was recruited in addition to working with him in the League CC.

A few days went by. I learned from Tito that Getachew was not only shot and killed by the squad member but that they had put acid on his face to disfigure him. They put his body in a sack and left it in a corner in a toilet. When the Derg found his body, Tito said, "It took *them* three days to identify him."

I thought I was going to lose consciousness. We were standing in front of Nyala Hotel. I wanted to sit on the ground and regain my consciousness. I couldn't say anything. *Wasn't killing him enough? Who is capable of committing such a horrendous crime?*

Years later, Nebiyu Aynalem told me that he knew an eye-witness account of Getachew's death. Nebiyu was the member of the Party IZ Committee who had told me about the genesis of *Anja*.

"The Derg's intelligence was wiretapping conversations and tracing calls at the time," he said. "They were able to identify twenty to thirty houses. The Party had warned its IZ that the house, the one Getachew was detained in, was one of the houses the secret service had eyes on. Getachew was at the time guarded by two squad members. Mezgebnesh, the wife of Berhanu Ejigu, lived there. Berhanu Ejigu had already been killed in Wolayita. The house was considered safe and we used to meet there."

By "we," Nebiyu meant members of the Addis Ababa Party IZ Committee.

He went on, "I used to inquire about Getachew after he was detained because I was the one who reported our meeting after the six of us had met. *They* said to me, 'We have no issue with Getachew's position. Is he going to take revenge? That is our problem. What if he creates a problem for us if we let him go? Is he ever going to forgive us?' At the time, Zeru Kishen had already gone to Assimba. I was already expelled from the IZ."

Zeru Kishen was one of the Central Committee members of the Party and by "they" Nebiyu meant the Party Politburo members.

"I think June 28, 1977 was the date the thirteen houses were raided," said Nebiyu. "The IZ had a meeting that day and when they found out that they were indeed surrounded, they had to make a decision about what to do with Getachew. They didn't want to leave him there because they didn't want the Derg to capture him alive. They decided to kill him and then they put his body in a sack and threw it away. I am not sure if it was a committee decision or the decision of an individual."

"Mezgebnesh came out of the house first but they let her go when she said she was going to buy oil," continued Nebiyu. "Then Girmachew Lemma and Asfaw came out. When they were told to stop, Girmachew told them that they were peaceful people. He then started shooting and a commotion was created but they escaped and went to a car wash and spent the night in a *Lonchina.* In the morning, they went to a house in Casanchis unaware that there were security people in the compound. They told them to stop but Girmachew ran on one side and Asfaw on the other. Then Asfaw saw Girmachew fall. He was shot dead. I heard it all from Asfaw. He has not been seen or heard from since."

The "benevolent" killing of Getachew appalled me. I thought it was even more vicious and callous. I asked Nebiyu about Getachew's alleged attempt to escape.

He said, "Somebody told me that Getachew had tried to escape when he was at the Casanchis house hitting the squad with karate. But there is no proof for that."

Getachew's friend, Shimeles Retta, told me that Getachew was at his place the day the Party detained him. "He left home around eight in the evening that night. My brother and I saw him off to a taxi. I told him to bring a gun with him. He got angry with me. 'How can I bring a gun with me when I am going to see comrades?' he said. I heard about his death when I was in prison. I was arrested on June 25. When I was there, I heard that squad member Surafel Kaba and his colleagues gave a statement during interrogation saying that Getachew was not shot dead. They beat him to death with a club. They put bleach on his face and encased his dismembered body in a sack. The Derg identified him by his ID card and by his thin mustache. I heard that in their interrogation statements, Surafel and Co. stated that, 'We beat a comrade like Getachew Maru to death. We didn't even have respect to a founding member such as him.'"

I found this account even more gruesome.

This was what I also found out from Nebiyu later. "They asked me to prove that I am not *Anja*. They told me that a death sentence has been passed on Berhanemeskel Redda and that the only way they could carry it out was through me. They said he was in Merhabete and he has EPRP's arms at his disposal. They told me that I should take an armed squad to Merhabete and meet a commando in Fiche. So I went to Merhabete."

By "they" Nebiyu meant the Party Politburo members.

"The squad members and I discussed the issue," went on Nebiyu. "We said, 'These people are cruel,' and we cried. We did not carry out the mission. I said to them, 'Berhanemeskel is very alert. He probably knows about our plan. There is no point in looking for him.' I told them to go back to Fiche and I came back to Addis. When *they* found out that the mission had not taken place, *they* killed the teachers, who they thought had possession of the arms that Berhanemeskel had allegedly taken. One of them, a school principal, survived being wounded. There was no Party leadership at the time. There was only one person. He was the one who made all the decisions."

Abiyu Ersamo, a member of the Addis Ababa Party Inter-Zonal Committee, has had custody of the organization's arms in a house located in Akaki, which is about twenty-two kilometers from Addis, before they were shipped to Merhabete.

Shimeles reminisced, "Abiyu had refused to surrender the arms, saying that he wouldn't give arms for the purpose of killing people. We transported the ammunition to Debre Berhan, gave them to some teachers, and came back to Addis safely. They killed the teachers and only one survived after a volley of seven bullets was sent through his stomach."

"Getachew used to live with me but he later got a shelter at Haile Wolde's house in Afincho Ber where Berhanemeskel was staying," continued Shimeles. "The house was located behind Sidist Kilo university campus, across Etege Menen School. Behind the house is Ketchene River, which runs past Arat Kilo assuming the name Ginfle. I used to pick up Getachew and Berhanemeskel from there and drive them to different places where they might have CC or Politburo meetings. Haile Wolde's house was rounded up one day and Berhanemeskel and Getachew almost got arrested. The house was exposed deliberately so that when the Derg eliminated Berhanemeskel and Getachew it would serve as an item of propaganda and a blessing in disguise to *them*."

By *them*, Shimeles meant the Politburo members Getachew called the "clique."

"Being CC and Politburo members in hiding, Getachew and Berhanemeskel shouldn't have shared the same shelter," Shimeles said. "The house at Afincho Ber was known by many members. A vehicle that transported arms taken from Sendafa, was parked right at the edge of the road leading to this house. The secret service knew the car. These actions say a lot to me. Getachew and Berhanemeskel escaped, anyway, and Getachew came to my house. He walked from Ginfle to Asko barefoot. That fateful day, Haile Wolde was at a *Kebele* meeting of election of officials. Unaware of the raid, he came home and was apprehended by *Nebelbal* forces and executed. His girlfriend and her parents were killed too later."

Haile Wolde was a member of the Party and a friend of Shimeles.

Shimeles told me that Getachew had written a seven or eight-page paper on three questions. I learned from somebody else that Getachew referred to them as the "three pillars." They were urban guerrilla warfare, Fascism and United Front.

According to Shimeles, "Getachew's paper was meant for discussion. He talked in the paper about the distinction between brutality and Fascism. He said, 'The Derg is indeed brutal. There is no question about that. However, that on its own cannot make it a Fascist regime. Labeling it as such is ignorance. Ethiopia's level of development cannot warrant such labeling.' He wanted to theoretically confront them citing the outstanding literatures of the day. Whatever his views, they had no mandate to take such brutal action on anyone, let alone on him, who was one of the founding members of the Party. It remains a paradox to see that someone who believed so strongly in negotiation has been killed."

"Regarding urban armed struggle, Getachew argued from two standpoints: from EPRP's principle and practical point of view," went on Shimeles. "It is stipulated in the Party's principle that liberation comes through armed struggle and politicization of the peasantry. Anything other than that was a shortcut to power. It became self-evident that urban guerrilla warfare was impractical. In the absence of liberated areas, the squad members had no place to hide after completing their mission. This is mere abuse of dear lives and unnecessary sacrifice. It is total disregard of ethical considerations. Based on these arguments, Getachew asked the immediate cessation of this practice and the referral of the issue to a new Party congress to be convened as soon as possible."

"His call for a new congress was based on the fact that the then congress was not representative of the current membership of the Party," Shimeles went on. "He noted that it was narrow and represented only those members present at the time of the formation of the Party. Since membership had grown tenfold, the Party should have had a new and a more representative congress. His opponents excused themselves by saying that the security situation could not warrant his call. Getachew refuted their excuse as sham because they were holding CC and Politburo meetings guarded by their infamous defense squads. They knew the upcoming congress would not condone such breach of principle and that it would hold them accountable for the damage sustained thus far. It seems to me that this was the reason that led them to a hasty decision to take his life."

"Getachew was clear about the need for a United Front with the Derg, however short-lived," Shimeles said. "It was intended to gain legality and reach the masses as much as possible. It was a tactical move to strengthen the Party and help grow its membership and support. He cited the example of Chinese Communist Party's temporary alliance with Chiangai Shek's Nationalist Party. When it is required, forming a United Front is tactical. His opponents gave it a different color because of his brother's presence in the Derg. They implied that he was pro-Derg. Unfortunately, our comrades gave it a blind eye and indulged in eliminating brilliant comrades like Getachew. Getachew was everything to us...an exemplary friend, a comrade, an organizer, a leader, a patriot...."

Getachew's older brother, who was in the Derg, was a sympathizer of the EPRP and Mengistu Hailemariam had given an order that he must be shot dead wherever he was found. He was outside of Ethiopia at the time as an envoy to the Derg. He never returned to the country.

Getachew had asked his position to be debated internally by members through the internal organ: Red Star. The "clique" denied the request.

Shimeles said, "I always said that 'I would have willingly died in his place because he was the one who would have benefited the country more.' Berhanemeskel was older. He was in the student movement longer, had worked for a while, and had lived abroad. He had all that life experience and was able to understand the intrigues and machinations of the people he worked with. Getachew was too young to understand all that. He trusted them and made us trust his judgment. He unquestioningly trusted his comrades, which finally resulted in his death. It was a weakness on his part to do that. They did not excel him in IQ or academically. They excelled him only in intrigue."

I was confused when Getachew's friend Mesfin said to me years later, "Let me tell you something. Getachew is responsible for the death of our guys."

Then I realized what he was trying to tell me. By "our guys," he meant *Abyot* members killed by the Party.

"*Abyot* was an organized body before the merger with the EPLO," Mesfin went on. "We had many members and EPLO had only a few individuals. We already had a constitution. Actually, one of the criticisms directed at us was that we had made it very difficult to join the group. The recruitment criteria were very stringent. We had embraced the youth and to some extent the labor force. For instance, we had good footing at Wonji Sugar Factory. The only group that could compete with us in the factory was *Woz League*. When talks began for the merger between EPLO and *Abyot*, we didn't like the way they were rushing the merger. Getachew was one of our representatives. *They* wanted to speed up the process because *they* wanted our people."

By *they*, Mesfin meant members of the EPLO.

"We didn't want to be rushed into the merger," went on Mesfin. "We wanted to slow it down so that we could discuss the issues at length and get to know one another better. We also wanted to know if some of the people we knew from campus were involved with the group. We didn't like those people. Getachew said they were 'militant' and 'comrades' after he talked to them. He was very trusting. He was pure…innocent. He was the one who trusted *them* and allowed *them* to push for the merger. He gave them the opportunity to do whatever they wanted to do. They pressed him to precipitate the merger too early. After the merger, he had a key position before he was elected to the Central Committee of the EPLO which was later re-named EPRP. He was chair of the Political and Organization Committee. That was a key position."

"I know why, but why do you think he didn't go to Merhabete with Berhanemeskel?" I interjected.

"He believed till the end that the issue would be resolved through discussion and that they would work together again. You know, Getachew loved discussion. He was very rational. We warned him several times not to go to *them* but he didn't listen. He trusted *them*. Berhanemeskel was not so positive about *them*. He used to say to him, 'You don't know *them*.' You know, Getachew made us even feel guilty. We felt bad about thinking that way about the comrades."

"He made me feel the same way too," I said.

"One day, they told me that *they* had killed him. I don't know...I just don't know. I was confused," he said, becoming emotional.

"Getachew had a positive attitude toward Tesfaye Debessay," he continued. "From what I learned from him the death of Tesfaye had hurt him."

Tesfaye Debessay was the chair of the Central Committee of the Party who threw himself out of a building during the first *assessa.* "But Tesfaye believed in everything that Getachew was against," I put in.

"Yes. But Getachew said that Tesfaye could compromise on issues. He could take a sort of middle-of-the-road position."

There was silence.

"You know, some of the comrades who came from abroad looked down upon homegrown revolutionaries," said Mesfin with a wry smile.

"Yes, Getachew told me that."

"Getachew never liked ESUNA. We never liked them. We used to call them Tupamaros."

By ESUNA, Mesfin meant students who were members of the Ethiopian Students Union in North America. The Tupamaros were a Marxist guerilla group engaged in urban guerrilla warfare in Uruguay from the early sixties to the mid-eighties.

I told Mesfin all that Getachew used to tell me about Fascism, the PPG and urban armed struggle. I asked him if he had heard them from Getachew.

"Those were not just Getachew's positions. They were *Abyot* positions as well. We had our study circle intact ever since we started it. We grew up together and kept the group for no reason other than being friends and comrades. We discussed theoretical issues all the time. I remember we spent the whole night one time discussing the transition – the transition from socialism to communism."

"We were against the Party claiming Fascism has held sway in the country," Mesfin continued. "We were against the use of the PPG as a strategic question and the launching of urban guerrilla warfare. We also believed that we had to accept the Derg's invitation to a United Front. What we suggested was that the underground structure remained intact and those who were already exposed worked overtly. There was of course danger in that. There is sacrifice…but we understood that. One day Getachew came and told us that the CC had made a decision to assassinate Mengistu Hailemariam and that he had spoken against it. We were outraged by the decision. He even argued on *their* behalf playing the devil's advocate. He had a habit of doing that. The next day, I met my contact person from the CC, Kiflu Tefera, and he told me about the assassination plan. I didn't do it on purpose but I told him that I had heard it from Getachew and we'd had an argument with him. He reported on him and Getachew was accused of breaching the principle of Democratic Centralism."

"Did you know about my relationship with Getachew?"

"You know," he laughed, "Getachew never told us directly about your relationship. He started saying, 'It is good to have a relationship. It is even good for the revolution. It is not necessarily a negative thing.' We knew about you and we used to laugh at him and say, 'Hiwot must have changed his life.' You know, *Abyot* had by-laws even on personal conduct such as drinking, smoking... Getachew was puritan. We used to do everything…smoke, party… He was puritan."

Matheos, Getachew's friend, once told me, "I heard that there was regret in detaining Getachew. Most of *them* had a soft spot for him. One thing in history… if the Chinese have to give him a medal or whatever, it was Getachew Maru who introduced Maoism in Ethiopia. In fact, Mao's books, *Peking Review…* all that came to Ethiopia…he must have been the first subscriber."

Melaku Takele, a former EPRP member, once said to me, "Just as Berhanmeskel Redda had changed a generation of students; Getachew Maru had transformed a generation of youth with Maoism. He was able to achieve all that at such a young age."

Getachew's "sin," as presented officially by the Party, was that he did not pass on the CC's decision to the League CC about the launching of urban armed struggle. He was also accused of talking to people out of the proper channel and that he had relationship with former *Abyot* members. He was accused of campaigning against the Party's decision to assassinate Mengistu Hailemariam, the killing of notorious *Kebele* officials, *Meison*, and other cadres, and damage to infrastructure.

Getachew became a CC member in August 1976, a little over a year after the merger of *Abyot* and EPLO. He was a Politburo member linking the committee with the CC. He was the youngest member of the CC and linked the Party CC with the League CC. He had worked in various important committees of the CC and was sent to various important missions.

He was only twenty-seven when he died.

I salute him for his courage for speaking out his convictions. He did not give a blind eye to what he saw around him, like most of us, for the sake of maintaining his position in the Party or for fear of being labeled. I admire his untiring effort to right the wrong through dialogue.

Getachew Maru, 1972

The Party, comrade, is more than you and I and a thousand others like you and I.
The Party is the embodiment of the revolutionary idea in history.
      -Arthur Koestler, *Darkness at noon*

I wanted to hope in spite of doubt and confusion clouding my world. Getachew's brutal death had left an indelible scar in my soul. My being was shaken to its core. It wasn't his death alone that had left me nonplussed, but the very idea that the Party could kill one of its own. The persecution of *Anja*s was as distant to me as the stars in the heavens; before Getachew's death, I simply refused to accept it. But Getachew's death brought it close. As a result, my attitude toward death changed: the halo surrounding sacrifice faded away, the lofty meaning attributed to it waned, the burning desire to lay my head under the guillotine cooled off. Revolution, change and progress became tainted with cynicism.

But in spite of it all, my love for the Party endured.

As the shock subsided, helped along by the escalating political repression and heavy workload, I began to see the future and not the present. True, it was not the same Party I had wanted to live and die for, but I still wanted to believe in it, and in the future. I had heard Getachew often say that the "struggle is above and beyond any one individual or group."

I wanted to emulate that.

I would be dishonest if I said my love for the Party was the only reason I stayed. I remained in the Party partly because there was no choice for me at that point. I couldn't and didn't want to go back home and endanger my family. I didn't know where else to go. The only alternative had been surrendering to the Derg, which would have caused the death of so many. In my own right, I knew enough to wreak havoc. I could never have done that. The only thing left for me to do was to keep going until I faced the same fate of thousands of other comrades.

At the beginning of September 1977, Tito told me that he was going away for a three-day meeting. He went for the meeting of the congress of the Youth League and when he came back, he told me that, with the recommendation of comrades, I had become an alternate League CC member. The "promotion" didn't excite me. I was dead inside.

Around the end of October or beginning of November, Tito informed me that I was transferred to the Party. It was a huge blow to me. I couldn't imagine myself leaving the League. Tito didn't like my transfer either but there was nothing that could be done.

A couple of days later, I met my Party contact person through the communication code that Tito had given me. He let me know that I would be working in the Party Shoa Inter-Zonal Committee. I would be secretary of the Zone that included towns like Nazaret, Debre Zeit, Awash and Metehara and Nazaret would be my home base.

It was the end of November and I was in *Mercato* trying to flag a cab around seven in the evening. None of them was willing to take me to Kidist Mariam even if I offered to pay more. The street slowly became deserted. I started getting anxious. I could be singled out standing in the dark and frantically looking for a cab. Staying that late in *Mercato* was suicidal. Finally, I decided to go to the apartment in Piassa instead and hopped in a taxi.

I spent the night there and left at six in the morning to change my clothes. When I got home, I saw the gate thrown wide open and wondered why. I lurched to the back of the house to see if *Etiye* was up. Hearing footsteps, the woman who baked *injera* for the family rushed out of the kitchen, located beside the house.

"Go away! Go away!" she said in a lowered tone, waving her hand.

"Why? What is the matter?"

"The house has been raided. Soldiers were at the gate when I arrived a few minutes ago. Haven't you seen them? "

"I didn't see any soldiers. Where is *Etiye*...?"

"She slept over at her sister's and came back this morning a few minutes after I got here. She went to the *Kebele* to report the incident. Please go away!" the old woman pleaded.

I went to the back door and found piles of wood at the entrance. The door was broken into pieces. When I went in, the door, which opened into the dining room, was smashed too. My bedroom was close to the back door and I went in. The mattress was hurled on the floor, cotton swabs scattered all over. My clothes were tossed on the floor. I anxiously opened the book sitting on the bedside table. I had taken pictures at Speedy Studio in Piassa to get a new ID. I found all four intact. They had ransacked the place but had not even touched the most important thing. I knew they wouldn't find anything. I never left anything incriminating in the house. I threw a few things in a bag and rushed out.

I wasn't sure if they were looking for me or Gezahegn, *Etiye*'s son. I was glad *Etiye* was not there when it happened above all, the two girls. They would have definitely taken them away. The girls have been hiding for quite a while at *Etiye's* brother's place in old airport.

I was amazed at how fate worked. I was willing to pay extra to get home but none of the taxis would take me. I thought of how many times I had cheated death. I considered myself the ultimate trickster. Had I known the story of Sisyphus then, I would have believed I was as much a match to death as he was.

Later that day, I learned that Tito and many League CC members were arrested the previous night. Tito had become Secretary-General of the League, replacing his brother Aklilu. Habteselassie, in whose house the IZ met, had also been arrested. I had become friends with him lately. I learned that the same League CC member who got Tito and Habte arrested was the one who came to look for me at three in the morning. He was the one who suggested I move to the shelter in the first place.

I learned that the comrade told his detainers that he would confess if only they would not touch him. They did not. The first person he got arrested was Habte. I was supposed to meet Habte at six-thirty the previous evening. He was the reason I stayed late in *Mercato* that evening. Tito always got home by seven. We all knew that. The CC member led the security to his shelter just after he stepped in.

I called *Etiye* in the late afternoon to ask her if I could see her. She thought it might be dangerous for me after what had happened and suggested I come the next day.

The following day, I took a cab around eight in the evening and got off beside Shoa Bakery, looked around carefully and went home slowly. The place was still in disarray. The *Kebele* had told *Etiye* that there was nothing they could do for her. She had waited for me until ten o'clock that night and went with her youngest daughter to her sister's house, who recently had a baby. *Etiye* and I had a pact. She would lock up the gate and go to bed if I stayed later than ten o'clock.

She learned from neighbors that the soldiers had come around three in the morning and had stayed there until about six. I got there after six, missing them by only a few minutes! I felt bad about the broken doors, since it had happened on my account. I had no money that I could offer *Etiye*. I packed the few belongings I had and left the house with tears in my eyes. *Etiye* was an amazing woman with so much kindness and generosity. She had treated me as her own child.

Since that fateful night, the entire League structure started crumbling. The CC member was there right from the beginning and knew everything. Our people in the security said, "Hide everything that *he* knows." It was impossible to do so. Another League CC member did the same thing. With most of the League CC members arrested, there was no leadership. Sirak Tefera would later be arrested. He had left the League IZ, like Samuel, to join the League CC. The League structure was battered every day with so many members arrested and killed and all that was blamed on *Anja*s.

But it was the Derg that had unleashed an untold terror in the country.

There, sighs, lamentations, and deep wailings
   resounded through the starless air,
so that at first I began to weep.
        -Dante Alighieri, *The Divine Comedy*

I remember dreading having to go out in the morning during Lent when I was in my early teens. Every morning, I listened to the *begena* – lyre-like instrument – on the radio, instead of the usual secular songs, while I was getting ready to go to school. The *begena* is many things at the same time. It is prayer, meditation, thanksgiving, an inquiry into the meaning of life and death and social and moral criticism through wax and gold (the literal and hidden meaning of a word). The melancholic tune on the radio matched the dark grey hanging clouds outside.

I felt the whole atmosphere was gloomy, morbid and foreboding.

That was exactly what it felt like in the country from October 1976 to February 1978. On February 4, 1977, Ethiopia saw Satan rise up like a bolt of lightning from its belly in the shape of a man named Mengistu Hailemariam. Mengistu drew his sword against everybody and anybody committing one of the most heinous crimes in history. He plunged the country into mourning, tears, trepidation and horror.

His "red terror" campaign reached cataclysmic proportions.

Particularly, September 1977 marked a heightened stage of the Derg's "White terror will be vanquished by red terror" campaign. By white terror, the Derg meant the killing binge of *Meison* cadres and others by the EPRP. It called EPRP members "mercenaries," "anarchists," "counter-revolutionaries," "revisionists," "sell outs," "CIA agents" and "instruments of imperialists." The "Life of one revolutionary will be avenged by the lives of a thousand counter-revolutionaries," Mengistu roared, letting his demons loose. When he spoke, his voice rumbled like a volcano, his body jerked with spasm, his mouth spewed foam, the ground beneath his feet quaked and the sky above his head whirled. On February 6, 1977, he smashed three bottles of a red liquid at the *Abyot* Square symbolizing the shedding of our blood.

Indeed, he slashed our veins and arteries open and spilled their contents in the streets, avenues and squares.

Marx would have been proud in his grave to have been proven right. All hell broke loose when Russia appeared on the political landscape. She gave ammunition to the Derg enough to annihilate its people, mainly the young. Her AK-47 rifles became the pride of every *Nebelbal, Abyot Tebaki,* cadre, and soldier. It was as if the weapon automatically spewed bullets.

The country trembled with violence.

Young people were rounded up and thrown into jail, tortured with ruthless brutality and executed. They were driven to the slaughterhouse in droves every single day. Their bullet-riddled corpses were displayed in the streets for days as a deterrent to the living.

The Derg reveled in voyeurism.

Blood flowed like water in the streets all across the country. Mothers wished they were sterile. Their tears of anguish drenched the earth and their wailings reverberated through the heavens. This woman's lamentations fell on the deaf ears of the notorious Major Melaku Tefera who had killed thousands in Gondar. But they were echoed by mothers from east and west and north and south.

መላኩ ተፈራ የእግዚር ታናሽ ወንድም
የዛሬን ማርልኝ ዳግመኛ አልወልድም

Meleaku Tefera God's younger brother
I beg your mercy, spare me this child today

And I promise, I will not bear another again.

Death struck everywhere. Family members scoured cities for their missing children only to find their corpses sprawled in the streets. The lucky ones found their children's bodies at their doorsteps at night or at daybreak. Others were not so fortunate. Their children's bodies were dumped in mass graves. It was not uncommon for a family to have lost three or four children in one day or in a short span of time.

Even God wept in regret.

Babies were wrenched from the breasts of their young mothers. Many were orphaned. Those who survived *Abyot Tebakis',* soldiers' and cadres' bullets trekked out of the country. Parents sold their belongings to sneak them out, but militias ambushed many of them in the jungle and either imprisoned or shot them dead point-blank. Some vanished in the jungle, devoured by beasts. Others perished in the desert, unable to endure the thirst and the scorching sun. Girls were violated. Parents were accused of being members or supporters of the Party or of hiding their children, and were thrown into jail. Some were mercilessly shot. Others were not allowed to mourn for their dead.

It was a reign of terror.

Ethiopia's proud children, who stood up valiantly against foreign invaders, whose blood boiled with the slightest affront to their dignity, watched with blank eyes when their country convulsed with violence. They gaped in utter horror, as the gates of "the first circle" of hell were hurled open in front of them. Gruesome killings and grisly torture numbed their faculties. The people who had risen up during the turbulent times of the revolution and shook the very foundation of the previous regime succumbed to the atrocities now perpetrated upon them. Violence shattered their existence to its core and they didn't know how to respond to it.

They became dazed and overwhelmed by shock, fear and grief.

Armored cars, uniforms, corpses in the streets, martial music, intimidations and warnings on television, radio and newspapers, forced meetings, rallies and demonstrations, constant raids, imprisonment, mass massacre and mass graves fragmented everyday existence. The whole array of government machinery – *Kebeles*, *Abyot Tebakis, Nebelbal*, army, police, secret service agents and cadres – not only altered the physical landscape of cities, but also the very fabric of social and human existence. It seemed like there were more armed people in the streets than civilians and more spies in bars, restaurants, hotels and hair salons than customers. The level of trust that existed among family members, friends, neighbors and colleagues became as ancient as Biblical times. The world they lived in was no longer recognizable.

They became strangers to themselves and others.

The people who spontaneously poured out into the streets with bold slogans during those tempestuous months were dragged out to support pro-government demonstrations with threats, intimidations and punishment. Television and radio reported as if they enthusiastically burst into the streets.

Marx, Engles and Lenin glared at us from a huge billboard at *Abyot* Square. The trio was mockingly called the "Trinity." A life-size statue of Lenin was later erected in front of the Jubilee palace. "Comrade" Mengistu's picture frowned at us wherever we went.

It was a travesty of the revolution.

Many believed that what was happening to them was an act of God. Churches and Mosques filled up more than usual as people sought answers from above. Marginal religious groups, such as Pentecostals and Jehovah Witnesses, mushroomed as people scrambled to make sense of what was happening to them. The buoyant spirit that characterized those seven months of the revolutionary period was smothered.

Hopes were dashed. Euphoria turned to despair. The rainbow, cast on Ethiopian skies during those revolutionary times, was rolled up.

Jokes, parody and social ridicule became the only weapons for getting even with the enemy. Mengistu, the Derg, cadres, *Kebele* officials, Russians, Cubans and heads of state, such as Castro and aging Soviet Union presidents, became subjects of cruel jokes.

A joke ran that a woman, who was worried about her dying daughter, went to see a sorcerer after medical treatments failed to cure her. The seer told her to hang a picture of the devil on the wall above her daughter's head. The woman couldn't find a picture of the devil, so she bought the picture of Mengistu Hailemariam instead, believing him to be the devil incarnate. The girl died instantly. Angrily, the woman returned to the magician saying he was a liar because her daughter died after she put Mengistu's picture over her head. But the diviner reprimanded her, saying if she had followed instructions everything would have been fine; by using Mengistu's picture instead of the devil's, she had given her daughter an overdose!

Meison, "the bad boy of the revolution," fell out with the Derg and went underground in August 1977. The Derg showed no mercy. Assisted by the other Marxist groups (*Woz League* and *Malerid*) it drew its dagger against it. Some of its prominent leaders, with PhDs from European universities, such as Daniel Tadesse, Kebede Mengesha, Kedir Mohamed, Terefe Woldestsadik and his wife Atnaf Yimam, were hunted down and massacred. Haile Fida,

Daniel's younger brother Desta Tadesse and his wife, Nigist Adane, were arrested and later executed.

Once *Meison* was out of the way, the Derg aimed its gun at *Woz League* and later at *Malerid.*

No one was spared.

EPRP, *Meison*, *Woz League* and *Malerid* fell one by one like "Autumn leaves." They swore by Marx but were unable to sort out their trivial differences and work together. Their behavior and actions caused bedlam in their respective organizations. In the process, they helped the Derg feast upon their corpses and have power all to itself.

They paid the ultimate price for their intolerance, rigidity and miscalculation.

Except for a handful on either side, whom Getachew might have called "power-mongers," they were genuine revolutionaries who wished their country the best. Many came from well-to-do families or were well placed in society. They were doctors, lawyers, engineers, university lecturers, teachers, pharmacists, geologists, economists, accountants, businessmen, nurses, military officers and students.

They were indeed tragic heroes. No matter what their flaws, they were the 'golden generation' – a generation of 'shameless idealists' with a great vision and altruism. They killed and died for equality, freedom, social justice and human dignity. Ethiopia will always remember them with weeping eyes for their selflessness and vision and with a forgiving heart for their follies. Alas! She was orphaned of her children in the twinkling of an eye.

The curtain fell on her. She receded into darkness. The revolution "froze."

Uprooted from their native land, survivors of those deadly years were "scattered like seeds" throughout the world. Many of those who fled to neighboring countries languished for years in sub-human living conditions. Others flooded European and North American cities. Wherever they lived, many of them became eternal strangers to the world and to themselves. Devoid of dreams and ideals, they lost meaning in the present or the future.

They kept chasing the elusive past.

I took the train to Nazaret around the beginning of December 1977. When the train pulled in the station in Debre Zeit (a small town about 45 kilometers south of Addis), a search was conducted. I had papers tucked in a small green bag, which I kept away from me. When soldiers came in, one of. them asked whose bag it was. Nobody responded. He poked at it with his boot trying to figure out what was in it. I watched him from a distance, my head covered with a *netela*. Finally, he left it alone and demanded passengers to show their IDs, while his colleagues were rummaging through our bags. When we arrived in Nazaret, I picked up the green bag and got off the train.

Nazaret is a small, yet bustling town about 92 kilometers southeast of Addis Ababa. It was an important town connecting the capital city through the railway and bus routes in different directions.

Kifle, chair of the Nazaret Zonal Committee, came to fetch me at the station and took me to meet a girl who came on a bike. The girl took me to her house where I spent the night. The next day, Kifle came and took me to an apartment that was going to be my home for as long as I stayed in Nazaret. I did not get the chance to meet the Zonal Committee members right away. They were supposed to come from nearby towns but were unable to travel for security reasons.

I was at home when I received a call a few days after I arrived in Nazaret. It was late afternoon and it was from a friend and co-worker of the comrade in whose house I was staying. He told me that my host has been taken away from his workplace and that I had to flee. He also told me that Kifle was apprehended and that he was the one who had gotten the comrade arrested. "They can be there any minute. Leave the place immediately," he urged.

I grabbed my bag, vaulted out, and took a cab to the bus station. I had nowhere else to go. I was new to the town and did not know anyone. I didn't know how to contact the girl in whose house I had spent the night I arrived in Nazaret.

My only bet was to go back to Addis.

There were a couple of buses standing at the station but there was no sign of movement. It was getting dark and I did not know what to do. I couldn't check in a hotel because I had only a few birr on me.

There were about seven or eight men at the station anxious to leave, like me. Around eight o'clock, I saw them talking at length to a short stocky man. I figured he was a bus driver. He probably didn't want to go because there were no more than eight people going to Addis. After what seemed an interminable negotiation, I saw the driver nodding. My heart skipped a beat. *Maybe there is hope!* It looked like the men had negotiated a fare with him. I couldn't believe it when he waved his hand for us to board the bus. Each of us contributed whatever we could. I gave ten birr. The regular fare was two. We arrived safely in Addis a little after eleven o'clock. The bus dropped us off at the Nazaret bus terminal near *Legehar*.

I didn't know where to go. I teetered between going to my cousin's and the Piassa apartment. I finally decided to go to my cousin's. But there was no taxi to be seen and the only cars swirling around were military patrol cars, machine guns mounted on them. I ran back and hid in the middle of two buses every time I spotted one.

Midnight curfew was fast approaching. I prayed for a miracle to happen. My prayers were answered. I saw a taxi accelerating toward Mexico square. "Taxi!" I yelled at the top of my lungs. When it stopped, I raced to the other side of the street, opened the door and dashed in. There were two passengers in the taxi. One was sitting down in the front, the other in the back.

"Where are you going?" the driver asked.

"Tobacco Monopoly."

"You are lucky. That is the direction I am heading. You are paying one birr."

"No problem." I was relieved.

The driver was kind enough to drop me off before my cousin's house, which was meters away from the main street. I knocked at the gate softly but insistently. I had to go in before the *Abyot Tebakis* saw me. It was past midnight by then. They were on the prowl and that was how they ambushed people, beat them, took them away and often killed them. After a few knocks, the guard heard me and opened the gate. I went to the back door and found the housemaid in the kitchen. Everybody else was sleeping. I went to the bedroom I usually slept in feeling safe, at least for that night.

The next day, I stayed home all day. I was watching TV in the evening when all of a sudden Kifle surfaced on the screen. He had conceded everything and had taken them to all the places that he knew. He had even taken them to a mountain where ammunitions were hidden. They found one buried during the Italian occupation! Nazaret and surrounding areas received a harsh blow after that. I later learned that the young girl with the bike, the one who let me sleep over at her place the day I arrived in Nazaret, was shot dead in the streets.

Coming back to Addis brought back memories of the times I had spent with Getachew. It had almost been six months since he had died. I was never able to come to terms with his death. Nothing could fill the void it created in my heart.

I got in touch with my contact person, secretary of the Party Shoa IZ Committee, and told him what happened in Nazaret. I learned that Kifle had given my description to the secret service. For the first time since I joined the struggle, I was known to the secret service. I was in a far greater danger than I had ever been. As a result, it curtailed my movement.

I learned that Nigist Tefera (the one who had the same brown skirt as me) had died. She had had no shelter and was living as a housemaid. She was supposed to be sent to Assimba since she was unable to function in Addis, but the Party wouldn't let her because of her relationship with someone related to Getachew. When the *Kebele* arrested her, she took the cyanide she always carried with her and died in a *Kebele* prison.

Talking of cyanide, the IZ had had a meeting at Habte's house one night. In the morning, Tito put on the table some cyanide pills he had brought with him. I picked one up like everybody else, but put it back. The idea of taking my own life revolted me. Leaving the place and walking down the street that morning, I wondered if I had done the right thing. I kept asking myself if I did not have the courage to die. I hoped, as I always did, to die instantly in the hands of my captors before betraying anyone.

There was break down in the League structure (the Party too). The organization had slid down the slope unbelievably fast. There was nothing much happening in Addis except for members being jailed and killed-not even daily, but hourly. Only the ghost of the League remained.

As it was battered on a daily basis, new members were recruited without the rigorous recruiting methods used before. The staunch discipline demonstrated by members over the past years had become a thing of the past. Many had neither the resolve nor the capability to protect their comrades as they had nothing to live or die for. There was nothing to bind them together. So they gave up names and information easily. Others continued with what seemed like a Sisyphean defiance.

According to Greek mythology, the gods condemned Sisyphus, the great trickster, to eternal punishment (after his death) in the underworld for sins he had committed on earth. He had to push a stone to the top of a mountain. Each time he pushed the stone to the top, the stone rolled down. According to Albert Camus, Sisyphus was *conscious* that his efforts were futile but rolled the stone to the top with defiance. He rose above his fate by the very fact of knowing his "wretched condition." He rose above his destiny because he scorned it.

EPRP members did not scorn their fate. They hoped they would win a war that they had lost a long time ago.

There was no more stamina for me to go on after so many League CC, IZ and Zonal Committee members had been arrested. The comrades I had struggled alongside had all been killed or thrown into jail. Only a couple had managed to flee. All that had taken its toll on me. I dragged myself daily with outward composure and equanimity, a trick I learned while nursing my affliction.

Around mid-December, the Secretary of the Party Shoa IZ Committee informed me that I was assigned to work in the sub-secretariat office (which was under the Secretariat of the Party Central Committee) and had to go to the South, as the secretary of the southern IZ Committee, comprising three provinces: Sidamo, Gomu Gofa and Bale.

My immediate task was to send a report to Addis on the insurrection that was staged in Wolayita in the province of Sidamo. Why did it fail? The Party has been waiting for a report and nothing had materialized. I was also to send a report on the Gomu Gofa strategic area chosen for armed struggle. The study report has been delayed. I was to go to Kuyera (a small town in east Shoa, some 240 kilometers from the capital city) first and stay there until I met IZ Committee members. I was given a contact name and address and another address in Gondar (the historic city in northern Ethiopia) I would have to use in the event that contact with Addis failed.

I took the bus to Kuyera, Getachew locked in the vault of my heart. Arriving in the late afternoon, I knocked at the door of a doctor's house which would be my temporary home.

I met Merid Gebrechristos, the comrade I was supposed to contact upon arrival, a couple of weeks later. Merid was a member of the southern IZ Committee. I knew him by sight at the university. He was my senior. He lived in Shashemene, a large town about 250 kilometers from Addis Ababa and about 12 kilometers from Kuyera.

Kuyera was famous for its hospital that catered to three provinces. The doctor who sheltered me lived in the compound of the hospital. Kuyera was also well-known for another reason: it was home to thousands of lepers. There was also the Kuyera Adventist Mission School.

Life in Kuyera was dreary, but safe. Merid and I had called a meeting of the IZ but the comrade in Bale couldn't travel because of security reasons. Merid came occasionally to Kuyera to update me on the developments. I had nothing much to do except for cooking, cleaning and doing other household chores. For once in my life I became domestic...too domestic for my liking. I pretended to be cheerful and carefree and never discussed Party or League with anyone. There was an opportunity for me to read, but I could not find the type of books I wanted.

As well, my health was not the best. I skillfully concealed my physical ordeal even from the doctor in whose house I lived. Now that I had all the leisure in the world to pay attention to my body, I found out that the swelling on the back left side of my neck was still there! I often had headaches, which I kept to myself.

I made up my mind to call home and ask my mother to bring me the herbal medicine she had brought me earlier. I went to Shashemene on a Wednesday, to call my sister in Addis, with a young boy who was a relative of the doctor. I asked my sister if my mother could bring me the herb to Mojo. Mojo is a couple of hours or so from Kuyera. She said she would send it right away.

Sunday morning, I took a taxi to Mojo instead of the bus. Only people with leprosy got on the taxi there. The driver opened the front door for me, but I did not want to attract attention sitting in the front. As all the seats in the back were taken, I sat on the floor wedged between several lepers. The stench was unbearable. I thought about the stigma and ostracism the people faced. They were the lowest of the low. I was moved to tears. At the same time, I was scared of seeing their maimed hands and toes and disfigured faces. But I quickly reminded myself that I was fighting for them and couldn't be afraid of them. I relaxed after a few minutes. After all, I was safe. No one would have suspected I was sitting amidst them.

Nobody stopped the taxi at a checkpoint as it spun on.

I arrived in Mojo and met my mother after so many months. I inquired after the rest of the family. They were all doing fine. She wanted to know where I lived. I made it seem like I lived in Mojo.

But she said, "A couple of weeks ago, somebody saw you in Shashemene and told your aunt." I insisted that it was a mistake. I had gone to the market on a horse-drawn carriage in Shashemene with the young boy to buy foodstuff. That must have been when the person saw me. I wasn't sure how the person recognized me since I always pulled my *netela* over my head to hide my identity. I took the herb from her and saw her off. I had to take the main bus that came from Addis since there was no taxi around. I arrived at Kuyera around three in the afternoon.

The next day, I took the herbal medicine, but only a small dose. Taking more would have meant diarrhea and vomiting. At the time, a guest from Addis had come to hide there for a few days. He was the person in whose house Getachew had been detained in Casanchis. I pretended I didn't know; I was as friendly and as sanguine as ever. Merid also came, and I did not want to appear sick in front of all those people. Merid told me that there would be a meeting of the IZ the following Tuesday.

I went to another doctor's house in the hospital compound for the meeting around six on Tuesday evening. It had taken over two months to bring the people to that meeting. The comrades came one by one: Taye Merid, Agere Miheretu and Mustefa and of course Merid, who had come from Shashemene a few days earlier. We also had an unexpected visitor from Addis: Mekonen Bayisa. It was the first time for me to see him since I met him in a small hotel in Alamata. He had come to hide in Kuyera.

Mekonen told us that there was neither Party nor League structure in Addis. Everybody had been thrown in jail, killed or had fled. He also told us Tito had given a television interview. I wept when I heard that not because I thought he had betrayed the Party or the League, but because I felt sorry for him having to go through that painful process. Of all the people I had worked with in the

League, he had impressed me the most with his youthful vigor and dynamism.

I mentioned to the committee members that I would go to Gondar to resume contact with the Party. I had never seen what was written in the piece of folded paper that I was given in Addis before I came to Kuyera. Mekonen laughed shaking his head and said I must have been out of my mind to even think of something like that. "How are you going to enter Addis, let alone go to Gondar? You have no idea of what is going on," he said.

We agreed that Yirga Alem, the then capital city of the province of Sidamo, would be my home base and that I would leave on Thursday. I was to make a tour of the three provinces and speed up the completion of the two reports. The meeting went on until five in the morning. We went to bed intending to continue the next day at one in the afternoon. Mekonen and I slept on one of the two beds in the room. Two others slept on the other bed and the rest in another room.

The next day was Wednesday, February 16, 1978. I awoke around eight-thirty in the morning and thought of going home to change and come back for the afternoon session. When I opened the door, I saw a girl whom I suspected was a member. I went back to bed feeling bad for having seen someone I was not supposed to. I slipped in beside Mekonen quietly and lay down for almost half an hour, figuring how to get out without bumping into anyone I was not supposed to see, when the door flew open and that very girl shouted, "Get up, the house is raided!"

The great mistake of the Marxists and of the whole of the nineteenth century was to think that by walking straight on one mounted upward into the air.

    -Simone Weil, Gravity and Grace

I pulled back the curtain on my left instantly and gaped through the window in disbelief. We were indeed fenced in! "Wake up!" I yelled, jumping out of bed. "Get up!" I screamed at Mekonen who was still asleep. I shook him and turned toward the others. They leapt out of bed and we crowded in the middle of the room. The rest of the IZ members rushed into the bedroom and joined us. It was then that I learned there were documents and even a rifle in the house.

It was utterly impossible to use the rifle. First, armed soldiers had encircled the house and second, there were two little girls inside. Is there enough time to hide the weapon and the documents? Can we try to escape? We questioned one another. Before we even got a chance to come to a decision, a male voice from outside urged us to surrender with a loudspeaker.

We opted to buck the odds, anyway. Somebody told me to go first; I ran into the hallway and saw the doctor's two daughters whisking around in utter terror. They may have been four and eight. I asked the older of the two to show me the exit. She led me to her parents' bedroom and pointed to a window. I dashed toward it and looked out. There was no sign of soldiers.

I dived out and fell on my knees.

"Halt!" I heard a voice shout when I got up and started running. I kept sprinting and then heard a blast. It was apparently shot in the air. My aim was to run to the end of the earth but I scooted into the back door of the house next door. I had no choice. I saw soldiers hiding in the lush garden beside the house. Had I kept running, they would no doubt have shot me. There was no one in the kitchen so I cruised into the living room. Wondering if the house was indeed empty, I burst into a bedroom. I found two frightened women looking out the window. I later learned that they were nurses.

I bluntly asked them if they could hide me somewhere, just anywhere. When they didn't respond, I climbed onto the unmade bed and curled up under a pile of blankets. I thought for a moment that a disheveled bed would perhaps be the last place to be searched. But I soon realized the futility of my effort and jumped back out.

The nurses stared at me as if I was a lunatic just escaped from the asylum.

I went to the window, abandoning the whole idea of hiding. I saw the doctor emerging from his house, hands up, followed by Mekonen, Mustefa, Taye, Merid, Agere, the girl who had announced the raid, and others whom I didn't know. I had thought that at least some of them had managed to escape. My eyes were still transfixed on the sad spectacle, when two soldiers came into the house through the back door and drove me out, hands raised high.

I was escorted to the open space before the doctor's house, where the other prisoners were. I was handcuffed behind the back, like everybody else, and ordered to sit on the ground. There were cadres and two men, whom I afterwards learned were security agents from the *Meakelawi Mirmera* – the central investigation agency. A huge crowd was watching the drama from a distance.

A man emerged out of a Land Rover, accompanied by a couple of armed cadres. He hid himself behind dark shades; the hood of his military green jacket pulled up over his head. He looked like a character out of a mystery novel. It was obvious that he was brought to identify people. I would find out later that he was an EPRP member. He had at some point taken shelter at the doctor's house or had worked in the area.

The cadres and security agents had come for the doctor and a nurse. The nurse lived with the two women into whose house I ran but was in Addis at the time. They didn't expect to find the rest of us in the doctor's house. They got so many in one place.

We were a windfall.

"Mekonen Bayisa! Isn't it interesting I found you here? I had gone as far as Gondar to look for you. I can't believe I found you here and so easily at that," one of the cadres, who accompanied the man with the dark shades, said to him.

"Don't I know you from somewhere? Don't I know you at the university campus?" the guy with the dark shades said, coming toward me.

May be that is where I know him. He certainly looks familiar. If only he could take off those dark sunglasses and the hood. "No. You don't know me. I never went to university," I told him quietly.

"I am sure I have seen you somewhere," he insisted, peering into my face.

The older of the two security agents came over and kicked my leg with his boot for no apparent reason. But Taye was the one who was subjected to the most abuse, probably because he was sitting at the far end. Every cadre or security agent passing by gave him a kick with his boot or a knock with a rifle butt.

Once the cadres and security agents got everybody out and thoroughly searched the doctor's house, taking away whatever evidence they could find, they shepherded us to the two Land Rovers parked on the side. The man with the dark sunglasses watched his former comrades struggle to get into the vehicles with their hands tied to the back.

"I am pretty sure I know this girl," he mumbled, while I was waiting in line to get into the back of one of the Land Rovers.

"She is probably the daughter of one of the feudal lords around here," I heard someone say and the next thing I knew was getting a hard whack in the face. It was the older of the two security agents. I wasn't aware he was standing beside me. He grabbed the strings my hands were tied with at the back and flung me into the back of one of the Land Rovers. I ended up on Merid's lap, face down. I struggled to get up and squeezed myself between Merid and the doctor's wife, Meskerem, who was a nurse. Finally, the Land Rovers moved and cut through the throng of spectators.

They turned south when we came out of the hospital compound. I had thought that we were being taken to Addis Ababa. They brought us to a militia training camp in Shashemene, which is about 12 kilometers from Kuyera. We entered into the compound and were directed to an empty room with an earthen floor.

Lying beside Mekonen on the floor, I pondered over what had happened that morning. I knew the inevitable would come one day either in the form of imprisonment or death. But when it happened, it seemed so unexpected. I have had several narrow escapes from death in Addis which I was lucky to circumvent with no skill of my own.

I had been sheltered from the savage witch-hunt taking place in Addis since I arrived in Kuyera. I had almost gotten used to the somewhat lackluster but peaceful life there. A moment came that I had come face to face with death. I just couldn't come to terms with my fate. I closed my eyes and was rehearsing the story that I've been concocting since we got at the militia camp when I heard someone say, "Haven't I seen you on the bus last Sunday?"

I instantly opened my eyes to a policeman standing in front of me, a rifle slung over his shoulder. He looked familiar. *I am ruined!*

"No, you haven't," I said sharply.

"What? What a liar? Are you telling me I haven't seen you last Sunday? You got on the bus at Mojo…you wore a *netela.* You came over and sat next to me. You bought oranges just before you got on the bus. You got off at the Kuyera hospital around 3:00 in the afternoon. Let me see if you can deny that."

Oh my God! He had indeed seen me just a week ago coming back from Mojo, after receiving the traditional medicine from my mother. "You must have seen somebody that resembles me," I said quietly.

"No, it was *you* that I saw. I remember your face very well. You were sitting right beside me. I have never seen such a liar in my life," he said, wiggling his head in disgust.

I did not intend to carry on the conversation so I kept my mouth shut. He left still shaking his head. Fortunately, there were no cadres or security agents around. That would have complicated things for me.

"This is not a good sign," Mekonen said, a faint smile crossing his face.

I had been telling him earlier that I was going to deny knowing any of them. I even told him that I would go to Gondar to reestablish contact with the Party if I managed to get released. The little note that I was given in Addis over two months ago with the contact information was still hidden in my bag. I had to deny I was on the bus that Sunday for my story to hold.

Around lunchtime, two soldiers came and led us out, and we lined up side by side on the veranda facing hundreds of militiamen, separated only by a small shade garden. The militias, peasants conscripted from all over the country, had been training and had just come back for lunch. Russians and Cubans were training them.

Someone, perhaps the administrator of Shashemene, addressed the officers, cadres and militia, claiming that "twelve counter-revolutionaries have been taken prisoner red-handed in Kuyera." Before he even finished his speech, the militia surged forward and demanded that we should be handed over to them so that they could take a "swift measure" against us. They had to be coaxed into having lunch. "The counter-revolutionaries will be turned over to you – the owners of the revolution – as soon as we are done with their interrogation. There is so much that they could give out," the administrator lulled them.

They were not to be pacified.

Standing beside Mekonen on the veranda, I was astounded and perplexed by their behavior. *Why are they overzealously hostile toward us? Wasn't the peasantry one of the main classes we've been fighting for?*

Suddenly, Getachew's words reverberated through my head like a thunderclap. "The peasantry, in a country such as ours, is not only the backbone of the army but also of the revolution. We have to educate and organize it in order to win its support. If we don't do enough in the rural areas and if we can't organize the peasantry on time, we won't be able to rally it behind us."

It was a moment of illumination. With sudden clarity, I saw the mistakes of the Party that Getachew had so earnestly been trying to make me see. *Did he have to die for me to realize this? Had we done something to educate and organize these people, had we not concentrated our forces in the cities, they would not be behaving this way.*

I felt in my being of beings the seeds of doubt, planted a few months ago, sprouting and tearing through every fiber in my body. When Getachew was killed, I had believed that it was a few individuals who had created all that mess, not the Party. It was the hope that those individuals would come to their senses that allowed me to carry on. But now, the edifice that I had painstakingly built around the Party was tumbling down right in front of my eyes. I felt my hopes and dreams dissipate into the oppressive atmosphere of the militia camp.

Tears pooled into my eyes.

I gawked at the militia who were still chanting and pressing forward. *Why are they doing this? Are they doing it to prove their loyalty to the same Derg that is sending them to war and getting them killed by thousands? Are they making us responsible for all the misery the Derg has brought upon them?*

The administrator tried to mollify them saying we would be handed over to them as soon as we were through with interrogation. I was relieved when the two soldiers convoyed us back into the room.

Emotionally drained, I fell asleep as soon as my back touched the floor, despite the heartache, the pain on my right arm, the few kicks and the slap that I had received from the older security agent and the burning sensation on my lacerated knee. My knee was hurt when I leapt out of the window of the doctor's house.

Around six in the evening, we were asked to come out on the veranda again and stand facing the militia. There were also military and police officers, district administrators, and cadres who had come from as far as Yirgalem. In a formal speech, the administrator of the province conjectured that the capture of twelve "counter-revolutionaries" was a huge victory for the revolution.

The militiamen once again shouted slogans and pressed forward only to be pushed back by soldiers. They were told once again that we would be all theirs once we were done with the investigation.

The soldiers untied our hands and allowed us to go to the toilet one by one. When we came back, we were handcuffed, our hands to the back, and were escorted to the two Land Rovers parked in the compound. When the two Land Rovers left the compound, the peasants banged the windows, hurled insults and wagged their index fingers at us.

I was relieved once we exited the compound.

Not long after we started our journey to Addis, the Land Rover I was in shook violently and almost slid to one side. I thought it was going to roll over, killing us all. For a fraction of a second, I regretted that the accident didn't happen. I was convinced we might have been better off dying in a car accident than face gruesome torture and execution.

I stared at the landscape through the window, unable to make sense of what had happened to us all that day. My senses had become numb. I looked at the comrades sitting facing me and beside me. They all seemed lost in deep thought.

My stomach turned from side to side.

I was wearing a short-sleeved blouse and a skirt. My right arm, the one I had a problem with, was so swollen I thought my muscles were going to burst any minute. At some point, I asked one of the cadres to please tear the sleeves off my blouse. He did, giving me respite.

We reached the capital city around the middle of the night. I thought we would be brought to one of those dreadful prisons: the prison in the compound of the Derg headquarters (which is commonly called the Derg office) or the *Meakelawi Mirmera*. Instead, the car made a left turn at Nifasilk, by the Gotera, and entered a villa compound. The first thing that I saw on our right was forty to fifty young men huddled in the garage. In a fleeting second, I realized that they were prisoners. The place was *Kefitegna* 19.

The Derg had created *Kefitegnas* to centralize and manage the activities of hundreds of *Kebeles*. Every *Kefitegna* had a number of *Kebeles* under its jurisdiction, and many of these *Kebeles* and all of the *Kefitegnas* had prisoners in their custody.

Once we got off the Land Rovers, we were steered into the villa. We settled on the cement floor and were given pen and paper to write our statements. I wrote that my name was Senait Hailu and had come from Assela (from the province of Arsi), which is about 175 kilometers from Addis and 60 to 70 kilometers from Kuyera, to seek medical treatment at the hospital.

I had gone to Assela a couple of times before the revolution. On one of my trips, I had stayed for over three weeks at my maternal uncle's, a police officer, and had just been transferred from Massawa. I thought I would be able to say a few things about the town if I had to. I didn't have to worry about making up an illness. I wrote that I was on my way to the hospital when I noticed the raid, and I was so frightened I went into the first house I came across. I didn't know what else to say for being in the house at the time of the roundup.

When we were done, some of us were directed to the independent service quarters in the back of the villa. They told me to come into a room, which was, in fact, a torture chamber. I had to stand at the door and watch the doctor being tortured.

The chamber had all sorts of torture paraphernalia devised by the ingenious human brain. It was dimly lit, and the older security agent and a cadre were busy hoisting the doctor on wooden poles. They blindfolded him and gagged his mouth with a rag. Then I saw a swinging baton violently falling and rising on his feet. Occasionally, the older security agent would loosen the rag on the doctor's mouth and ask him to tell the truth. Unable to watch, I closed my eyes, forgetting that was the reason they made me stand there. I then let my eyes wander in the ominous room.

Finally, they untied the doctor and two men carried him outside. I had the chance to look at his blue and inflated feet when they took him past me. The security agent then beckoned me over.

"Do you want to tell the truth or go through what you just saw?" He glared at me when I stood in front of him.

"I have already told the truth in my statement," I said calmly.

He nodded to the cadre and before I knew it I was hanging on the poles upside down, my feet tied with a rope. They blindfolded me and gagged my mouth with the same rag that the doctor was gagged with. The same cadre beat me with a yellow rubber pipe. He would stop beating me for a few minutes and the security agent would untie the cloth on my mouth and ask me to tell the truth and I would say I had already told him and the cadre would resume his beating.

The worst part of it was when the security agent chocked me for a few seconds. Just when I thought I was going to pass out, he would remove his hand and then ask me to tell the truth. I stuck to my story. When I was finally led out of the room, Mesekerem, the wife of the doctor was called in.

Those of us who were tortured were told to walk barefoot on the cemented ground outside. It was the most painful sensation I had ever experienced. A couple of *Abyot Tebakis* sauntered around us, rifles on their shoulders, to ensure we moved along. Since I couldn't take the pain any longer, I squatted to take a few minutes break. "Keep walking!" one of the *Abyot Tebakis* shouted. I stood up. "Keep walking!" I heard someone else yell, and the next thing I knew was receiving a huge slap on my right cheek. I thought it was from another *Abyot Tebaki*. It was the older security agent. He had come out of nowhere. *He really hates me.*

They led us back to the villa. Mekonen, the girl who notified us of the roundup in Kuyera and I were taken into a room. There were a few girls sleeping on the floor. They sat up when we came in and offered us a *gabi*. Mekonen took off his light blue jacket and gave it to me. I folded it and put it under my head. The three of us shared the *gabi* to cover ourselves and we lay down on the bare cement floor. My feet hurt badly when I stretched my legs. It had been a long and grueling day. Instantly, I fell asleep.

I opened my eyes when I heard someone shout, "Make sure the Shashemene group stays in!" I looked around and tried to figure out where I was. Then I saw girls across the room getting dressed in a hurry. I remembered that they were the ones who gave us the *gabi* the previous night. I saw Mekonen sleeping beside me. I felt pain on my feet and remembered the beatings. *I am in jail!*

It was five in the morning and prisoners had to go out for their daily compulsory exercise. A cadre came into the room and told us that the three of us should not come out. I wondered where the rest of the comrades were.

"How are your feet?" Mekonen asked, looking at me sideways.

"Okay," I said, trying to cover them with the *gabi*.

"It is amazing how fast you fell asleep," he said, smiling and shaking his head.

I forced a smile and went back to sleep.

The girls offered us breakfast later in the morning. Mekonen, the girl and I headed out to meet the rest of the Shashemene group, as we were referred to. We went to the back of the villa where we found them sitting in a circle outside. I noticed a beautiful young woman, Konjit, talking to Meskerem, the doctor's wife. I learned she was one of the nurses in whose house I sought refuge in Kuyera. She had come to Addis Ababa the night before we were arrested and had been brought in that morning.

There were twelve rooms in the service quarters and were all filled up with prisoners. There were hundreds of them outside, some strolling and others sitting and chatting. There was absolute silence when the radio announced (through a speaker tied onto the office window) that twelve "counter-revolutionaries were apprehended the previous day in Kuyera." We, the Shashemene group, looked at one another in surprise. Around mid-morning, we were summoned to the office and asked to give our statements once again.

I did not change my story.

One morning, about a week after we were brought in, I was in room #3 when I heard someone call out, "Senait Hailu!" Limping out, I was told to come to the office. At the front of the villa, I saw the girl who had warned us about the raid and a young boy, also arrested with us, standing beside a Land Rover. The older security agent and Muluneh, one of the cadres who had come to Shashemene the day we were arrested and had tortured the doctor, his wife and me, were with them. Muluneh motioned to me to come. I went up to him.

He told me that I was released and that they were taking me back to Kuyera. It was too good to be true. I was not prepared for such an early and easy exit and didn't know how to react. I didn't have to go back to the dorm since I had no possessions of any kind. "Get in the back," cadre Muluneh called out to the three of us, pointing to the Land Rover. Just when I was about to climb in the vehicle, the older security agent said, "I have changed my mind. This girl is staying. The others can go."

"Why? Didn't we agree she was to be released?" asked Muluneh.

"I don't believe a word she has told us. I have a feeling she is not telling the truth," he said, looking at me with hostility.

"I told the truth. I don't know any of those people," I protested. His eyes told me that his decision was final.

"Please let me go," I pleaded.

"You will go through another round of interrogation and if you are innocent, I will drive you back to Kuyera. For now these two can go." He closed the back door of the truck after the girl and the boy.

The girl and the boy were released because they had stated in their statements that they were personal servants of the doctor. I went back to my room, brooding on the missed opportunity.

Getting released was not going to be so easy, after all. The next morning or the morning after, Mekonen signaled to me when I came out of room #3. He was sitting outside with Taye and Agere. "It is over," Agere said when I sat on the lawn. Agere was a student at Leul Mekonen Secondary School and a political science major at Haile Selassie I University. He was one of the earliest recruits of *Abyot* and had worked in Wolayita before the merger of *Abyot* and EPLO. He was a straight-A student from high school to university. He had an exceptional sense of humor. In the sophomore year, he was one of the few theoreticians on Marxist theory on campus. In third-year, he was in the executive of USUAA congress. He was arrested in February 1972, by the Haile Selassie government and held in the *Meakelawi* and in the Kolfe and Gibe (Boater) camps for about 6 months. He went to Woldya to teach after he was released. He returned to campus in 1974, but went to Dejen (in the province of Gojjam) for *Zemecha*.

"What is over?" I asked.

"They know everything," Mekonen said.

"How do they know? What happened?" I asked, shifting my eyes from one to the other.

"They have been told by one of the comrades brought with us. He is in the office right now. He was there last night, too," said Taye. Taye was a university student and had gone to Shimeles Habte in high school. He was president of the Students' Council at the school. He was also a member of the Students' Council of Councils representing his school. The Council of Councils was formed in 1970.

Minutes later, they summoned us to the office. Zerihoun, the lead cadre of the *Kefitegna*, told us that they are trying to handle our case "democratically," and that we should cooperate for our own sake. The security agents from the *Meakelawi* would like us transferred to the prison at the Derg office. Going there would mean undergoing severe torture and much more. Later, they let us go so that we could mull over what we had been told.

The next morning, we were all called back to the office and asked to give our statements anew. So our identities had become known. Berhanu, one of the cadres, led me into an office and pointed to a pen and paper neatly placed on the desk. I sat on one of the chairs and began writing down my confession. There was nothing to confess. Before I was arrested, I always prayed to die instantly before I betrayed anyone. The idea of giving up my comrades was what really worried me whenever I thought of going to jail.

But this time, there wasn't anything to give up. Almost everybody I had worked with was either in prison, dead or had fled. I hadn't worked in Kuyera or in the South, so I had no knowledge of what was going on. It was my first time to meet all the IZ members brought in with me except for Merid, whom I met upon arrival in

Kuyera. I had never met the rest of the people except for the doctor and his wife. They occasionally came to the doctor's (my host in Kuyera) house, but I had never been to their house before the meeting date and never knew they were involved with the EPRP.

My detention hadn't even given me the chance to see for myself if I had the resources to withstand torture. I knew that what I had gone through the night I arrived was just a slap on the wrist compared to the horrendous torture many were subjected to. The cadre was sitting across the desk and watching me write, when the phone rang. He jumped to his feet, walked over to a desk in the corner and answered it.

"Hello! Yes sir! We've started working with them, sir. Right now, I am in the middle of taking the statement of one of the girls. Sir, I don't think they need to be transferred at this point. If there are some who do not cooperate, we will definitely move them there. Yes, the security here is very tight, sir. Don't worry, sir. We watch them carefully. No, they have not yet notified their families, sir. We make sure that they won't until the investigation is completed. Yes, sir, I understand that," he said, a thin line of sweat running down his temple.

"The comrade was a high ranking Derg member. He wants you all transferred to the prison at the Derg office. I assured him you are cooperating. I hope you will, for your own sake. If you don't, it is going to be bad for you and for us too," Berhanu said.

Soon after, the girl and the boy who had been released were brought back with a few more girls, perhaps from Wolayita and Shashemene. The boy and the girl would eventually be released again, a couple of months later.

The day after I gave my statement, I was outside sitting on the steps of room #3 when I noticed someone trying to get my attention through the office window. It was an older man, one of the

Kefitegna officials I had seen in the office during my interrogation. I pulled to my feet and went to the office. He was the only one there and asked me to have a seat. He handed me a pencil and a red cardboard. I stared at him, not understanding.

"I want you to draw the youth organization structure. Actually, that is not what I called you for," he said.

I looked at him with questioning eyes.

"If someone comes in, you have to pretend you are drawing the League structure. You know...I feel sorry for you," he said, looking me in the eye with a touching sympathy.

"Why?"

"Because I know they are going to kill you. I hear what they say about you and your friends. I know you are not allowed to notify your family about your arrest until you are through with the interrogation, but I want to help. Call your parents and let them know you are here. Remember if somebody comes in, you are drawing the youth organization structure." He pushed the phone toward me.

"Thank you, but no. I want them to forget about me and live their lives. I know they have suffered the past few years because of me and I don't want them to suffer more."

"You fool, it is even worse for them not to know what has happened to you. You should call them and let them know you are here. Do you think they will forget you just like that?" he said, snapping his thumb and middle-finger.

He went on, "Don't be so cruel. It is much better for them to know you are dead than wonder what had happened to you for the rest of their lives. Hurry up! What is the number? I will dial it for you. Tell me the number please before somebody shows up."

I gave it to him reluctantly.

"Here, it is ringing," he said, handing me the receiver and a smile of encouragement crossing his face.

"Hello!" It was my sister Almaz.

I almost hung up on her. "Etete!"

"Hiwot! Where are you?"

"I am in… I am in prison."

"Oh, which prison? When were you arrested?"

"About ten days ago. I am at *Kefitegna* 19. It is by the *Gotera*"

"I will be right there."

I hung up the phone and stared at the older man.

"God bless you. Now I am relieved. I felt so sorry for you ever since I heard about your case. I wish I had never seen you. I will always remember you. I will pray to God to save your life. You have touched my heart. Now go. Keep this to yourself. I have a family to take care of. I know I can count on you. Be brave and believe in God. He will look after you," he said with a heart-wrenching sympathy.

"Thank you so much and trust me I won't let you down," I said with a lump in my throat.

He came over, grabbed my hand, blessed me and wished me good luck one more time. Just when I was about to go, a cadre came in. I had no idea who he was. I looked at the older man who was standing and staring at me. He winked at me and looked down at the cardboard. I seated myself back on the chair, picked up the pencil and started drawing the Youth League structure. The cadre went to another room, came, stood behind me, and watched what I was doing. The older man went back and sat down on his chair.

He said to the cadre with a nervous smile, "It is the youth organization structure - you see? That was how they divided the city. Isn't it amazing?"

The man did not seem to understand. He listlessly stared at the red cardboard and without saying a word. A few minutes later Muluneh came in, his Kalashnikov dangling from his shoulder. He came over and looked on silently.

"She is drawing the youth organization structure," the older man said with a feigned excitement.

I felt sorry for him for desperately trying to cover up what he has done earlier. Muluneh was impressed. When I was done, he picked up the cardboard from the desk and told us that he was going to paste it on the wall. He was asking for a tape when I slipped out.

I went back to room #3 thinking about my family. *What I did was wrong. I shouldn't have made that call. It would have been better for them not to know. There are so many families who don't know what had happened to their sons and daughters.*

My family had been through an ordeal because of my illness, and in the past year and a half I had caused them much fear and anxiety by running away from home. The last thing I wanted was to make them suffer more. I became morose and lay down. A few minutes later, I heard a girl asking for me. I ran out and found her carrying plastic containers, a thermos, clothes and a pair of flip-flops. She was on duty to deliver food that day.

"It is from your sister. She sends her regards," she said.

"Tell her I am doing fine," I said, taking the clothes from her. She brought the food and the thermos to room #12. I was assigned in room #12, but I went there only in the evening to sleep since my two friends, Meskerem, the doctor's wife, and Konjit, the beautiful nurse, were in room #3.

I ran to room #12 and immediately changed into jeans, a top and a brown sweater. They were clothes that I had left behind when I had walked out in September 1976. It felt good to have something to change into. I was tired of borrowing clothes and washing mine at night. I had no shoes either (I had lost my flip-flops the day I was arrested) and walked barefoot and put on somebody's flip-flops from the pile at the door to go to the toilet.

I came back from room #12 and sat at my usual spot: on the doorstep of room #3. I sensed someone watching and saw the older security agent peering through the office window. Moments later, I saw him coming toward me. Every time he came to our quarter, girls would tell me to hide since he had made it a habit of either kicking me with his boots or slapping me on the face for no reason. He looked furious and walked faster than usual, his chest puffed up and swinging his arms violently. He came over, kicked me with his boot on my legs, and barked, "Where did you get those clothes?"

I did not respond. I simply stared at him.

"Tell me where you got those clothes! Come to the office. Actually, bring your belongings with you. You are going to the Derg office," he growled.

I went to room #12, grabbed the plastic bag that contained the few clothes my sister had sent, and followed him to the office. There were several cadres in the office chatting noisily. The older man, who made the phone call, was among them.

The agent demanded, "Tell me how you got those clothes. How did you manage to inform your family about your arrest?" He then turned to the head cadre, Zerihoun, and screamed, "If this is how the Shashemene group is being handled, I should report the matter to the authorities and have them all transferred to the Derg office. How can we continue with the investigation if they alert their people and help them escape or hide or destroy evidence? The hell with your idea of democratic method! What these people need is a good beating."

I saw the old man through the corner of my eye. His eyes implored me.

"Do we have any evidence that she had informed her family? Hiwot have you informed your family?" Zerihoun asked.

"No, how would I inform them?"

The agent roared, "Where did you get those clothes then? You have been wearing the same thing since you got here. All of a sudden you show up in wrangler and fancy slippers?"

I didn't say a word, which seemed to make him even more furious.

"I know she won't say anything. Why would she? She knows nothing is going to happen to her. She is being handled democratically," he said sarcastically.

There was clearly antagonism between the security agents and the cadres. The agent came over and struck me on the face, saying, "Follow me; I am taking you to the Derg office."

"You can't. She is under the authority of this *Kefitegna*. It is the chair of the *Kefitegna* or I who have authority here. You need an authorization letter from the Derg office if you want to take her away," said Zerihoun firmly.

The security agent came over and hit me on the face again so hard that I became dizzy for a second.

"Please stop it. We will investigate the matter," Zerihoun said visibly upset. He then turned to me and said, "You can go back now. Please respect the rules for your own sake."

About a week or so after our real identities were known, I was told that I had a visitor. I limped to the gate and saw Azeb's mother outside the prison compound. I was excited to see her. We were standing too far apart to hear each other. I asked after Azeb and she nodded indicating that she was doing fine. I didn't know how she had found out I was in jail. It was only afterwards that I learned it was Azeb who had asked her to come and visit me.

A month or less after I was arrested and two weeks after Azeb's mother came to visit me, Tayech, a former EPRP member, asked me to come to the toilet with her. As soon as we went in, she put her arms around me, tears streaming down her cheeks.

"What happened?" I asked, getting alarmed.

"Azeb Girma has been executed!"

For a moment, I didn't know where I was. We cried on each other's shoulders. We wiped our tears and went back to room #3. Meskerem, the doctor's wife, knew that Azeb and I were friends and didn't know how to break the sad tidings to me. Tayech must have heard of Azeb's execution from her.

I cried all that night. I remembered everything Azeb and I did together. Even though we had never worked together, we were inseparable and had shared so many things. I closed my eyes and thought of the ordeal she must have endured. I remembered her courage and determination, which I had heard so much about. Her sincerity and innocence came back to me. I could see her shy smile. I could feel her pushing me away when I leaned on her sitting in a cab.

She was the sensible one in our group on campus, holding us back every time we crossed the line. Her sense of responsibility and discipline was unparalleled. The image of her walking in front of the Post office kept coming again and again. That was the last time I saw her.

I thought of Semegne and Getachew. *Oh my God! They are all gone.* The pain became unbearable. The only solace was that I was going to join them soon. It was about a month since I'd been arrested and I didn't believe I was going to last long.

I kept crying under my blanket and couldn't sleep for several nights. I dragged myself through the days that followed, wondering when some of us would be executed or simply expire under torture. I wondered if Sara and Kidist had learned about

Azeb's death. I didn't even know if Sara was still in prison. I later learned that she was released after a year. Kidist had her second child, a boy, around the time I was arrested.

I had no doubt in my mind, until I was brought in to the *Kefitegna*, that what we had started would continue no matter what the obstacles. I had believed that our goal had a linear progression, which could not be stopped no matter how bumpy the road was. Tossed in prison, I realized our project had failed, our comrades were wiped out, and our very lives were hanging on a thin thread.

I found out the hard way that the Party had not only made grave errors, but had at the time been totally quashed. How it could have been vanquished so quickly and easily was beyond my grasp. *Where did we go wrong? It started so beautifully; but what happened? Didn't the Party claim victory was ours...that it would turn its enemies into dust? Where did all that might go?* My dreams were shattered, my heart throbbed with grief, and my mind became numb with disillusionment.

Only my spirit struggled to persevere.

Man never made any material as resilient as the human spirit.
   -Bernard Williams

Even though executions and torture were meant to break our spirits, we survived daily tensions through a variety of ploys. It wasn't just what was taking place at *Kefitegna* 19 that created suspense and nervousness but also lurid accounts of torture and executions at other prisons and *Kefitegnas*.

Kefitegna 19 was originally a villa. It belonged to a feudal lord, Dejazmach Kebede Bizunesh, a war hero during the Italian occupation and executed by the Derg in the western part of the country, in Jibat ena Mecha. He had been fighting against the Derg and was killed in action.

There were close to four hundred prisoners at the *Kefitegna,* almost all of whom were EPRP members or suspected members. The Derg had shifted its fury to *Meison* after it had cleaned the country of EPRP. Most of the new prisoners, jailed after we were brought in, were either *Meison* members or others who had no political affiliation. One day, even a sorcerer was brought in, accused of duping people. There were also those thrown in for contraband arms sales. The illegal arms trade flourished in those days, the network extending from Addis to Ogaden, in the eastern part of the country.

The *Kefitegna* compound was spacious. The service quarters had about ten individual rooms filled with prisoners, except for room #8, which was the torture chamber. Torture later took place in one of the rooms in the villa. Room #1 used to be a traditional kitchen with clay hearths. Room #12 is a kitchen inside the villa. It adjoined the dining room turned office. There were on average twenty-five prisoners in each room. The garage had the most number of prisoners, about 40 or so. Women occupied rooms #2, #3 and #12.

Room #12 was the cleanest and brightest. There was a bathroom past the kitchen, where the four of us slept, as there was not enough room in the kitchen. We used the bathroom only for sleeping. The pipe below the sink leaked and we had to get up several times in the middle of the night to fold our blankets and *gabis,* as the water threatened to wet our beddings. Oftentimes, we found a blanket or a *gabi* drenched in water. It was only after a few girls were released that we moved into the kitchen.

Torture was routine at *Kefitegna* 19. Some of the cadres, like Muluneh, were experts in the trade and were sought after when new prisoners were brought in. There was this EPRP member, Tesfaye Kebede, whose feet looked horrendous with charred flesh and deep wounds from beatings and burning at another *Kefitegna* (perhaps at *Kefitegna* 15). They had sprinkled gasoline over his feet and ignited them. They said he had never given in to the brutal torture. He couldn't walk and room-mates carried him out and back in his room. He gradually started walking with a cane. Of all the prisoners I had met at *Kefitegna* 19, he was the one who had really touched my heart. He was quiet and smiled all the time despite his horrific injuries.

It was not only political prisoners who resisted torture and protected their "comrades-in-arms." This older man, taken in for contraband arms sales, was tortured like no other. Fellow prisoners asked him why he would not give up names instead of going through all that. He told them that it was "un-Christian" to give up a fellow human being. His torturers finally gave up, unable to force a word out of his mouth and later released him.

Death was a constant threat, but we were not paralyzed by the fear of it. We did chores, chatted, laughed, loved, hated, played, and read. The only time it showed its power over us was when a cadre or a *Meakelawi* agent came to a dorm and asked to light a candle in the middle of the night. Except for rooms #8 and #12, none of the dorms had electricity. When cadres or security agents came in the dead of night, everybody sat up and watched with an unnerving silence. The question on everybody's mind was, "Would I be the one to go tonight?" The cadre or cadres may have come to drop off a new prisoner or they were simply drunk and were making a "round" in the middle of the night, sending waves of terror across dorms.

Another spine-chilling moment was when we heard cars coming into the compound at witching hours. We would be at our wits' end, thinking they had come to take prisoners away for execution. Often, the cadres were only coming back after a night out, usually drunk.

Once, cadre Berhanu was going from dorm to dorm late at night when he stopped at the door of one of the men's dormitories. Everybody instantly covered their heads with blankets, pretending to be asleep. He stood at the door silently for a few minutes. One of the prisoners poked his head out of the covers thinking he had gone. Berhanu, tipsy as usual, commanded the prisoner to get up and follow him to the torture room. He beat him, simply out of spite.

Since room #12 was adjacent to the office, we could hear every move from the cadres. After the torture chamber moved inside the villa, we even heard prisoners being tortured. Everybody sat motionless, in torture jitters.

Samrawit was one of those people who was constantly racked with these jitters. She was my dorm-mate and the daughter of one of the richest men in the country. Samra and some friends, also from wealthy families, were arrested during the mass mobilization denunciation and self-denunciation frenzy, which took place in *Kebeles* earlier.

When people were forced to denounce themselves and others at a *Kebele* meeting, Samra and her friends had nothing to say, for they had no political involvement. At the same time, they worried they might be suspected of holding back. So they chose to 'confess' that they had read *Teyik* – inquire – a glossary of revolutionary terms sold in bookstores. The cadres were so enraged over what they thought was an indefeasible apathy they brought the girls in so that they could be "enlightened." They kept them there for about four months.

Samra was so terrified of being tortured she often flared up when someone called her name at night.

"Samra!"

"Who is calling my name?" she would say, rolling her big eyes.

"It is me. Have you seen…?"

"Why are you calling my name at night? I don't want anybody calling my name at night!"

"She is scared of *Megelbet*." Someone would say. *Megelbet* means to be hung upside down on a pole and be tortured.

"When they hear her name the cadres might remember that they have to torture her," somebody else would say to tease her.

"Can you please keep it down? Don't you know that they can hear you? I don't want to be called to the office at night. I don't even want amorous moments at night, let alone being called to the office," Samra would implore.

We enjoyed those Samra moments. They put smile on our faces.

Love was another potion that made news of executions from other prisons and tortures at the *Kefitegna* bearable. Many were paired and nestled together or took a walk. Some even went on a date outside the prison compound, with the excuse of seeing a doctor, if they were one of those prisoners whose cases were not serious.

The *Kefitegna* allowed many prisoners to go to school during the day and come back in the evening. They took turns to go home every Friday afternoon and came back Sunday evening. A few older prisoners also went to work and returned before dusk.

During the day, most prisoners sat outside in small groups and chatted or told jokes to lighten up the tense atmosphere. Some walked up and down with friends. Most prisoners took their daily walks around five in the afternoon. Others stayed inside and read books.

Two male prisoners, whom we called police, were assigned every day from each dormitory. At six in the evening, they clapped their hands, which meant we had to go inside. Their main responsibility was to make sure that everybody in each dorm used the only toilet by eight o'clock. We were not allowed to go out after that. If there was an emergency, we called the *Abyot Tebakis*.

The two "police" passed around cigarettes, books, tea, notes and other items from room to room. Sunday was a busy night for them. Some dorms had more goodies than others did, and boys and girls sent them to their friends and sweethearts.

Volleyball was an important pastime for some. I had a passion for it, and had played for my school in junior high. At the *Kefitegna*, we bought a medium-sized latex ball for seventy-five cents and played for hours.

Life at the *Kefitegna* was communal. We shared many things, but each "house" had absolute ownership of all the food that came in every day. There was not enough food to go around after many prisoners were released. To mitigate the shortage of food, every dorm designated two individuals to serve as its "Food Committee." Food Committee members counted the number of "dishes" that came in each day, and reported it to two prisoners who would go from dorm to dorm and get all the numbers. This was my job for a while. These two individuals tallied the number of "dishes" received and redistributed them to each dorm based on the number of prisoners they housed. The Marxian maxim, *from each according to his ability, to each according to his needs* was thus put into practice.

The Food Committee also made tea in the morning, washed cups, and raised money to buy bread for breakfast. After breakfast, they took out the double folded blankets – mattresses were not allowed – out into the sun and shook them well before they brought them back in.

Other duties included keeping the cement floor swept and mopped; no one entered the dorm with their shoes on. They also received our lunches and returned empty containers. Around noon, they served lunch. We sat on the floor in the middle of the room in two or three groups and ate from large trays. After lunch, the Food Committee washed the dishes and kept them apart, so that they could be returned to the families the next day.

In the evening, they served dinner if there were any leftovers. A few family members, who lived nearby, also brought food in the afternoon. My sister and my cousin took turns to bring mine every morning. My mother often came in the afternoon, despite my insistence that she should not. She had to come all the way from Semen Mazegajia and without fail told the prisoners who received my food that she was just passing by and thought she might as well drop off my supper.

That was her way of making sure that I was still alive.

Mandatory Marxism-Leninism sessions took place for two hours every morning. Each dorm was provided with a handout on the basics of Historical Materialism. The idea was to "raise" our political consciousness. None of us liked these sessions. To begin with, many of us were familiar with the literature. Most importantly, no one seemed to be interested in it any more. It was in a way a reminder of our failed dream. There was this older woman called *Etiye* Zenebu. She was accused of being involved in the teeming contraband arms sales. After most of her roommates in room #2 were released, she came to room #3 to participate in the daily Marxism-Leninism study sessions, which was meaningless as far as she was concerned.

"Do you have a supplementary *Etiye* Zenebu?" the chairperson asked her one day, while a discussion was going on.

"I have more important things to think about than worry about your supplementary. I have four kids at home. I am concerned that my ten-year old daughter will burn herself trying to cook for her younger siblings. She asks me if I have a supplementary! You are all good for nothings putting your parents into trouble. They go to such lengths to bring food for you every day and all you do is sit here adding and subtracting nonsense," she snarled.

We burst out into a roar of laughter. We were too immature to understand her motherly concerns.

Afternoon sessions were torturous. It was singing time, and almost all the "revolutionary" songs were denouncements of the EPRP. A general assembly was also held in the garage once a week. Questions that were not answered in each dorm during the Marxism-Leninism sessions were brought to the general assembly for discussion. Every so often, we organized "camp fire" (even though there was no fire). Talented boys and girls performed skits, sang songs or read poems. Those moments brightened our lives and gave a sense of normalcy to the otherwise uncertain and often tense situation.

When visitors came on Sunday, we stood a few steps away from the gate and waved at them. If the *Abyot Tebakis* were kind enough, we could have a quick look at them on a weekday, too. The

Shashemene group was not allowed to enjoy this privilege for a period of time.

Cadres and officers trooped into the *Kefitegna* to have a glimpse of the most famous member of the Shashemene group: Mekonen Bayisa. He was the highest-ranking Party member in their hands at the time, and cadres from the Political School or other *Kefitegnas* and even some military officers (perhaps Derg members) came to see him. I was often called in with him on such occasions. They would say, "Is this Mekonen's secretary?" They spoke as if I were Mekonen's personal secretary just because they had heard that I was a member of the sub-Secretariat office in the Party structure.

The *Shashemene* group was inspirational to many prisoners. Some of the members of the group were high-ranking Party members and the rank-and-file looked for opportunities to hear from them about the Party and the League.

Mekonen, in particular, was highly regarded by the prisoners. He had been a charismatic president of the Students' Council at Leul Mekonen High School in Addis Ababa when he was in grade eleven. He was elected twice to the Students' Council of Councils representing his school. He left for the Sudan in 1970 when the security was after him. He came back and in June 1971 he went back, this time with Taye Merid, when the secret service started looking for him again. He re-appeared in 1974, when the revolution broke out.

It was years later that I learned that Getachew and Mekonen knew each other, when the former was secretary of USUAA in 1970. Mekonen was an *Abyot* member and had close relationship with Getachew. Prisoners at the *Kefitegna* were often eager to sit and talk with Mekonen because of his high position in the Party hierarchy and his knowledge of history of the Party and the student movement.

That was not meant to last long.

...people hastily accept whatever they have heard from their fathers and shy away from critical examinations. But God created man to be the master of his own actions, so that he can be whatever he wills to be.
-Zere Yakob, *17th century Ethiopian philosopher*

Even Zerihoun, the lead cadre instrumental in keeping us (the Shashemene group*)* at the *Kefitegna,* didn't last long. One day, we found out that he was executed. He was a member of *Woz League,* one of the Marxist/Leninist organizations that had sprung up and made a marriage of convenience with the Derg. The Derg had been unleashing its fury on them as it earlier did on *Meison.*

I wondered if the "democratic" era was coming to an end.

A new cadre, Daniel, was assigned to the *Kefitegna* in place of Zerihoun. Daniel was one of those EPRP members who had "returned to the revolutionary camp." Many EPRP and *Meison* members were all the while switching organizations (some of them more than once) in order to flee from the Derg's wrath. *Malerid* and *Seded* (Mengistu's Party) were their last refuge until the former was spurned by the Derg. Some of the turned-*Seded* EPRP members became cadres of many *Kefitegnas.*

Daniel held a one-on-one meeting with a few former members of the EPRP in his office the day after he arrived at our *Kefitegna.* I was one of those individuals called for the meeting. When I went into his office, he greeted me flashing his snow-white teeth and told me to sit in a chair across his desk.

"The reason I called you today is to gauge your understanding of the Party's positions on issues...such as the Provisional Peoples Government, the nature of the Derg, United Front and so on," he said.

The image of Getachew flickered before me. He had worked so hard to ensure I had a clear idea of what was what. I answered the questions as best I could and went back to my dorm.

The next day, Daniel called a meeting in the garage. It was his first appearance in front of the general prison population.

"I have had a discussion about EPRP's positions on various issues with ten individuals who were in the top echelons of the Party and the League. I picked out three amongst them whom I thought had a clear understanding of the points in question. From now on, these three individuals will chair meetings at the general assembly. I will provide the topics. The individuals are Mekonen Bayisa, Taye Merid and Hiwot Teffera," he announced, standing at the periphery of the crowd.

I couldn't believe my ears and squinted at Mekonen who was sitting next to me on the dirt floor. He looked astounded too. Daniel told the three of us to stand up so that all the prisoners saw us. They all clapped when we got to our feet. Daniel smiled at us and walked away quickly. Mekonen, Taye and I caught up with him and asked him why he did that without our consent.

He smiled thinly. "I didn't realize I needed permission to help you save your life. But never mind, if you want to become martyrs, go ahead, don't accept the assignment...Hiwot you're going to chair the first meeting. The discussion topic will be the national question. You can come and pick up the handout from my office."

I just stared at him, startled.

He left and came back, took me aside and said, "You know, Hiwot, your family is leaving no stone unturned to save your life. You understand how serious your case is. If you want to die, go ahead and make yourself a martyr. But I think you should think about your family who are doing everything they can to save your life." He walked away, leaving me where I was standing.

I joined Taye and Mekonen and we stood there nervously talking about the new responsibility entrusted upon us. We were reluctant to accept the task owing to the different color it might be given by the general prison population. Other prisoners came and advised us to accept the appointment. "More than enough people have died and we don't want any more to die," they reasoned.

A couple of days later, I went to Daniel's office to collect the handout. He gave me a few days to prepare myself for the meeting. Finally, the day I dreaded the most arrived. I hated speaking in front of a group. I was the quietest even at IZ meetings.

I installed myself on a chair in the middle of the garage, surrounded by hundreds of fellow prisoners. I summed up the content of the handout, which was a theoretical analysis of the national question. It was also a critique of the Eritrean Liberation Fronts' claim that the Eritrean question was a colonial question (i.e., that Ethiopia had colonized Eritrea), which raised the disquieting issue for the Derg of the right of nations to self-determination, right up to secession.

I kept saying the Eritrean *tagayoch* – fighters – instead of *tegentayoch* – separatists – as they were referred to in the handout. I was so much used to saying *tagayoch* I couldn't force out the word *tegentayoch*. Every time I said *tagayoch,* I looked at Daniel from the corner of my eye. He watched me, smiling. I then opened the floor for discussion. To my relief, the discussion went smoothly.

That was the first and last time I chaired the meeting.

On March 21, a little over a week later and less than two months since we had been arrested, *Etiye* Zenebu was standing at the door of room #2 when she signaled me over. It was just after breakfast and I wondered why she would call me. I had never talked to her.

"I have good news for you," she said.

"What kind of good news?"

"I dreamt about you last night. It was such a vivid dream. Everybody was lining up over there to make tea," she said, pointing to the spot where we made tea on an improvised hearth. Each dorm took turns making tea in the morning at the wood fire. That was before each dorm bought portable kerosene stoves.

"I saw you standing in line behind one of your friends," she said.

"Mekonen?"

"I don't know his name. It is that one, the one wearing a jacket." She pointed toward where Taye and Agere were sitting.

"His name is Taye."

"Your friend had made tea and was filling up his thermoses, while you were waiting. When he was done, you picked up a pail and were about to pour the water into the pot when I grabbed your arm. I lifted up the pot from the hearth and threw out the tea that you friend had left, washed the pot with soap and water and splashed clean water into it and put it back on the hearth to boil."

I wasn't quite sure what she was getting at, but listened to her, nevertheless.

"When I woke up, I was amazed by the mercy of God. I said, 'God has saved this girl's life.' I have heard that your case is serious. God has given you another chance at life. I am telling you, I don't usually dream, but when I do, it always comes true. Your life is spared. I threw out the old tea, washed the pot and poured clean water into it. That is the beginning of a new life for you. Mark my words!" she ended excitedly.

I thanked her and went back to my room. I didn't think much of the dream.

Around five o'clock, we were all told to go inside. I went to room #12 and dashed to the bathroom window, along with a few girls, to watch what was going on behind the house. We saw two men, who looked like security agents, heading toward the prisoners' quarters, accompanied by Daniel. One of them was wearing a navy blue T-shirt.

They went door to door calling names. Nine prisoners were called out. They were Taye Merid, Agere Miheretu, Merid Gebrechristos, Fatuma Ali, Meseret Lemma, Tesfaye Kebede (the one badly tortured at another *Kefitegna*), and three other prisoners whose names I did not know. Everybody knew what that meant. The first three were members of the Party IZ Committee in southern Ethiopia. Meseret, who was in her teens, was the youngest among them. I saw Fatuma coming out of room #3 twirling a green scarf over her head. She was a member of the Shashemene group brought in after us.

I couldn't stand there and watch all that. It was so painful. Then it occurred to me that I too might be called out! I took off the green scarf twined around my hip, threw it over my shoulders, went, and stood quietly beside the hand-washing sink. The girls were still looking through the window and suddenly they lowered their heads down whispering, "They are coming to our dorm! They are coming!"

We scurried to the kitchen and sat on the folded blankets on the floor. The two men and Daniel came and paused at the foot of the stairs. My eyes darted from the stocky man with the navy blue T-shirt to his colleague. Their sinister eyes were fixed on us sending out a whirl of terror in the dorm. Daniel was standing behind them, head down.

I was the only candidate there as all of the girls were rank-and-file members of the League or have been thrown in for practically nothing. But the authorities were unpredictable. I expected to hear my name any minute. I was numb, unable to think of anything. I knew the end had finally arrived, but couldn't even make out my feelings. My head felt light and empty. I sat there frozen like everybody else.

What seemed like an endless stare lasted only a few instants forcing upon us an unbearable suspense. All of a sudden, the men turned around and headed to the office. Everybody was relieved. Many even shed tears of joy. At least, for that day, none of us had been taken away. Some girls came over and kissed me for being spared. But the tears of joy and relief were short-lived. We remembered the less fortunate ones. We cried quietly. I suddenly remembered *Etiye* Zenebu's dream. *Oh my God! Taye is taken away!*

I was astounded.

The next morning, news of the nine prisoners came. They had all been shot and their bodies displayed in the streets! It was a horrendous and atrocious day. Some of us were not able to sleep after the prisoners were taken away that evening, and had heard several gunshots at night in the vicinity. It had never occurred to us that the nine prisoners were killed so close to where they have been held. We were told to stay in that morning and were not even allowed to cry; we had to hide our tears. We sat in the dorm with sullen faces and bloodshot eyes.

News of the slaughtered prisoners spread far and wide. Parents flocked to the prison. They demanded to see their children. We heard women wailing. Family members by then knew what it meant when the *Abyot Tebakis* refused to accept a prisoner's food from a visitor. It meant that the prisoner had been killed or, if lucky, transferred to another prison. It was a desperate moment for the family members crying and sobbing that day, suspecting the worst.

Only one woman saw her son. She was screaming and wailing and the *Abyot Tebakis* were unable to manage her. The cadres finally gave in. When the boy came out to wave to his mother, she ululated. In the afternoon, they told him to come to the gate again. When he returned, he brought a new shirt with him. His mother had bought him a new shirt for defying death! Everybody awkwardly smiled despite the sadness.

My mother brought my lunch that morning and was in line when she heard about the execution. Her hands shook and the lunch containers slipped off when she heard that one of the girls, whose body was thrown in one of the streets, wore a green scarf. Helpless, she ran to call my sister Almaz at work.

The previous day, I was doing the dishes under a pipe in the front yard of the villa and had waved at my mother when I saw her standing a few meters away from the gate. I had a green scarf draped around my hip.

She and my sister found out right away that I was not among the slain prisoners. They came in the afternoon with my aunt, anyway. The girl who brought my supper to the dorm told me that they wanted me to send them something that would prove to them that I was still alive. I gave her a green food container telling her it belonged to my aunt. That was how they knew for sure that I had survived the execution.

The prisoners' death had made my own imminent; I knew it was only a matter of time before I drank from its cup with my departed comrades. Death was no longer the existential horror that shattered 'our everyday world.' Its banality had dulled my senses.

I awaited my fate with a come what may attitude.

Days after the execution of the nine prisoners, the gloom that hung over the compound started to give way and a semblance of normalcy set in. But another tragedy struck. One afternoon, Tayech (the girl who told me about the execution of Azeb) asked me once again to follow her to the toilet. I was trembling with panic walking behind her. She threw her arms around my shoulders sobbing as soon as she closed the door behind her. She told me that Askale Nega was dead. She took the cyanide hidden in her collar when she was apprehended. It was indeed a very sad moment. Azeb and I had become friends with Asku during the *Zemecha*. The last time I saw her was at the apartment in Piassa the day those safety pins were scattered on the floor.

Soon after came the day that changed the trajectory of my life. Daniel called an early morning meeting. We had to go straight to the garage after our morning exercise. I wondered what it was about.

They forced us out every day at five in the morning to the front yard for the most hated drill. Muluneh rudely awakened us banging the door and barking "Wake up!" Women were given special consideration during their periods, but we used that excuse as often as we could get away with sleeping in. "How often do you have your periods... every week?" grumbled Muluneh. After exercising, we lined up and chanted a few slogans to condemn our enemies and ourselves.

"Down with feudalism!"

"Down with imperialism!"

"Down with EPRP!"

"Anti-revolutionaries will be vanquished!"

Daniel was standing at the edge of the crowd when I got to the garage. Another cadre, Berhanu, stood beside him. Mekonen Bayisa, bundled in a *gabi*, got up to speak. He gave an analysis of Fascism and said that the Party had made a theoretical error when it said that Fascism had reigned in a country like ours. He said that he held that view even before his incarceration. A huge commotion ensued and Mekonen was bombarded with questions.

Some of the prisoners asked, "How is it that those of you at the top hierarchy of the Party believed that the Derg was not Fascist but convinced us that it was and had us hoist banners, distribute leaflets and hold demonstrations and got us killed and imprisoned in thousands?" They asked him why he did not leave the Party if he did not believe in its position on an issue as important as this one.

Mekonen sat poised and responded to the questions, at times smiling. He said he did not see the need for leaving the Party but had tried to make his view heard through the proper channels. He said, "There are people in other prisons who have worked with me in committees and they can testify to that. You might think I'm saying all this to save my neck, but believe me I have no illusions about that."

Nothing could abate the fire that erupted in the crowd. When the meeting ended, people broke into small groups and engaged in heated discussions. "Did you know he held such views?" a couple of prisoners asked me, while I was walking toward room #3. "No, I did not. It wouldn't have mattered if I did. It is his right to hold any view. I knew people who said the same thing," I responded.

As of that day, a very funny thing happened in the compound: Mekonen became an outcast. Many had lived by the words that came out of his mouth. Besides his top position in the Party, he was an eloquent speaker with a ready smile and a handsome face. Girls particularly worshipped him. After that famous speech, he was not only unseated from his pedestal but also dubbed "opportunist," which was totally insupportable.

I maintained my friendship with him, over the concerns of some of the other prisoners. Soon, I too became excommunicated. What Mekonen and I called a clique was created in the prison compound that mobilized the prisoners against us.

I was very popular among the general membership of the League. It was like high schools days for me. I laughed, played volleyball and took a walk, rain or shine, with many League members. I felt I was sixteen again, forgetting that death was hovering over my head.

After Mekonen's speech, many avoided me like they did Mekonen because they would be cast out off the community for talking to me. I had moved earlier to room #3, where all the ardent female EPRP members were. The *girls* were also members of the clique created in the prison compound.

Interestingly enough, the issue of chairmanship, forgotten after the death of Taye, was retroactively taken up to support some of the accusations against us. Mekonen chaired his first and last meeting a week after I did, a few days before the nine prisoners were killed. In fact, the Marxist-Leninist sessions in the dorms and at the general assembly had been held off after the execution. The general assembly since then had focused on "campfires" and performances.

To my mind, the comrades were not vexed because they felt they were misled. They were incensed because Mekonen had spoken the unspeakable. He had uttered the taboo word: mistake! He had said publicly that the Party had erred. Blasphemer! The Party could not make a mistake! Even if it did, one should not say it in public, not even to oneself.

The Party had indeed made a mistake, as pointed out by Getachew, Berhanemeskel and others. They had warned of the danger and tragic consequences of embarking on the path of urban guerrilla warfare. We had seen the truth of their words in a very short time at that.

I had never heard anyone mention the names of Getachew, Abiyu, Endreas, Bekri and Getachew Assefa, all killed by the Party. It was as if these people had never existed. Talking about them would have been as much a sacrilege as saying the Party was mistaken. The prisoners were all of one mind on this (though some of them wouldn't have known who they were), silently echoing the chorus in Agamemnon.

The rest I did not see,

Nor do I speak of it.

It was all about the Party, not about the revolution, the future of the country or the thousands of its members who had perished in the blink of an eye.

But Berhanemeskel Redda, Getachew Maru, Abiyu Ersamo, Endreas Mikael, Getachew Assefa, Bekri Mohamed and others who spoke out should have been credited for their courage and clairvoyance. They may have lost their lives, but when they fell, they were the victors.

I too had difficulty accepting the idea that the Party could err. Even Getachew believed that comrades had erred, not the Party. As Matheos Abera, Getachew's friend, once told me, "Getachew believed that the Party was good. It was comrades who had made a mistake." Only two days after I was arrested, I remember cringing in horror and shame when one of the comrades remarked at the general assembly, "EPRP is responsible for the death of so many young people." I thought that even the slightest questioning of the Party would have somehow lessened my dedication. Earlier on, I had compartmentalized Getachew and the Party and did not do or say anything to rectify the situation.

I was a member of the Entertainment "committee" in the good old days. That was around the time I moved in room #3. Lemlem, a former EPRP member, and I were the "committee" members. Sunday night, we made tea on a coal brazier and served it with whatever desert we happened to get that day. Our role was to entertain the "house." We had people tell jokes or stories or had them solve puzzles. After the excommunication, I saw no reason to cheer up my former comrades. I restricted my responsibilities to that of making tea.

It was a Sunday afternoon in July 1978. I heard the *girls* (the clique members) whispering that the wife of one of the Central Committee members of *Meison* was being interrogated in the office. We had heard that the Derg had killed her husband outside of Addis almost a year ago. That night, Lemlem and I had just put the cups and the brazier away and gone to bed when someone pushed the door open. That was a most dreaded moment. It might mean for a prisoner to go and vanish from the face of the earth. We peeked our heads out of our blankets to see who was at the door. "Light a candle!" a cadre yelled. A couple of girls got up and scrambled to find a candle. One of the cadres then made his entry into the room carrying a woman in his arms. He put her on the floor close to the door and left.

I knew she was the wife of the *Meison* leader. I immediately got up and asked Lemlem to heat water. I went over and made the woman lie down comfortably. Her feet were swollen and blue. I had never seen anyone tortured the way she was in that *Kefitegna*. I wondered why she had so many layers of clothing as I struggled to remove them one by one. She was probably trying to run away, I thought.

She threw up when we gave her tea. One of the *girls*, who used to be her neighbor, got up finally to help me. She was a more or less moderate follower of the clique. After cleaning the mess, I soaked Emebet's feet in warm water, gave her a massage, and rubbed them with Vaseline.

While all this was going on, the *girls* interrogated the traumatized woman about the whereabouts of her husband. Emebet did not know he had been killed! It was cruel, especially considering the situation she was in.

I knew very well that what I had done that night for Emebet was going to be taken against me. It was bad enough to stand by Mekonen, but showing such humanness toward a *Mesion* was unpardonable. Yet it would have been the ultimate betrayal of my humanity had I not stepped up that night. Even then, I knew a political person was a human being before he or she was a *Meison* or an EPRP member. I shuddered at the behavior of my comrades. Surely, there must be something that made them behave this way.

What was interesting was that day marked the development of a close and lasting friendship between Emebet and me. I found meaning and comfort in her sober outlook toward the political differences between *Meison* and EPRP. She believed that both organizations had made mistakes and that both lacked proper leadership, which precipitated their downfall. Her great sense of humor and wit was a fresh breath of air in the bleak atmosphere of the *Kefitegna*. I also befriended other *Meison* members, which of course, augmented my sins to unconscionable levels.

It took Emebet quite some time to walk on her own again. She had suffered many slights in the dorm, which she took with maturity and equanimity. She was devastated when she later learned of the death of her husband.

Her three kids (two boys and a girl) were staying with her mother-in-law and came to visit her with their nanny a few days after she was brought in. I went to the gate with her to see them. Emebet, aghast, stood there speechless. They all appeared leaner to her. She did not even recognize the youngest child, who had grown up in a few months and appeared to her mother skinny. She was happy to see them but at the same time she was utterly shocked. She looked like she wanted to cry but couldn't. Watching the reactions of the kids and their mother many visitors and some prisoners were moved to tears.

I started suffering from rheumatism in my right arm. The double folded blankets were not padded enough to buffer the cold coming from the cement floor. My right hand was usually swollen, particularly after having played volleyball. Finally, I sent a message to my sister Almaz to smuggle me some more traditional medicine.

A few days later, I was summoned to the office of the chair of the *Kefitegna*. For a fraction of a moment, I thought it was the older security agent who'd wanted to see me. When I went into the chairman's office, I saw Fasika, a cadre whom my paternal aunt knew, sitting on a chair and talking to the chairman.

I felt my heart skipping a beat. *Who is it this time?* I thought he had come again to take me to the funeral of a family member, as he did when my paternal uncle died a few weeks after I was incarcerated. I had stayed at my uncle's for three days. It was a miracle at the time for someone like me, who was in the higher committees of the Party, to go home.

"You are going home for twenty days for treatment. But I don't want you to be seen in public. Neither do I want anyone outside of this compound to know that you are going home," the chairman said to me. "I hope I can count on you on that one," he said, looking at Fasika.

"Of course, you can count on me," Fasika reassured him and told me to go and get my belongings.

I ran to the dorm and told Emebet that I was going home and threw some of my clothes in a plastic bag and bid her goodbye and went to Mekonen's dorm and babbled something about going home. He stared at me with a mixture of smile and surprise written on his face. Before he even spoke, I took off, waving at him.

Fasika was waiting at the gate. He gave the permission slip to the *Abyot Tebakis* stationed at the gate when we went out. I spotted my sister Almaz's car when we came out; my sister, my mother and my aunt were sitting in it. I went over to greet them and they told me to come home with Fasika. I went in his car.

We went to my sister Almaz's house. It felt strange to go back home after so many months. I didn't realize how much I had missed my family until I got there. My younger sister Negede was at school and so were my niece and my nephew. I was eager to see them from up close. Only my little nephew was at home.

We had lunch and my sister Almaz asked me to thank Fasika. She divulged that he was the one who was able to get my name successfully crossed off from three execution lists. I thanked Fasika.

At home, I once again had to go through the horror of the crystal like traditional medicine buried in my elbow in addition to taking the herb every day. For twenty days, I went through hell, crying daily.

I came back to prison to find the situation worse. I had committed another cardinal sin: I had gone home for twenty days! My comrades were furious, as if I was on vacation in some exotic island. They had no idea what I had been through and they wouldn't have cared less, anyway. However, going home by itself was proof, as far as they were concerned, for some of the slanders leveled at me.

One of the *girls* was heard saying, the night I came back from home, "Others who have done less than she did are killed but she gets to go home. It is not fair." I didn't know what I did for them to wish my death.

I was confused and didn't know how to respond to what was happening around me. It threw me off balance. I nested in my dorm and buried my face in books to shield myself from hostile and icy stares. I read Anna Karenina, The Resurrection, The brothers Karamazov and a few others.

But the opportunity helped me turn inward and look at myself as I had never done before. My comrades, in a way, were like a mirror reflecting back at me. I was astounded by the realization that I was once a blind follower. I had obeyed the Party and had remained steadfast in my loyalty even when there were enough grounds for me to question its actions. The Party was an abstract entity to me, insulated from human limitations. Despite Getachew's cold-blooded murder and what I had witnessed after I was arrested, I'd still believed with all my heart that it was good, omniscient and omnipotent.

I became engrossed in internal monologue.

Why do people imitate others? Why do they follow them blindly? Except for the few who manipulate them, many of these people are not bad; so why do they behave this way? Is it because they are afraid to stand on their own? Doesn't each of us know the difference between right and wrong? Isn't each of us endowed with the ability to think for ourselves? Don't people know they are hurting others when they wrongly accuse them?

Appalled by what I observed as a crowd mentality, something in me rebelled. My inner cynic awoke, surmising, albeit rudimentarily, that we are "plastic" beings easily shaped by others.

I knew my comrades suffered from the "death of an illusion." We'd lived in a make-believe world: trying to build a utopia inspired by Marxism. It was difficult to go on after what had happened to our project. All that passion, sense of purpose and the idea of building a redemptive future were gone, never to be retrieved again. There is nothing sadder. It was obvious that it would be difficult to pick up the pieces and move forward, even if our lives were spared. But this didn't explain why Mekonen and I had become scapegoats. Were we responsible for the shattering of our comrades' dreams? Why do people blame others for things that go wrong in their lives?

I often asked myself whether my comrades had to project their frustrations and disappointments on us for being relatively senior members in the Party within the prison community. I came to realize that people somehow lost their individuality and moral independence when they belonged to a crowd whose collective mind dictated their life. *Will I ever belong to a group again? How can I steer clear of the crowd mindset? How can I remain an individual? What was it to me that our intentions were good if the means made me lose my moral integrity?*

I kept examining my thoughts and actions constantly so that I did not backslide into the group mindset. I resolved to remain true to myself and to the world around me. Whatever I did, I wanted to do it with the full awareness of the moral consequences. This became the single most important concern in my life. I often said to myself, "I will never join a group again, if I live through this." Turning inward gave me the will to hold onto the decisions I had made. Yet I realized there was no guarantee I could stick to my decision except for being forever vigilant and becoming acutely aware of my beliefs, behavior and actions.

I became cognizant that the group is everything for its members regardless of the reality, which stares at them individually. This helped me discern that the Party was equated with the revolution and the ideal society we had set out to bring forth. Rather than being a vessel for change, it had become the end. As a result, it had to be armored from the gaze of others even if it meant false allegations. It had to be defended at any cost so that its sacred memory would live on.

Until that point, I had never really seen myself as an individual. I was part of a group with a shared sense of identity and destiny. I was at home with myself and with the world. My belief about the direction of our struggle and what we would be able to achieve was as robust as could be. The internal world of the Party seemed to be suffused with certainty and trust, until the detention and liquidation of Getachew. Even then, my love for the Party overpowered all the doubts and questions that I harbored. I'd believed that all was going to be well again.

After all, life was what we made it out to be, or so I thought.

But at the *Kefitegna*, life became imbued with enigma, confusion and doubt. We no longer controlled our destiny. The Party was totally decimated. It had not proved to be as invincible as I'd imagined. The deaths of Afework, Getachew and my little brother, Minasse, had taught me that life was impregnated with tragedy. The demise of thousands of comrades whom I had never met and of close friends such as Azeb and Semegne had opened up my eyes to the fact that the price we pay for the 'greater good' was costly. What is more, I knew execution would not be long in coming.

But what am I dying for? How lucky were the comrades who had died? They knew what they were dying for. They knew their deaths would be worth the while. There was nothing left for me to die for, except for struggling to maintain my integrity.

I had become an outcast for sticking to what I believed was right. I could have mimicked others and shunned Mekonen, but that would have cost me my integrity and I would never have been able to forgive myself had I done that. I took responsibility for the decision I'd made and lived with the consequences. I lost my comradeship with others but was able to reclaim myself.

As for Mekonen, he never gave in to the sad treatment he was subjected to. He always smiled and opened his heart and mind to whoever wanted to talk to him. He was the one people still turned to learn about the history of the Party. He continued doing that for those who wanted to know, he became their passport to sanity.

He stood tall because of his maturity, patience and gracefulness.

Whatever had happened at the *Kefitegna* meant nothing compared to the grand scheme of things. But my heart ached at the time, and the comrades were oblivious to their hurtful behavior and actions. Defending a Party that no longer existed was more important to them than showing empathy.

In my world before the prison, people were good. Life was good. After the *Kefitegna*, not only people but also life itself became suspect. It wasn't so much what the comrades did but the knowledge that something like that could happen between comrades that threw me off-guard. What kept me from plunging into the abyss was the sheer love of life, the knowledge that I was innocent and the resolve to be true to myself and to the world around me.

A difficult choice presented itself to me in the form of renouncing or not renouncing the Party. For the first time in my life, I was at a crossroads, unable to choose one way or the other. I labored to mute the nagging voice that called upon me to disavow *my* beloved Party. My heart simply refused to let go. *How can I turn away from the pillar of my life that gave me so much hope and meaning? Who am I and what am I without it? What about our noble project? It was all for naught? Didn't we promise the masses a better future?*

A shiver went through my entire being at the very idea of forsaking *my* Party. Turning away from it amounted to turning my back on all those comrades who had sacrificed their lives. *Did they die in vain? How about the thousands who languish in prison?* This and other questions hammered my mind and tormented my soul.

But my mind connived against *my* cherished Party and slowly I tore up the sacred veil draping my eyes. Without the illusions, myths and sacred taboos surrounding it, to my horror it became just an ordinary bunch of people trying to find their way in the dark. I turned away not because the Party had made a mistake, *but because collective entities like it turned their members into blind followers.* I was also revolted by the hatred they instilled in their members who thought differently from them.

But why does this happen? Is it because of their underground nature? Is it the ideology they swear upon? Is it Marxism-Leninism itself, which we tried to follow to its logical conclusion? *Is Marxism flawed, or is it us who distorted it trying to translate it into practice? How can I turn away from the theory that taught me how to change the world?*

I dared to lift up the sacred halo surrounding Marxism. I questioned its Promethean vision: a vision that was so sure of itself. How did it dare impose inevitability on life that is too uncertain, too ambiguous, too fleeting and too arbitrary? The nationwide massacre perpetrated by the Derg and its allies, the death of Getachew and the *Kefitegna* experience had taught me that life did not go in a straight line: projects could be thwarted, dreams shattered, and humans could be turned into automatons.

But who amongst us would have doubted the theory? Who would have challenged its validity? The Russians and the Chinese may have gotten it wrong, but *we* were going to do it *right*. We never doubted ourselves and the ideology, which we surrendered our lives to.

Now that I took off the lens, the world appeared different. It wasn't the black and white world that I had painted it to be. I learned the dangers of trying to uncritically implement an ideology. Marxism taught that the history of society is the struggle of antagonistic social forces; progress comes only through the destruction of one of these forces by the other. We took that as the ultimate truth, and destroying the real or perceived enemy became the driving force in our struggle.

How can we do good if what we do is achieved at the cost of human life? I had seen too much violence and bloodshed. The very idea of violence induced an aversion in me. Urban or rural armed struggle engendered violence and I rejected both. The supreme value of any change should be human life. Any change should come peacefully, I resolved.

What I learned at the *Kefitegna* and thereafter was that I could not be innocent just because my former comrades had brushed me off. What I loathed about crowd mentality was not simply becoming a cipher, but also the idea that I might hurt others without realizing it. After so much soul searching, I came to realize that I too was answerable for every mistake committed, for every blood spilled and for every name defamed in the name of the revolution. As E.M. Cioran says, *"I shall no longer say "I am" without blushing."*

My decision did not come without a price. I was rocked from side to side like a ship in high seas. I felt the axis of my existence wobbling beneath me. *How am I going to hold out without the Party?* I reckoned I had cast its love out of my heart. I trembled with the very idea of turning my back on it. *Would life have any meaning for me again? What am I to hold on to maintain my sanity?* I became lonely amidst hundreds of comrades for whom I would formerly have gladly died. Even though the loss of meaning in life was the main issue confronting me at the time, I strove to keep my composure. I was not totally successful. At times, I did not feel like talking to the few people around me, such as Mekonen and Emebet. For the most part, I kept my poise.

Slowly, I felt a *new person* surging in me. I gained confidence in the knowledge that I can define and redefine myself. I could determine who I wanted to be and where I wanted to go. I didn't need a Party or a group of people to tell me who I am and where I'm going. I tasted the beauty of freedom. I embraced it and vowed to stand by it no matter what the ramifications.

I developed the consciousness that I would prevail in the end, if only my life could be spared.

Farewell my sister, fare thee well.
The elements be kind to thee, and make
Thy spirits all of comfort: fare thee well.
      -William Shakespeare, *Antony and Cleopatra*

Around November 1978, nine months after I was arrested, news came to the *Kefitegna* that the Derg had formed a committee that would review the cases of political prisoners.

It may have been around January 1979, I was in the dorm when I heard my name being called. I wasn't feeling well that morning. When I went out, I was asked to come to the office. I noticed that others, including Mekonen, had been called. In the office, I saw several men sitting behind desks at different stations. That was when I understood that the people were members of the committee who would go over our cases. The first person I saw was the older security agent. I was disconcerted. I hadn't seen him for quite a few months. I sent a quick prayer toward the heavens so that I won't be called to his station.

He had enjoyed abusing me physically through spanking and kicking. His efforts to take me to the Derg office prison had been frustrated. He was not able to do as much harm to me as he would have loved to as long as I was at the *Kefitegna*.

I remember one afternoon, about a week after the identity of the Shashemene group became public and after we started giving our statements, he called me to the office and told me that he was going to take me to a series of different prisons so that I could pinpoint people I had worked with. He said he was sure there were individuals who had worked with me whose names I had not yet given up.

He took me to the *Meakelawi* first. Girls were asked to come out and stand in line. He asked if I knew any of them. I looked at all the girls and I saw Yordanos, Sara's cousin, whom I knew at the

university. I said I did not know any of them. The girls were asked
if they knew me. No one spoke. I felt so humiliated I couldn't even
look up.

I prayed he would not take me to the Third Police Station,
where Azeb was held. The Police Station was adjacent to the
Meakelawi. When we came out of the compound, the driver told the
security agent that he had to go to an appointment. I was waiting for
the agent's response in trepidation. I would have loved to see my
friend after so long, but not in such an undignified appearance. I
knew Azeb would know that I would not betray her, or anyone else,
for that matter. I heard the agent say, "Well, then let's take her
back."

I was relieved.

The car went past the Police Station. The agent turned to me
and said, "I will take you to the Military Police and the Derg office
prisons another day. I am sure you know a lot of people there." I
surely did. There were people like Tito, Habte, Sirak, Gebeyehu and
Alemayehu Egzeru. They dropped me off at the *Kefitegna* and left.
That night, tears poured down my face under the cover of the
blanket, burning with shame. The last time I had seen the agent was
when I was called into the office one day.

I had been taken to *Kefitegna* 15 by a cadre shortly after the
identity of the Shashemene group had been disclosed. I didn't know
why I was being taken until I got there. Martha, Mahlet, Hanna and
the rest of residents of the Piassa apartment were thrown in because
of me. I had to testify that they had no political involvement and
that I went to the apartment just because we were friends. They
were released after a week.

Since the day I got back from Kefitegna 15, one of the
cadres had fancied that he could come anytime and have me called
to the office and talk to me. The day I was called to the office, I saw

the cadre from *Kefitegna* 15 chatting with Zerihoun, the older security agent and other cadres. They were standing in the middle of the room. The cadre from *Kefitegna* 15 shook my hand and recklessly said, "So you were the secretary of Nazaret area which made you my boss! I thought I was in control. You are a heroine. Take this as a token of your heroism." He unstrapped his empty cartridge pouch off his waist and handed it to me.

I held the pouch in my hand puzzled.

The older security agent became so indignant he snatched it from my hand and gave it back to the cadre saying, "You can't spoil prisoners like that. Praise is not what this girl needs. She is an enemy of the state and she has done more than most people around here. As to you," he said, turning to me, "as to you, I will be a dead man if I don't throw your corpse in the streets."

I shrugged my shoulders.

"You see how arrogant she is? She must have some relative that she is counting on. There is no reason for this kind of impudence. Who is that relative of yours you are counting on, huh?" he growled, giving me a hard slap on the face.

I felt I had lost my sense of sight.

Zerihoun, upset, asked the agent to restrain himself. The agent was so outraged by the friendly attitude of the cadres toward me he kept ranting. He said he would make sure that I would be transferred to the Derg office prison and stormed out.

My prayers must have been lost half way through the heavens because I saw the security agent trying to get my attention. I went up to him filled with sudden disappointment and hatred. He told me to sit down in a chair across his desk. I had spotted a pleasant looking man from among the committee members and had hoped he would call me. Instead, Mekonen was asked to go there.

"What is wrong? Why are you wearing a *gabi*?" the agent asked me without looking up. He had a file in front of him and was scribbling something.

"I am not feeling well."

"Let's get down to business. Your name?"

"Hiwot."

"Father's name?"

"Teffera"

"Grandfather's name?"

"Minda"

"Teffera Minda? Which Teffera Minda?"

"Teffera Minda," I muttered. I did not know another Teffera Minda.

"Is Teffera Minda the Teffera Minda from Jijiga? Is he the brother of Meharene and Mamite Minda?"

"Yes."

"Are you Teffera Minda's daughter?"

"Yes."

"Oh, God! What have I done? I've been torturing my brother's daughter all along. I lived in Jijiga when your father was a police commissioner. I am indebted to him forever. Like father, like daughter. No wonder you are brave."

I never grew up with my father. My parents were separated when I was little. My father was a maverick and an avid reader of English novels. He had a bit of Western education and spoke fluent English, Italian, Arabic and Somali besides Amharic. I assumed the security agent said, "Like father, like daughter," because he probably knew the story about my father. My father was in jail (before I was born) accused of "defiling the Emperor's name."

He was kept in prison for six months and was later sent to the Supreme Court in Addis. The Emperor presided over the court and gave him amnesty saying his father had done them (the government) a favor.

"My dear child, your case is very serious," began the security agent. "I'm sure you know and I won't try to hide it from you. The penalty is death. But I will see to it that you won't die. No, I will not see Teffera's daughter die. Where is your father now? He used to work in Dire Dawa."

"He is here in Addis. He is retired."

"Does he come and visit you?"

"He came only a few times. His knees hurt. He can't be on his feet for long."

"How come your aunt didn't tell me about you?"

"I don't know."

I didn't know what to make of this sudden outburst of emotion on the part of the security agent. I couldn't believe it was the same ferocious and evil man I had known all along. He looked gentle and caring. When I was done, he told me not to worry too much and let me go.

It was only later that I learned that my aunt has been desperately looking for him in vain. Years later, her son told me, tears trickling down his cheek, that he once met the security agent in a bar. When he told him his mom's name the security agent said to him, "I once tortured and abused a girl without knowing that she was Teffera Minda's daughter, but I saved her life."

It was sometime in March and I woke up one morning and thought about the dream I had seen overnight. I don't usually dwell on dreams, but there was something sinister about this one. I wished *Etiye* Zenebu was there to interpret it for me. She was set free a few months ago.

I dreamt that there was a dark alleyway adjacent room #3, lined with barren trees on both sides. People were walking in a straight line and I couldn't make out their faces. I was last in line. I could vaguely identify Tito among them. The only person I could clearly recognize was Mekonen. He was walking right in front of me and had his light blue jacket on. I was tagging after him when I suddenly saw a wider and brighter street on my right. I hesitated for a moment but took it.

In the afternoon, I was in my dorm still mulling over my dream when Mekonen's name was called out. I rushed out to see what was going on and saw him shaking hands with some people. I went over and shook hands with him, bid him goodbye and wished him good luck. He was smiling as usual and it was hard to know what his feelings were. I returned to my dorm, tears welling up in my eyes. *Why would they take him to the Meakelawi after over a year?* The answer was obvious.

It was a devastating blow.

Just about a month before that, we had heard Party alternate CC member, Fikre Zerga, had been executed. He was captured in Wollo in October 1978. Mekonen and I felt bad when we learned about his execution. Fikre was the comrade I accompanied to Tigray in May 1977.

Then in April, just before Ethiopian Easter, sad news came to the *Kefitegna*. Mekonen Bayisa and League CC members Tito Hiruy, Sirak Tefera, Gebeyehu Dagne, and Alemayehu Egzeru were executed. Among them were also Habteselassie and Meron Assefa, and others whom I did not know personally.

I felt bereft.

It was an enormous tragedy. I could still vividly see Mekonen's smiling face and kind eyes and the clothes he wore just before he left. The image of Tito in his black leather jacket and Meron's beautiful face is still memorable. All those bright young people were mercilessly butchered. The sadism of the Derg never seemed to let up.

It was as bloodthirsty as it has ever been.

To our dismay, we also learned that Ashenafi, Tizazu (I Say) and Tesfaye Pettie had been killed. The three had been brought to our *Kefitegna* from *Kefitegna* 21 some months previously, along with others, when a death list, which included their names, was sent to their *Kefitegna*. Their cadre, Getahun, a friend of our cadre Daniel, hid them in our *Kefitegna* until their cases were forgotten. They were locked in one of the dorms so that the rest of us would not see them. We had to be inside when they had to go to the toilet or take a shower.

They were later taken back to their *Kefitegna* and then brought back when another death list came. Getahun took them back later, and the three were finally executed despite his efforts. That was another heartbreak we had to deal with after the death of Mekonen and League CC members.

It was interesting that many prisoners were against cadre-turned EPRP members such as Daniel and Getahun. Even though they claimed that they had returned to the "revolutionary camp," in order to escape death and imprisonment in the hands of the Derg and went around rifles hanging on their shoulders, these individuals played a crucial role in saving the lives of many of their former comrades.

Not long after the execution of Mekonen and League CC members, we also learned that Berhanemeskel Redda was arrested and was held at the hellish dungeons of the Derg Headquarters. The legendary revolutionary finally fell in the hands of the enemy. I wondered what had happened to his wife. I had looked forward to meeting her.

Ayalew Temesgen, a former EPRP member, once told me that he was at the Derg office prison with Berhanemeskel Redda. He said, "They took away Berhanemeskel every day, from morning till evening, for interrogation. Sometimes they brought him back for lunch and took him away. He often played chess with a fellow prisoner. I played with him once. The pieces were made of torn slippers. Generally, Berhanemeskel kept to himself but he was always relaxed. He also told me that he had told Getachew not to trust *them* and had warned him not to go near *them*. He said, 'When I told Getachew not to trust *them*,' he said to me, 'what is this talk of not trusting comrades?' 'I had warned him but he didn't listen. He believed he would change things through dialogue.'"

Everything had seemed quiet at the *Kefitegna* before all those executions took place. The deceptively quiet situation had prompted the will to live. The sense of resignation has been ebbing. Death had lacked its immediacy. But the slaying of Mekonen and other comrades jolted me out of my dream like existence. I once again was sure my own death was imminent. As the days went by, pangs of survivor guilt began to gnaw at me, even though I did not yet know my fate. It seemed almost a shame to be alive after all those comrades were gone.

Life didn't make sense.

At the time, I went home for treatment, I had learned about the efforts made by my family to save my life. I could not totally rely on it. There were families who did their best and gave all they had, but ultimately were unable to save the lives of their children. Other families, who could grease the palms of security agents, cadres, Derg members or *Kebele* officials or who had the "right connections" were more successful. Prisoners' files were destroyed, their names changed, and they were finally released. The most painful blow was when others were unscrupulously executed in their place for the sake of money!

What I learned during those tough times was how we humans put things at the back of our minds quickly in order to survive. Were it not for our capacity to forget, we would have perished as a species, unable to take in the magnitude of tragedies we faced on a daily basis. The life we lived at the *Kefitegna* was make-believe. We moved *as if* all was well, to maintain our sanity. That was the only weapon at our disposal to face the terror shadowing us.

Once the shock over the death of Mekonen, Tito and others subsided, I felt the will to live creeping in again. All of a sudden, life seemed precious. I wanted to cling to it. I felt sheer delight in being alive. I was grateful and humble before the force that kept me alive. It did not matter what the future held. I was alive and that was what mattered.

I was going to take each day at a time, and did, until my world was shaken up once more in the beginning of June 1979. It was around ten in the morning and I was washing cups after breakfast beside the water pipe in the front yard of the office. I looked toward the gate, causally, and saw a military truck pull into the car park outside the compound. I saw an officer with a Lieutenant's badge get off the truck and enter the compound. He was carrying a piece of paper in his hand. I knew what that piece of paper meant.

I gathered the cups quickly, dashed to the dorm and told Emebet that our sentences had come. Since the interview by the committee, we had been awaiting our verdict. We suspected that Mekonen and all the comrades executed with him were sentenced to death by the recommendation of the committee.

Minutes later, someone started calling out names. Mine was one of them. They told us to get our belongings and come to the office. I stuffed whatever I had into a plastic bag, said goodbye to Emebet and rushed out.

There were about fifteen or so of us. They commanded us to get into the back of the truck. While walking, I saw a young man carrying the orange and white plastic containers in which my lunch came. My cousin Elsa had hired him for just that purpose. It was my first time seeing him in person, and he didn't know me by sight. I secretly waved at him just before I climbed into the truck.

I saw him turn back, sprinting.

It was when we reached Menilik II Square that I realized that they were taking us to the *Meakelawi*. I had always dreaded that place. It was one of the bloodiest prisons in the country. They dropped us off at the compound and led us through a narrow passage to the dormitories.

There were two small rooms for women. I was taken to one into which about twenty-five to thirty women were herded. After about an hour, the *Capo* (a prisoner who has certain privileges and duties) came and asked for me. He had brought my lunch and told me that my mother, my sister Almaz and my aunt were outside, and had sent me their greetings. He told me he knew my aunt. I was relieved but wondered how they had managed to discover my whereabouts in such a short time.

The next morning, I was in the dorm when I noticed for the first time a young pregnant woman surrounded by a few girls. They called her Tady. A couple of days later, a newspaper circulated in the dorm, which announced the execution of Berhanemeskel Redda! I was shocked. That was when I learned that the young pregnant woman was his wife. Her name, Tadelech Hailemichael, was on the newspaper. She was about six months pregnant. Some of the girls hid the newspaper so she would not find out about the execution.

The death of Berhanemeskel felt like it was the end of an era.

I was excited to see Tadelech. Getachew had wanted me to meet her. I had always been reserved, but the *Kefitegna* experience had made me even more so. Besides, the room was so overcrowded it was hardly possible to talk in private. Almost all of us stayed indoors since there was nowhere else to go. We had to take turns to sit on the small bench outside. I got the chance to talk to Tadelech, albeit briefly, when we were waiting our turn at the washroom one day, and we exchanged a few words.

Another day, we ended up beside one another on the bench outside. Somehow, Mekonen Bayisa's and Meron Assefa's names came up during our conversation. She had heard from one of the *girls* who had come from our *Kefitegna* about Mekonen. To her shock, the *girl* had told her that, "Mekonen got what he had deserved." I was as shocked to hear that as she had been. Tadelech and I also talked about Anna Karenina, a book that I had read at the *Kefitegna*. I was smitten by her charisma.

I instinctively knew we were kindred spirits.

Life in *Meakelawi* was boring, to say the least. I had no books to read and no one to talk to. I never got the chance to talk to Tadelech again. There was little or no movement. The longest trip one could take was going to the washroom which was only steps away. The days dragged on painfully slowly. *How long are they going to keep us here? Are they going to execute us? Is that why they brought us here?* I wrestled every now and then with those questions.

One morning around the end of June, after twenty-five days at the *Meakelawi*, prisoners who had come from *Kefitegna* 19 and other *Kefitegnas* were called out. I stepped out when I heard my name.

All of a sudden, there was a commotion in the dorms and outside. People were walking rapidly back and forth. I was standing at the door of our dorm when the *Capo* came over and anxiously asked me if my name was from one to five on the list. I did not exactly remember but I knew it was among the first names called out.

"Why? What happens to those whose names are called one to five?"

"Nothing...nothing. I can assure you that you are all given sentences. I just wanted to know if your name was one to five on the list," he said and walked away hurriedly.

I stood there trying to make sense of what he had said. *Why is he so anxious if I am given a sentence? Maybe those whose names are one to five on the list are the ones to be executed.* The *Capo* was concerned because my aunt had told him to look after me. I saw him coming back taking long strides.

"You are given only three years. It is okay. You are young and you will still be young when you come out," he tried to reassure me.

I knew better than that.

"Why do you say that if I am given only three years? I've already been in for more than a year, which means I will be out in less than a year and a half. I don't expect to get a light sentence. Tell me the truth. Am I on the execution list?"

"No, no, no! I swear to you. You are given---three years," he said, avoiding my eyes.

I suspected that one to five were given life imprisonment or were slated for the firing squad. While I was ruminating, we were told to come out with our belongings. I darted into my dorm, grabbed my plastic bag and proceeded to the spot we were told to stand in a line.

I saw Lieutenant Shimeles, the one who brought us to the *Meakelawi,* standing next to a truck. A soldier was standing beside him, a piece of paper in hand. Lieutenant Shimeles instructed us to go on the trucks when our names are called out. I heard my name and I was number five on the list. I saw the Lieutenant look at the paper and heard him say "Puuh!" slapping his forehead with the palm of his hand and shaking his head incredulously. I got onto one of the trucks.

Nebiyu Tefera, who was only nineteen and had come with us from *Kefitegna* 19, was left behind. I wasn't sure where we were being taken but I worried about him. If we were going to *Kerchele* – the central prison – then Nebiyu would definitely be executed. I couldn't take my eyes off him when the trucks left the compound. He wore a navy blue sweater.

I felt a knot in my stomach.

Kerchele was our only hope. *Kerchele* is a corruption of the Italian word c*arcere* – prison. I knew from the behavior of the *Capo* and the reaction of the Lieutenant that my sentence was long. *How long is it? Ten? Fifteen, Twenty? Life?* But I did not care about that.

What mattered was that my life was spared.

When the truck went down Menilik II Square and passed by the old Post office, it all came back to me. I saw the spot where I accidentally met Getachew the day he got off the taxi and tugged at my elbow. I remembered my appointment with Tito that day and all the days we met there. There was the street that led to the Piassa apartment: my friends Martha, Mahelet, Hanna, and Kidan!

The truck rolled down Churchill Road to Tewodros Square and I saw the street leading to Gola Mikael and to the *Ij meschia*, where the League IZ often met. We passed by Noh, our hang out, and then by the Post office building. I remembered the last time I saw Azeb walking in front of the building. Then I saw Mimo Bar, where I had gone with my Zonal Committee members... and

Semegne! *Will I ever get to see these places again? What if I die of natural causes? What if the sentence was a mistake and is reversed? How is my family going to take it if I am given life? Am I going to be a burden on them my whole life?* The questions spun in my head.

When the trucks went down towards Kera, I was relieved because I knew for sure we were being taken to *Kerchele*. I didn't know where it was exactly, but I knew it was somewhere there. The trucks burst in through the gate and came to a halt. We got off one by one. There were several male wardens at the gate watching us as we descended from the trucks.

Kerchele was bigger than I had imagined. It looked barren. Everything around it was old and shabby. We were led to an old building, which was the office. A Major, the prison administrator, came out, talked briefly to Lieutenant Shimeles, and made a short welcome speech to us. Lieutenant Shimeles then wished everyone good luck and came up to me.

"Have those who gave you the sentence seen you?" he asked, shaking his head.

"Yes...well...I don't know...I think so," I answered. I didn't know what to say.

"They are going to tell you your sentences in a minute. You will still be young when you come out. Besides, only God knows what is going to happen. You may get amnesty and come out before you finish your term. Be strong, make yourself busy and take good care of yourself. The best thing is to keep oneself busy. I wish you good luck," he gave me words of encouragement. He was still shaking his head when he walked away, shoulders slumped. I was touched by his kindness. It was consoling to know that there were people like him among *them*.

We went inside the office and they directed us to a room where a man was sitting behind a desk. We were told to go one by one and tell him our names. He looked down a list and told each individual his or her sentence. There were different reactions. Some walked away in disbelief. Others sighed with relief. I went up and told him my name.

"Fifteen years!" he said, a look of disbelief coming over his face.

I laughed.

"Are you laughing?"

I shrugged my shoulders.

He shook his head again incredulously. The Major was sitting on the desk and looked at me in utter horror.

"Were you an executive?" he asked.

"No."

"You must have killed, then."

"No," I said and walked away.

I was soothed. By the look of the Lieutenant's and the *Capo*'s reactions, I thought I had gotten life. I was lucky to be alive and get fifteen years. There were so many who did not get that chance. What mattered was that I was alive.

After all, life had become precious again.

I am given a second chance and I am going to take it happily. I am not going to take anything for granted. I would make the most out of life in Kerchele. Of course, there was no guarantee that the Derg would not change its mind, given its whimsical nature. But I left that to the future and seized the moment. I remembered Azeb, Semegne, Mekonen, Tito, Aklilu, Habte, Sirak, Taye, Agere, Merid, Fatuma, Ashenafi, and others who didn't get that chance. As for the other prisoners from our *Kefitegna*, four (two of whom were female) were given ten. The *girls* in room #3 got three and four, and they had already served over a year.

I was contemplating my new lease on life when we were led out of the office. I saw a couple of female wardens standing outside.

They were there to accompany us, the women, to the female quarter. Walking down to our destination, I saw hundreds of male prisoners strolling in the large courtyard.

Kerchele was built around the end of the 1930s. Men and women lived in separate quarters and men were jammed into different quarters such as *Ketero* (for those with pending court cases), *Firdegna* (for those serving sentences) *Alembekagn* (for those with life sentences and those convicted of murder awaiting execution), *Fitabiher* (for those in for civil law violations) and the women's compound. With the influx of political prisoners in the prison, this classification no longer held true as political prisoners were thrown into any quarter.

I was in for a surprise when the gate of the women's compound was flung open. I saw a woman, whose name I later learned was Zergi, in dirty clothes, colorful beads on her forehead and her legs chained and screaming at the women around her. I was terribly scared of her. *So much for Kerchele*!

Cans of all sizes, mostly of tomato sauce and milk powder, were arrayed on the gravel-covered courtyard and a woman was scooping something out of a coal black medium sized barrel and filling up the cans. I had learned that water was rationed at *Kerchele*. *They must be getting their daily water ration. Oh no! They can deprive me of anything but not water. What am I supposed to do with water in a tomato sauce can?* At a closer look, it was tea that the woman was pouring out into the cans. It was just before lunchtime when we got there and there were a couple of pails near the tea barrel, with ladles inside. The pails looked filthy and the sauce unappetizing.

My stomach turned.

Someone yelled "*Delday* Committee!" and a woman, whose name I later learned was Hilina, emerged out of *Adarash* and came down the stairs and welcomed us and ushered us in. *Adarash* – hall – was a rundown building built by the Italians during the five-year occupation. It was the largest building in the compound at the time.

Women were sitting inside on their beds or mattresses, chatting or knitting, when we went in. I was surprised to see beds since we slept on double-folded blankets at the *Kefitegna*. There were double-decker beds on opposite sides of the hall and mattresses, rolled up in white, blue and green plastic covers, were lined up in the middle. It was quite a spectacle. It looked like a bazaar. Those who slept on the cement floor in the middle of the hall had to bundle up their mattresses during the day so that people could freely move around.

On the right side of the entrance were three double-decker beds; on the left, there were mattresses on the floor lined up against the wall. Those who slept on those mattresses didn't have to roll them up during the day.

A few moments after we'd been in *Adarash*, a couple of girls, whom I knew from the university, came and took me out to the "teahouse." Tea was made outside on a huge coal hearth. We sipped our tea sitting on the ledge of the *Emechat Bet* – a rather small building that housed mothers and their babies. Right away, my name was called out. I ambled to the spot where two women were standing. They were assigned to call names when food was brought to the gate by male prisoners. I took the food and signed my name in the book. I was once again amazed at how quickly my family had learned of my whereabouts.

News spread of the longer sentences and many women came over to see us. I learned that there was a girl who was given life and another twenty years from among the former prisoners. They were members of the Eritrean Liberation Fronts. I was the first female EPRP member, and would remain the only one to get the longest sentence.

Like any new prisoner in *Kerchele*, I was curious to see members of the royal family who had been in prison since September 1974. They came out to the volleyball court for their late-morning stroll. The rest of the prisoners were not allowed to go on the court during those walks. The royal family was kept in a room at the back of *Adarash*.

Hilina, chair of the *Delday* Committee (the committee that looked after sleeping arrangements), later took us to *Sostegna Bet* – house number three. I was with a couple of girls who had come with me from the *Meakelawi*. They were from another *Kefitegna*. We swept the semi-dirt floor to make our "bed" and put our blankets and linen on one of the top bunk beds, when this elderly woman came over and threw them on the floor. She had a scarlet headscarf tied around her head in a funny way. She was carrying a huge sack on her back.

We were shocked. "*Emama*, we are sorry. We are new and didn't know the rules around here," said one of the girls.

The woman was outraged and babbled, "He tried to get to her. She is no one's fool. She threw it off her bed."

What? Who is he? Is the woman normal? I then heard a couple of girls say, "Bogeye! Bogeye! Why are you throwing their stuff on the floor?"

Bogeye? How can they call this old woman Bogeye? Shouldn't they be calling her Emama as an old woman deserves to be addressed? I later ended up calling her Bogeye, an endearment of the name Bogalech.

My greatest worry since I was brought in *Kerchele* was how to break the news of my sentence to my family when I saw them during visitation time on Sunday. The day we arrived in *Kerchele* was a Wednesday. The days crawled, prolonging my agony.

Sunday morning, at nine o'clock the first name was called out. Criers stood ten meters apart at designated spots and their voices echoed throughout the compound. Some were stationed at the door of each *bet* – house – and yelled out names, knitting, chatting with friends or sitting or standing.

I was about to face the most dreadful day of my life. I was anxiously pacing the volleyball court when, Zeleka, a former EPRP member and a friend, came and joined me. Zeleka was a member of the *Mekrus* I had joined. *Mekrus* was a group of individuals who pooled their resources to survive in jail.

Zeleka tried to cheer me up, to no avail. When my name was called, I exited the compound, my heart racing and my eyes blurred with tears. At the visiting place, I paused, astonished at the sheer number of people standing behind the wooden bars that separated prisoners from them. I was apprehensively looking for my family when I spotted Tsedey, my sister Almaz's friend, waving at me. I was so happy to see her, I felt like crying. Her big, beautiful eyes were red and I could see that she, too, was restraining herself. She told me my mother and sisters were in the lineup. I breathed a sigh of relief when she told me that they knew about my sentence. They had brought food every day since I was transferred, but I had no idea they knew how many years I was given.

Unlike *Kefitegna,* where we could only wave at visitors from a distance, here we could actually talk to them, albeit separated by two wooden rail fences running parallel to each other. Female wardens stood every few meters between the fences and passed things like food, money and clothing from visitors to prisoners, or empty food containers and other items the other way. The only hitch was the noise, as visitors and prisoners had to out-shout one another to be heard.

Finally, I saw my family coming down. My mother started to cry, but my older sister nudged her so as to say "don't make her (meaning me) cry." I put on a brave face. I was spared of the burden of breaking the long sentence to them. We chatted until one in the afternoon, till the end of visitation time. I told them that they didn't have to come every day to bring me food. We ate in a group and each member was assigned to provide sustenance one day of the week. No one was responsible for Sunday, as everybody's family visited. My sister said Saturday worked best for them. Finally they left. It had been an eventful and overwhelming day.

I became an object of curiosity and pity in the compound for a few weeks as a result of my long sentence. I was treated a little bit like a celebrity, given priority at the water pump or in the toilet lineup. Sunday visits were very awkward, as prisoners pointed their index fingers at me (of course secretly), telling their family and friends in hushed tones that I was in for fifteen years, causing them to recoil in horror or shake their heads in disbelief. As the weeks went by, the curiosity wore off and I became more relaxed.

"The day you arrived here," a wealthy lady, a resident of almost four years, said to me one day, "they told me that this girl has been given fifteen years. I wanted to check her out. I saw you at the teahouse, sitting with girls, chatting, smiling and drinking tea as if nothing had happened. For heaven's sake, you'd just been told your sentence! Allow me to ask you a question. How did you manage to swallow the tea?"

I smiled awkwardly. I didn't know what to say. She had no idea how relieved I was at that point. The most important thing for me then was that my life was spared. I appreciated that even more when news about Nebiyu Tefera's (the nineteen-year-old from our *Kefitegna*) execution came. I was never able to erase the look in his eyes that day at the *Meakelawi*.

I was naïve enough to believe that whatever had happened at the *Kefitegna* would be behind me. No such luck. No sooner had I arrived in my new home than a rumor started that I was someone to watch out for. I didn't have a friend except for Zeleka. I was transferred to *Adarash* a couple of weeks after I arrived in *Kerchele* due to my long sentence and didn't make any friends there. I was not even at home in the *Mekrus*, yet I couldn't think of leaving. Not because I didn't have the means to support myself, I could. But I found the very idea of sitting and eating alone terrifying.

There was nothing left for me but to patiently wait for better days.

Berhanemeskel Redda, 1979

Agere Miheretu, 1973   *Abiyu Ersamo, 1967*

Semegne Lemma

Mekonen Bayisa

Your friend is your needs answered.
　　-Kahlil Gibran, *The Prophet*

Better days came one evening in August 1979, a couple of months after I was brought to *Kerchele*. I was standing outside when I heard the gate clank open and Tadelech walked through with a belly that looked like a distended balloon. I thought she was going to have the baby that night. Brikti and I ran to welcome her. Brikti was associated with one of the Eritrean Liberation Fronts; she had been at the *Meakelawi* at the time I was there and had come to *Kerchele* perhaps before me. Tadelech was assigned at the *Emechat Bet,* since she was expecting. We became fast friends. She was Berhanemeskel Redda's wife and the ultimate *Anja,* and an outsider to the general EPRP prison population.

　　The day was September 18, 1979. Just after the *Adarash* door was opened at six in the morning, I heard that Tadelech was in labor. I jumped out of bed and ran to the clinic in fear and trembling. I found her lying on a bed with a nurse prisoner assisting her. It was my first time to see a woman giving birth. I prayed hard nothing would happen to her or to the baby. Tadelech lay quietly on the bed in obvious pain, sweat trickling down her temple. I helped the nurse passing forceps, my hands shaking. The nurse kept telling her to push and all of a sudden Tadelech screamed and I saw the baby's head coming out.

　　She gave birth to a beautiful baby. Its lips were blue and its body covered by a yellow paste. It was a girl! I shed tears of joy when the nurse held her upside down and smacked her on her buttock. The baby gave a shrill. The nurse then swaddled her in a white cloth and gave her to Tadelech, who kissed her and held her in her arms. It was the most beautiful sight. Tadelech was taken to the hospital after about an hour or so, and stayed there for a month.

A woman in labor was usually sent to the hospital. In some cases, as in the case of Tadelech, the woman may deliver at the women's prison clinic because of delay. But she'd still be taken to the hospital for fear of complications. The female wardens did not usually respond as quickly when they were called in the middle of the night or simply refused to call the health workers as they did in the case of Tadelech. This is because they had to walk to the main gate, which was at least a ten-minute walk from the women's compound, to have the male wardens relay the message to the health assistants stationed at the Health Center, which is another ten-minute walk from the main compound.

The health assistants on duty were the only ones who had the authority to refer prisoners to the hospital and it might take them two or three hours before they came to attend to a situation. There were two of them for seven thousand prisoners. When there was such a delay, a woman could give birth at the clinic with the help of a female prisoner, who could be a nurse, a doctor or a midwife with no formal training.

Tadelech had not learned about her husband's, Berhanemeskel's, death. Brikti and I were waiting to tell her until after she had the baby. Even then, we were afraid to break the sad news to her. One morning a prisoner, whose cadre daughter was killed by the EPRP, told Tadelech indirectly about Berhanemeskel's death, knowing very well that she didn't know about it. I wasn't sure what the woman was in for, but she was very bitter towards the EPRP. When I was at the *Sostegna Bet*, every time she saw me making tea she would start to jabber, wagging her head, "Some of them had gotten what they deserved. He has cloaked them with long sentences." The *some of them* was me and the *he* was Mengistu Hailemariam. That was her way of getting even with EPRP members.

Tadelech was distraught, and wanted to know what the woman was trying to tell her. Brikti and I led her out of the area telling her not to mind the "crazy woman." We took her to the *Emechat Bet* and she was sitting on her bed when Brikti finally told her that Berhanemeskel had been executed. She gave her the newspaper that announced his execution.

Tadelech stared blankly past us and then tears poured down her cheeks. Her entire body crumpled with grief. It was a very poignant moment. All we could do to alleviate her heartache was remind her that she has three kids to remember him by. She leafed through the newspaper and gazed at his picture with red and misty eyes.

Shortly afterwards, I felt the time had come to tell her about Getachew. It hadn't seemed right to broach the subject when she still didn't know about her own husband's death. "I knew about you," I began. "Getachew Maru was my friend. He used to tell me about Berhanemeskel and you. He wanted me to meet you both. But Berhanemeskel left before I got the chance to meet you."

My revelation blew her away.

"I remember Getachew saying something about a girl. I remember also Berhane talking about this girl that Getachew was involved with. Was it you? Well, this is amazing! What happened to Getachew was really sad."

"I know. I often wonder if it was better if the Derg had killed him."

"Getachew believed in dialogue," she said. "He believed he would work things out with *them*. Berhane warned him not to trust *them* and not to go to them whenever they called. The day he was detained, Melikte Yohannes and Bekri had warned him not to go."

"I also told him they might harm him. He wouldn't listen," I lamented.

"One day, Getachew told Berhane and me," continued Tadelech, "that when the negotiation for the merger between *Abyot* and EPLO was taking place, he asked *them* who actually the EPLO people were. He said, 'They told me they were with Berhanemeskel Redda. That was when I thought we could work with them.' One of the things that Berhane was accused of by the Party was cultivating a personality cult around himself. It's ironic, then, that *they* were using his name to convince others to work with *them*. Getachew used to come to our house wearing khaki, white rimmed reading glasses and a black berretta hat."

"That was his usual camouflage. It made him look old. I never liked it, especially the hat. I feel bad for keeping silent about what he used to tell me. I had never said anything to anyone. That is the shame I have to live with for the rest of my life."

"Our faith in the Party prevented us from questioning. When Berhane and Getachew talked about the weaknesses of the Party, I used to get angry with them. They used to say to me, 'Here comes the little Anarchist,'" Tadelech said.

Anarchist was the name the Derg gave to EPRP members.

Since that day, Tadelech and I never stopped talking about the two men. We went over and over again about how we met them, what we did with them and what they had told us about the Party. That was one way of keeping their memory alive.

Years later, I told her that all we talked about whenever we met revolved around Berhanemeskel and Getachew. She looked up at me and said, "You know, we treated these men as if they were alive and that is why we have been unable to move on."

It is so true.

I had always known that if ever I came out of prison alive, I would write a book about Getachew, that I would tell his story to the entire world. As the years went by, I even became convinced that my life was spared to tell his story.

"You know what I think?" I said to Tadelech one night after she put the baby to bed. "We should write a book about Getachew and Berhanemeskel and get it published when we get out. We have to tell their stories. I've always felt that I should tell Getachew's story."

"I want to write a book about Berhane too. Let's do it."

"Let's start right now."

We started working on our project right away. We sat down every Monday night, after the baby has been put to sleep, to talk about what we have written the whole week. News came to the compound that there was going to be a search. I didn't know what to do with my notes. After debating with myself, I tore them to pieces. I didn't even tell Tadelech until after I did it. Tadelech had destroyed hers too.

Tadelech's arrival at *Kerchele* made a huge difference in my life. I didn't have close friends there. Loneliness and alienation had taken their toll on me. Without hesitation, I left my *Mekrus* and joined that of Tadelech's.

I found a good friend in her. I was often impressed by Getachew's insight. He knew we could be friends. I often found it impossible to believe that Getachew and Berhanemeskel had died and Tadelech and I had become friends. Since she came, I regained confidence in myself and trust in others. I allowed myself to make friends and learned that the world is not that bad a place, after all.

A few months after Tadelech had her baby, my friend Emebet came to *Kerchele* from *Kefitegna* 19. She was given four years. It was so good to see her again after so long. Emebet and Tadelech also became good friends. They had a lot in common. Emebet studied at Haile Selassie University and then went to France for further study and spoke French like Tadelech. The Derg had killed their husbands and they had kids at home.

The story of Emebet and Tadelech was the story of many prisoners in *Kerchele*.

What cannot man live through!
  -Fyodor Dostoevsky, *The House of the Dead.*

Kerchele was different from *Kefitegna* in terms of the composition of prisoners. It housed murderers, thieves, political prisoners and others, unlike *Kefitegna* where almost all were political prisoners. It was also home for those who had lost their mind or who feigned madness like Zergi – the woman with the colorful beads that I saw the first day I got there.

The overwhelming majority of political prisoners had no sentences. They languished in prison year after year without knowing their fate. Some of them had no affiliation to any organization and were in jail for no reason at all. Length of sentence or length of stay in prison did not necessarily reflect a person's rank in the Party or the League or any other organization for that matter. Some prisoners had no files. Nobody even knew who had put them in and for what.

It took years to sort that out and set them free.

Two or three year sentences were treated as days compared to ten or fifteen. When a girl had only one more year to go people talked about it as if she was leaving the next day. "You are lucky. You have only one more year left," was a common remark. One night, Hanna Tefera – Nebiyu Tefera's sister and a fellow *Kefitegna* prisoner and who was given ten years – sat up on her top bunk and clapped her hands and cried with excitement, "Attention everyone! After four years, I would have only two more years to go!" Most of us burst out with laughter but the older ones shed tears.

Long sentences were harder on those who were married and had children. Marriages broke up and families were torn apart. Even worse, children died, while their parents were languishing in prison. This was the most tragic thing of all. The entire compound would be gripped by grief but mothers were stricken with terror and panic.

We lived in crowded *bets* - houses. *Sostegna Bet* sheltered over one hundred prisoners at the time I got there. This was nothing compared to the men's houses that took in up to seven hundred! *Sostegna Bet* was a dungeon. It was made of corrugated zinc sheets and was almost dark inside with no windows. It was stifling hot during the day and chilly at night. There were single and double-decker beds and, except for newcomers, almost everybody slept on a bed. There was no toilet inside and a urine bucket was stuck in the corner during the night. As a newcomer, I used to sleep on the dirt floor near the door and the urine bucket. The stench was unbearable.

There were all kinds of prisoners in *Adarash,* unlike *Sostegna Bet,* whose population was mainly EPRP. There were wives and children of bureaucrats, ministers, army generals, and feudal lords of the previous regime. They had already been there for more than four years when I was brought in. Their crime was that they were the children and/or wives of officials of the former regime. There were also Eritrean prisoners of war, EPRP and *Meison* members and at times a few murderers and thieves.

One hundred and seventy-five women were crowded into *Adarash.* But it was cleaner and brighter than *Sostegna Bet.* Two fluorescent lights glared at us all night. Unlike *Kefitegna,* where we slept in the dark, lights were kept on during the night in *Kerchele.* If the lights were out for any reason they were restored at once for fear that we might escape.

There were two windows on opposite sides of *Adarash.* Since they were in the middle area, it was stifling hot at night in the upper section of the hall. It was called "the oven." At night, some of the women in the "oven" section sat topless, their boobies covered with scarves. The other section was called "the fridge." It was chilly at night because of the draft coming in through the two windows. Those in the "fridge" section usually wrapped themselves with *gabi,* particularly during the rainy season. There was a "water room" inside *Adarash* with a small window open twenty-four hours a day. The air coming in through the window on cold nights made the area even cooler.

Even though *Adarash* was better than *Sostegna Bet* in every sense of the word, it had its own setbacks. There were women with mental health disorders and they screamed incessantly in the middle of the night. One of them shrieked every day around two in the morning. It was a terrible screech and most of us were kept awake for hours on end. At one time, about four women took turns screaming in the middle of the night. One night it was so unbearable many shed tears. The Discipline Committee member would call the wardens when it became intolerable. The guards often pretended they did not hear. At times, they called the health assistants on duty, who sedated the women with *Largarctil.* Other times, the screeching woman would be taken to the mental institution only to come back a few months later with screams worse than before.

It was a vicious circle.

Thieves had a section by themselves. We called them *Oola* – slang for thief. Their house was a small room with a dirt floor and mud walls. It was overcrowded during the rainy season. Many of the *temelalash* – repeat offenders – stole and got caught on purpose to be sheltered from the rain and the cold weather. Most *Oolas* were proud of their trade and unabashedly called themselves *leba* – thief. Some of the novices, including those from middle-class families brought in for peccadilloes, usually felt embarrassed of what they did and showed discipline and restraint. By the time they had served two or three months, they had become unrecognizable. They had by then learned the art of thievery from the veterans, who readily and proudly imparted their expertise.

Water shortage at *Kerchele* was the most talked about subject when I was at the *Kefitegna*. But never had I imagined it to be so dire. There was only one standpipe outside for over five hundred women. *Adarash* had a small one inside the building but the precious drop clocked in after midnight, and briefly, too.

Women lined up their jerry cans, pails and water cans under the large water pipe outside for days in the hope that a miracle would take place under the plumbing. The pipe showed mercy twice a day – in the morning and in the evening – and very often only the lucky, the brawny and the bullies got water. Most took off frustrated. It was usually *Oolas* who fetched water for political prisoners and others for money or food.

The pipe was always left open and when water abruptly gushed, a great deal of chaos ensued. Brawls broke out as people always accused one another of jumping the queue. Fistfights were not uncommon sights as "victims" seized the opportunity to release pent-up energy. One or two women were often rushed to the clinic with a bleeding nose or a scratched cheek. Precious water was also wasted in the process.

Leaders arise in every crisis situation. The row around the water pipe had been going on for quite a while until this woman arrived on the scene. I didn't know what she was in for. She was tall and commanded respect and inspired fear. She handled the situation with an iron fist for which she was nick named *dictu* – diminutive for dictator. *Dictu* would burst forth out of nowhere when the pipe started running and silenced everybody with one word: *Zor bey* – keep away! Or she would yell, "Put that jerry can back where it was!" Everybody obeyed her. The self-appointed leader brought sanity and order around the water pipe.

When I was with my previous *Mekrus*, each individual was allowed to use only three jugs of water to wash herself. For someone like me, who loved water, it was hard to adjust to such meager ration. There was only one "shower room" for all female prisoners. Each individual was allocated two fifteen-minute shower time slots on different days of the week. The list was posted at the door of the clinic.

When it was my turn, I poured three jugs of water into a pail and headed to the "shower room," wondering how I would be able to "shower" and wash my hair with half a pail of water. What was even worse was the "shower room," which used to be a toilet, was locked from outside by a sliding lock. The woman before me locked the door for me and I was just pouring the cold water on my body when I heard a knock at the door. I heard someone warn me I had only five minutes left. *Oh, my God!* Before I knew it, the door was flung open. "Your time is up!"

I stood there naked with soap all over my body. The interesting thing was that the "shower room" faced the gate, which opened every second in the morning as male prisoners brought in food to the gate. Men were not allowed into the compound. I splashed water on my body and came out wrapped in a towel. Since that day, I washed myself in a toilet used by everybody, including the wardens. It was located mid-way between *Sostegna Bet* and the clinic. Passersby popped in every minute, did their business and left, while I was washing myself. The place was stinky and the traffic heavy but I didn't mind. I also got used to taking a "shower" with three jugs of water.

Roll call took place at six in the evening. We rushed to make tea or cook supper on a coal-fire brazier before then. We feverishly fanned the coal-fire with *maragebia* – a small and round straw fan. *Mekrus* members may not necessarily be in the same house and even if they were, supper was served before roll call. Supper for most people might be a piece of bread and a cup of tea. The noise in the compound was at its peak around roll call as individuals called roll call mates: *"Kotari meta! Kotari meta!"* - roll call!

We had to stand in pairs in a straight line during roll call. A newcomer or someone who had moved from another *bet* had to find a roll call mate. The mate may not even be someone that person usually talked to. But they queued up together every evening. The sequence of the lineup remained the same day after day, year after year. If a pair was number one, they remained number one until they were both released. If only one of them is released, the other one retained the number and found another roll call mate.

That served a purpose. There was only one toilet, Turkish style, inside *Adarash*. One's turn to use the toilet was determined by the roll call lineup sequence. The first woman on the lineup used the toilet right away (even before roll call is over). Unless she was sick, she was done for the night, or else she would have to wait till number 175 has used the toilet, which was usually around twelve o'clock at night. There were a few known individuals who took too long and made the waiting even longer. However, we didn't need to use the toilet before or after our turns unless there was an emergency.

The roll call lineup also maintained our turns at the water pump in the "water room." Water came after midnight and flowed thin and painfully slowly. We had to fill up our jerry cans in the dead of night. Many of us fell asleep holding our jerry cans under the water pipe.

Privacy was unthinkable, but many who slept in the lower bunks draped their beds to make their own spaces. Those in the top tier had to tough it out. The 'curtain' could be an old bed sheet or a scarf tied around the bed.

Life in *Kerchele* could have been even worse were it not for us prisoners who made it out to be what it had become.

You desire to know the art of living, my friend? It is contained in one phrase: make use of suffering.
       -Henri Frederic Amiel

"We set out to build a utopia in the outside world but settled for reforming *Kerchele,"* my friend Dawit Sibihatu once observed. Dawit was a former EPRP member thrown into *Kerchele* for years without a sentence. Indeed, having spectacularly failed to build a utopia in the nation at large, we turned things around and made *Kerchele* habitable.

Proof of the triumphal power of the human spirit.

We formed committees that looked after our needs and interests and pushed for many reforms. Committees such as *Delday* (that looked after sleeping arrangements), Sports and Recreation (that organized entertainment and sports), Food (that advocated for better food provision) and Health (which pressed for adequate provision of health care) met once a week and pressured the administration to make changes and reforms in our interest. Chairs of all committees met once a month to discuss issues and to further exert influence on the administration to yield to our demands and needs.

We had learned how to struggle for our rights and we made use of it.

I became chair of the Sports and Recreation Committee and Secretary of the *Kinet* – Arts – Group. The Group rehearsed every week and performed to the prison audience. It was formed and was active around the time of the Derg's *Enat Hager Tiri* – a call of the motherland campaign – to raise funds to the war against the Eritrean Liberation Fronts in the North and the Somali invaders in the East. During the campaign, famous singers such as Tilahun Gessese and Mohamed Ahmed performed at *Kerchele* in front of thousands of prisoners.

The overwhelming majority of prisoners did something to make their dreary existence bearable. There were, of course, a few who merely marked time. But most of these women suffered from mysterious illnesses. Knitting was the most common pastime for many. Others devised ingenious survival strategies. They sold cigarettes and matches, sweaters, scarves, embroidered pens, plaques, colorful baskets, and coin pouches. We bought them and proudly gave them as gifts to family members on holidays, birthdays and weddings. Embroidered pens with names of our loved ones engraved on them, plaques with poems and sweaters were the most favored gifts. Eritrean prisoners of war mass produced baskets and sold them to the outside world through networks.

Oolas sold their labor to the 'elite.' They washed clothes, made beds, cooked, washed dishes, and on Sunday called names on behalf of their 'employers.' They were usually paid in-kind in the form of food or articles of clothing. Some were paid in cash on Sunday.

A new *bet* was added from the men's compound to address over-crowding. The building swallowed up all the residents of *Sostegna Bet* and many more. It kept the name *Sostegna Bet*. It was by far better than the one before.

A cooking stall was built with corrugated zinc sheets. Some entrepreneurial non-political prisoners squatted with tomatoes, potatoes, hot green peppers and coal, turning it into a teeming market place. Others sold such niceties as Nivea Cream and Vaseline. *Oolas* and other non-political prisoners, who did not have the luxury of indulging in such extravagances, nevertheless purchased fingerfuls when they were about to go to the soccer match, to school, or on a Sunday with the hope of receiving a visitor. They threw fifteen cents on the vender's outstretched palm and stuck their index fingers in the containers to scoop out the cream. They showed their fingers to the vender to reassure her that they had not taken more than they have paid for. They spread the cream on the extremities and off they were with lubricated faces and limbs.

School was the best thing that happened to us in *Kerchele*. It was also our greatest achievement. The first political prisoners taught literacy under a tree. Soon a school was built in the main compound. It was a large building with a dirt floor and mud walls and no partitions. Several classes went on simultaneously in the same room. Grade 12 might be going on beside a literacy class. Several classrooms were later built and the school that started with literacy, expanded to high school and vocational training.

Vocational training in horticulture, poultry, auto-mechanics, drafting and building construction was given. There were many success stories about those who graduated from these courses and made use of their skills when they got out. Language instructions in French, Italian, German and Arabic were also given.

I took French, building construction, drafting, a six-week criminal law course, soccer refereeing, first aid and some Italian. I did a few weeks of Primary Health Care. A female warden had to escort me to Primary Health Care classes but later they complained that there were not enough wardens to take me back and forth. I was told that I wouldn't be able to do the practical aspect of the course at a hospital, so I was obliged to discontinue.

At first, men and women were not allowed in the same classroom, and classes took place in shifts. After painstaking negotiations with the prison administration, 'co-education' started. A female warden sat outside the classrooms and watched any 'improper' behavior between men and women.

Grade twelve students sat for the ESLCE (Ethiopian School Leaving Certificate Examination), a requirement to enroll at the university, as with any other school in the country. The school scored the highest in the country and was rated number one for several years in a row.

There were all kinds of prisoners who were qualified to give the courses: medical doctors, accountants, mathematicians, lawyers, chemists, historians, economists, elementary and high school teachers. I taught literacy and science in grade eight and English in grade nine for a short time. Tadelech taught history in grade twelve and gave French lessons. She had gotten her degree in Switzerland in History.

A night school was opened for the wardens. The prisoners not only taught one another, but the wardens as well. Older wardens were able to complete elementary school and the younger ones, who had discontinued their education, got the opportunity to graduate from high school.

The women's compound had a clinic managed by a female health assistant. When a volunteer at the clinic was released, her position was up for grabs. I got the position after writing a test. I was able to write the test because of the length of my sentence. I moved to the *Emechat Bet*, where Tadelech and her daughter were staying. That was the reward for giving free service to the clinic. It was the best thing that happened to me.

There were less than twenty women at the *Emechat Bet*. The room had a parquet floor and was clean, with a water pipe inside the washroom. The children had cribs and the mothers slept on beds. I was the only one who slept on the floor.

I later moved to the ward, which was even better. I got the permission to bring a friend of mine, Chuchu Negussie – a former EPRP member – from *Adarash* to work with me. The ward was big and had about twenty or so beds. Chuchu and I slept on a double-decker bed. I slept on the top bunk and Chuchu on the lower. We waxed the parquet floor and covered the wall with newspaper and beautiful pictures torn from magazines. We made glue from a paste of semolina gruel.

There was a shower in the Turkish style toilet in the ward. Even some of our friends from *Adarash* took their daily showers there. It was clean and for the most part only Chuchu and I used it. The ward also served as the "dining room" for our *Mekrus* and a meeting place for all my friends. We ate, chatted, dressed, danced, sang, combed our hair, laughed, and cried in that room for over three years. Often, Chuchu and I got permission from the good wardens for our friends to sleep over.

We even smuggled in a tape recorder a couple of times to listen to songs and tape ourselves singing and talking. Samson Gashaw, a former EPRP member and Chuchu's *aynuka* – sweetheart by sight – was the one who lent us the tape recorder, which we managed to keep a secret.

Our friends gathered in the ward to listen to music. When rumor floated around that there was a tape recorder in the ward, we immediately returned it to Samson. Radios and tape recorders were forbidden items. Later, the tape was confiscated from the men and my friend Dawit Sibihatu had to spend all day in a punishment cell for one month for being found with it. He had to be on his feet for eight hours a day because of the urine soaked floor.

Family visits were periodically allowed in the office. It was an exciting and anxious moment, especially for those who had children. The permission, which could be obtained either at the request of the prisoner or family members, may not be granted all the time. The feeling we experienced after a family visit in the office was indescribable. We talked about it for days.

Sunday was the biggest prize of all. Family members and friends came to visit. We looked our best to show that we were doing fine. Some prisoners even looked better than many family members. Sunday also meant, pay day, for many of us. Visitors gave us money. That saw us through the week and we awaited the next Sunday with great anticipation.

Occasionally, family members or friends brought wedding, christening or birthday pictures, which were considered great treasures. We proudly showed them around and studied every detail. Some of our siblings, such as my younger sister Negede and Tadelech's younger sister, were abroad at the time, and we looked at the pictures they sent us with so much joy and pride.

Those were our links to the outside world, to normal life.

Water became available after more pipes were installed. Shower stalls were built, which eliminated the shortage of shower rooms. A teacher who taught drafting built them. I was one of his students. Some of my classmates and I helped him install the pipes and shower heads. Water shortages became a thing of the past. Suddenly, there was water flowing everywhere. Time slots for shower became history.

Unlike *Kefitegna,* life in *Kerchele* was less communal. *Mekrus* members were on the whole friends, siblings, fellow *Kefitegna*, *Meakelawi* or police station prisoners or members of a religious group. *Mekrus* played many important roles in our lives. It provided material, emotional, psychological and social support. Without it, many prisoners would have had serious health problems. As it was, many suffered from various kinds of psychological ailments. *Mekrus* also alleviated the burden on family members. Many couldn't afford to bring food to their children, even once a week. Those who had the means accommodated individuals who could not provide for the *Mekrus.*

The prison had a small library stacked with books mainly confiscated from prisoners. Later on, a nicer and bigger library was built with money raised through the prisoners' shop. Female prisoners were allowed to go to the library only on Thursday mornings. We were led like a flock of sheep by two women wardens. We checked out books overnight; my friend Dawit Sibihatu, the librarian, brought them to us, just before roll call. He came back to collect them in the morning.

There were six soccer teams in the compound. Membership was usually assigned, just like sleeping areas when prisoners first arrived at the prison. We were recruited based on our political affiliations. The teams were politically charged and there was much animosity amongst some of them. Political differences, especially between *Meison* and EPRP, had been imported into *Kerchele.*

The prison administration threatened to ban the teams unless the names were changed. *Netsanet* (freedom) was renamed *Nyala* (antelope), *Andenet* (unity) was christened *Nib* (bee), *Abyotawi Netsebrak* (revolutionary spark) became Walia (walia ibex), *Wozader* (proletariat) was renamed *Gureza* (colobus monkey), *Tegbareid* (technical) became Blue Nile and *Teramaj* (progressive) was renamed *Awraris* (rhinoceros).

The overwhelming majority of members of Nyala, Nib and Walya were former EPRP members. I was assigned to Nyala. Gureza membership was for the most part *Meison* and Awraris members were mainly security agents, former cadres, *Kebele* members and soldiers.

Soccer was the biggest attraction in the compound. If there was anything, even if temporarily, that transported prisoners to another blissful world, it was soccer. It glimmered on *Kerchele* like a shining star, giving meaning and purpose to life. It alleviated boredom and anxiety which were typical of prison life. In the early days, many girls vented pent up emotions through fistfights when they returned from a soccer game because of the passion surrounding soccer as well as the politically charged atmosphere.

Saturday morning or Friday afternoon, women curled their hair and sat in the sun all morning to look their best at the soccer games. Saturday afternoon, just after lunch, they lined up in pairs at the gate to go to the game. The young, the old and the sick came out in droves to pour out passion and enthusiasm around the soccer pitch. Besides the Saturday and Sunday entertainment by the six teams, the once-a-month "all star" game drove spectators to intoxication. The "all star" team played a few times professional soccer teams from outside, which was a bonus.

Each team built its own "tearoom" in the men's compound. All prisoners went to "opening parties," including women. I went to the *Ketero* compound for the housewarming party of one of the teams. That was my only trip to men's compound. A tearoom was built in the women's quarter and a ping-pong table was set up. Only a few of us played the game. But one of the royal family members made good use of the place. She taught children drawing, writing and reading there.

We played volleyball for leisure or team tournament. I played as a defender for *Nyala* for a good while. An "all star" team once played a very famous professional volleyball team – *Etu Mela Michi* – from outside the compound. I played in that match.

The best team in town trashed us.

The only occasional hurdle to playing volleyball in the compound was *Adey* Silas. She was an old woman jailed because of her son who had joined one of the Eritrean Liberation Fronts. She weaved a basket sitting under one of corners of the volleyball net. She always refused to go elsewhere, when a game was going on. Every time the ball bounced on her head, she pricked it with her owl. We were not discouraged so easily. We would immediately raise money and ask one of the wardens to buy us a new one.

Aynuka spiced up life in prison. Before the arrival of political prisoners, male convicts had women *aynukas* whom they may have never talked to. They fell in love with them by sight. In olden times, the only time men set eyes on women prisoners was when the latter were on their way to court. The only thing a man could do when he saw his *aynuka* was wink at her from a distance, and that was if she happened to see him. The woman may not even know she was somebody's *aynuka* unless she received winks on her way to court or a gift through a warden. Men often fought over a woman without her knowledge.

When political prisoners came to the scene, they took *aynuka* to a higher plane. Before 'co-education' started, they exchanged love letters tucked under books and passed on through female teachers, who had limited access to men. After 'co-education' started, *aynuka* took center stage in school life. Almost everybody had an *aynuka*. No longer was it done through an intermediary. Men and women could sit and talk for hours under the watchful eyes of *Etiye* Feleku – one of the female wardens. If *Etiye* Feleku was in a good mood, she would let *aynukas* or any male and female friends sit and talk for as long as they wanted. If she was in a foul mood or if she wanted one of the well-to-do prisoners to slip a note in her hands, she would walk around telling everybody to get up *benekis* – one by one. There were many serenades for *aynukas* sung by women during farewell parties or other occasions.

ግንቡ ሽፍኖኝ ነው ዘቡ ከልክሎኝ ነው
ሳላይህ አልቀርም ምኞቴ ብዞ ነው
አንተ ወዲያ ማዶ እኔ ወዲህ ማዶ
አንገናኝም ወይ ክልሱ ተንዶ
እስቲ ውሃ ውሃ በደረቴ ላይ
ያንተም ልብ እንደኔ ይዋልላል ወይ
ያንተም ልብ እንደኔ የዋለሰ እንደሆን
በታትነው ልምጣ መቼም እስር አይሆን

We organized farewell parties for prisoners who had finished their terms. The day before a girl was released; she placed curlers in her hair and sat in the sun all day. She washed, scrubbed, and gave away things that she would not take home with her. There was a feeling of elation among her friends. At night, a party would start; tea and treats would be served, and then all would start singing.

> ልብሷን በፌስታል አዘጋጅላት
> ነገ ሚሚዬ መንገደኛ ናት
> አይዞሽ ሚሚዬ አይበልሽ ከፉ
> ሁሉም ይፈታል በየ ወረፉ

> አንቺ መንገደኛ ወዬት ነው ያሰብሽው
> በክርኜ ጎዳና ጉዞ የጀመርሽው
> እጭንሽለሁኝ ገብተሽ ተሳፈሪ
> ለዛሬው እኔ ነኝ ተረኛ በራሪ
> ጥያቄ ቢመጣ ወይ ተቆጣጣሪ
> ተፈኜ ነኝ በይው ማንንም ሳትፈሪ

The farewell party was also an occasion for prisoners to express their own anxieties, hopes and wishes.

> ያሳ ሽማግሌ ዳር ዳሩን ይዋኛል
> አትሽበር ልቤ እፈታ ይሆናል
> እባክሽ ወፊቱ ልግልልሽ ፍሬ
> ታመጭልኝ እንደሁ የመፈታት ወሬ
> አልታይሽ አለኝ ያገሬ ሰማይ
> እንዲህ ሆዬ ቆርጦ ታስፈያለሁ ወይ
> መሄድ መሄድ አለኝ ጎዳና ጎዳና
> አልግደረደርም እስቲ ይፍቱኝና

Blen was a former EPRP member who was in about the same time I was. She came up with an ingenious plan of making money. When she exhausted her supply of cigarettes, she placed a bowl on a mattress, stood in the middle of the room and sang English songs. Bettye Swann's 'Make me yours' was her favorite. We got up and threw cigarettes or coins in the bowl. That saw Blen through the rest of the week.

Books became more and more accessible and even abundant in *Kerchele*. In the beginning, Marxist books were not allowed, even though the Derg professed to be Socialist. No one wanted to read them, anyway. The authorities did not allow philosophy books either as they were suspected of politically corrupting prisoners.

Videos became available. We went to watch them at the school, paying fifty cents per movie. We watched films such as The Champ, Amadeus, Gandhi, The Deer Hunter and Endless Love.

The food ration was a nightmare. For the most part convicts depended on it. The bread was so sour many suffered from stomach ailments. What is more, on one side of the room, a woman may sit with a piece of dry bread and tea in a tomato sauce can. Next to her, someone else might be having *injera* with chicken or beef sauce. It was often difficult to witness that. However, we shared with others whatever we had.

Every fortnight was a barbecue day for us. Meat was rationed out and served an hour or so before roll call. We crowded around the middle of the gravel-capped courtyard to welcome the meat, excitedly fanning the coal-fire in our braziers. The meat came in a half-barrel, hanging from two wooden bars carried by two female wardens. Everybody got a fistful of boiled meat. We called it *ye menge sega* – sega – meat and *menge* diminutive for *mengist* – government – or Mengistu – for Mengistu Hailemariam. We barbecued the boiled meat on the coal-fire until it turned brown. Some even prepared *awaze* (a hot condiment prepared from ground red pepper, salt and lemon or lime juice) ahead of time in anticipation of the *menge sega.*

It was so divine we could forgive Mengistu his brutality.

We earned the respect of the wardens as our relationship with them evolved. In the pre-revolutionary era, prisoners in *Kerchele* were mainly thieves, murderers and others convicted for civil violations. It was common for wardens to treat cons as their personal servants. They brought all kinds of chores from home such as grinding, washing and weaving, and had convicts do it for them for free. Often they beat them for disobedience or for not performing personal chores properly. They stripped them of their dignity and subjected them to sub-human treatment. Things changed after the arrival of political prisoners. We gave convicts back their dignity and freedom as permitted by prison conditions. Some of the older wardens hated us for changing the status quo. They could not treat prisoners as chattel anymore and whip them at will. Cons went to school instead of slaving for guards.

Hibret Souk (a prisoners' shop) was opened and run by the prisoners. Besides providing basic items to us, it gave employment opportunities to some prisoners. Most importantly, it provided freed prisoners, who had come from the provinces and had been a long time in prison, with transportation and start-up money. Many of the prisoners who had committed murder had lost their social networks and had to start life from scratch.

Searches took place in the compound from time to time. The plan always leaked and we hid things not allowed in the compound such as knives, radios, tape recorders and bottles. The wardens, who were also the ones who confiscated them, smuggled most of these items in. Knives were either smuggled or carved out of the corrugated zinc fencing. We gave money to trusted wardens to buy us radios.

Those who owned radios listened to music laying down on their beds, radio stuck to their ears and their heads covered with *gabi*. The volume was so low, even the person sitting on the next bed might not hear. We called our favorite songs *medeberia* – blues. If a favorite song of a girl was playing when she was socializing with friends, somebody would call out, "Hey Aster! Your *medeberia!*" She would rush over to her bed, cover her head with *gabi* and stick her radio on her ear. Many newcomers and convicts never knew what *medeberia* meant. Most cons wouldn't think twice to report us to the wardens if they suffered the slightest offense by a political prisoner.

Moged is the slang term for prison rumor. It was jocularly defined as an acronym for *Morale Genbi Dirijit* (organization to build morale). *Moged* was essentially unsubstantiated news of release or amnesty, which spread like waves (the real meaning of the slang term) throughout the prison community. It was these stories of hope and release that kept most prisoners going.

Moged usually started circulating in the compound around July or even as early as June. It went wild particularly in August as we approached September 12 – the date the Derg took power, officially celebrated as Revolution Day. The Derg released a few prisoners for the occasion as a token of amnesty.

Sometimes *Moged* was just made up by individuals. It diffused in the compound with lightning speed. By the time it came back to its creators, it had become so elaborate with many additions and omissions that they didn't even recognize it. Other times, *Moged* was based on facts leaked from security or the Derg office, often intentionally. The chief of security, Colonel Tesfaye Woldeselassie, was rumored to be the number one creator of *Moged*. Parents would come to *Kerchele* and confide in their daughter or son that they had been told by the Colonel that she or he would be released on Revolution Day. It may or may not be true, but that was how the Colonel sent many weeping parents home. June, July and August seemed like running down a slope. The months flew by, even for those of us not taken in by the *Moged* hype. After Revolution Day, it was like going uphill all over again for many prisoners.

Most prisoners were superstitious when it came to being released. *Gede* – a species of falcon, which also meant luck – is believed to be the harbinger of good news. She was the ultimate lucky charm. A *gede* usually showed up just before roll call and installed itself majestically on the roof of *Adarash*. Women assembled in the courtyard and watched it with reverence, as if it had been sent down directly from the heavens. Some swore in the name of the Good Lord that some people would soon be released. Even the release of one prisoner the next day or the day after was proof that *gede* had brought the good news. At times a *Moged* coincided with the arrival of *gede*.

That sparked a wave of euphoria in the compound.

The prison compound was so shabby it was hard to believe human beings actually lived there. Sara Cosio, a half-Italian, half-Ethiopian former EPRP member, completely transformed the courtyard. She had the area dug to plant flowers and grass. We named it Cosio Square. It was nice to see something green for a change. Many lay down or napped in the "garden." During searches, many, including me, hid radios and knives there.

Gabi and a warrant (*gabi ena* warrant) usually meant a definite release in *Kerchele*. In previous times it could have meant an execution or a transfer to another prison. A prisoner was asked to come out with *gabi* and a warrant (a piece of paper with the name, date of detention, reason for detention, length of sentence and date of release, if any). A male friend of mine had mounted mine (with the fifteen-year sentence) on a piece of wood frame to preserve it for posterity.

Prison life would have been even more difficult had it not been for the unfailing support of family members, visiting twice a week standing in line for hours rain or shine. It was never easy. I felt particularly guilty when my mother and sisters had to come on holidays. They came first to *Kerchele* and then went home to celebrate. Those were the most painful moments.

We might have been in prison, but they were the ones who carried most of the burden. We were indebted to them with boundless gratitude. As for me, it was the support from my family that helped me cruise through my prison years with human dignity.

Man---that is the mystery....I work with this mystery, because I want to be a man.

        -Fyodor Dostoyevsky

What does it mean to be human? What is human nature? Kerchele was the place where I came face to face with these questions. We were conditioned and streamlined in the Party, and almost all of us behaved uniformly. In my pre-prison days, I was too green to understand the ebb and flow of existence. Whatever took place at the *Kefitegna*, I saw it in terms of political context. Here in *Kerchele*, I learned the complexity of human nature. It lay before me in its naked state. Here evil is raw and frightening. It wasn't disguised under politics, which made it look understandable when it really was not. There was no ideological justification. It was just stark. *What does it mean to be human?* The answer was often scary, sometimes a mystery. But life would have been depraved, atrocious and depressing were it not for its redeeming aspects.

      There were murderers in *Kerchele* who had committed heinous crimes. Every time I saw one of these, I asked myself, how could a human being do what she did? To my horror, only humans were capable of committing such crimes.

Among those who committed murder was Zinash. She was tall, slim, beautiful, and had long hair. She came in for killing a four-year-old boy. She quarreled with the boy's mother and in order to punish her, she crushed a razor and made the child swallow it with water. When the boy didn't die, she hanged him from the rooftop of his parents' house. What could have a four-old boy done to deserve that? It was sickening. We were all stunned and repulsed by such atrocity. I could feel my blood run cold in my veins every time I saw that beautiful woman standing at the doorstep of *Adarash,* leisurely combing her long and lustrous hair. How could such an angelic figure commit such a horrible crime?

It was beyond my comprehension.

Zinash was on the news and on the *Polisena Ermijaw* – newspaper of the police force. Her crime has been so horrific it caused quite a stir both in and outside of the prison compound. But her story did not end there.

She got life, having children being the extenuating circumstance. That was nothing compared to what she did to herself. She started losing weight to the point of being emaciated. She became bed-ridden and was admitted into the ward. All kinds of tests were done and the doctors affirmed that there was no organic cause to explain her condition. Finally, she was sent to the hospital. The day before her departure, I went to the ward with clean sheets to change her bed. The woman who was caring for her lifted her up with both hands so that I could change the sheets.

Zinash slowly and painstakingly turned her head and turned her eyes toward the woman with hollow and lusterless eyes. Her cheekbones were protruded and her muscles wasted. She had shrunk to a skinny twelve-year-old girl. Her hair had fallen off almost completely and whatever remained had become thin and dull. She couldn't move her arms or her legs. The soiled sheet was covered with peeled skin. I had never seen anything like it. I stood there staring at her with almost veneration.

It was compelling.

This woman has gone through a terrible penance and bears tremendous suffering. She has quietly precipitated her own death. Compassion and admiration stirred in me for the woman who had committed the most horrible crime I had ever heard of.

I admired her capacity to suffer.

Some of those who had committed no less crimes feigned madness in the hope that their sentences would be reduced. Those who had killed children had become mad, but I doubted their insanity. When they became nuisance to the rest of us, they were sent to the mental institution. I believed that was where they became mad, if at all. I had not seen in them the capacity to suffer as Zinash. Their insanity seemed an escape, to me at least, from whatever was troubling them deep inside.

Zinash didn't simulate madness. She faced her guilt squarely and succumbed to suffering for what she had done. I came to believe that there was no harsher punishment than one meted out by a person's conscience. I became mystified by the workings of the human conscience. Though I was in no position to forgive or condemn anyone, I forgave her because of her capacity to suffer. What Zinash went through appeared to me repentance par excellence. I found it humbling.

She later died in the hospital.

Zergi was jailed for killing her step-son with rat poison. She was given twenty or twenty-five years. She, like Zinash, had killed a child, but showed no contrition, or so it seemed. We didn't see any telltale sign of repentance. Did I have to see it to believe it? As humans, we always demanded to see remorse in others for wrongdoing. Perhaps this satisfies some deep-seated need in us for reassurance. Perhaps it was a sublime human quality we desired to possess and to see in others. All I knew was that Zergi was too coarse to have such a refined human quality.

She was no Zinash.

Zergi was what we called *Awko abed* – one who habitually feigns madness. The potential to do evil was also palpable in her. If you wanted to irritate her, you just had to say "rat poison." She would roll her eyes and fix them on you in a way that warned you your days are numbered. I always recoiled in utter terror when I saw those chilling eyes. They were small but carried the seeds of danger.

What really intrigued me about Zergi was why she simulated madness. Was it her way of telling us that whatever she did was prompted by circumstances beyond her? Was it her way of coming to terms with guilt? One thing was certain: her simulation had given her the freedom that other prisoners could not enjoy, such as hurling a torrent of insults at the guards or not taking a shower for a year or two.

Bogeye, the old woman who threw our beddings away the day we arrived at *Kerchele*, was in for murdering her Italian husband. She was given twenty-five years. She had already served eighteen when I got there. We all believed that she was crazy. Whether or not she was crazy because of what she did or due to her long stay in prison wasn't clear to me. She was surely a subject of psychotherapy.

Bogeye had so many superstitions that forced her to constantly be on the lookout for malevolence intended on her. For instance, she believed that odd numbers were a bad omen. Male wardens came just before six to help out with roll call. The sick, the old and the mentally challenged were allowed to stay in, while the rest were lining up in pairs outside to be counted. A male and a female warden would go in and count those inside. "One, two, three, four, five," counts a male warden.

"Six!" shouts Bogeye, sitting on her top bunk bed.

"Oh, was it six? I thought I counted five. One, two three, four, five…"

"Six!" shouts Bogeye again.

"You counted five. Don't listen to her. She is crazy. Bogeye, shut up so that we can do the roll call," would interject a female warden.

Bogeye did that every time the number was odd and a new warden always went through the same ritual every time she did that.

It was around the time I came to *Kerchele*. I was reading a book lying down on one of the girls' bed, when I heard these two older women chatting. "I was so happy I ululated upon hearing the five-year sentence," said *Etiye* Alemitu.

"How can you ululate when you are given five years?"

"I thought they were going to kill me. I didn't care how many years I got as long as they didn't kill me. That was why I ululated."

Bogeye, who was sitting and knitting on her top bunk, looked down and said, "Alemitu, six years is nothing. It will be gone before you know it!"

Bogeye didn't like certain kinds of names, such as Hiwot or Sophia. She believed they had an ominous import. Since she didn't like my name, she gave me a few, one of which was Emebet. She didn't like many people either. She liked me despite the dislike she had taken to my name. She believed that I was one of the very few who were not spell-casters.

To Bogeye, people were always on the lookout to bespell her, so she is always on guard. If she saw a woman scratching or simply touching her chin, her forehead or her eyes, she would automatically do the same. That was her way of "aborting" an impending magical spell. She never missed any movements that signaled a looming spell. If you passed by her without even realizing that she was walking beside you, she would circle you to untangle the magical spell you'd just cast on her, or were about to.

Bogeye could be fun during the day, but she was annoying at night. She would start her unceasing and senseless monologue after ten o'clock and many newcomers found themselves unable to sleep. She talked about how one day she was so dressed up and went to the market and met him there… She did the same thing early in the morning, rudely awakening us all. People at *Sostegna Bet* had to cope with that every day. I believed that Bogeye was crazy, but there were times she knew what she was doing. Was she really crazy? I would never know. Like Zergi, her craziness allowed her certain liberties. For instance, she would open apart the zinc sheets of the fence and watch the men in the ward adjoining the women's compound which was unthinkable for another prisoner to do.

Biri came from the central province of Shoa. Biri was a respectable, generous and kind person. She was stoic and did very well at school. She killed her husband and buried him in her one-room house, then continued to live there, sleeping directly above the dirt floor where she had interred her husband's body. She told her neighbors that her husband had gone to visit his family in another town. They eventually got suspicious when the husband had not returned even a year later, and reported his disappearance to the police. When Biri got wind of it, she burned her house and took flight to the South, where she lived for three years married to another man.

The police had publicized her photo nationwide. One day they apprehended her, while she was shopping at a market. They brought her to *Kerchele* and she was given life.

There was something about some of those who had committed murder, like Zergi, that bespoke their capability to commit crimes. There was nothing about Biri that indicated that. I often said to Tadelech, "If somebody like Biri is capable of committing a crime, there is no reason why I wouldn't be able to. What is in Biri must be in me too."

Growing up, I'd always thought that murderers belonged to a separate set of people who had some overpowering reason to kill. *Kerchele* had taught me that they are like everybody else and that, as humans, we all have the seeds of evil planted in us. Some of these people had committed crimes with premeditation and others in a fit of anger often for trivial reasons. *But what prompts people to take such actions? How can a person as kind, generous, and correct as Biri kill another human being?*

The human mind is quite a mystery.

It is interesting to see why and how human beings would do anything in their power to do things that are prohibited. In *Kerchele,* many people would die for a glass of alcohol. Going to the hospital provided an excellent opportunity for drinking. If you could bribe the wardens (family members usually did it for us), you could meet your family members at the hospital and go home. Some didn't even have to go to the hospital.

We female prisoners were escorted by male and female wardens when we went to the hospital. The best excuse was to complain of persistent toothache. Once we left the compound, the male wardens would leave us with the female wardens at the hospital and go their own way. We would meet them at the end of the day at the hospital or near *Kerchele,* and walk together to the compound.

If a prisoner escaped, the warden who was responsible for him for that day was jailed for three months. Only a few political prisoners managed to escape. For the most part, every one returned at the end of the day.

Once, four of us were taken to Menilik II Hospital, all complaining of tooth pain. The female wardens who escorted us couldn't have been more different. One of them was *Emama* Tarikua, a very kind and lenient elderly woman, and the other was Madam Brown, who was indeed very inflexible. She was called Madam Brown because of the henna that turned her hair into red brown. As soon as we arrived at the hospital, Madam Brown sat on the pavement and started crying.

"What happened?" inquired *Emama* Tarikua, putting her hand on her cheek.

"I know what the girls are up to. They are poised to go home. They will have me lose my job," she sobbed.

"Who is going home? Am I not responsible for the girls as you are?" asked *Emama* Tarikua a look of disgust imprinted on her wrinkled face. *Emama* Tarikua went to have us registered and came back. We then asked both wardens if we could go and get something to eat. Madam Brown let a torrent of tears saying she "knew it was coming."

Emama Tarikua convinced her that nothing was going to happen and we went and sat behind the fruit stall outside the hospital. We contributed money to buy beer. Madam Brown watched us with resignation. She knew that there was nothing she could do at that point. Once we collected the money, Gifti Ebba, a non-political prisoner – and I went to buy beer accompanied by *Emama* Tarikua.

Gifti and I had two bottles of beer each and *Emama* Tarikua one at the store. We went back to the back of the fruit stall. We had bought each of the girls and ourselves two bottles of beer, besides the two Gifti and I had at the store. Everybody kind of got tipsy and started giggling. Madam Brown watched the drama with half disgust and half resignation.

I had earlier had one of the wardens call Sisay Abdulkadir, a friend of mine from campus days, before we left *Kerchele*. He came and took us to an eatery to have lunch. We had another round of beer with lunch and by then everybody was quite mellow. When we got back to the hospital, we had become so unmanageable *Emama* Tarikua surmised to get us all an appointment for another day. "I cannot let you see the doctor in this state," she enjoined concern and regret inscribed on her creased face.

That meant another opportunity to drink! The truck that brought us arrived late in the afternoon. All of us went in the back and Gifti and I begged the driver to take us for a joyride through Piassa. The two of us stood up on the back of the truck and *Emama* Tarikua pleaded with us to be seated like the other girls. We refused. Madam Brown watched us with aversion. We waved at every passerby, including at police and army officers riding in Land Rovers.

When we arrived in *Kerchele* the driver dropped us off at the gate. Before entering the compound, *Emama* Tarikua begged us to walk in a straight line and not giggle so that no one would suspect we'd been drinking. She told us to hold hands so that we could walk in a straight line.

On occasion, alcohol was smuggled into the prison compound. On the eve of one *Genna* – Ethiopian Christmas celebrated on January seventh – my friends and I wanted to throw a party in the ward. We contributed money to buy alcohol. We spent the day cooking, cleaning and making beds for everybody.

Around four in the afternoon, one of the wardens working on the liquor smuggling project, broke the news that the "ship had sunk," which meant the drinks have been confiscated. There was a huge garden behind the women's compound and that was the "pier" where the "ship docked." It was usually there the confiscation occurred. We were not going to give up so easily, and we raised money again and gave it to a warden. We anxiously awaited the arrival of the drinks. To our relief, the warden brought them safely to the clinic in a box.

The second hurdle was getting the permission for all our friends coming from *Sostegna Bet, Adarash* and *Emechat Bet.* Permission depended on the wardens on duty. You wouldn't know who would be on duty for the night till after four in the afternoon. On a day like that, prayers are sent to the high heavens that wardens like Madam Brown would not be working. Fortunately, they were not that night.

Chuchu covered the door and the window of the ward with blankets so that the wardens couldn't peek through the crevices. She then turned the tape recorder on. Dinner was served. There were about ten of us. Normally, it was just Chuchu and me. After dinner we planned to spend the night dancing till our feet hurt. Drinks were served and in no time most of us were knocked out. Tadelech, Alemash and Genet were the only ones who were sober. The party was over even before it began.

In the morning Tadelech told me that there was a half-bottle of brandy left over and that we had to hide it. We looked frantically for it but couldn't find it. It was a mystery. There was a patient admitted into the ward a few days prior to *Genna.* Suddenly, I saw a bottle sitting on the small table beside her. Then I noticed that the woman was staring upwards lifelessly. I believed she was dead. I ran to the clinic to call the health assistant.

The health assistant found out that the patient's blood pressure had spiked. She had drunk the half-bottle of Brandy after everybody had fallen asleep! Fortunately, she was okay and the incident was covered up since the health assistant was a friend of ours.

There were political prisoners who would have made good specimens for Sigmund Freud. At night or during the day, a cluster of girls rushed an "unconscious" girl into the clinic. The health assistants would inject the girl Vitamin B Complex without the girl knowing what it is, just to make her feel that she is being given a medication. At times the male health assistant, working at the clinic, injected a girl with distilled water, used to dissolve penicillin or streptomycin, when he ran out of Vitamin B Complex shots. Seconds after they were given the injections, these girls "regained" consciousness and opened their eyes.

The health assistants would wink at each other and smile. Some of the girls, who transported the "patient" to the clinic, would tell their friends to go back to their *bet* so that they too won't "start." The "disease" was like an epidemic. Once it started, at least two or three girls were hauled into the clinic every day.

Some of these girls would throw insults at their interrogators or refuse to confess, giving the impression to people around that they were reliving the torture experience. Most of them, however, had never been tortured according to accounts by prisoners tossed in with them at some *Kefitegna* or police station.

I thought that was their way of coping with reality in prison.

When I let go of what I am, I become what I might be.
     -Lao Tzu

My own coping mechanism was reading. It gave meaning to my life. I wanted to find an answer in books to what had happened to our project and to me personally, and how I should live my life in *Kerchele*. Material possession had never appealed to me except for the insatiable urge to possess books. I was delighted by the sheer sight of them. It was as if they would open up the mystery of existence and of the whole universe to me. Perhaps that was because of the environment in which I grew up.

Books were like gold or diamonds in our house. My mother collected books, magazines and newspapers, discussed them with her male friends and locked them up in a huge light blue wooden box. She always kept the padlock key hidden. It was only when she left it unlocked or forgot the key hanging on the padlock that my little sister Negede and I got the chance to rummage through the box and glimpse its contents. My sister was fascinated by the medals our older sister Almaz had won for every kind of sport imaginable. She caressed them, examined them and put them one by one around her neck. I assuaged my curiosity peering into old and new Amharic books, old newspapers and magazines.

Before I started reading in English, I borrowed Amharic books from my mother and returned them as soon as I finished reading them. Then they would disappear into the wooden box where they would not see the light of day.

My reading career started with *Tsehay Mesfin,* which my mother gave me when I was eight years old. My mother was an avid reader of Amharic books and well-versed in Ethiopian history and Amharic literature. She was schooled in traditional education at home and had done the Psalms.

Traditional education in Ethiopia was mainly religious and entrenched in churches and monasteries. For the most part, sons of rich peasants ran away from home to escape the life of a peasant and pursued the long journey to becoming members of the traditional elite. Education included writing, reading, numerals, translation, poetry, church music, liturgy, astrology and commentary. The traditional elite were also chroniclers of the history of the church and of kings and of their dynasties. The students, commonly called *yekolo temari* (for subsisting mainly on roasted grain) traveled on foot from monastery to monastery in search of renowned *Memhirs* (traditionally educated religious scholars), under whose apprenticeship they started the long journey to becoming one themselves. This long journey usually took from 15 to 20 years. Aleka Gebrebrehana was the most legendary traditional intellectual and was known for his brilliance, elegant poetry, witticisms and a daring critique of Emperors and the nobility.

When my mother gave me *Tsehay Mesfin*, I read it and wept for Tsehay, the leading female character, who suffered and died of tuberculosis.

Little did I know that I would weep for myself years later.

In grade seven, I started reading English books borrowing three or four at a time from the library at Ras Mekonen School in Harar. The books were children's books. I would finish them all and return them on Monday. The librarian, seeing my thirst for reading, started selecting books appropriate for my age.

Before I finished grade nine, I had already read most of the Longman abridged editions such as *A Tale of Two Cities*, *Oliver Twist, Jane Eyre, Portrait of a Lady,* and other abridged editions such as *The Thirty Nine Steps and The Prisoner of Zenda.* In grade ten, I outgrew the abridged editions. I read *The Three Musketeers, Montezuma's Daughter, The Count of Monte Cristo, She, The Woman in White* and *The Scarlet Letter*. Before I finished grade eleven, I had already read *Les Misérables, Gone with the Wind, Exodus, Madame Bovary, Germinal, Wuthering Heights, Sense and Sensibility, Lady Chatterley's Lover, The Comedians* and most of Harold Robbins.

Most of the books that were available in *Kerchele* were thrillers by authors such as Irving Wallace, Robert Ludlum, Ken Follet, Frederick Forsyth, Jeffrey Archer, Arthur Hailey, and Sidney Sheldon. I rabidly consumed them all, but got tired of them. I read only a few non-fictions such as *Roots* and Adler's *On Human Nature*.

I then came across *The True Believer, Darkness at Noon, The Gulag Archipelago, The First Circle* and *Cancer Ward*. Alexander Solzhenitsyn was widely read in the compound, particularly *The Gulag* and *The First Circle*. We wrapped the books with newspaper to protect them from the gaze of the authorities. The books resonated with our experience. I found myself and my fellow comrades in all of those books.

I read *Darkness at Noon* twice and it stirred something in me that had been bothering me since Getachew's death: the idea of the end justifies the means. I was astounded by the similarity of our experiences. How is it possible that people who grew up in different cultures and lived in different times thought and behaved the same way? My conclusion pointed to the ideology they espoused and to their nature.

The *True Believer* gave me access to the group mind that had puzzled me for over three years. I was once a true believer and was shocked to find my former comrades and myself in Eric Hoffer's book.

However, Hoffer simplifies our motives for self-sacrifice. It is not always negative experiences such as alienation or external factors like ideology that propel us humans to self-sacrifice. Largely, it is compassion, the "sole non-egoistic motive," innate in us that thrusts us to self-sacrifice.

The way I looked at my past and the world in general took another sharp turn on my first visit to the prison library. Even if I read, I had never set foot in the library for the very reason I avoided many of the activities in the prison compound, staying away from my former comrades. I had stopped teaching or even taking courses, just to avoid being with most EPRP members.

That day at the library, I dawdled around the shelves and found out that many of the books were Marxist-Leninist. The very sight of them turned a knot in my stomach. I quickly moved away to the Art section. A large book caught my attention: *A History of Art and Music* was the title. I casually found myself a seat and opened it; little knowing that it would change the direction of my thinking forever.

I read short biographies of Vincent Van Gogh, Mozart and Beethoven. Van Gogh's and Beethoven's personal lives and tragedies moved me. I had to wipe my tears several times, reading about those two giants. When it was time for us to leave from the library, I told Dawit Sibhatu, the librarian, that I would like to sign out the book. "You can't sign out a book before the end of the day, but I will bring it for you later this afternoon," he told me, jotting down the title.

I stayed up till three in the morning that night reading the book. Dawit came in the morning to collect all the checked out books. I asked him to bring mine back in the evening. I did that every day until I finished reading it. I took notes upon notes. I learned about the different forms of art and music.

What am I to do with all that I've learned? I needed an outlet. I bought an exercise book and started writing to my niece, who was at the time nine or ten. She was a gifted piano player and I had seen her play pieces from Mozart. It was from her that I had learned the name Mozart for the first time. She started piano lessons when she was five or seven. I became obsessed with taking notes of the biographies and works of artists and composers, and smuggled them out to my niece. Every week, I bought a new exercise book, filled it with all the things that I had learned, tucked it in a food container and sent it away on Sunday.

To crown it all, I came across *Lust for life,* a biographical novel about Van Gogh by Irving Stone. Then other books surfaced in the compound by the same author: *Depths of Glory,* about Camille Pissarro and *The Agony and Ecstasy,* about Michelangelo. I also read *Of Human Bondage* by Somerset Maugham.

I felt my head reeling.

I discovered an exciting world. I found myself attracted to the bohemian lifestyle of the artists and writers. I wondered if I would ever go out of prison and lead the "authentic" existence I imagined it to be. Their detachment from material possession and the life of poverty attracted me.

Then there came to *Kerchele* my future friends, Sabela and her younger sister Ariam. The two were incarcerated along with their brother for refusing to condemn "counter revolutionaries" at Youth Association meetings because of their religious beliefs. Ariam was only fourteen when she was taken into custody.

Sabela was an accomplished sculptor, painter and musician. She was a genius. She was the bohemian artist that I had read in books about. She made sketches of everything in *Kerchele,* dazzling us with her talent. She played the guitar and *kirar* (a five or six-

string lyre). She tried to teach me how to play the latter and how to
draw. It was a futile effort.

I was cut out for neither.

Marxism-Leninism had taught me that change was possible as
groups and in an organized way, and I had tussled with the idea
since *Kefitegna* days. I knew I could never shy away from doing
what changes peoples' lives for the better after having gone through
the EPRP experience. But what I asked myself all along was how I
could do it without compromising my individuality and moral
integrity.

After reading *A History of Art and Music,* I concluded that it
was individuals who changed the world for the better through their
genius and inspiration. It may not have been an earth-shaking
discovery, but it was, to me at the time, something that helped me
see the world in a new light. Now that I came to realize that it was
individuals who changed society, I was able to shake off the belief
that had kept teasing my heart: that change comes only through
collective and organized effort.

I was acutely aware of the strong aversion that I had
developed toward politics. At times, I wondered if that was the right
thing to do. I was happy leading my life the way I wanted, but there
were constant questions in my head whether my focus in my own
personal development was completely acceptable--not to others, but
to myself.

Even though books gave color to what otherwise might have
been a monotonous existence, it was also the acute awareness of
why I was there that made prison life bearable. I did not brood over
my long sentence, not because I believed poetic justice had been
served but because I was bound by the vow that I had made when I

subscribed to the struggle. I knew very well the price I had to pay for getting myself into something like that.

Life in *Kerchele* taught me that what people were actually going through was much more important than striving to build a rosy future, which they may never live to see, if it happened at all. Guarding my own freedom and integrity is much more *important* and has *primacy* compared to trying to build a utopia, I concluded.

At the *Kefitegna*, I had learned to be suspicious of human nature and of even life itself. It was not based on any philosophical reflection but from something that had sprang out of my being.

I learned in *Kerchele* that I could still believe in the beauty of life and the fundamental goodness of people. *Kefitegna* and *Kerchele* had taught me that there were people who made me forget the painful existence I was living, people who showed me the sunny side of life and the good side to human nature and made me put all that painful experience into perspective.

I had long ceased to believe that the struggle was my true essence, in short who I really was. I had to deal with the sense of hollowness and nothingness after I renounced the Party. I still believed that what we set out to do was genuine, but it had gone wrong and had serious consequences. It was only then it had occurred to me that Getachew had believed that peoples' lives were much more important than implementing an idea.

That was the legacy he had left me with.

I learned to stand away from the Party and see it critically without nostalgia or regrets. Standing away from it was also a way of standing away from myself, which helped me realize what is most important to me and become focused on it. Once I learned the uncertainty and unpredictability of life, I became humbled in the face of the power that governed my life.

Without even being conscious of it, I adopted a dispassionate attitude toward life. Deep inside, I felt I would always be that "homeless hitch-hiker" who spun around the edges of existence, looking for that something…which I "cannot lose." I knew in my heart of my hearts the kind of life most people led (even in the context of *Kerchele*) was not really for me. Neither had I sought their company all the time. I loved my solitude and locked myself in the clinic dispensary for hours and read books, or sat in silence away from the hubbub of *Kerchele* life. Sitting in that small room, I felt I was in my element - my 'mandala'- where I could connect with my inner self. I struggled to find the perfect axis where I could balance personal freedom and responsibility and the situation around me.

A women's *Hibret Souk* (branch prisoners' shop) was opened in the women's quarter and I started working there after my *Mekrus* member, Sophia, quit. I applied for the position and got the job after sitting in an interview. I quit my volunteer job at the clinic after three years of service. I managed the shop and the tearoom and was paid 54 birr per month, which was a substantial amount in the prison context. A real tearoom was built where people were able to sit and have tea chatting with fellow prisoners.

The shop was another retreat for me. I locked myself inside on weekends just before roll call and read, did school assignments and regained my sense of being. The downside of it was I had to go back to *Adarash*. It was by then less crowded, and the most vehement and former *Kefitegna girls* have been released long ago.

Every now and then I suffered from bouts of moodiness like everybody else. I often kept to myself when that happened. Betty Kassa was the only one who knew how to lift me out of that state. Betty was a former EPRP member. She was ebullient, loud and hilarious. I usually locked myself in the shop and sat in the dark. She would come and knock on the door.

"What do you want?" I would snap.

"Please open the door for me!"

"No! Go away! I want to be by myself."

"Please, *Hiwotiye* let me in." She would never give up.

Annoyed, I would fling the door open.

"So what do you want to do? Talk? Laugh? Cry? I am ready to do all," she would say, laughing.

We would sit there in the dark and talk and laugh until roll call. By the time we came out, I was in a good mood again.

Mimi, Tadelech's daughter, also gave meaning to my life. I played with her, fed her, washed her clothes, braided her hair and cooked for her. I often slung her on my back with a *gabi* and took a walk. Those were my soothing moments, my lullabies. She was my pet and my friend. She used to say I was her best friend.

Whatever pain I experienced at the *Kefitegna* receded to the edges of my existence. I chose to focus on the new and fascinating life *Kerchele* had offered me.

The memory of the Party lives with me despite my vow to stay away from the crowd mentality it had inspired. There is no awe, no sense of sacredness, no adoration, no throbbing of the soul, no illusion nor nostalgia; but there will always be respect and admiration in my heart for what it stood for, for making us dare to believe, for letting us dream, for bringing out the best in us, and for giving us perspective about life. I am grateful for all the good things I learned in the Party. It helped me tone up with discipline, commitment, hard work, composure in the face of hardship, and detachment from material possessions.

Every so often I questioned myself if I could really blame what I had suffered at the *Kefitegna* on crowd mentality or if each of us has personal responsibility. What put me off guard at the time was the same thing that shook me out of my depth when Getachew was killed. I had never thought that comrades would hurt one another and breach the trust they bestowed upon one another. I was too raw to understand the complexity of human nature and the workings of ideology and politics. I came to realize that our comradeship was based on our dedication to the same goals, and that brought our relationship to extraordinary and almost sacrosanct and ethereal levels. I came to believe that was the reason I saw my comrades as more than mortal beings. That knowledge, the sense of my own fallibility and human frailty, and the longing to remain human helped me heal, let go and set me free.

I'm coming home, I'm coming home
Tell the world I'm coming home.
 -P. Diddy

Kerchele had become depopulated, as many prisoners were set free. Emebet was released in July 1982, after completing her four-year term. As difficult as it was for us, we were happy for her. Chuchu was released in mid-1983, after five years in prison, three years in *Kerchele* and two elsewhere. Life in the ward had become boring after she left. It had been a huge blow for me. We had become like sisters, sharing everything and having so much fun living together in the ward. Sabela and Ariam were also released after four years. It was another blow for me. As much as I loved to be by myself, I loved my friends and enjoyed their company.

It was sometime in 1985. I was playing volleyball one afternoon when I could lift my right arm no more. I immediately ran to the ward and examined it. It was red and swollen. A little worried, I took a shower, put my nightgown on and went to bed. I didn't say anything to anybody. The next day, it was even worse. I stayed in bed reading a book.

Tadelech came and asked me why I was in bed. I showed her my arm. She urged me to see the health assistant right away. I did and I was referred to the doctor who came once a week to *Kerchele,* but had to wait a few days to see him. When he saw my arm, he referred me to Black Lion Hospital (where he worked) right away.

But I was told by the office I could only be sent to Menilik II Hospital. I told my sister Almaz about what had happened when she came on Sunday. The next day, I was called to the Major's office. He asked why I had complained to the authorities. I wasn't aware my sister had gone to the *Meakelawi* and had lodged a complaint about me not being sent to Black Lion Hospital. When the Major saw my inflamed and swollen arm, which hadn't changed much since the day I played volleyball, he didn't hesitate to give me the permission to go to Black Lion.

Through my brother-in-law, I managed to be seen by Professor Asrat Woldeyes, one of the two renowned surgeons in the country. I was admitted right away. One of the bones on my right elbow had developed osteomyelitis (infection of the bone). The Professor curetted the bone and I stayed for over two months at the hospital. I could have stayed for as long as I wanted to, but I didn't want to saddle my sisters with high hospital fees. Besides, my family visited me every day and I worried it would be an additional burden on them.

After nearly fifteen years, I eventually got respite. For the first time, I felt I was rid of the curse that had been following me around. I had put my pains and anxieties aside when I was struggling under the banner of the EPRP. But in prison, the fear of losing my arm someday had come back.

It was one of the most horrendous acts of the Derg. It was late afternoon in September 1985. Zaid Belay and another woman's names were called. They were detained, accused of being members of the Eritrean Peoples' Liberation Front. We went to *Adarash* to congratulate them thinking that they were going to be released. About forty male prisoners have been called out too that afternoon. They were ready to go home but all of a sudden, they were told that they would be released the next morning. It was strange. It diluted the euphoric mood. Then the sordid news surfaced that they were actually going to be executed. A wave of terror swept through the compound.

The next morning Zaid and the male prisoners were summoned to come out. Close to forty of them were executed after being in prison for seven or eight years! Amongst the male prisoners were Yohannes Girmachew, Zewdu Belayneh and Getachew Kumsa, who were EPRP members. Yohannes used to coach us volleyball and he was the only male allowed in the compound for that purpose. Most of the executed were former EPRP members and the rest were members of the Eritrean Liberation Fronts, the Tigrian Liberation Front and even Jehovah Witnesses. At the time, many Pentecostal and Jehovah Witnesses were thrown in prison because of their beliefs.

We didn't know what to do with this sadistic measure of the Derg. It was inconceivable how people, who have been jailed for over eight years, could have been taken out and cold-bloodedly killed. It was a reminder that the Derg was still bloodthirsty. For those who had been awaiting freedom for many years, it seemed like the end of the road.

It was as if we were back to square one.

Tadelech and her daughter, 1983   *With Tadelech's daughter, 1983*

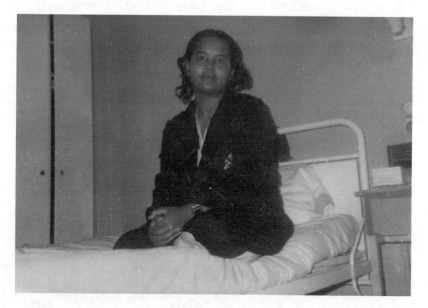

Black Lion Hospital, 1985

"Guard! Guard! People are dying! People are dying!" we heard male voices shouting in the middle of one night from the male ward, located beside the female compound. All of us in *Adarash* sat up on our beds and listened to the desperate calls with utter consternation.

The prisoners sounded desperate and their voices got louder. Many of us cried. We knew something grave was happening in the men's ward. The voices died down later and we went back to sleep still wondering what had gone wrong. In the morning, we learned that some men had died in the ward that night. They had died of dysentery. The next night, we heard the male prisoners call the wardens again. In the morning, we learned that there was a cholera outbreak in the prison compound!

More people died and many more got sick. There was panic and desperation. Every night we heard men screaming, "Guard! Guard! Someone is dying!" The male ward became overcrowded with more people getting sick. The school had to be turned into a triage. In the women's compound, only one woman, who happened to be pregnant, got the dysentery. She was immediately quarantined and miraculously survived.

The Red Cross donated blankets and clothes of the dead and the sick were burned. Tents were pitched before the school, where patients were quarantined and treated. School was closed and prisoners were not allowed to step out of their quarters. In order to contain the outbreak, no food containers were allowed to go out of the prison compound.

We (women prisoners) were given Tetracycline capsules three times a day, as precaution. Most people stayed in bed to keep away the cholera. They were scared of shaking hands with others or even touching one another, and the best prevention was staying in bed all day. I opened my shop at the usual time but had no customers, as most people stayed in bed.

Many took matters into their own hands and concocted potions out of garlic, lime, ginger, hot green pepper and other hot spices. They went to the clinic by the dozens complaining of stomachache, nausea and vomiting.

At the *Emechat Bet,* there was even more terror because of all the children. The moms burned incense to ward off flies. We stopped kissing the kids.

We never learned how many people died in the men's compound owing to the outbreak. The numbers ranged from fifty to one hundred and fifty. Death hovered over us, once again becoming an immediate existential threat. Fear and terror ruled the day. My greatest fear, like many prisoners, was to die in prison. The cholera threatened to make that fate reality. It had me thinking that it would be a tragedy to die of dysentery in prison after surviving the Derg's bullet and after being there for over eight years. I wondered if there was any justice in that. *Is this a mockery of our existence?*

I had recently heard about existentialism. A non-political prisoner was said to have talked about it at a meeting held at the school; others rebuffed him for his frivolity. Marxism was not yet fully cast out of the heads of many political prisoners.

When the cholera outbreak occurred, I started contemplating on the meaning and purpose of life. I was at the time reading one of the most popular books in the prison compound: *The story of philosophy,* by Will Durant. I was reading Arthur Schopenhauer, the 19th century German philosopher, and it was as if I was reading from the pages of life in *Kerchele.*

How can we die of cholera in prison? Where is the justice in that? I asked myself repeatedly. Death had meaning eight years ago when we were struggling under the leadership of the EPRP. We knew why and what we were dying for; but to die of cholera in prison seemed obscene. The previous three years have been brighter and more meaningful to me because my friend Sisay Abdulkadir has been visiting me every Sunday. I was ready to finish my term with courage and determination, but I felt courage slipping out of my existence. Life became gloomy and ironic. Schopenhauer's idea of life as "evil" and as "suffering" snuck into my head, threatening to tear down the edifice I had been building around the meaning of existence.

All that feeling of desolation was washed away a few weeks later. We heard that a Derg member, Major Endale Tessema, was coming to visit the prison. The new prison administrator, Colonel Abera Ayana, promised that he would have Mengistu Hailemariam visit the prison and get us released.

We were forced out to wash, scrub, dig, sweep and paint the prison compound to make it as clean and as presentable as possible for the chairman. No matter how hard we tried, the place still looked shabby and dirty. After a month's clean up, it was said that Mengistu was finally visiting. The day he came, except for a few selected prisoners, the rest of us were locked in. He did not even come to the women's compound. After he left, a series of *Moged* started to spread and a sense of euphoria swept through the compound. *Gede* started to appear more often.

I was sitting in the store, when the male health assistant working at the clinic came over one morning. He was smiling shyly when he leaned on the counter and greeted me.

"Hiwot, I know you're going to be released soon," he said.

"How do you know?" I asked, smiling. I liked the old man. We had worked together at the clinic for three years and he was a fatherly figure.

"I dreamt about you last night. You were paddling a wooden raft. I saw you coming ashore," he answered.

"So what does it mean?"

"You know, a wooden raft is a relative. You will be released through the help of a relative."

"Well, I hope it is true." We chatted for a few minutes and he left.

It was Friday evening and word floated around that an amnesty was given to one thousand prisoners and that the list had arrived in the office. That night was a sleepless night for many.

Moged had never affected me. I never imagined I would shake the remaining years of my sentence off my back and go home. Therefore, I did not think I would be released, but I was uneasy about remaining with only a few people for the rest of my term.

The next morning was Saturday, June 6, 1986. I was taking a shower around eight thirty in the morning when Tadelech came in the shower room. "They say people are going to be released today. Do you think we will be released?" she asked excitedly.

I didn't want to disappoint her. I wished her release more than anybody else did. Her daughter was then seven years old and would soon be forced to go home. No child above the age of eight was allowed to stay in prison. There were also her two daughters. At the same time, I did not want us to get excited and then feel bad later. "I don't know. I am not expecting to be released today," I responded, sounding a bit serious. She went out without saying a word. I felt bad for being so cold and so serious.

Around ten o'clock, my lunch arrived as usual. Then the most incredible thing happened. We heard a voice over a megaphone calling the names of male prisoners. The list was endless. Every time a name belonging to a person we knew was called, we screamed. Everybody came out and congregated in the courtyard. We froze with disbelief where we were standing. Then the gate was swung open and two male soldiers came in. One of them started calling names. I was standing at the door of my shop.

People ran around when their names were called out. Others rushed to congratulate them. All of a sudden, all that shock and disbelief was turned into excitement, tears and nervous laughter. I did not know what to think or expect. It would be very disastrous if all those people were released and I was left standing there. I did not know if I should cry for being left there alone or be happy for the others.

Finally, I heard my name. It was unbelievable. People came and kissed me on the cheeks and ran away to kiss somebody else. I did not kiss them back. I stood there unable to even move. Once I heard mine, I waited anxiously to hear Tadelech's name. Then I heard her name! That was when I woke up from my reveries and ran to where she was standing. I fell on her chest with an outburst of excitement.

A few minutes later, disaster struck. Somebody came and shocked us with the news that Tadelech's and another girl's names were called by mistake! What? I could not believe what I heard. We approached the gate to make sense of what we had just learned. Sadly, they broke the news that she was called by mistake.

It was inconceivable. I just could not see myself going and leaving them behind, especially Mimi, who was as much my daughter as she was Tadelech's. I sobbed uncontrollably. All the released prisoners left. I stayed behind leaning on Tadelech's lap and crying. Two female wardens came over and pulled me away. I could no longer walk and tumbled on the ground outside the gate. I screamed wildly lying there. The wardens did not know what to do with me. "You know they might change their mind if you are behaving this way," they warned.

I didn't care.

It was after so much cajoling that the wardens were able to lift me up and help me walk. They held my elbows on both sides and begged me to stop crying and walk straight. I just could not. My knees had given way. I felt desperate. When we approached the office, where the *Meakelawi* people and all the 700 or so released prisoners were crowded, the wardens got jittery that I might indeed be sent back.

They wiped my tears and once again beseeched me to walk on my own. I joined the prisoners and the two wardens stood on the side. Among the released were my friends Tibletse Asmelash and the librarian Dawit Sibhatu. It was raining and we stood there for what seemed like an endless time. Then I saw Lieutenant Shimeles charging through the crowd and coming up to me. It has been almost seven years since he brought us to *Kerchele* from the *Meakelawi*. "Congratulations! I am so glad you are out. You see there is God, after all. What did I tell you? Don't cry now, you are free," he said, smiling and shaking my hand.

I did not have the heart to appreciate my release. I could not say anything to the good man. The words would not come out. Tears started rolling down my cheeks again.

"No! Don't! It is not good for you," he cautioned, looking around. He left after he gave me a few more words of encouragement.

After what seemed an endless wait, we were taken to the *Meakelawi* for "orientation" and then I was free after eight years and four months!

When we came out, we faced a multitude of family members in the compound pressing forward to find their loved ones. They pushed and shoved to look for their sons, daughters, sisters, brothers, husbands, wives, relatives, and neighbors. They laughed, wept and ululated.

Tibletse and I drifted through the crowd, hands clenched, disoriented, overwhelmed and numbed. The two female wardens, who had escorted me to the office, had asked me for my phone number to call my sister Almaz and let her know about my release. While Tibletse and I were walking, still dazed, I spotted one of my aunts. She ululated when she saw me and fell on my shoulders, tears of joy streaming down her cheeks. She held my hand and jostled her way through the crowd, taking me to my mother, my sisters, my brother in-laws, my aunts and my cousins. We all went to my sister Almaz's house, including Tibletse. My mother refused to go and set off instead to St. Mikael's Church, to fulfill her pledge.

The society we had left behind, the idealism and concern for social justice was no longer there. The EPRP experience was so near and so fresh to us, but when I came out people talked about it as if it were something that had happened in a distant era. They referred to it as "the EPRP era."

Tadelech was released in 1991 when Mengistu Hailemariam was ousted. She got out after twelve years and five months!

However, that was not what mattered. What mattered was that we had pulled through it all with courage, determination, integrity, dignity and cheerfulness.

Prison was meant to crush our spirits and depersonalize us. However, it turned out to be the place where I learned what it means to be human. It was there that I discovered the value of freedom, and realized that personal responsibility, individuality and moral integrity are much more important in life than trying to build a utopia.

However, it was what I learned from Getachew Maru, the hero of my life, that I always wanted to emulate: respect for human life, tolerance and peaceful resolution of conflict.